The American Political Dictionary

The American Political Dictionary

Second Edition

JACK C. PLANO ◇ MILTON GREENBERG

Western Michigan University

Holt, Rinehart and Winston, Inc.

New York • Chicago • San Francisco
Toronto • London

TO ELLEN AND SONIA

Preface

The reception accorded the first edition of *The American Political Dictionary* has reinforced the authors' belief in the utility of this unique approach to lexicography. The new edition maintains the format within which materials basic to an understanding of American government and politics are arranged topically within chapters and discussed in the context of their relevance to the contemporary political scene. New developments in civil rights and liberties, foreign affairs, defense, social welfare, space exploration, education, and national-state relations demanded a revision of most entries and the inclusion of numerous new terms. In addition, at the suggestion of many colleagues and students, an extensive cross-reference system has been incorporated.

The American Political Dictionary developed out of the authors' experiences as teachers of political science. Students are generally reluctant to recognize that the social sciences, like the natural and physical sciences, have a technical language, a grasp of which is crucial for the understanding and solving of social and political problems. This book represents an effort to overcome this language difficulty. It defines more than 1100 terms, agencies, court cases, and statutes which we consider the most relevant for a basic comprehension of American governmental institutions, practices, and problems. Each definition is followed by a statement of its significance to American government and the citizen. Items have been selected for their pertinency to the general introductory course in American government and to an understanding of contemporary political events.

As teachers, we have found ourselves faced with the dilemma of how to present the "realities" and "processes" of American government while, at the same time, providing the student with the basic facts and essential language tools needed for such a probe into the excitement of government in action. We have attempted here to meet this problem in a novel way—

by a discussion of individual terms within subject-matter categories so that the term is placed in its proper frame of reference. This book should, therefore, enable the teacher and student to decrease the time spent in the classroom on defining terms and explaining their significance, and permit more time for a fuller analysis of the American governmental process. It can be used most effectively as a supplement to texts or groups of readings in American government and other political science courses.

It has become commonplace to speak of the need for an informed citizenry in order to maintain a free society. This necessity is, nevertheless, both real and urgent. The authors hope that this volume will contribute to more effective use of classroom time to attain this goal.

KALAMAZOO, MICHIGAN   JCP
JANUARY 1967   MG

A Note on How To Use This Book

This book can be used in two ways. It is a *dictionary* in which terms are listed alphabetically by subject matter; the reader can find a term by consulting a particular chapter, or, when in doubt as to the usage of a term, by consulting the index. It is also a *study guide;* a complete reading of a chapter will provide the reader with basic information in a subject area and help in preparation for class discussions or examinations.

The material is divided into 18 chapters which dovetail with the chapters or groups of chapters found in most textbooks on American government. State and local governmental issues and procedures are integrated with national governmental practice in most instances. For example, terms used to describe legislative, executive, or judicial functions are essentially the same at all levels of government. A separate chapter on state and local government is included which focuses on terms that have specific application to state and local governmental problems and practices.

With few exceptions, each chapter has four sections. The first and longest in each case is an alphabetical listing of terms. Each is defined and then followed by a paragraph on its significance as it relates to overall operations, theories, and problems of American government. A few terms are used in more than one chapter because they have more than one meaning or application. In such instances, the definition and significance are related to the subject matter of the particular chapter. When deemed useful, cross references are provided to similar or closely related terms.

The listing of terms is followed by sections on important agencies, important cases, and important statutes, each of which contains an alphabetical listing of definitions or descriptions of items and a statement of their significance. Many terms found in the first part of a chapter contain mention of agencies, cases, and statutes, but detailed treatment is given to a highly select group. United Nations agencies and other international organizations in which the United States plays a role are treated as regular items in Chapter 16.

The index contains a complete listing of all major entries as well as all significant terms discussed within major entries.

Contents

One

Political Ideas

Absolutism   Unrestrained powers exercised by government. Absolutism is the opposite of constitutionalism, which provides for government limited by law. *See* TOTALITARIANISM, page 16.

Significance   Prior to the American and French Revolutions, absolutism took the form of absolute monarchy based on the theory of the divine right of kings. In modern times, it has taken the form of dictatorship of the right (fascism) or dictatorship of the left (communism). The American Founding Fathers feared absolutism and established a system of separation of powers with checks and balances to safeguard against it. The historic struggle between absolutism and democratic constitutionalism continues today, both within and between nations.

Accountability   The concept underlying democratic representative government that elected officials are responsible to the people for their actions. Accountability under law is one of the features distinguishing governments based on the concepts of liberal democracy from those embracing the principles of absolutism. *See* DEMOCRACY, page 6; REPRESENTATIVE GOVERNMENT, page 14.

Significance   Accountability implies that citizens in a democracy are familiar with their elected officials and the decisions they make, and have an opportunity to pass judgment on them. This, in turn, requires short ballots, frequent elections, and an effective opposition. In the national government, the voters can hold the President accountable for all decisions and actions undertaken in the executive branch because under the Constitution he alone is accorded authority and responsibility for them. In Congress, accountability is based on individual performance; frequent roll-call votes on important bills enable voters to judge their congressman every two years and their senators every six years. When bills are killed through minority blocking tactics, or when parliamentary maneuvers are used to conceal political motives or to confuse voters, accountability is reduced.

Alienation   Indifference fostered by an individual's estrangement from society. Political alienation results when individuals believe they have lost their

1

ability to participate effectively in the political process and to influence its outcome.

Significance   Various theories have sought to explain the alienation of modern man and have offered, through political and economic ideologies, the means for overcoming it. Marxism, for example, posits that the destruction of capitalism will restore man's societal and cooperative nature. Modern society has produced widespread feelings of anomy and rootlessness through the impersonalizing forces of machine technology and mass culture. Underlying mass movements and protest demonstrations by minorities, for example, is the alienation of such groups from the rest of society. Those alienated often fail to vote or participate in the regular arena for making political decisions.

Anarchism   The doctrine that government is an unnecessary evil and should be replaced by voluntary cooperation among individuals and groups. Anarchists regard the state as an instrument used by the propertied classes to dominate and exploit the people. Anarchist thinking varies from individualism to collectivism, from pacifism to advocacy of violent revolution. All anarchists, however, hold the state's coercive system responsible for the warping of man's personality and look to the day when every form of government will be abolished.

Significance   In Europe, anarchism has been represented primarily by syndicalist parties; similarly, in the United States, anarchists have worked through the organization, the Industrial Workers of the World. Anarchism has never been a successful political ideology, but its advocates have had considerable influence on other political theorists and movements. Marxian communism, for example, views government as an evil instrument of class exploitation and provides for a "final stage" in which government "withers away" and people in a "stateless, classless society" spontaneously cooperate with one another.

Aristocracy   The exercise of political power by a small ruling clique of a state's "best" citizens. The selection of the aristocrats may be made on the basis of birth, wealth, or ability.

Significance   Aristocracies are characterized by limited suffrage and great emphasis on property rights. Post-Revolutionary America had characteristics of aristocracy, with property and religious qualifications for voting and holding office. The "Jeffersonian Democracy" of that era emphasized rule by an aristocracy of ability. The democratic reforms ushered in during the age of Jackson provided a leveling influence.

Authoritarianism   Concentration of political authority in one man or a small group. Authoritarian regimes emphasize obedience by the people to their rulers and the absolute power of rulers over their subjects. *See* ABSOLUTISM, page 1.

Significance   Political history has been characterized by continuing struggles between the rival doctrines of authoritarianism and democracy. Although authoritarianism was set back by the defeat of the Axis powers in World War II, today it threatens again with the spread of communism and military takeovers in the new states of Asia and Africa. In many cases, modern authoritarian regimes operate behind a façade of democratic and constitutional institutions.

Capitalism   An economic system based on private ownership of the means of production and on a supply-demand market economy. Capitalism is based on the laissez-faire theory, which emphasizes the absence of governmental restraints on ownership, production, and trade. *See* LAISSEZ FAIRE, page 9.

Significance   Capitalism as a working economic system developed in Europe and the United States in the late eighteenth and early nineteenth centuries, replacing the state-fostered mercantilist system. Historically, capitalism in its pure state has never been practiced for long, since each major economic group has soon looked to the government of its country to improve its own economic position, and since each government in time has assumed a substantial promotional and regulatory role. Today, all capitalist states have mixed economies in which private ownership and market economies are matched with extensive governmental intervention. Free trade, a hallmark of capitalism, has been replaced by national and regional international trade restrictions, and the concepts of economic freedom that characterize capitalism are being challenged by socialism and communism.

Collectivism   A generic term that describes various theories and social movements calling for the ownership and control of all land and means of production by the state or groups rather than by individuals. The term is often used synonymously with the more specific doctrines of socialism and communism, for collectivism rejects the economic freedoms of capitalism. *See* COMMUNISM, page 3; SOCIALISM, page 15.

Significance   The major ideological conflicts of modern times have involved clashes between supporters of collectivist doctrines and defenders of the concepts of individualism. The former have emphasized the advantages of cooperation and group effort, the latter the advantages of competition and individual enterprise. Many Communist countries are increasingly substituting profit motivations for collectivistic planning and control in their economies.

Communism   A political, economic, and social theory based on a collectivistic society in which all land and capital are socially owned and political power is exercised by the masses. Modern communism is based on the theories and practices of Karl Marx, V. I. Lenin, Josef Stalin, Nikita Khrushchev, and contemporary Soviet leaders, with some new variations provided by Mao Tsetung and the Chinese Communists. Communism in theory espouses the doctrines of historical inevitability, economic determinism, labor value, the "inner contradictions" of capitalism, class conflict, capitalist colonialism and imperialism, world wars resulting from competition for markets, the destruction of the bourgeoisie, the dictatorship of the proletariat, the socialist revolution, and the final "withering away" of the state. Plato and other political theorists have also advocated communism in the form of communal living and various church and social groups have practiced it. *See* ECONOMIC DETERMINISM, page 8.

Significance   Since World War II, communism as an ideology has been used by the Communist states, especially the Soviet Union, in a world-wide offensive against capitalism and democracy. Communism in theory is largely destructive, basing its main attack on the evils and weaknesses of nineteenth-century capitalism. In practice, communism has been highly pragmatic: Soviet leaders often use capitalistic practices to provide incentives and to secure some degree of political stability and economic viability. During the period of transition from socialism to communism the "dictatorship of the proletariat" has proved to be a quite permanent dictatorship by one man or by a ruthless oligarchy. Communists have been unsuccessful in winning mass support and political elections, but they have been highly successful in infiltrating and capturing control of mass independence movements in Asia and Africa.

Concurrent Majority   The political doctrine, expounded by John C. Calhoun of South Carolina prior to the Civil War, that democratic decisions should be made only with the concurrence of all major segments of society. Without such concurrence, Calhoun argued, a decision should not be binding on those groups whose interests it violates. *See* NULLIFICATION, page 37.

Significance   The idea of concurrent majority was central to a systematic effort by Calhoun to justify the secession of southern states from the Union. He held that the decisions made by Congress concerning tariffs and slavery were inimical to the interests of the South. Each southern state, therefore, had to decide whether it would accept these decisions or would reject them and withdraw from the Union.

Consensus   Agreement approaching unanimity, usually without a vote. Consensus relates to the acceptance of a society's basic values or to a concurrence in specific decisions by members of a group. In a democracy, "government by consensus" sometimes replaces majority rule and reduces the role of the opposition.

Significance   Consensus provides the cementing force for a society. When consensual bonds are broken by revolution or civil war, new ones must evolve if stability is to be restored. The process of building a consensus for a specific decision within a group is usually based on compromise or strong leadership.

Conservatism   Defense of the status quo against major changes in the political, economic, or social institutions of a society. The philosophy of conservatism has been expounded most effectively by the English statesman, Edmund Burke. He held that political stability could be maintained only if the forces of change could be moderated by a slow and careful integration of new elements into time-tested institutions. *See* LIBERALISM, page 10.

Significance   Both major American political parties have conservative wings that frequently unite in opposing liberal legislation. Today in American politics the term "conservative" has no precise meaning and is often used accusatorily against a rival party or candidate. The general conservative position on issues, however, has been fairly consistently opposed to governmental regulation of the economy and civil rights legislation, and in favor of state over federal action, fiscal responsibility, and decreased governmental spending and lower taxes. Although conservatism received a setback in the 1964 defeat of Republican presidential candidate Barry Goldwater, conservative groups in the United States are well organized and remain powerful in American politics.

Constitutionalism   The political principle of limited government under a written or unwritten contract (constitution). Constitutionalism assumes that the sovereign people draw up a constitution by the terms of which a government is created and given powers. In the American system, the Supreme Court acts as the guardian of the constitution through its powers to void governmental actions that exceed these limitations (judicial review). The Founding Fathers also incorporated into the system various limitations that restrain the individuals who exercise power. The most significant of these include the separation of powers, checks and balances, federalism, subordination of military to civilian control, and the Bill of Rights. *See* DEMOCRACY, page 6; CONSTITUTION, page 21.

Significance   The American system of constitutional government has been fairly effective throughout most of its history in maintaining limitations upon government. In recent years, however, public sentiment has favored bigger government with expanded powers. The Industrial Revolution, depressions, wars, alien ideologies, and other domestic and foreign threats have overridden the fear of stronger government. Expanding democratic government is viewed by many as a means of achieving better protection for their personal rights, values, and welfare, rather than as a threat. The problem remains essentially one of maintaining an equilibrium between the needs for liberty and for order, and of enabling government to meet new and challenging responsibilities, while still maintaining the restraints of constitutionalism.

Contract Theory   A class of theories that seeks to explain the origin of society and government and to set out the respective authority and responsibility of government and individuals under their contractual obligations. Contract theorists regard man as having lived in a state of nature prior to the organization of civil society. Once a "body politic" has been created through a contract or compact among the people, a government is then founded and empowered through a second contract or constitution concluded between the people and the government. The nature of the relationship established by the governmental contract varies, in these theories, from the individualism of John Locke's popular sovereignty and limited government to the authoritarianism of Thomas Hobbes's *Leviathan*. *See* DEMOCRACY, page 6.

Significance   The contract theory was developed by various political philosophers during the Middle Ages as an intellectual challenge to the existing absolutism based on the theory of the divine right of kings. Progressively the new doctrine gained adherents and the absolute power of some monarchs was mildly curtailed, but its full flowering and broad democratic implications emerged during the Age of Enlightenment. The advocacy of the doctrine by John Locke, Jean Jacques Rousseau, and James Harrington helped to gain the support of the intellectual classes and laid the foundations for the English, American, and French Revolutions. The American Declaration of Independence, described by Thomas Jefferson as "pure Locke," based its justification of revolution on the violation of contract by the English government. Although the theories of a social contract are somewhat out of vogue today, the great ideas they fostered remain part of the concept of democracy based on limited government and individual rights.

Democracy   A system of government in which political power is exercised by the people. The term is derived from the Greek words "demos" (the people) and "kratos" (authority). Democracy may be direct, as practiced in ancient Athens and in New England town meetings, or indirect and representative. The Democratic Creed includes the following concepts: (1) individualism, which holds that the primary task of government is to enable each individual to achieve the highest potential of development; (2) liberty, which allows each individual the greatest amount of freedom consistent with order; (3) equality, which maintains that all men are created equal and have equal rights and opportunities; and (4) fraternity, which postulates that individuals will not misuse their freedom but will cooperate in creating a wholesome society. As a political system, democracy starts with the assumption of popular sovereignty, vesting ultimate political power in the people. It presupposes that man can control his destiny, that he can make moral judgments and practical decisions in his daily life. It implies a continuing search for truth in the sense of man's pursuit of improved ways of building social institutions and ordering human relations. Democracy requires a decision-making system based on majority rule, with minority rights protected. Effective guarantees of freedom of speech, press, religion, assembly, petition, and equality before the law are indispensable to a democratic system of government. Politics, parties, and politicians are the catalytic agents that make democracy workable. *See* ACCOUNTABILITY, page 1; CONSTITUTIONALISM, page 5; CONTRACT THEORY, page 5; DIRECT DEMOCRACY, page 7; INDIVIDUALISM, page 9; MAJORITY RULE, page 10; NATURAL LAW, page 11; POPULAR SOVEREIGNTY, page 13; REPRESENTATIVE GOVERNMENT, page 14; RULE OF LAW, page 15.

Significance   Democracy, for many centuries regarded as a dangerous but unworkable doctrine, swept the western world during the nineteenth and twentieth centuries as one of the forces unleashed by the American and French Revolutions. In the twentieth century, democracy has clashed with new authoritarian ideologies, and the struggle continues, particularly in the new nations of Asia and Africa. Democracy is under attack not only from the ideologies of the extreme right and left, but from within as well—by those who oppose it as a mob rule that vulgarizes society and makes a virtue of incompetence and mediocrity; and by those who charge that democracy is a sham, impossible in practice because of an "iron law of oligarchy." Supporters of democracy reject such attacks, pointing to the evidence of the superiority of democracy as practiced in the United States, Britain, and Scandinavia. Yet façade democracy exists in many nonwestern countries where, despite forms and appearances, a small oligarchic group manipulates all power. Workable democracy seems to require a special environment, including an educated and responsible people, some degree of economic stability, and some social cohesion and consensus. Above all, it demands an acceptance of the democratic "rules of the game," viz., that there will be fair and frequent elections, that the losers will accept the verdict of the voters and allow the majority to govern, that the majority will respect the right of the minority to furnish opposition, and that if the minority wins a future election it will then be permitted to take over the reins of government. Although democracy in practice will never achieve the perfection of the Democratic Creed, yet so long as such goals are held worthy and efforts are made to move in their direction, the system may be called democratic. American democracy, like its British counterpart, is an evolutionary and organic system that has pragmatically overcome obstacles and crises.

Democratic Socialism   An economic system established by a democratic nation in which the people, through their government, take over ownership and direction of basic industry, banking, communication, transportation, and other segments of the economy. The extent of the government's role in the economy is determined by free elections rather than by ideological dogma. Although a private sector of the economy may continue to exist, much effort is expended by government in planning, directing, and regulating it, and in providing welfare services for the needy. *See* SOCIALISM, page 15; WELFARE STATE, page 17.

Significance   Democratic socialism has been partially instituted in several countries, particularly in Britain and the Scandinavian countries. Some observers regard it as the best answer to the economic challenge of communism. Communists are especially hostile toward democratic socialism because they fear it will correct the evils and "inner contradictions" of capitalism upon which they place their hope for economic collapse. American conservatives also oppose it as a dangerous leftward step toward communism.

Direct Democracy   A system of government in which political decisions are made by the people directly rather than by their elected representatives. Under direct democracy, the citizens assemble periodically and function as a legislative body. *See* REPRESENTATIVE GOVERNMENT, page 14.

Significance   Direct democracy has been used in ancient Greece and Rome, in some Swiss cantons, in New England town meetings, and in some midwestern township meetings. A modern adaptation of direct democracy is found in fewer than one-half of the American states—those that provide for initiative, referendum, and recall action by the people. Many local units of government also use binding and advisory referendums in reaching decisions on important issues. Direct democracy, however, is not provided for nor recognized by the United States Constitution. Ordinarily, direct democracy is practicable only in small communities and in resolving simple issues.

Divine Right   A theory supporting absolutism based on the divinity of a person or his office, or on a right to rule inherited from ancestors believed to have been appointed by a Supreme Being. *See* ABSOLUTISM, page 1.

Significance   The political philosophy of the divine right of kings was accepted in theory and practice throughout most of the western world from the fifteenth through the eighteenth centuries. The system was perpetuated through the family inheritance of the ruling power and the intermarriage of ruling families. Any challenge to or revolt against a king was regarded not only as a treasonable act but as a sin. In time, the divine right of kings was first weakened and then overcome by the new contract theory, which held that a ruler's power was granted to him not by God but by the sovereign people.

Economic Determinism   The theory that the economic factors of the methods of production and exchange of goods control the form of a state's political and social organization and shape the intellectual and moral development of its people. Economic determinists view history in terms of epochs in which the prevailing economic system pits the servile class against the dominant class, a struggle that eventually results in a new alignment. *See* COMMUNISM, page 3.

Significance   Vague beliefs in some aspects of economic determinism are widespread and are held by people of many persuasions. The most celebrated systematic theory was set forth by Marx and Engels, who used it to explain the movement of history in response to changing economic relationships. Economic determinism is the core of such concepts as class struggle, the predicted collapse of capitalism, and the eventual victory of communism.

Fascism   The political system of the extreme right, which incorporates the principles of the leader (dictator), a one-party state, totalitarian regimentation of economic and social activity, and the arbitrary exercise of absolute power by the regime. After 1922, Benito Mussolini fashioned the fascist prototype in Italy and was emulated in the 1930s by Adolf Hitler in Germany, Francisco Franco in Spain, and Juan Perón in Argentina. Fascism's glorification of the leader makes the system vulnerable and unstable, and poses serious problems of succession. Unlike communism, fascism retains the private ownership of land and capital, but most economic activity is controlled and regimented by the state through a system of national socialism. *See* TOTALITARIANISM, page 16.

Significance   Fascism is contemptuous of democratic parliamentarianism and personal liberty, but is actively hostile toward communism. Fascists generally have come to power during a crisis in which the landed or industrial leaders of a state have feared the rise of communism. Although fascism was dealt a destructive blow by the defeat of the Axis powers in World War II, neofascism in the form of military dictatorship is on the rise throughout much of the world.

Government   The political and administrative hierarchy of an organized state. Governments exercise legislative, executive, and judicial functions; the nature of the governmental system is determined by the distribution of these powers. Government may take many forms, but it must be sufficiently powerful and stable to command obedience and maintain order. A government's position also depends on its acceptance by the community of nations through its diplomatic recognition by other states.

Significance   Questions concerning the form of government and who will exercise political power within a state have always been matters of contention. Government has helped to bring peace and order to many states, but it has also been the cause of civil wars, revolutions, ideological struggles, and conflicts between states. As populations grow and technology develops, people become increasingly interdependent and turn to government for help in solving their problems, making government an increasingly significant force for good or evil.

Ideology   The "way of life" of a people reflected in terms of their political system, economic order, social goals, and moral values. Ideology is particularly concerned with the form and role of government and the nature of a state's economic system. Ideology is the means by which the basic values held by a party, class, or group are articulated. *See* IDEOLOGICAL WARFARE, page 326.

Significance   Ideology serves to justify for the individual or for groups an existing social system, or postulates a desirable future social order. Two rival ideologies—communism and democracy—are dominant today. Other ideologies exist, but they are overshadowed by the size and intensity of this major struggle. Ideology provides the basic propaganda ammunition for psychological warfare. Each side seeks to sell its ideology by emphasizing its own good points and its opponent's weaknesses.

Individualism   The political, economic, and social concept that places primary emphasis on the worth, freedom, and well-being of the individual rather than on those of the group, society, or nation. *See* DEMOCRACY, page 6.

Significance   Individualism is the central idea in the political doctrine of constitutional democracy and in the economic theory of laissez faire. The broad guarantees afforded to each person and to his property right by the Constitution exemplify the American focus on the worth of the individual.

Jacksonian Democracy   A political and social equalitarian movement in the United States that rejected political aristocracy and emphasized the "common man." The chief apostle of the new equality and democracy was Andrew Jackson, who brought to the presidency the leveling influences of the frontier. *See* LONG BALLOT, page 105; SPOILS SYSTEM, page 191.

Significance   The election of Jackson in 1828 ushered in an era of democratic changes on the national, state, and local governmental levels. Jacksonian democracy emphasized and largely brought about universal manhood suffrage, popular election of officials, short terms of office, and the spoils system.

Laissez-faire   The economic theory, propounded by the French physiocrats and popularized by Adam Smith (*The Wealth of Nations,* 1776), that calls for a "hands-off" policy by government toward the economy. Laissez-faire rejects state control and regulation and emphasizes economic individualism, a market economy, and natural economic laws to guide the production and consumption of goods. Tariffs and other trade restrictions are rejected in favor of a world-wide system of free trade. The economic system becomes self-regulatory in nature and each individual's pursuit of his own self-interest contributes to the well-being of all. *See* CAPITALISM, page 3; FREE TRADE, page 324.

Significance   The wide acceptance in practice of the theory of laissez-faire in the western world during the eighteenth and nineteenth centuries ushered in the new economic era of capitalism. Laissez-faire was largely a reaction to the severe production and trade restrictions imposed by governments under the previous system of mercantilism. The American Revolution was a product of these economic forces of change as well as of new political ideas, all of which were based on individualism. Today, laissez-faire has been modified by the expanding role of government in economic affairs, so that the United States now has a "mixed economy" combining capitalism with governmental promotion and regulation.

Leftist   An individual or a political group advocating liberal or radical political or economic programs, an expanded role by democratic government, or empowering the masses. Leftists include such categories as "welfare-statists," democratic socialists, Marxian socialists, Communists, and anarchists. The use of the term stems from the practice in European parliaments of seating radical parties to the left of the presiding officer. *See* RADICAL, page 13.

Significance   The moderate leftist has played a significant role in advocating governmental action to correct injustices and shortcomings in existing societies. Leftists have been particularly active in calling for changes and modifications in capitalism and political democracy. American leftist movements have included the Progressive, the Socialist, the Socialist Labor, and the Socialist Workers parties. The "new left" in American life shuns political parties in favor of direct action through mass protests. Leftist views on social, economic, and political matters have often been in advance of popularly held beliefs. Extremes of the political left, like those of the right, tend to culminate in dictatorship.

Liberalism   A political view that seeks to change the political, economic, or social status quo to foster the development and well-being of the individual. Liberals regard man as a rational creature who can use his intelligence to overcome human and natural obstacles to a good life for all, without resorting to violence against the established order. Liberalism is more concerned with process, with the method of solving problems, than with a specific program. *See* CONSERVATISM, page 4.

Significance   Liberalism evolved in the eighteenth and nineteenth centuries as a doctrine emphasizing the full development of the individual, free from the restraints of government. The twentieth-century liberal, conversely, looks to government as a means of correcting the abuses and shortcomings of society through positive programs of action. In civil rights, for example, today's liberal views government as a positive force that can ameliorate wrongs and expand the freedom of the individual, rather than as, in the traditional sense, the major threat to individual freedom. Liberals have fought totalitarianism of the left and right by pursuing policies that seek to reduce economic and social inequalities and to produce political stability.

Majority Rule   A basic principle of democracy which asserts that the greater number of citizens in any political unit should select officials and determine policies. Majority rule is justified on the grounds that it rests on superior force, that it is commonly accepted in practice, and that, pragmatically, no reasonable alternative exists. *See* DEMOCRACY, page 6.

Significance   Political philosophers have long debated whether it is any more justifiable for the majority to impose its will on the minority than for the minority to rule. Some theorists reject majority rule in favor of government by consensus or by a concurrent majority. In the United States, majority rule is not rigidly adhered to, as in most cases only a plurality is needed to win an election. Other practices that depart from majority rule include the equal representation of the states in the Senate, gerrymandering, districting on other than a population basis, and the election of the President by the Electoral College.

Monarchy   Any form of government in which the supreme powers of the state are exercised, or ceremoniously held, by a king, queen, emperor, or other regal potentate. Monarchs may acquire their position through inheritance or election, although the latter is unusual. Absolute monarchs exercise full ruling powers, whereas constitutional monarchs either share governmental powers with elected parliaments or are mere figureheads. *See* DIVINE RIGHT, page 7.

    Significance   Absolute monarchs once ruled nearly all of the states of Europe. Today in the few that retain their monarchs—Britain, Sweden, Norway, The Netherlands, for example—the king or queen is assigned a ceremonial role as chief of state. In several semifeudal states of Asia, Africa, and the Middle East, however, monarchs continue to have absolute power.

Nation   Any sizable group of people united by common bonds of geography, religion, language, race, custom, and tradition, and through shared experiences and common aspirations. The term is often used interchangeably with *state,* but not all national groups have achieved statehood, although they all aspire to it. Modern nations began to emerge from feudalism in the ninth century. The community of nation-states was given political and legal recognition by the Peace of Westphalia in 1648. *See* NATIONALISM, page 330; STATE, page 15.

    Significance   In the modern era, the nation has provided the unifying concept with which the individual can identify himself. The results have not always been good, for many national groups have built their unity on a shared hatred of other groups or on a desire to bring others under their dominion. These conflicting national interests, which characterize the world's state system, have contributed to the instability of international relations and to the outbreak of wars.

Natural Law   The concept that human relations are governed by an immutable set of laws, similar to the physical laws of the universe and recognizable through human reason. The theory of *jus naturale* was expounded by the Stoics and was highly developed by the eighteenth-century natural-rights philosophers. *See* NATURAL RIGHTS, page 67; DEMOCRACY, page 6.

    Significance   The concept of natural law has been influential in the development of legal and political theories and institutions, morals and ethics, and religion. Its main significance historically has been its use as a moral standard for judging individual and governmental conduct. Its ambiguities, however, subject it to conflicting interpretations and challenges. It constitutes the basis for the natural-rights philosophy that underlies democratic systems of government.

Oligarchy   Any system of government in which a small group holds the ruling power. Oligarchical systems are usually based on wealth, military power, or social position.

Significance   Oligarchs traditionally rule with absolute power unencumbered by democratic restraints. Even in democratic systems, however, oligarchic groups may temporarily hold a decisive influence over the government because of their economic position or social status. Two European philosophers, Robert Michels and Vilfredo Pareto, developed a theory of the "iron law of oligarchy" which propounds the impossibility of democracy in practice because of the tendency of small groups to dominate and control the majority.

Parliamentary System   A system of government, often based on the British prototype, in which governmental authority is vested in the legislative body (parliament) and in a cabinet headed by a prime minister or premier. The cabinet exercises political leadership and directs the administration. Cabinet ministers are entirely or largely selected from the membership of parliament and the cabinet continues in power so long as it commands the support of a majority of the parliament. Substantial disagreement between the parliament and the cabinet results in either the appointment of a new ministry or the election of a new legislature. *See* PRESIDENTIAL GOVERNMENT, page 13.

Significance   The major advantage of the parliamentary system is that it avoids continuing controversy or deadlocks between the legislative and executive branches and provides for clear accountability to the people. These advantages, however, result in the loss of checks and balances and the American people have never seriously considered adopting this system. Most of the world's democracies are patterned after the British or continental European parliamentary systems, rather than after the American presidential system with its separation of powers.

Pluralism   The concept of modern society as made up of heterogeneous institutions and organizations that have diversified religious, economic, ethnic, and cultural interests. *See* PRESSURE GROUP, page 114.

Significance   The greater the variety in a population, the greater is the degree of pluralism likely to exist. Some react with fear in the presence of differences; others derive satisfaction thereby. While diversity is a potential threat to unity, uniformity is a threat to freedom. In countries like the United States, pluralism has given rise to a tremendous proliferation of organized groups, many with some impact on public policy, representing all manner of interests. It has also resulted in a greater variety of solutions to problems than will be found in homogeneous societies.

Political Science   One of the social sciences, dealing with the theory and practice of politics, government, and administration. Political science as an academic discipline includes the fields of political theory, governmental institutions, public law, politics and public policy, public administration, and international relations and foreign policy.

Significance   Political science in its broadest sense dates back to Plato and Aristotle and to even earlier philosophers. For many centuries, the study of politics was mainly concerned with deducing the characteristics of the ideal or utopian state. In the modern era, students of government have used scientific methods, to create an intellectual discipline based on the postulating of hypotheses followed by empirical verification and the ascertainment of probable trends, and on generalizations concerning state and individual political actions.

Popular Sovereignty   The natural-rights concept that ultimate political authority rests with the people and can be exercised to create, alter, or abolish government. In practice, popular sovereignty is ordinarily exercised through representative institutions. *See* DEMOCRACY, page 6.

Significance   Popular sovereignty was enunciated by the natural-rights philosophers in their attack on governmental absolutism based on the theory of divine right. The concept that the people possess supreme political power pervades the Declaration of Independence and is implicit in the United States Constitution. Popular sovereignty is most directly practiced by the American people when engaged in the writing, amending, and revising of federal, state, and local constitutions or charters.

Presidential Government   A system that features a separation of powers between the legislative and executive branches and the independent election of an executive serving a fixed term. *See* PRESIDENT, page 169.

Significance   The main advantages claimed for the presidential system are the choosing of the executive by the voters rather than by the legislature, the effective use of checks and balances, and the encouragement of strong executive leadership. Critics, however, claim that the system creates a gulf between the legislature and the executive, encourages disagreement and deadlock, and disperses responsibility. In presidential government, the executive tends to emerge as the central figure in the system.

Radical   An advocate of substantial political, social, and economic changes. Although no precise use of the term exists, a radical is generally regarded as a leftist who is extreme in his demands for change. *See* LEFTIST, page 10.

Significance   The American guarantees of freedom of speech, press, and association have encouraged the expression of radical views. Some radical parties have played a significant role in gaining popular support for some of their proposals, and these have been incorporated into the platforms of the major parties. Extreme radical parties are often Marxist-oriented. Ultra conservative groups in contemporary American politics are referred to, however, as the "radical right." The term radical is freely used in political campaigns in attempts to discredit opponents or their proposals.

Reactionary   A person who advocates substantial political, social, or economic changes favoring a return to an earlier, more conservative system. A reactionary believes that most social problems result from democratic excesses favoring the propertyless masses, and usually prefers government by oligarchy. Although the use of the term is not precise, reactionaries are political rightists who are more extreme in their views than are conservatives. *See* RIGHTIST, page 14.

Significance   Some of the new nations of Asia and Africa have come under the control of reactionary regimes after early failures of democracy following independence. In American politics, reactionaries have generally favored laissez faire and have opposed social welfare legislation. The term is freely used in political campaigns in attempts to discredit opponents or their proposals.

Representative Government   Any democratic system of government in which the people elect representatives to act as their agents in making and enforcing laws and decisions. Authoritarian regimes often have a façade of representative institutions, but they lack the vital element of accountability of democratic governments. See REPUBLIC, page 14; DEMOCRACY, page 6.

Significance   Any large and populous political unit must resort to some form of representative government, although small units may provide for direct decision-making by the people. Representatives may act for a special class or group, as in medieval assemblies; for an occupational or social group, as in a system of functional representation; or for a geographical community, as in most contemporary legislatures. One theory, expounded by the English statesman, Edmund Burke, holds that a representative should exercise his own intelligent discretion in reaching decisions; another views his role to be that of an agent of the people who is expected to vote according to their wishes and interests.

Republic   A form of government in which sovereign power resides in the electorate and is exercised by elected representatives who are responsible to the people. Republican government stands in contradistinction to monarchical or oligarchical government in which the rulers have a vested right to office. It is also to be distinguished from pure democracy in which the people govern directly. See REPRESENTATIVE GOVERNMENT, page 14.

Significance   In the century following the American and French Revolutions, republican government emerged in many countries to replace monarchical systems. The Founding Fathers significantly wrote into the Constitution a guarantee by the national government of a republican form of government in every state. In American politics, the distinction between a republic and a democracy is one frequently drawn by conservatives to emphasize the representative character of the American system in contrast to what they consider the "excesses" of democracy.

Rightist   An individual or group advocating conservative or reactionary political or economic programs, a restriction on the power of the masses, and oligarchical rule. Rightists tend to favor laissez faire and strong executive power; the extreme right wing supports fascist dictatorships. The term is derived from the common practice in European parliaments of seating conservative parties to the right of the presiding officer. See REACTIONARY, page 13.

Significance   Rightist parties exercise considerable influence in most democratic states. In the United States, both major parties have conservative members who hold many positions of influence in Congress. Prominent American rightist movements include the John Birch Society, the Ku Klux Klan, the

Conservative party, and the Young Americans for Freedom. Extreme right-wing forces have never found much support in American politics.

Rule of Law   An Anglo-American concept that emphasizes the supremacy of the law and restricts the discretionary power of public officials. The rule of law particularly stresses the protection of individual rights from the arbitrary interference of officials. *See* DEMOCRACY, page 6.

Significance   The rule of law provides the foundation for democratic constitutionalism. In the United States, for example, the rule of law requires that each individual accused of crime be treated equally under the law, receive a fair trial with established procedures, and be accorded due process in all official actions undertaken against him. Guarantees provided by the rule of law are in contrast with the operations of a police state. A vital maxim of democratic government is "government of law and not of men."

Socialism   A doctrine that advocates economic collectivism through governmental ownership of the means of production and distribution of goods. Its basic aims are to replace competition for profit with cooperation and social responsibility, and to secure a more equitable distribution of income and opportunity. Though these aims are common to all socialists, a wide variety of schools of thought have arisen, distinguished mainly by their approaches to the problem of how best to achieve socialism. These vary from the peaceful and democratic ideas of utopian and Christian socialists to the aggressive, and sometimes violent, approaches of anarchists and Communists. *See* DEMOCRATIC SOCIALISM, page 7.

Significance   Socialism has been a significant force, particularly in Europe, since the middle of the nineteenth century. In the United States, socialist parties have had little success at the ballot box, but their ideas have gained some measure of acceptance through liberal economic and social welfare programs. The democratic Socialist party of Eugene Debs and Norman Thomas has had great influence on American politics, but has waned in recent years. The more radical Socialist Labor party still runs a presidential candidate, but has few adherents.

Sovereignty   The supreme power of a state, exercised within its boundaries, free from external interference. The idea behind sovereignty is an ancient one, but it was first developed into an elaborate doctrine by philosophers of the fifteenth and sixteenth centuries, who sought to justify the absolutism of the kings of the new state system. *See* SOVEREIGNTY, page 338.

Significance   The early absolutist implications of sovereignty developed by Jean Bodin and Thomas Hobbes gave way in time to the new concept of popular sovereignty developed by Jean Jacques Rousseau and John Locke. The idea of sovereignty remains a significant factor in international relations. The concept of absolute sovereignty, however, has been modified by state consent, as is demonstrated in treaties, international law, and world organizations.

State   A political community occupying a definite territory, having an organized government and possessing internal and external sovereignty. Recognition of a state's claims to independence by other states, enabling it to enter into international engagements, is important to the establishment of its sovereignty. The term is also used to describe territorial divisions within a federal system, such as in the United States. *See* NATION, page 11.

Significance   More than 130 states comprise the community of nations. The state, the basic political unit of the world since the sixteenth century, is slowly giving way to evolutionary internationalism in the form of world and regional organizations. The basic challenge today is whether a stable system of international cooperation can be created before the state system destroys itself in a world war.

Theocracy   Any political system in which political power is exercised directly or indirectly by a clergy, and in which church law is superior to or replaces civil law. The implication is that decisions are made by a Supreme Being and are transmitted to man through agents who rule in a theocracy.

Significance   Theocracies typically are nondemocratic systems in which political power is exercised by an oligarchic council of priests, ministers, monks, or other church officials, or by a single church leader. Examples of theocracies include Geneva under John Calvin and Tibet prior to the Communist conquest.

Totalitarianism   A modern form of authoritarianism in which the state controls nearly every aspect of the individual's life. Totalitarian governments do not tolerate activities by individuals or groups, such as labor unions and youth organizations, that are not directed toward the state's goals. Totalitarian dictators maintain themselves in power by means of a secret police, propaganda disseminated through all media of communication, the elimination of free discussion and criticism, and widespread use of terror tactics. Internal scapegoats and foreign military threats are created and used to foster unity through fear. *See* ABSOLUTISM, page 1.

Significance   Totalitarianism has developed in the twentieth century through new techniques that mobilize entire populations in support of an authoritarian government and a political ideology. The main totalitarian governments have included Nazi Germany, Fascist Italy, the Soviet Union, and Communist China.

Utopia   An imaginary human paradise created in the mind and writings of Sir Thomas More. More's ideal commonwealth was located on an island untouched by worldly vices and provided a nearly perfect society. The word "utopia" means literally "no place" and is taken from the title of More's book published in 1516.

Significance   More's *Utopia* is part of the body of speculative political theory that has fostered the imaginative creation of ideal states and social systems, such as are found in Plato's *Republic* and Tommaso Campanella's *City of the Sun*. The adjective "utopian" is also used to describe the idealistic nineteenth century socialistic programs offered by Robert Owen, Claude Saint Simon, and François Fourier. American democracy has been influenced by utopianism and has established ideals of perfect freedom, equality, and brotherhood in the Democratic Creed.

Welfare State A concept that stresses the role of government as the provider and protector of individual security and social good through governmental economic and social programs. This role for government represents a shift from that of a minimal protector of persons and property to that of a positive promoter of human welfare.

Significance The welfare state is a product of the Industrial Revolution, urbanization, and the social and economic consequences of depressions and wars. Opponents of government's welfare role charge that "cradle to the grave" security destroys the individual's initiative and enterprise and promotes fiscal irresponsibility. Supporters point out that programs involving social security, health, subsidized housing, and the like provide necessary minimum standards of life for all, and that no civilized society can avoid this responsibility. Nearly all modern governments have engaged in some such practices, but only rich, industrialized nations have been able to afford extensive welfare programs.

Two

The United States Constitution: Background, Principles, Development

Amendment   Changes in, or additions to, a constitution. In the United States Constitution, Article V spells out the methods. Amendments may be proposed by a two-thirds vote of both houses of Congress or by a convention called by Congress at the request of the legislatures of two-thirds of the states. Only the first method has been used. Such proposals must be ratified by either the legislatures of three-fourths of the states or by conventions called for that purpose in three-fourths of the states, as determined by Congress. Only the Twenty-first Amendment (repealing prohibition) was submitted to conventions. The President may not veto an amendment proposal. Congress may stipulate a time limit, usually seven years, within which a proposal must be ratified. A state that has rejected an amendment may change its mind, but once a proposal is ratified by a state legislature, it stands. Ratification by a state may not be accomplished by a referendum of the people, but only by the legislature or convention. Though thousands of proposals have been made in Congress to amend the Constitution, only thirty have received endorsement from both houses; of these twenty-four have been adopted. Amendments are appended to the Constitution and not placed within the article or section that may have been changed, as is done in some state constitutions. *See* AMENDMENT, page 127; CONSTITUTIONAL AMENDMENTS, STATE, page 363; *Coleman v. Miller,* page 27. (For specific amendments, *see* Index.)

    Significance   A constitution, no matter how well designed, requires adjustment from time to time. A reasonable amendment procedure makes adjustment possible, without resort to force, in basic governmental arrangements. The Founding Fathers considered that proposal of amendments by the national government, with ratification controlled by the states, would safeguard the basic division of powers under the federal system. While most amendments adopted to date have not involved fundamental changes in American government, a few, such as the Fourteenth, have had a profound effect. The present methods of amendment have been criticized largely on the ground that minorities may block the majority will because of the two-thirds- and three-fourths-vote requirements. However, other less formal methods of change, such as judicial interpretation and custom and usage, have made frequent resort to the amendment process unnecessary.

18

Annapolis Convention   A conference called by the Virginia legislature in 1786, inviting the states to send delegates to Annapolis, Maryland, to discuss trade regulations. Only five states were represented. Under the leadership of Alexander Hamilton and James Madison, the group urged Congress and the states to call another convention in Philadelphia in 1787 to consider revision of the Articles of Confederation.

Significance   The Annapolis Convention was an important prelude to the framing of the Constitution of the United States, accomplished in Philadelphia the following year. Dissatisfaction with the Articles of Confederation, particularly in the areas of trade and commerce, led to this movement for reform.

Antifederalists   Persons who opposed adoption of the United States Constitution framed in Philadelphia in 1787. They opposed the centralist tendencies of the Constitution and attacked the failure of the framers to include a bill of rights. The group included many who had signed the Declaration of Independence or had strongly supported the Revolution.

Significance   A substantial number of people opposed ratification, but strong opposition to the Constitution rapidly dwindled after its adoption. The Antifederalist group, however, became the supporters of Thomas Jefferson whose views on the nature of the Union, as distinguished from those of Alexander Hamilton and other Federalists, continue to be influential and controversial in American politics today.

Articles of Confederation   The compact made among the thirteen original American states to form the basis of their government. Though prepared in 1776, the Articles were not officially adopted by all states until 1781 and were replaced in 1789 by the United States Constitution. The Confederation was a league of sovereign states. Each state had one vote in a one-house legislature. No provision was made in the Articles for a separate national executive or judiciary. The congress was assigned a limited number of powers, but the approval of nine states was necessary for effective action. The central government lacked significant powers, including the powers to tax, to regulate commerce or the currency, or to make its laws directly applicable to the people without further state action. In short, the congress could not force states or individuals to comply with its decisions, resembling, in many respects, an international organization. Any amendments to the Articles required the unanimous approval of the thirteen states. *See* CONFEDERATION, page 29.

Significance   The Articles, and the lessons learned under their operation, formed the backdrop against which the states could move toward "a more perfect union." The Confederation brought the Revolutionary War to a conclusion, accomplished much toward the development of the American continent through the Northwest Ordinance, and established the principle of interstate cooperation through such means as interstate rendition and full faith and credit. Many of the defects of the Articles were rectified in the United States Constitution.

Charter Colony   One of the three types of colonial governments—charter, proprietary, royal—found in colonial America. Charter colonies, namely Rhode

Island and Connecticut, operated under charters agreed to by the colony and the king. The legislature was elected and was allowed much autonomy by England. The governor was chosen by the legislature.

Significance   Charter colonies enjoyed the greatest degree of independence from the Crown. The charters of Connecticut and Rhode Island proved so satisfactory for local self-government that they served as state constitutions until 1818 and 1842 respectively.

Checks and Balances   A major principle of the American governmental system whereby each department of the government exercises a check upon the actions of the others. The principle operates not only among the legislative, executive, and judicial branches but between the two houses of the legislature and between the states and the national government. Each department has some authority to control the actions of one or more of the others by participation in their functions. Examples include the President's veto power and the congressional power to override the veto; judicial review of legislative and executive actions; presidential appointment of judges with senatorial approval; and the congressional power to impeach. See SEPARATION OF POWERS, page 25.

Significance   Through the various devices of check and balance, the framers of the Constitution sought to prevent the accumulation of all power in one branch, or in one or several persons, by giving each branch the authority to prevent the encroachment of the others. The check and balance system stresses the interdependence (rather than the complete separation) of the various units of government. It stresses the need for compromise and prevents the usurpation of power. Major defects of this system are its tendencies to create deadlocks and to prevent swift action during crises.

Commerce and Slave Trade Compromise   An agreement reached at the Constitutional Convention of 1787, giving the national government power to regulate foreign commerce, required the consent of two-thirds of the Senate to treaties and prohibited the national government from taxing exports or from interfering with the slave trade until 1808.

Significance   One of the major purposes for which the convention was called was to strengthen national control over commerce. Southern delegates, however, feared that northern majorities might cut off the slave trade and discriminate against the profitable cotton trade. They agreed to grant the national government control over foreign commerce provided that the South was given a check over treaties and that Congress would not tax exports. It was believed that a sufficient number of slaves would be available by 1808. The treaty and foreign commerce provisions continue to influence the making of American foreign policy.

Connecticut Compromise   The agreement reached in the Constitutional Convention of 1787 that resolved the question of representation in the national Congress. Each state is represented in the House of Representatives according to population and in the Senate each state is represented equally. The Compromise, also called the "Great Compromise," satisfied the small states in particular and made it possible for them to agree to the establishment of a strong central government. *See* BICAMERALISM, page 127.

Significance   While the Connecticut Compromise was the "price of union" in 1787, it has had lasting significance. The equal representation of states in the Senate has resulted in a disproportionate influence of sparsely settled states and regions. Though the states are represented by population in the House, bills must pass both houses to become law. Thus the Compromise of 1787 is felt in the daily workings of Congress. It is generally agreed that the Compromise was the crucial step in the formulation of the Constitution.

Constitution   A fundamental or "organic" law that establishes the framework of government of a state, assigns the powers and duties of governmental agencies, and establishes the relationship between the people and their government. Constitutions may be written or unwritten. The English operate under an unwritten constitution, that is, one consisting largely of legislative acts, legal decisions, and customs that have never been comprehensively gathered in one document. American constitutions are written, but much fundamental law is unwritten and is in the form of custom and usage. The United States Constitution went into effect on March 4, 1789, and has been amended twenty-four times. It is the supreme law of the land. Its basic principles include limited government, popular sovereignty, separation of powers, checks and balances, and federalism. *See* CONSTITUTION, STATE, page 362; DISTRIBUTION OF POWER, page 23.

Significance   The United States Constitution, the oldest and most successful written constitution in history, has served the nation with remarkably little formal alteration during periods of rapid social change. This is due to the wisdom of the framers who wrote a brief and flexible instrument, and to the policy of liberal construction that has characterized Supreme Court decisions. The Constitution has not only served as an effective instrument of government and a guardian of human rights but has come to be a revered symbol of how free men with diverse interests, and spread over a large area, can live together in freedom.

Constitutional Construction   The method of interpreting the Constitution. Some favor a "loose" or "liberal" construction of constitutional phrases; others, a "strict" interpretation. The difference is largely expressed in terms of the interpreter's attitude toward broad grants of power to the national government (loose construction) as opposed to the retention of as much power as possible in the states (strict construction). *See McCulloch v. Maryland,* page 42.

Significance   The issue of loose versus strict construction arose early in American history and contributed to the emergence of political parties. The Federalist party favored a broad interpretation of national powers, while the Jeffersonian Anti-Federalists stood for a narrow construction of such powers. The legal issue arose in the famous case of *McCulloch v. Maryland,* 4 Wheaton 316 (1819), which involved the question of whether the national government was limited to those powers *expressly* delegated to it or whether it had *implied* powers. Chief Justice Marshall resolved the issue in favor of the implied-powers doctrine and established the principle of, and the necessity for, a loose construction of the Constitution. From time to time, the strict constructionists have had their way, depending largely on the party in power and the attitude of the Supreme Court. Loose construction, however, remains the basis for constitutional interpretation and has facilitated adaptation of the Constitution to the needs of the time.

Constitutional Convention of 1787   The convention held in Philadelphia from May 25 to September 18 that framed the Constitution of the United States. Called by the Confederation Congress to revise the Articles of Confederation, the delegates proceeded to draft an entirely new document. Rhode Island sent no delegates and only fifty-five of the seventy-four men originally appointed as delegates attended. George Washington presided. The deliberations were conducted in secret but have been made known through notes kept by James Madison. The delegates made compromises on various differences between large and small states, North and South, agrarian and commercial interests, and advocates of a strong or a weak central government. They not only ignored their instructions merely to revise the Articles of Confederation. They also ignored the provision of the Articles requiring unanimous consent of the state legislatures for revision, by providing that the new constitution would go into effect when nine states ratified it in state conventions. See COMMERCE AND SLAVE TRADE COMPROMISE, page 20; CONNECTICUT COMPROMISE, page 20; ECONOMIC INTERPRETATION OF THE CONSTITUTION, page 23; MADISON'S JOURNAL, page 24; NEW JERSEY PLAN, page 24; VIRGINIA PLAN, page 27; THREE-FIFTHS COMPROMISE, page 26.
    Significance   The convention was a conservative reaction to the excesses of the Revolutionary period and to the commercial disorder under the Articles of Confederation. Its membership was young and well-informed on government and politics, and was representative of propertied and commercial interests. The convention has been the only national constitutional convention in American history, but by law, another can be called by Congress on the request of two-thirds of the states.

Continental Congress   The body of delegates representing the colonies that first met to protest the British treatment of the colonies and eventually became the government of the United States. The First Continental Congress met in 1774 and drafted a Declaration of Rights. The Second Congress, meeting the following year, adopted the Declaration of Independence, conducted the War of Independence, and served as the national government until the Articles of Confederation went into effect in 1781.
    Significance   The First Congress met in an atmosphere in which the colonists still considered themselves Englishmen who were being abused. The Second Congress convened after open conflict with England had begun. Though the Second Congress rested on no legal base, it served as a *de facto* government. Delegates were selected by the state legislatures. While the states did not feel bound by decisions of the Continental Congress, it succeeded in bringing the war to a successful conclusion. It also developed an American conscious-

ness, which led to the adoption of the Articles of Confederation and, eventually, to the Constitution of the United States.

Declaration of Independence   The document adopted by the Second Continental Congress on July 4, 1776, declaring the independence of the American colonies from Great Britain and justifying the rebellion. It was drafted by a committee composed of Thomas Jefferson, John Adams, Benjamin Franklin, Roger Sherman, and Robert Livingston. The draft was largely the work of Jefferson, who drew heavily from the natural-rights doctrine of the English philosopher, John Locke. The Declaration enumerated the grievances against the Crown and contained an eloquent defense of the rights of man and the right of self-government.

Significance   The Declaration of Independence does not have any legal effect today. Nevertheless, it is recognized throughout the world as a basic statement of the American creed. Its opening passage declares the equality of man, the natural rights of man endowed by God, the principle of limited government, government by consent, and the right of people to rebel against tyrannical government.

Distribution of Powers   An underlying principle of the American constitutional system designed to prevent tyranny by assigning powers to different governments and agencies and by checking the exercise of power. The distribution takes the following forms: (1) dividing power between the national and state governments under a federal system; (2) separating power among the three major branches of the government—legislative, executive, and judicial—giving each branch a check upon the operations of the others; (3) selecting the personnel of the three branches by different procedures and electorates, making them responsible to different pressures; (4) limiting all governments by specific constitutional restrictions. *See* FEDERALISM, page 32; SEPARATION OF POWERS, page 25.

Significance   The framers sought to prevent all governmental power from falling into the hands of any individual or group. They feared majority tyranny as much as minority or individual tyranny. Hence they provided for a wide distribution of authority, limited in scope, and designed to effect a balancing of interests. The distribution of powers has been modified by the expanding role of the national government, the increasing influence of the President over legislation and foreign affairs, and the development of independent regulatory agencies that exercise some legislative and judicial power in their supervision of the economy.

Economic Interpretation of the Constitution   The theory that the framers of the Constitution represented the well-to-do classes and that the Constitution was designed to protect their interests. The theory was developed by the distinguished historian Charles A. Beard in his *An Economic Interpretation of the Constitution of the United States* (1913).

Significance   Beard did not attribute any malice to the framers but tried to show that they had much to gain from the creation of a strong and stable national government. He pointed out that the delegates were professional or propertied men with extensive holdings in public securities, land, manufacturing, shipping, and slaves. Although the framers were a conservative-minded group who were affected by their own backgrounds and interests, Beard and other historians have emphasized that economic interest was only one of the factors that motivated them.

Federalist Papers   A series of eighty-five essays written by Alexander Hamilton, James Madison, and John Jay (all using the name *Publius*), which were published in New York newspapers in 1787 to convince New Yorkers to adopt the newly proposed Constitution drafted in Philadelphia. These essays have been collected and published under the title *The Federalist*.

Significance   *The Federalist*, though written in haste and for the specific purpose of winning support for the Constitution, is widely regarded as the best single commentary on the Constitution. Governmental officials, especially judges, often rely on *The Federalist* in interpreting the meaning of the Constitution. Moreover, it is considered to be the outstanding American contribution to political theory.

Madison's Journal   Notes kept by James Madison of the proceedings of the Constitutional Convention of 1787. Though an official journal of the convention was kept, it contained only formal motions and votes by states. Madison kept a record of the debates as well. These notes were not published until 1840, four years after Madison's death.

Significance   The proceedings of the convention were conducted in secrecy and Madison's notes are the only reliable source of information. For more than fifty years, the Constitution was interpreted without the benefit of these materials, which cast important light upon the intentions of the framers.

New Jersey Plan   A plan submitted by William Patterson of New Jersey to the Constitutional Convention of 1787 representing the views of the small states and states'-rights advocates. It was expressly designed as a counterproposal to the strongly nationalistic Virginia Plan. The essence of the New Jersey Plan was a single-house Congress with each state having an equal vote. Moreover, the Plan looked toward a moderate modification of the Articles of Confederation rather than toward the drafting of a new document. *See* VIRGINIA PLAN, page 27.

Significance   The New Jersey Plan, along with the Virginia Plan, drew the major battle lines of the convention. Though the basic idea of the New Jersey Plan to retain the Articles of Confederation was defeated by the convention, the demand for equal representation resulted in the Connecticut Compromise. The assurance that the states would receive equal representation in one house of Congress made it possible for the convention to complete its deliberations.

Preamble   The statement affixed at the beginning of the Constitution, stating the source of its authority and the purposes it is to serve. The Preamble to the United States Constitution is of no legal effect but may serve as a guide to the intent of the framers.

Significance   Particular importance is attached to the fact that the Preamble begins with the words "We the people" rather than "The states of New York . . . ." The wording establishes the supremacy of the national Constitution as emanating from all the people rather than as a contract among sovereign states. This was of particular significance in the great debate over the nature of the Union prior to the Civil War. The Preamble is also noted as a concise statement of the enduring principles of a free people.

Proprietary Colony   One of the three types of colonial governments—charter, proprietary, royal—found in colonial America. Proprietary colonies were governed by charters issued by the "proprietor," an individual to whom the king had made a land grant. Pennsylvania was established under such a charter bestowed by William Penn. Other proprietary colonies were Delaware and Maryland. Though the lower house of the legislature was elected, the upper house and the governor were chosen by the proprietor, subject to approval of the Crown.

Significance   The proprietor represented the Crown, and the colonies were largely ruled from England, Nevertheless, important lessons in self-government were learned. Increasing efforts by the Crown to control these colonies was a contributing factor to the Revolution. The "frame of government" drawn up by William Penn for Pennsylvania, was a relatively democratic document.

Royal Colony   One of the three types of colonial governments—charter, proprietary, royal—found in colonial America. Eight colonies were royal colonies. The lower house of the legislature was elected but the upper house and the governor were appointed by the king. Royal governors exercised almost complete authority over the colony through instructions received from England.

Significance   It was in the royal colonies that much of the resentment against the king grew, resulting in the Revolution. The royal governor, in particular, was the object of resentment and fear, and the first state constitutions reflected this by giving little authority to the governor. This tradition has lasted until recent times, but the current tendency is to strengthen executive power in the states.

Separation of Powers   A major principle of American government whereby power is distributed among three branches of government—the legislative, the executive, and the judicial. The officials of each branch are selected by different procedures and are independent of one another. The separation is not complete, in that each branch participates in the functions of the other through a system of checks and balances. The separation, however, serves to ensure that the same person or group will not make the law, enforce the law, and interpret and apply the law. *See* CHECKS AND BALANCES, page 20.

Significance   The separation of lawmaking, law enforcement, and law interpretation is designed to prevent tyranny. It also serves to make the three branches responsive to different pressures. At the same time, the system frequently results in lack of unity between the legislative and executive branches, particularly when they are controlled by different parties. This fragmentation of power is a major factor in the operation of the American governmental system. The judiciary plays the critical role in maintaining the branches within their assigned powers.

Shays' Rebellion   An armed revolt by farmers in western Massachusetts in 1786-1787, seeking relief from debts and possible foreclosures of mortgages. Led by Daniel Shays, a Revolutionary War officer, the group prevented judges from hearing mortgage foreclosure cases and attempted to capture an arsenal. They were repelled by the state militia.

Significance   While its seriousness may be questioned, Shays' Rebellion is credited with being a major factor in the demand for a revision of the Articles of Confederation. The event highlighted the economic difficulties facing the states at that time and caused alarm among the creditor and commercial interests.

State Sovereignty   Independence of a state from external control. The concept of state sovereignty was an integral part of government under the Articles of Confederation and was part of the great debate on the Union that took place prior to the Civil War. In effect, state sovereignty is a rejection of the principle of national supremacy under the United States Constitution. *See* STATES' RIGHTS, page 39.

Significance   The states of the Union were sovereign under the Articles of Confederation. Prior to the Civil War, it was claimed by southern states that the Constitution was a compact among states rather than among the people and that the states were free to secede. State sovereignty as a legal doctrine is rejected, although the states' rights political argument reappears from time to time, invoked by the opponents of expanding federal power.

Three-Fifths Compromise   An agreement reached at the Constitutional Convention of 1787 to count only three-fifths of the slave population in determining representation in the House of Representatives and in apportioning direct taxes.

Significance   At the Constitutional Convention, the issue of whether to count slaves for representation and tax purposes sharply divided the northern and southern delegates. The resultant compromise was one of many made at the convention. This provision of the Constitution (Art. I, sec. 2) is no longer pertinent.

Usage   A custom that, because it is well-established, is regarded as a part of the American constitutional system. Though not precisely provided for in the words of the Constitution, such practices form an important element of the actual operations of government. Among these are such vital components as the role of political parties, the operations of the Electoral College, the presidential Cabinet, and the inner organization of Congress.

Significance   Little can be learned about how American government works solely by a reading of the Constitution. Usage is one of the major methods by which the Constitution has been developed to meet practical problems. A full understanding of the American constitutional system requires knowledge not only of the written document itself, but also of the various usages. A well-established usage becomes part of the "unwritten constitution" and may have the same effect as, or greater than, an actual constitutional amendment.

Virginia Plan   A plan, submitted by Edmund Randolph of Virginia to the Constitutional Convention of 1787, that called for scrapping the Articles of Confederation and establishing a new and strong national government. It provided for a two-house legislature based on state population or wealth, a national executive, and a judiciary. Congress would have had power to disallow state legislation and was to be invested with broad power over matters of national concern. *See* NEW JERSEY PLAN, page 24.

Significance   The Virginia Plan served as the major basis for discussion in the convention. Once a compromise over representation (equal representation in one house) that satisfied the small states was reached, the delegates proceeded to draft a constitution as envisaged by the Virginia Plan. A strong central government was established with power to act directly on individuals rather than through the states.

IMPORTANT CASES

Coleman v. Miller, 307 U.S. 433 (1939): A case establishing the principle that the process of amending the Constitution is essentially political in nature and not subject to judicial interference. Specifically, the Supreme Court held that a state legislature may ratify the child labor amendment proposal after once rejecting it, and that whether the pending proposal was still valid after many years is a political question for Congress to determine.

Significance   No case involving the amending clause of the Constitution has come before the Supreme Court since *Coleman v. Miller.* The decision has had the effect of removing the Court from involvement in the amending process, leaving Article V to the political branches of the government.

IMPORTANT STATUTES

Northwest Ordinance   An enactment of the congress under the Articles of Confederation providing for the government of the territory north of the Ohio River and west of New York to the Mississippi River. The Ordinance provided for the eventual statehood of areas of the territory when they acquired 60,000 inhabitants. Liberal provision was made for local self-government, civil and political rights, and education. Slavery was forbidden in the territory. A previous ordinance of 1785, establishing the township system of dividing land and providing for local schools, was reaffirmed in the Ordinance of 1787.

Significance   The Northwest Ordinance was the most significant measure passed by the Confederation Congress. It was readopted by Congress under the Constitution and served as the basis for later territorial acts. It established the important policy that territories were not to be kept in subjection but were to be developed for admission to statehood on an equal footing with other states.

Three

The Federal Union

Admission of New States   The Constitution empowers Congress to admit new states to the Union (Art. IV, sec. 3). Limitations on this power are, that no state may be created within an existing state, nor may any state be formed by the union of two or more states or parts of states without the consent of the states concerned and of Congress. The usual procedure for admission is (1) the people of the territory through their territorial assembly petition Congress; (2) Congress passes an "enabling act" that, when signed by the President, authorizes the territory to frame a constitution; (3) Congress passes an act of admission approved by the President. Though Congress and the President may insist upon certain conditions for admission to the Union, a state, once admitted, is equal with all other states. No state may constitutionally withdraw from the Union. *See Coyle v. Smith,* page 41; TERRITORY, page 40.

   Significance   The Founding Fathers recognized the desirability of expanding the federal Union by giving Congress power to admit new states. Political considerations, such as which political party the people of the area are likely to support, may influence the majority party in Congress. With the exception of the thirteen original states, thirty were elevated from territorial status; five (Vermont, Kentucky, Tennessee, Maine, and West Virginia) were formed by separation from other states; and two, Texas and California, were formed from an independent republic and by acquisition from Mexico, respectively.

Centralization   The tendency for political power and authority to gravitate from state governments to the national government. Though the functions performed by all governments in the United States have increased, the nation-wide impact of economic, social, and defense problems has led to an increased assumption of responsibility by the national government.

   Significance   The proper division of powers between the national and state governments has been a cause for controversy throughout American history. It is argued that centralization permits more efficient handling of problems that are nationwide in scope. Opponents contend that decentralized activity prevents tyranny, permits experimentation, and encourages local solutions to problems. Various groups tend to support the management of a function by that level of government most responsive to their needs.

Commerce Power   The authority granted to Congress by the Constitution to regulate commerce with foreign nations and among the states. The term "commerce" has been interpreted to include the production and buying and selling of goods as well as the transportation of commodities. Any of these functions are subject to national regulation and control if they affect more than one state. *See* COMMERCE, page 259; *Gibbons v. Ogden,* page 276.

   Significance   The commerce power is one of the major constitutional provisions used by Congress to expand national power. A broad interpretation of what constitutes interstate commerce has enabled Congress to regulate such matters as manufacturing, child labor, farm production, wages and hours, labor unions, civil rights, and even criminal conduct that involves the crossing of state lines, such as car theft or kidnaping. Any activity that in any way "affects" interstate commerce is subject to national rather than state control. So many functions are now interstate in character that the role of the states in the federal system has been considerably altered.

Concurrent Powers   Authority possessed by both the national and state governments. Examples include the powers to tax, to maintain courts, and to charter banks. The states may exercise concurrently with the national government any power that is not exclusively conferred on the national government by the Constitution and that does not conflict with national law. *See* DELEGATED POWERS, page 30; RESERVED POWERS, page 39.

   Significance   Under the American federal system, it is essential that both national and state governments possess those powers necessary to enable them to function. The power to tax is a noteworthy example. The fact that this power is delegated to the national government does not mean that the states may not also tax. States frequently legislate in areas in which the national government has not, despite its power to do so, sought to legislate. Should the national government determine to occupy a particular field of activity delegated to it under the Constitution, then the principle of national supremacy prevails. In the regulation of interstate commerce, the national government has frequently allowed state control over some elements of such commerce. The Supreme Court has disallowed state action when it has determined that national uniformity is desirable.

Confederation   A league of independent states. A central government or administrative organ handles those matters of common concern delegated to it by the member states. The central unit may not make laws directly applicable to individuals without further action by the member units. The governments under the Articles of Confederation and the Confederate States of America are two examples from American history. The United Nations is often referred to as a confederation. *See* ARTICLES OF CONFEDERATION, page 19; FEDERALISM, page 32.

   Significance   A confederation is generally distinguished from a federation in which, as in the United States, the central unit is invested with supreme authority and may act directly upon individuals. American experience under the Articles of Confederation is credited with being an essential step toward the formation of the "more perfect union." A confederated structure enables sovereign states to cooperate in seeking solutions to mutual problems without giving up their autonomy.

Contract Clause   Article I, section 10 of the Constitution prohibits any state from passing laws impairing the obligation of contracts. This clause applies to contracts between individuals and to contracts made by the states. The state may neither weaken the effect of a contract nor make it more difficult to enforce. All contracts, however, are subject to the limitation that they may not endanger the health, safety, and welfare of the people—the areas of the states' "police powers."

Significance   At one time, the contract clause was a major constitutional defense against state regulation of private property. The framers of the Constitution sought to guard against state practices of relieving private persons (such as debtors) of their contractual obligations. The clause was also used to favor corporations receiving charters from the states by making it impossible for the states to change the charters at a later date (*Dartmouth College v. Woodward,* 4 Wheaton 518 [1819]). State constitutions or statutes now make specific provision permitting revocation or alteration of corporation charters and other state contracts, subject to the limitations of due process of law. This development, along with police power limitations, has modified the restrictive nature of the contract clause.

Cooperative Federalism   A concept that views the state and the national government as cooperating partners in the performance of governmental functions rather than as antagonistic competitors for power. The grant-in-aid programs typify this relationship between the national and state governments. *See* GRANT-IN-AID, page 32.

Significance   Many current problems cut across traditional divisions of authority between the national and state governments. Cooperation between these units to meet common problems has enabled American federalism to adjust to new problems and to find some middle ground between extreme centralization of power and unworkable decentralization. For example, a vast interstate highway system would be unlikely without national and state cooperation.

Delegated Powers   Powers granted to the national government under the Constitution. Generally, the delegated powers are those found enumerated in the first three articles of the Constitution, relative to the legislative, executive, and judicial branches of the national government. Article I, section 8 contains the main compilation of these powers. The terms "delegated," "enumerated," "granted," and "specific" may be used interchangeably. *See* IMPLIED POWERS, page 33; RESERVED POWERS, page 39.

Significance   Under American federalism, the national government is a government of delegated powers. With the exception of foreign affairs, it must find justification for its actions in a specifically authorized power, or in one that can be reasonably implied from those specifically authorized. The national government does not possess unlimited or general governmental power but only such power as is given to it in the Constitution.

District of Columbia The seat of government of the United States of America, commonly called Washington, D.C. It consists of some seventy square miles of land carved out of the state of Maryland. Article I, section 8, of the Constitution grants Congress exclusive control over the capital. The District is governed by a three-man Board of Commissioners appointed by the President, one of whom is an Army engineer. Congress is the legislative body for the District and in effect acts as the city council. Funds for the District are secured largely through local taxation. The District is a highly urbanized area of about one million inhabitants. The people of the District do not choose local officers, but, under the Twenty-third Amendment adopted in 1961, they may vote in presidential elections .

Significance In recent years, attention has turned toward securing a measure of self-government for the people of the District. Major obstacles appear to be the inability of Congress to agree on a scheme of government, and southern opposition based on the fact that a large portion of the residents are Negroes. Criticism has also been made of the great amount of time devoted by Congress to affairs of the District, which would be unnecessary if home rule were granted.

Enabling Act An act of Congress authorizing the people of a territory to take the necessary steps to prepare for statehood. This would include calling a convention to frame a constitution. *See* ADMISSION OF NEW STATES, page 28.

Significance The enabling act constitutes an official indication that Congress and the President look with favor upon a territory's petition for statehood. Congress and the President are vested with considerable authority over what areas and under what conditions statehood will be granted. They must still approve the territory's constitution before officially granting statehood. On occasion, such as in the case of Alaska, a state has bypassed the petition and enabling act steps and has gone directly to Congress with its proposed constitution.

Exclusive Powers Those powers that, under the Constitution, belong exclusively to, and may be exercised only by, either the national government or the governments of the various states. An example of an exclusive national power is that over foreign affairs; an exclusive state power is control over local government. *See* CONCURRENT POWERS, page 29.

Significance The concept of exclusive power emphasizes the federal nature of the United States—two governments, existing side by side, each supreme within its own sphere of authority. Many problem areas, once considered within the exclusive realm of state power, have, however, under changing social conditions, fallen under national control. Civil rights and welfare programs illustrate how the national government has moved into fields previously under exclusive state control.

Federalism   A system of government in which power is divided by a written constitution between a central government and regional or subdivisional governments. Both governments act directly upon the people through their officials and laws. Both are supreme within their proper sphere of authority. By contrast, a "unitary" system of government is one in which the central government is supreme and in which regional and local governments derive their authority from the central government. Federal systems are found in the United States, Canada, Switzerland, Mexico, Australia, India, and West Germany, among others. In the United States, the term "federal government" is used as a synonym for the national government. See UNITARY STATE, page 41; CONFEDERATION, page 29.

Significance   Federalism is a compromise between an extreme concentration of power and a loose confederation of independent states for governing a variety of people, usually in a large expanse of territory. At the Constitutional Convention of 1787, this compromise was essential in order to convince the independent states to join together. Federalism has the virtue of retaining local pride, traditions, and power, while making possible a strong central government that can handle common problems. In the United States, federalism has facilitated growth through the admittance of new states to the Union. The basic principle of American federalism is fixed in the Tenth Amendment to the Constitution, which provides that the national government is to have those powers delegated in the Constitution, with all other powers reserved to the states. In some countries using the federal system (for example, in Canada), the pattern is reversed, with the regional governments possessing only delegated authority. Federalism is one of the major principles underlying the American Constitution and has a continuing impact upon American life and politics.

Full Faith and Credit   One of the obligations of each state in its relations with other states. Article IV, section 1, of the Constitution provides that "Full faith and credit shall be given in each state to the public acts, records and judicial proceedings of every other state." The clause applies to civil but not criminal proceedings. It ensures that rights established under wills, contracts, deeds, and other property rights will be honored in all states. A judicial decision in one state will be honored and enforced in all states. One area of difficulty has arisen with regard to divorce decrees. Some states have refused to recognize uncontested divorces granted by sister states because of questions over domicile (*Williams v. North Carolina,* 325 U.S. 226 [1945]). See HORIZONTAL FEDERALISM, page 33.

Significance   This clause was originally put into the Articles of Confederation to promote "mutual friendship and intercourse among the people of the different states in this Union." It was carried over to the Constitution and has contributed to the unity of the American people. It protects the legal rights of citizens as they move about the various states and prevents evasion of legal responsibilities. The increasing mobility of the American people and the expanse of business operations have increased the importance of the clause.

Grant-in-Aid   Funds made available by Congress to the state and local governments for expenditure in accordance with prescribed standards and conditions. State legislatures also make such grants to local governments. Some measure of supervision over the expenditure of the funds accompanies the grants. In addition, the receiving government is required to match the contribution dollar-for-dollar or in some other ratio. Highways, airports, agriculture, education, welfare, and health are among the major functions financed through the grant-in-aid device. *See Massachusetts v. Mellon,* page 42; FEDERAL AID HIGHWAY ACT, page 43; COOPERATIVE FEDERALISM, page 30.

Significance   Extensive use is being made of grants-in-aid to make available the superior tax resources of the national government for financing activities administered by the state and local governments. It has enabled the national government to enter fields formerly considered to be within the reserved powers of the states. The states have accepted some national control, because they need federal funds. Often, because state governments have been unwilling or unable to deal with pressing problems, people have turned to Washington for help. In recent years this has also been true in local areas. This has enabled all sections of the country to benefit from governmental services that otherwise might be available only in wealthier states. In addition, states have been stimulated to undertake needed activities and to improve their administrative and technical standards. The major disadvantage of the grant-in-aid system is that it transfers policy-making authority to the national government in areas formerly handled by state and local governments. The system, however, represents an alternative to extreme centralization of the administration of services.

Horizontal Federalism   The relationships among the states of the Union either imposed by the Constitution or undertaken voluntarily. This term is used to distinguish state-state relations from national-state relations (denoted by the term "vertical federalism"). Requirements imposed by the Constitution are that each state afford full faith and credit to the public acts, records, and judicial proceedings of other states, grant the citizens of each state the privileges and immunities of citizens of their own state, and return fugitives from justice. Voluntary arrangements include interstate compacts, uniform laws, reciprocal agreements, and cooperation through consultation. *See* FULL FAITH AND CREDIT, page 32; INTERSTATE COMPACT, page 35; INTERSTATE RENDITION, page 36; PRIVILEGES AND IMMUNITIES, page 37; UNIFORM STATE LAWS, page 377.

Significance   Under federalism, the relationships among the states may be of equal importance to the relationship between the national and state governments. Since each state retains a good deal of authority, certain requirements have been laid down to assure cooperation. The requirement of full faith and credit, for example, helps to guarantee legal rights of citizens throughout the country. The states have sought to forestall national intervention into problem areas that cross state lines by entering into voluntary agreements. States have not, however, shown sufficient initiative in meeting mutual problems, resulting in increasing dependence by the people upon the national government.

Implied Powers   Authority possessed by the national government by inference from those powers delegated to it in the Constitution. For example, the power to draft men into the armed forces may be deduced from the power delegated to raise armies and navies. The implied power concept derives from the "necessary and proper" clause in Article I, section 8, which empowers the national government to do all things necessary and proper to carry out its delegated powers. This principle was officially enunciated by the Supreme Court in *McCulloch v. Maryland,* 4 Wheaton 316 (1819). *See* CONSTITUTIONAL CONSTRUCTION, page 21; *McCulloch v. Maryland,* page 42; NECESSARY AND PROPER CLAUSE, page 37.

Significance   In the early days of the Union, conflicting opinions arose over whether the national government was limited to exercising only those powers expressly delegated to it in the Constitution. It is unlikely that the national government could have emerged as a powerful force had the more limited view prevailed. Through the use of implied powers, the national government has been able to strengthen and broaden the scope of its authority to meet many problems not foreseen by the framers.

Inherent Powers   Authority vested in the national government, particularly in the area of foreign affairs, that does not depend upon any specific grant of power in the Constitution. Inherent powers derive from the fact that the United States is a sovereign power among nations. The Supreme Court has pointed out that even if the Constitution made no mention of it, the national government could still, for example, make international agreements or acquire territory. Whether or not the President has inherent powers to meet emergencies in internal affairs by virtue of his position as chief executive, is a matter of dispute. *See* INHERENT POWERS, page 326; *United States v. Curtiss-Wright Export Corp.,* page 342; *Youngstown Sheet and Tube Co. v. Sawyer,* page 178.

Significance   Since the national government is one of delegated powers, justification for its actions must be found either directly or by implication from a specific grant of power. In the field of international affairs, however, the United States must be presumed to have the same power as any other nation in the world. Many Presidents have taken unauthorized action to meet emergency situations, notably Abraham Lincoln during the Civil War. However, in 1952, during the Korean conflict, the Supreme Court ruled that the President could not seize private property (steel mills) without authorization from Congress (*Youngstown Sheet and Tube Co. v. Sawyer,* 343 U.S. 579).

Intergovernmental Tax Immunity   The exemption of state and national governmental agencies and property from taxation by each other. The doctrine of intergovernmental tax immunity had its origin in the case of *McCulloch v. Maryland,* 4 Wheaton 316 (1819), in which the Supreme Court declared that the states may not burden the national government by the taxation of its agents or functions. This doctrine was later extended to national taxation of state agents and functions. For a time, even the salaries of governmental employees and contractors were exempt from taxation; this is no longer the case. National governmental functions and properties are exempt from state taxation, but where hardship may result, because of extensive federal holdings in a state, payments in lieu of taxes may be authorized by Congress. State or local activities may be taxed by the national government if the function is nongovernmental in character. An example of this is national taxation of state-owned liquor stores. *See McCulloch v. Maryland,* page 42; *Graves v. New York,* page 41; *South Carolina v. United States,* page 254; PROPRIETARY FUNCTION, page 265.

Significance   Intergovernmental tax immunity prevents undue interference by one government with the proper exercise of power by another government. This rule is essential to the effective operation of a federal system of government. Without such a rule, one level of government might use its tax power to weaken or to destroy operations of the other. National taxation of state nongovernmental functions remains a matter of controversy, since it is questionable whether any state or local activity can be classified as nongovernmental in character. The courts have been reluctant to interfere with congressional judgment on this matter.

Interposition   A concept that holds that a state may place itself between its citizens and the national government so as to prevent the enforcement of national law upon its citizens. According to this doctrine, each state may be the judge of the legality or constitutionality of national action, and may "interpose" its sovereignty to nullify invalid federal action. This theory was propounded by Thomas Jefferson and James Madison in the Kentucky and Virginia Resolutions of 1799 protesting the Alien and Sedition Acts, and by the South prior to the Civil War. Southern leaders reactivated the theory in opposition to the desegregation rulings of the Supreme Court. The federal courts, however, have rejected the doctrine as contrary to the national supremacy clause of Article VI. *See* NULLIFICATION, page 37.

Significance   Interposition represents a challenge to national supremacy in an extreme form. Obviously, fifty different interpretations of the Constitution would dissolve the Union. From time to time, the right to interpose state sovereignty has been claimed by states in all sections of the country. This claim of state sovereignty has generally been made to cover up underlying social and economic interests of particular groups that feel themselves threatened by national policy. When interposition is claimed, it is a sign that the federal principle is under strain.

Interstate Compact   An agreement between two or more states. The Constitution (Art. I, sec. 10) requires such agreements or compacts to have the consent of Congress. Many agreements on minor matters, however, are made without such consent. Generally, any compact that tends to increase the power of the contracting states relative to other states or to the national government requires consent. One of the earliest and best-known compacts was concluded between New York and New Jersey, in 1921, to establish the Port of New York Authority for purposes of regulating the New York harbor and other facilities. A great variety of other compacts are in existence covering a wide range of subjects from flood control to petroleum conservation. Congress has, at times, granted advance blanket approval to certain kinds of compacts, as in civil defense matters and water pollution. *See Virginia v. Tennessee,* page 43; HORIZONTAL FEDERALISM, page 33.

Significance   One intent of the requirement that congressional consent be acquired was to prevent the states from threatening the Union through alliances among themselves. Today, interstate compacts serve as a means for the states to solve regional problems without resort to national aid. In this way the states may avoid the centralizing tendencies of recent years.

Interstate Rendition   The return of a fugitive from justice by a state upon the demand of the executive authority of the state in which the crime was committed. This is one of the obligations imposed upon the states by Article IV, section 2. Though the language of the Constitution is positive on this obligation, the federal courts will not order the governor of one state to deliver a fugitive wanted in another state. Compliance by a governor is viewed as a moral duty. Rendition is routinely followed in most cases but, on occasion, a governor has refused to comply. Refusal may be based on such grounds as the good behavior of the fugitive since his escape, the suspicion that a fair trial will not be granted, or for political or other reasons known only to the governor. Congress has supplemented the requirement by making it a federal crime to flee across state lines to avoid prosecution for certain felonies. When apprehended by federal agents, the fugitive is usually turned over to the state from which he fled. The term "extradition" is used to describe this practice among nations under international law. *See Kentucky v. Dennison,* page 41; HORIZONTAL FEDERALISM, page 33; EXTRADITION, page 323.

Significance   The practice of rendition is designed to prevent "beating the rap" by leaving a state. Although the governor may refuse to return the fugitive, he may invite retaliation of the other state by such action. Considerable doubt exists as to whether Congress could compel a governor to return a fugitive, despite a Supreme Court decision suggesting that this could not be done (*Kentucky v. Dennison,* 24 Howard 66 [1861]).

National Supremacy   A basic constitutional principle of American government that asserts the superiority of national law. This principle is rooted in Article VI, which provides that the Constitution, laws passed by the national government under its constitutional powers, and all treaties, are the supreme law of the land. The Article requires that all national and state officers and judges be bound by oath to support the Constitution regardless of any state constitutional or legislative provisions. Thus, any legitimate exercise of national power supersedes any conflicting state action. Determination of whether such a conflict exists rests in the hands of the judiciary, with the final decisions made by the Supreme Court. *See McCulloch v. Maryland,* page 42; *Cohens v. Virginia,* page 228.

Significance   National supremacy is crucial to the successful operation of the federal system. The national government is the government of all the people; a state speaks for only some of the people. The application of the principle of national supremacy has been a source of constant conflict, with such extreme results as the Civil War. The major *legal* challenge to national supremacy was expounded by the Supreme Court in the concept of "dual federalism," which held that a grant of authority to the national government does not destroy local power reserved to the states. Since 1937, the Court has rejected this concept and applied a broad construction of national authority. A contemporary example of the application of national supremacy is the controversy over ending racial segregation.

Necessary and Proper Clause   The final paragraph of Article I, section 8, of the Constitution, which delegates legislative powers to Congress. It authorizes all laws "necessary and proper" to carry out the enumerated powers. This clause, sometimes called the "elastic" clause, was used by the Supreme Court in *McCulloch v. Maryland,* 4 Wheaton 316 (1819), to develop the concept of "implied powers." *See McCulloch v. Maryland,* page 42; IMPLIED POWERS, page 33.

Significance   Congressional authority is limited to its delegated powers. The necessary and proper clause, however, allows Congress to choose the *means* by which it will execute its authority. Broad construction of this phrase has enabled the national government to adapt its powers to the needs of the times. It has given elasticity to our constitutional system and has reduced the need for frequent constitutional amendment.

Nullification   A declaration by a state that a national law is null and void, and therefore not binding upon its citizens. South Carolina, in 1832, attempted to nullify the Tariff Acts of 1828 and 1832. The theory of nullification, a logical extension of the theory of interposition, was formulated by John C. Calhoun. The theory holds that the Union is a compact among sovereign states and that the national government is not the final judge of its own powers; a state may nullify any national law and even secede from the Union. *See* INTERPOSITION, page 35.

Significance   Though nullification is a discredited theory, the racial segregation problem of recent years has given rise to nullification talk by some southern leaders. The Supreme Court has rejected the theory as contrary to the principle of national supremacy. Nevertheless, some southern states have continued to thwart the national government's efforts to achieve full desegregation.

Police Power   Authority to promote and safeguard the health, morals, safety, and welfare of the people. In the context of the American federal system, police power is reserved to the states. The national government, exercising only delegated powers, does not possess a general police power. Many national laws enacted under the commerce and postal powers, such as those which prohibit shipment of impure drugs in interstate commerce or mailing of obscene literature, are, however, examples of what may be termed "federal police power." State laws enacted under the police power may legally invade national jurisdiction if such laws are pertinent to the health, safety, or welfare of the people of the state, such as a state law regulating grade crossings for interstate trains. *See* POLICE POWER, page 68.

Significance   Police powers are the most vital powers reserved to the states under the Constitution, in recognition of the responsibility of state government to safeguard individual well-being. The judiciary plays a large role in determining the proper scope for the exercise of the police power. The police power has greatly enlarged the area of state and local control over the individual as well as over business, labor, and property.

Privileges and Immunities   Special rights and exemptions provided by law. The Constitution contains two clauses that use the term "privileges and immunities." Article IV, section 2, provides that, "The citizens of each state shall be entitled to all privileges and immunities of citizens in the several states." The Fourteenth Amendment provides that, "No state shall make or enforce any law which shall abridge the privileges or immunities of citizens of the United States." The first provision is considered to be an instrument of federalism, one of the obligations of states in their relations with each other. Basically, it means that a citizen of one state is not to be treated as an alien when in another state; he may not be discriminated against by denial of such privileges and immunities as legal protection, access to courts, travel rights, or property rights. Out-of-state residents, however, may be denied certain political rights, such as voting, or other privileges reserved to that state's residents, such as lower tuition at state institutions. The full and precise meaning of the term has never been established by the courts. The Fourteenth Amendment's privileges and immunities clause has, similarly, not received complete definition. It is basically an instrument of civil liberties, placing certain restrictions upon each state in its dealings with United States citizens. The clause has been interpreted to apply only to those privileges that apply to the individual by virtue of his national citizenship (*Slaughterhouse Cases,* 16 Wallace 36 [1873]). These include the rights to travel, to have access to national officials, and to engage in interstate and foreign commerce. As interpreted, the clause confers no new rights upon citizens nor does it affect the citizen in those privileges that he enjoys by virtue of his state citizenship. *See* HORIZONTAL FEDERALISM, page 33.

Significance   Neither of these clauses has proved to be of great importance in American history. The narrow interpretation given by the courts to the Fourteenth Amendment has disappointed those who saw in it a boon to Negro rights after the Civil War. Article IV has served, in part, to strengthen economic and social ties among the people of the various states, but the vagueness of its language, and its uncertain judicial interpretation, has limited its use.

Regionalism   A method of decentralizing power on a geographical basis. In the United States, regionalism is often proposed as an alternative or supplement to the states. For example, the country could be divided into nine or ten regional subdivisions instead of into fifty states. The term is also applied to regional administration of federal projects, such as the Tennessee Valley Authority, and to regional interstate compacts.

Significance   Advocates of regionalism argue that since the states do not reflect realistic economic and social patterns, they should be united into regions having genuine unity, such as the Missouri Valley area and New England. People of the United States tend to take a regional or sectional rather than state outlook on many problems. The strong tradition and constitutional power of the individual states make their elimination unlikely, but states are increasingly acting together to meet common problems.

Republican Form of Government   A government that operates through elected representatives of the people. It is generally distinguished from a pure democracy, in which the people govern directly. Article IV, section 4 of the Constitution, known as the "guarantee clause," provides that the national government shall guarantee to each state a republican form of government. *See Luther v. Borden,* page 42; *Pacific Case,* page 161.

Significance   The precise meaning of the guarantee clause has never been determined; the Supreme Court has held this to be a "political question" to be answered by Congress or the President. A state government is considered to be republican in form if the houses of Congress accept the elected representatives of the state. In addition, the President could conceivably use the armed forces to dispossess a state government considered by him to be other than republican in form. This guarantee is classified by political scientists as one of the obligations of the national government toward the states in maintaining the federal system. State citizens are thereby protected against arbitrary seizure of power of state government and abuse of state electoral systems.

Reserved Powers   Powers of state governments under the American federal system. The states retain all powers not delegated to the national government, or prohibited to them, by the Constitution. These powers are frequently referred to as "residuary." It is not possible to make a definitive list of state powers since, in the very nature of the federal system, the states may exercise any power that is not delegated to the national government. Generally, this includes authority over internal affairs of the state and general police power over the health, safety, morals, and welfare of the people. State constitutions may place specific restrictions upon state powers. *See* DELEGATED POWERS, page 30.

Significance   The division of authority between national and state governments is a basic principle of American federalism. The concept that certain powers are "reserved" to the states is stated in the Tenth Amendment. Exactly what constitutes a reserved power is often a matter of dispute. With problems continuously changing in scope, a power formerly exercised by a state may fall under national control. This is particularly true in matters of commerce, as these increasingly become interstate in character. The judiciary is frequently called upon to determine the proper division of authority between the nation and the states.

Resulting Powers   Powers of the national government derived from a combination of delegated or implied powers; hence, powers that "result" from a number of powers, rather than inferred from one of the delegated powers. *See Legal Tender Cases,* page 253.

Significance   Resulting powers are an extension of the implied-powers doctrine. They make possible an exercise of national power that logically follows from a series of granted powers. For example, the United States Criminal Code provides that the violation of any national law is subject to punishment. The Constitution does not explicitly delegate this power, nor is it implied by any single grant of power. Rather, it "results" from the aggregate of power delegated to the national government.

States' Rights   A term used to connote opposition to increasing the national government's power at the expense of that of the states. States' rights adherents call for an interpretation of the Constitution that would place limits on the federal assumption of implied powers and give expanded interpretation to the reserved powers of the states. *See* STATE SOVEREIGNTY, page 26.

Significance   Strong support for states' rights usually comes from those groups who feel that their particular interest will be better served by state than by national action. Though the term is common in American political life, it has rarely been used with consistency. For example, southern politicians who oppose national action in the field of civil rights actively seek federal grants-in-aid for state projects. The proper balance between national and state power is a continuing American problem under the federal system. The balance is usually determined by the strength of political forces rather than by the language of the Constitution.

Tenth Amendment   The final item of the Bill of Rights in the Constitution, which defines the principle of American federalism: "The powers not delegated to the United States by the Constitution, nor prohibited by it to the states, are reserved to the states respectively, or to the people." *See* FEDERALISM, page 32.

Significance   The Tenth Amendment was added to the Constitution to make clear the position of the states in the Union. Though it was generally understood that the framers intended that the states would retain all powers not prohibited by the Constitution or delegated to the national government, the people insisted upon an express provision to that effect. Exactly what is meant by the phrase "or to the people" has never been determined.

Territory   An area belonging to the United States that is not included within any state of the Union. Though the Constitution does not expressly grant the power to acquire territory, Article IV, section 3 authorizes Congress to make rules respecting the territory of the United States. Power to acquire territory also results from the national government's power to make treaties, to admit new states, and to make war that might result in conquest. The District of Columbia, though not part of any state, is not considered a territory. Major territorial possessions of the United States now include Guam, Puerto Rico, the Panama Canal Zone, Samoa, the Virgin Islands, and the Territory of the Pacific Islands. The Office of Territories in the Department of the Interior supervises the territories except for the Panama Canal Zone, which is under the Department of the Army. *See* ADMISSION OF NEW STATES, page 28.

Significance   Most of the territory acquired by the United States through purchase, conquest, or treaty has eventually become part of the United States. Current possessions are important mainly for strategic reasons. The United States has rarely used its territories as "colonies" to be exploited. Rather, inhabitants have been trained for self-government and given independence (the Philippines) or statehood (Hawaii).

Twenty-First Amendment   An amendment to the Constitution, adopted in 1933, permitting the sale of intoxicating beverages in the United States. The amendment protects states that retain prohibition, by barring the importation or transportation of liquor into such states. It repealed the Eighteenth Amendment, which had imposed prohibition on the entire country.

Significance The Twenty-first is the only amendment that repeals a prior amendment. It is also the only one to have been ratified by conventions in the states rather than by state legislatures. (It is notable that ratification was accomplished in just one year.) By prohibiting the transportation of intoxicants into "dry" states, the amendment lends national support to state laws.

Unitary State A centralized government in which local or subdivisional governments exercise only those powers given to them by the central government. It differs from a federal system, in which power is constitutionally divided between a central and subdivisional government. The United Kingdom and France are examples of the unitary form. In the United States, local governments, such as cities and counties, stand in a unitary relationship to the state governments that assign specific rights and duties to them. An exception to this is found in those states in which cities are given "home rule" by constitutional provision. *See* FEDERALISM, page 32.

Significance A unitary system provides a unified and consistent administration of policy while at the same time permitting variations to be made by the central authority. It allows more efficient handling of nation-wide problems and is more sensitive to national majorities. Opponents of unitary government claim that federalism is superior in that it permits more experimentation in local government and greater freedom in meeting local needs.

IMPORTANT CASES

Coyle v. Smith, 221 U.S. 599 (1911): Established the principle that all states are admitted to the Union on an equal footing. Congress may not enforce conditions that would undermine the equality of the states. In this case, the Court upheld the right of Oklahoma to change its capital city contrary to a requirement in the congressional enabling act that preceded statehood.

Significance Congress may stipulate any conditions it chooses for the admission of a state. Once admitted to the Union, a state may not be compelled to abide by any condition that would interfere with its right to manage its internal affairs or that would create different classes of states.

Graves v. New York ex rel. O'Keefe, 306 U.S. 466 (1939): Held that a state may tax the income of a federal employee and that such a tax does not impose an unconstitutional burden upon the national government.

Significance This was one of the last in a long line of cases that arose out of the decision in *McCulloch v. Maryland* that a state may not tax an instrumentality of the federal government, since the power to tax is the power to destroy. This doctrine was carried to the point that neither the state nor the national government could tax each other in any way, including the salaries of their respective employees. In the *Graves* case, the Court reversed its position and sustained congressional authorization of state taxation of federal employees' incomes. Federal taxation of state employees had been upheld the previous year in *Helvering v. Gerhardt,* 304 U.S. 405 (1938).

Kentucky v. Dennison, 24 Howard 66 (1861): Decided that the constitutional duty of a governor to return a fugitive to the state from which he fled is only a moral obligation rather than a mandatory one. The Court found that a national statute of 1793 dealing with the return of fugitives provided no means by which a governor could be compelled to perform his duty and, in any case, that the national government lacked authority to coerce a state officer.

Significance   The *Kentucky* case enabled the Court to shun the difficult practical question of how a state governor could actually be compelled to perform his duty. Though the supremacy of the national government is clear in most national-state controversies, this decision has been respected by the national government and all states, thereby keeping interstate rendition a discretionary act for the governors.

Luther v. Borden, 7 Howard 1 (1848): Held that the question of whether a state has a republican form of government is a political and not a judicial question. The Supreme Court refused to define a republican form of government, holding that Congress and the President must decide. The case arose out of Dorr's Rebellion in Rhode Island in 1841, when rival groups claimed to be the true government of the state.

Significance   The constitutional requirement that the national government guarantee each state a republican form of government will not be enforced by the courts. Congressional power to accept the state's representatives, and the President's power to use force to quell a rebellion are the means by which the guarantee is honored.

Massachusetts v. Mellon and Frothingham v. Mellon, 262 U.S. 447 (1923): Rejected claims by a state that the federal grant-in-aid program to protect the health of mothers and infants was an unconstitutional invasion of the reserved powers of the states guaranteed by the Tenth Amendment. In a companion case (*Frothingham v. Mellon*), the Court rejected the claim of Mrs. Frothingham that the grant-in-aid program would take her property under the guise of taxation.

Significance   Three important rules were established by these cases: (1) A state cannot validly seek to protect its citizens who are also citizens of the United States from the enforcement of federal laws; (2) A grant-in-aid system based on voluntary acceptance of programs by the states is a political and not a judicial question; (3) An individual taxpayer who cannot show suffering and injury different from that of the general taxpaying public has no standing in court to challenge the constitutionality of tax laws (Frothingham rule). Today, under this rule, it continues to be impossible for an individual to test the constitutionality of a tax law in the federal courts.

McCulloch v. Maryland, 4 Wheaton 316 (1819): Upheld, in a landmark decision of the Supreme Court, the power of the national government to establish a bank, and denied the state of Maryland the power to tax a branch of the bank. In the opinion by Chief Justice John Marshall, the Court held that it was not necessary for the Constitution expressly to authorize Congress to create a bank. Rather, the power to do so was implied from Congress' power over financial matters and from the "necessary and proper" clause of the Constitution. Maryland could not tax a legitimate instrumentality of the national government, said the Court, since this would be an invasion of national supremacy. "The power to tax is the power to destroy. . . ." From this was derived the principle of intergovernmental tax immunity.

Significance   Two important principles of American government were firmly established by this decision: the doctrine of "implied powers," which has given the national government a vast source of power; the principle of "national supremacy," which denies to the states any right to interfere in the constitutional operations of the national government. Had the decision favored Maryland, the national government would not have been able to meet the problems of an expanding nation and the Constitution would not have become a "living" document.

Virginia v. Tennessee, 148 U.S. 503 (1893): Denied a suit brought by Virginia to void the boundary line between it and Tennessee on the ground that the line had been established by agreement between the states without the consent of Congress. The Court held that the agreement did not constitute a compact between the states that required the positive approval of Congress. The only compacts or agreements requiring approval are those that tend to increase state power at the expense of the national government. In other instances, Congress may give its approval by implication.

Significance   Although the Constitution prohibits states from entering into agreements or compacts without consent of Congress, this decision made it clear that the restriction did not apply to every agreement between states. This has made it possible for states to solve mutual problems without involving Congress. Yet Congress is always free to step in if it feels that the agreement threatens the national government in any way.

IMPORTANT STATUTES

Federal Aid Highway Act   A major example of federal grants-in-aid to the states; the first such grant was given in 1916 for the building of highways. From this time, grants have been given for trunk roads, secondary roads, urban extensions of highways, and, since 1956, an extensive interstate highway system. The states must meet national requirements regarding matching funds, maintenance of roads, location, and engineering details. The 1956 Act provides for a thirteen-year program for the building of 41,000 miles of multilane highways connecting all major cities. The national government is financing ninety percent of the cost. The program is administered by the Bureau of Public Roads in the Department of Transportation.

Significance   This is a leading example of a successfully operated grant-in-aid. Through it, the national government has shaped state and local road policy, although it does not actually build the highways. Highway expenditures of state and local governments are exceeded only by expenditures for education. The grant-in-aid program has provided states with substantial revenue, but it has limited the discretion of the state and local authorities over a major function.

Four

Immigration and Citizenship

Alien   An individual who is neither a citizen nor a national of the state in which he is living. Aliens generally owe allegiance to a foreign power, but may acquire citizenship by following prescribed procedures. *See* ALIEN REGISTRATION ACT, page 52; *Truax v. Raich,* page 52.

   Significance   In the United States, aliens enjoy many of the civil rights that the Constitution accords to "persons" as distinguished from citizens. These include most provisions of the Bill of Rights and freedom from arbitrary discrimination. Aliens are subject to the laws of the United States, must pay taxes, and may be drafted. Military service and other duties and rights of aliens are generally in accord with treaties between the United States and other nations. An alien who refuses to be drafted forfeits his right ever to become a citizen. Under the laws of most American states, an alien may not engage in certain professions, own firearms, hold government employment, or, in some states, own real estate. In no case may he enjoy such political rights as voting or holding public office. The most serious disability imposed upon an alien is the continuing possibility of deportation. Since an alien has no *right* to live in the United States, he may be deported for moral turpitude or for past or present affiliation with the Communist party. In time of war, aliens who are subjects of enemy states may be severely restricted. Under present law, all aliens must register with the Attorney General every year.

Citizen   An individual who is a native or naturalized member of a state, owes allegiance to that state, and is entitled to the protection and privileges of its laws. Citizenship in the United States is defined in the Fourteenth Amendment to the Constitution: "All persons born or naturalized in the United States, and subject to the jurisdiction thereof, are citizens of the United States and of the state wherein they reside." Citizenship is based mainly on one's place of birth (*jus soli*) but may be acquired through naturalization and, under circumstances defined by Congress, through blood relation (*jus sanguinis*). *See United States v. Wong Kim Ark,* page 52; NATIONAL, page 48; *Jus Soli,* page 47; *Jus Sanguinis,* page 47.

   Significance   Two basic problems were raised prior to the Civil War:

(1) Should Negroes born in the United States be considered citizens? (2) Is state citizenship secondary and incidental to national citizenship? The Fourteenth Amendment provides affirmative answers to both questions. Recent developments include the extension of citizenship by birth to American Indians and to the people of Guam, Puerto Rico, and the Virgin Islands. Prior to 1922, a married woman took the citizenship of her husband, but under the Cable Act of 1922 women are treated the same as men, with the exception that an alien woman marrying an American citizen may be naturalized after a shorter period of residence. Children of foreign diplomatic agents who are born here are not citizens, since they are not "subject to the jurisdiction" of the United States.

Denaturalization   The revoking of citizenship that has been acquired by naturalization. This may be done only by court order in accordance with due process of law.

Significance   The most common ground for denaturalization is fraud or willful misrepresentation when being naturalized. Lengthy residence abroad by a naturalized citizen, once a ground for denaturalization, may no longer, under Supreme Court ruling, result in termination of citizenship (*Schneider v. Rusk,* 377 U.S. 163 [1964]). Recent legislation permits denaturalization of those who affiliate with subversive organizations within five years after naturalization, or those who are convicted of contempt of Congress for refusal to testify in an investigation into subversive activities within ten years after naturalization. Many observers charge that such provisions make "second-class" citizens of naturalized persons, since native-born citizens are not affected by such laws. A commonly held assumption, that one loses his citizenship when convicted of a serious crime, is not true. One may lose certain privileges of citizenship, such as the right to vote or hold certain jobs, but citizenship is retained.

Deportation   Compulsory expulsion of an alien from a state to his country of origin. Deportation is a civil rather than a criminal proceeding under American law, hence, various constitutional safeguards do not apply. With the exception of naturalized citizens who lose their citizenship, a citizen may not be deported. *See Fong Yue Ting v. United States,* page 50.

Significance   Aliens remain in the United States at the sufferance of Congress, which has virtually unlimited power to establish grounds for deportation. Illegal entry is the most common cause of deportation, but in recent years Congress has considerably increased the number of grounds for deportation, particularly for Communists and other political undesirables and for aliens convicted of serious crimes. Constitutional safeguards with regard to bail and ex post facto laws, for example, do not apply to deportation proceedings, and great discretion is vested in the Attorney General. Many public officials and citizens have questioned the fairness of procedures used in deportation cases. The courts have been reluctant to interfere since the issue involves the plenary powers of the national government in international affairs.

Dual Citizenship   Holding citizenship in two or more countries. This may occur because most countries recognize as citizens those born within their boundaries as well as children of their subjects born abroad. Thus, a person born abroad of American parents is an American citizen (*jus sanguinis*) and may also be a citizen of the country in which he was born (*jus soli*).

Significance   Dual citizenship has become widespread because of increasing mobility. It may cause hardship when, for example, conflicting claims are made over the right to require military service. Under American law, a person who, after reaching the age of twenty-two, lives for three years in another country that also claims him as a citizen, forfeits his American citizenship unless he takes an oath of allegiance to the United States before a diplomatic official.

Expatriation   Voluntary withdrawal of allegiance or residence from the country in which citizenship is held. Since 1865, Congress has expressly recognized the right of expatriation, setting forth specific grounds. Actions that constitute expatriation include: naturalization in a foreign state, taking an oath of allegiance to another state, serving in a foreign army without consent, taking a job open only to citizens of another state, voting in a foreign election, and conviction of treason or attempt to overthrow the government by force. A citizen living abroad may voluntarily renounce his citizenship before a diplomatic officer but renunciation is permitted within the United States only during wartime with the consent of the Attorney General. *See Perez v. Brownell,* page 51; *Trop v. Dulles,* page 51.

Significance   Congress recognized the right of expatriation as "a natural and inherent right of all people," essential for the rights to life, liberty, and the pursuit of happiness. The major purpose of this declaration was to justify before the world the great number of people from foreign lands who were emigrating to the United States. The expatriation laws assume that the person committing certain acts, whether or not they intend them to be acts of expatriation, acted voluntarily and with full knowledge of the consequences. Supreme Court decisions have declared unconstitutional statutory provisions to the effect that leaving the United States to avoid military service constitutes expatriation (*Rusk v. Cort,* 372 U.S. 144 [1963]), and those stating that a person convicted of wartime desertion expatriates himself; the latter decision was made on the ground that expatriation for desertion was cruel and unusual punishment (*Trop v. Dulles,* 356 U.S. 86 [1958]). The Court, however, upheld the taking away of citizenship if a person voted in a foreign election (*Perez v. Brownell,* 356 U.S. 44 [1958]).

Immigration   Admittance of a person to a country of which he is not a native for the purpose of establishing permanent residence. Early attempts by seaboard states to regulate immigration into the United States were invalidated by the Supreme Court, which declared immigration to be an exclusive function of the national government, incidental to its power over foreign affairs. Immigration into the United States was unlimited until 1882, when Congress began to impose restrictions on the admission of criminals, the mentally ill, paupers, diseased persons, illiterates, the Chinese, anarchists, and advocates of violent governmental change. In 1924, Congress barred Asiatics and established the "national origins quota" system, which limited annual immigration and assigned a quota to each country based on the numerical contribution it had made to our national stock as of 1920. In 1952, Congress erased racial exclusions but retained the quota system and the annual limit. Restrictions against the admission of Communists or other suspected subversives were increased. In 1965, Congress abolished the national origins quota system and established a new annual limit of 170,000, with preference given to relatives of citizens and persons with special skills. Immigration from the Western Hemisphere was restricted for the first time. Immigration laws are administered by the Department of State and the Department of Justice, and each has been given extensive discretion to determine who may enter the United States. *See* IMMIGRATION ACT OF 1965, page 52; *The Passenger Cases,* page 51.

Significance   More than forty million people have come to the United States from all over the world. From time to time, Congress has relaxed quota restrictions by admitting large numbers of refugees and displaced persons from war-torn and iron curtain countries. Pressures for limiting immigration have come largely from labor organizations, from those who fear the introduction of alien ideologies, and from those who, though immigrants or descendants of immigrants themselves, look down upon new groups seeking admission. Criticisms of the quota system as discriminatory led to passage of the 1965 immigration law, which eliminates race and ancestry as the basis for immigration policy. Many continue to protest the red tape required for admission to the country and the vast discretion vested in immigration officials to deny entrance to aliens. The United States has, however, a proud record of achievement in absorbing millions of immigrants and, in turn, the nation has benefited immeasurably from the contributions of many people of varied backgrounds and talents.

Jus Sanguinis   "Law of the blood"—a principle by which citizenship is determined by parentage rather than by place of birth (*jus soli*).

Significance   The Fourteenth Amendment recognizes only birth and naturalization as bases for citizenship, but Congress has adopted the rule of *jus sanguinis* to apply in special circumstances. Thus, one may be a citizen of the United States if born abroad, provided that either or both of one's parents are citizens. If only one parent is a citizen, that parent must have lived in the United States or one of its possessions for ten years, five of them after the age of fourteen; and the child, in order to remain a citizen, must live in the United States for five years between the ages of fourteen and twenty-three. Because large numbers of Americans are working and traveling abroad, *jus sanguinis* has taken on increasing significance.

Jus Soli   "Law of the soil"—the basic rule under which American citizenship is determined by place of birth rather than by parentage (*jus sanguinis*). *See United States v. Wong Kim Ark,* page 52.

Significance   The Fourteenth Amendment's provision that all persons born in the United States are citizens (with minor exceptions, as for example, children born to foreign diplomats who are not under American jurisdiction) is far-reaching. Anyone born here is a citizen whether his parents are resident aliens or merely visitors. For purposes of citizenship, Congress has declared that the soil of the United States includes Puerto Rico, Guam, and the Virgin Islands.

National   A person who owes allegiance to a country, though not a citizen thereof. The term is used at times, however, in the same sense as the term "citizen." Under American law, a national is an inhabitant of an outlying possession of the United States to whom Congress has not granted citizenship. Residents of the Philippine Islands were considered nationals until independence was granted, whereas the people of Puerto Rico were granted citizenship in 1917 after a period as nationals.

Significance   The term "national" is basically a concept of international law. American nationals are accorded most of the protections that citizens have, and the actual distinction is hazy. By granting the status of nationals to a people, Congress identifies them as belonging to and entitled to the protection of the United States, particularly for purposes of international relations.

Natural-born Citizen   A native of the United States. The term is used in Article II, section 1 of the Constitution, which stipulates that "No person except a natural born citizen" may be President of the United States.

Significance   The language of Article II is the only place in the Constitution where a distinction is drawn between a natural-born and a naturalized citizen. Whether or not a person born abroad of American parents, and, therefore, a citizen under the rule of *jus sanguinis,* is eligible for the presidency has never been resolved. Although the Constitution makes no other distinctions between natural-born and naturalized citizens, the former cannot be denaturalized or deported.

Naturalization   The legal procedure by which an alien is admitted to citizenship. Congress is authorized by Article I, section 8 of the Constitution to establish uniform rules for naturalization. Naturalization may be individual or collective. Collective naturalization confers citizenship upon entire populations by statute or treaty as was done in the cases of Alaska, Hawaii, Texas, Puerto Rico, Guam, and the Virgin Islands. An individual over eighteen years of age may be naturalized after meeting certain qualifications. These include his (1) residence in the United States for five years, (2) ability to read, write, and speak English, (3) proof of good moral character, (4) knowledge of the history and attachment to the principles of American government, (5) neither advocacy of Communist or other subversive doctrine nor membership (unless involuntary) in any subversive or totalitarian organization, and (6) taking of an oath of allegiance to the United States and renunciation of allegiance to his former country. Detailed administration of naturalization is handled by the Immigration and Naturalization Service of the Department of Justice with final examination and administration of the oath by a judge of a federal court or a state court of record. The residence requirement is lowered for spouses of citizens and for aliens who serve in the armed forces. Minors become citizens when their parents are naturalized. *See Girouard v. United States,* page 51.

Significance   Millions of people have met the requirements established by Congress and have become American citizens. Some critics maintain that efforts to measure moral standards and political views are not always fair, particularly during times of crises, since officials may abuse their discretion. Others, though not critical of the naturalization procedure itself, point out that a naturalized citizen is a "second-class" citizen, since he may lose his citizenship under conditions that would not affect the citizenship status of the native born. The procedure is designed, however, to foster the "Americanization" of the alien, many of whom become more knowledgeable and appreciative citizens than some of the native born. Through collective naturalization, the United States has demonstrated to the world its desire to give equal rights to all people under its control and, in some cases, to prepare them for eventual statehood.

Nonimmigrant   One who comes to the United States on a temporary basis. This includes visitors, seasonal workers, tradesmen, crewmen, students, members of the press, and accredited representatives of foreign nations. Nonimmigrants must meet many of the qualifications imposed upon regular immigrants.

Significance   For a time, a good deal of controversy raged over the stringent red tape that visitors, many of whom were distinguished persons, had to face to enter the United States. This included many searching questions, delays in securing visas, and even fingerprinting. Some of these requirements have been relaxed but rather close inspection continues.

Passport   A certificate, issued by an official governmental agency, that identifies a person as a citizen of a country and authorizes him to travel abroad. Passports are granted to Americans by the Passport Office of the State Department, by territorial governors, and by diplomatic officials abroad.

Significance   No American citizen may leave the country without a passport (except for trips to Canada, Mexico, and certain other nearby areas), and few countries will admit a traveler without a valid passport. A passport entitles a person to the privileges accorded travelers by international custom and various treaties. In 1958, the Supreme Court ruled that the Secretary of State could not deny a passport to a citizen because of his political beliefs or associations without explicit authorization from Congress (*Kent v. Dulles,* 357 U.S. 116). The Court also struck down the section of the Internal Security Act of 1950 that forbids issuance of passports to members of Communist organizations, on the ground that such denial constitutes a violation of the right to travel (*Aptheker v. Secretary of State,* 378 U.S. 500 [1964]). The State Department has refused to issue passports for travel to Communist China, Albania, Cuba, North Korea, and North Vietnam. The Supreme Court has upheld such limits on the right to travel if travel to such countries is likely to prove detrimental to the foreign policy interests of the United States (*Zemel v. Rusk,* 381 U.S. 1 [1965]).

Visa   A permit to enter a country. Persons seeking admission to the United States must get a visa from a United States consul located abroad. Many countries require visas as well as passports. Visas are usually stamps of approval affixed to the passport by an official of the country to be visited or entered permanently.

Significance   The visa procedure is an instrument of national policy that enables a country to screen applicants prior to their departure for that country. In the United States, before 1924, screening was done at ports of entry, causing great hardship to those rejected. Consular officers stationed abroad have unlimited discretion to grant or refuse visas, resulting in occasional charges of abuse of power.

IMPORTANT AGENCIES

Board of Immigration Appeals   A board appointed by the Attorney General to hear appeals from decisions of the Immigration and Naturalization Service relative to the exclusion or deportation of aliens.

Significance   Only on rare occasions will the courts hear appeals on immigration or deportation matters, since Congress has broad authority in these areas. Hence, for most aliens, the Board is the "court of last resort" on matters of entry or deportation.

Bureau of Security and Consular Affairs   The part of the State Department that supervises the issuance of passports and visas. The Bureau was established by the Immigration and Nationality Act of 1952 and, under its supervision, consular agents abroad determine whether foreigners will be permitted to enter the United States.

Significance   Fear of Communist and other subversive elements has led to the extensive screening of applicants for visas to enter the United States. The decisions of consular officers are final.

Immigration and Naturalization Service   The part of the Department of Justice that administers the laws regarding the admission, naturalization, and deportation of aliens. The Service investigates the credentials of immigrants at ports of entry. Immigration and Naturalization Service officers also patrol the Canadian and Mexican borders to prevent the illegal entry of aliens. Aliens seeking to become citizens are investigated by agents of the Service, who recommend to the courts whether or not the alien should be naturalized.

Significance   Agents of the Immigration and Naturalization Service exercise considerable discretion in determining whether persons may enter the United States, become citizens, or be subject to deportation. Some critics have charged that the Service does not always follow fair procedures in reaching its decisions, particularly with regard to determining the character and political beliefs of aliens. Decisions of the Service may be appealed to the Board of Immigration Appeals in the Department of Justice.

IMPORTANT CASES

Fong Yue Ting v. United States, 149 U.S. 698 (1893): Supported the authority of the national government to deport aliens under its sovereign power in the field of international affairs. The Court upheld a federal law that authorized the deportation of Chinese laborers who had failed to get certificates of residence.

Furthermore, the Court held that deportation is not criminal punishment and, therefore, does not require a judicial trial.

Significance   The major points of the case, that Congress has full power to deport aliens and that such action is not considered to be punishment, remain basic to American law. While the Court has, in subsequent cases, demanded that basic elements of fairness or due process be observed in deportation proceedings, it has not insisted that a judicial trial is required.

Girouard v. United States, 328 U.S. 61 (1946): Established that an alien may be admitted to citizenship even if he refuses, on religious grounds, to swear that he will bear arms in defense of the United States. In this case, the Supreme Court reversed its earlier stand on this question and upheld Girouard's right to become a citizen since he was otherwise eligible and was willing to perform noncombatant duties.

Significance   In the Immigration and Nationality Act of 1952, Congress voiced its approval of the *Girouard* decision. The Act provides that conscientious objectors may be admitted to citizenship if they are willing to perform noncombatant service. It specifies that the exception applies only to persons who object to bearing arms on religious and not on general philosophical grounds.

Perez v. Brownell, 356 U.S. 44 (1958): Upheld a law providing that native-born citizens forfeit their citizenship by voting in a foreign election. The Court reasoned that this problem fell within the realm of foreign affairs and that voting abroad by American citizens could prove embarrassing to the conduct of foreign relations.

Significance   The Court rarely, if ever, interferes with the conduct of foreign affairs and here extended this principle to expatriation. Under current law, two other acts by a citizen in relation to a foreign state—serving in its armed forces or assuming public office therein—may result in loss of citizenship.

The Passenger Cases, 7 Howard 283 (1849): Declared that immigration is the exclusive concern of the national government and is not subject to state control. The seaboard states had sought to regulate the heavy flow of immigrants to their shores by levying a tax on ships carrying immigrants.

Significance   This decision helped to promote a uniform immigration policy prior to the great influx of immigrants in the late nineteenth and early twentieth centuries. It was not, however, until 1882 that the national government assumed the full responsibility of regulating immigration.

Trop v. Dulles, 356 U.S. 86 (1958): Decided that the deprivation of citizenship for wartime desertion is a cruel and unusual punishment. The Supreme Court held that native-born citizenship is a basic right and cannot be taken away without voluntary expatriation. The Court noted that desertion does not always indicate disloyalty to one's country.

Significance   This case raises citizenship to the level of a constitutional right and declared unconstitutional the law that provided that a citizen expatriates himself if he is convicted by court-martial for wartime desertion.

Ordinarily, when a person expatriates himself, he becomes a citizen of another country, but this law would leave a person completely stateless.

Truax v. Raich, 239 U.S. 33 (1915): Declared unconstitutional an Arizona law requiring that at least eighty percent of the employees of any private business must be citizens, as a denial of equal protection of the law. The Court held that a state may not deny a person the right to earn a living, regardless of his race or nationality.

Significance   This case and others that have followed it underscore the fact that an alien is entitled to most of the rights of a citizen, since the Constitution speaks of "persons" rather than citizens with regard to most rights. While an alien may be denied access to specific jobs, such as governmental employment, he may not be deprived by law of any right to work in ordinary occupations.

United States v. Wong Kim Ark, 169 U.S. 649 (1898): Established that all persons born in the United States are citizens of the United States, even if the parents are aliens ineligible for citizenship. The only major exceptions are children born to foreign diplomats stationed here. The Court held that a Chinese person born in California who went to China for a visit could not be denied readmission to the United States.

Significance   This was a major interpretation of the meaning of the Fourteenth Amendment, which confers citizenship upon "all persons" born in the United States and subject to its jurisdiction. The Court made it clear that citizenship by birth, regardless of parentage, is the basic rule of American citizenship.

IMPORTANT STATUTES

Alien Registration Act of 1940 (Smith Act)   An act requiring the annual registration of all aliens over the age of fourteen. Aliens are required to be fingerprinted, to inform the government of their address, occupation, and other data, and to carry registration cards at all times. *See* ALIEN REGISTRATION ACT, page 89.

Significance   The Alien Registration Act is a major sedition law that makes it criminal to teach, advocate, or join an organization advocating violent overthrow of government. The alien-registration requirement is designed to make it easier for the government to know the whereabouts of aliens who might prove dangerous in time of war.

Immigration Act of 1965   A major revision of American immigration policy that eliminated the national-origins quota system. Under the quota system, in effect since 1924, American immigration policy discriminated against Asians, Africans, and southern and eastern Europeans. The overall quota was set at less than 157,000 immigrants per year, with nearly 127,000 assigned to northern and western Europe. It was often criticized as racist in philosophy and as detrimental to the American international position. The 1965 law ended the quota system, established an annual limit of 170,000 immigrants (no more than 20,000 from one country), and gave preference to relatives of citizens and persons with special skills. For the first time, a limit (120,000) was placed on immigrants from the Western Hemisphere.

Significance   The Immigration Act of 1965 climaxed a forty year effort by ethnic groups to eliminate race and ancestry as bases of American immigration policy. The new law's stress on reuniting families and on admitting skilled persons regardless of ancestry reflects growing national concern with domestic racial problems and foreign-policy considerations.

Immigration and Nationality Act of 1952 (McCarran-Walter Act)   A major revision and restatement of the immigration and citizenship policies of the United States. The Act maintained the quota system for immigration and placed restrictions upon the immigration and naturalization of Communists and other totalitarians. All racial barriers to immigration were eliminated by the Act, but Asians, Africans, and southern and eastern Europeans were assigned small quotas. (The Immigration Act of 1965, however, eliminated the quota system.) Communists or other persons advocating violent overthrow of the government are denied admission to the United States. Further, such persons residing in this country may not be naturalized, and citizenship may be taken from naturalized persons who join the Communist party or refuse to testify before a congressional committee investigating subversive activities.

Significance   The Immigration and Nationality Act of 1952 is a comprehensive collection of the immigration and citizenship laws of the United States. Most opponents of the Act protested its retention of a discriminatory immigration policy and its continuation of the policy of making naturalized citizens subject to loss of citizenship on grounds not applicable to native-born citizens. In 1965, Congress, in response to extensive ethnic-group pressures and foreign-policy considerations, eliminated the discriminatory national-origins quota system. The Supreme Court has moved in the direction of ending the "second-class citizenship" of naturalized citizens.

Five

Civil Liberties

Academic Freedom   The principle that teachers and students have the right and the duty to pursue the search for truth wherever the inquiry may lead, free of political, religious or other restrictions except those of accepted standards of scholarship. Important corollaries to the principle are that alleged violations of academic freedom will be investigated under procedures consonant with due process, and that the tenure of teachers will not depend upon adherence to any orthodoxy.

Significance   Academic freedom is not a legally enforceable right, although it is commonly recognized as a major element of a free society. Academic freedom is continually under stress. Its degree and nature vary with the political, religious, and social values of a community. The major contemporary problem of academic freedom involves the fear of communism and disloyalty, which results in loyalty oaths for teachers and investigations into school and college activities. Another problem in academic freedom results from the segregation controversy in the South where attempts have been made to control teaching about integration and the civil-rights activities of teachers and students.

Attorney General's List   A list of organizations, deemed to be subversive, compiled by the Attorney General of the United States. The Attorney General's list was drawn up as part of the loyalty program established by President Truman in 1947. Membership in any listed organization has been taken into account in determining the loyalty of governmental employees. In *Joint Anti-Fascist Refugee Committee v. McGrath,* 341 U.S. 123 (1951), the Supreme Court declared that an organization could not be listed without being given notice and an opportunity to be heard.

Significance   The Attorney General's list of subversive organizations does not carry any legal weight. The legal determination of what constitutes a subversive organization is the responsibility of the Subversive Activities Control Board, established under the Internal Security Act of 1950. The Attorney General's list may, however, be used informally in determining the loyalty of particular persons. Some critics of the list point out that it does not distinguish between organizations in terms of the date of their inception or the degree of their subversive connections, and that its very existence imputes guilt by association to the members of these groups. Some state and local governments have accepted the list at face value in determining the loyalty of employees. The list does put innocent individuals on notice of the possible subversive character of their organizations.

Bad Tendency Rule A test used by the Supreme Court to determine the permissible bounds of free speech. The bad tendency rule holds that speech or other First Amendment freedoms may be curtailed if there is a possibility that they might lead to some evil. It is to be distinguished from the "clear and present danger" doctrine, which holds that an individual's liberty may not be curtailed unless it presents some imminent danger of illegal action. *See Dennis v. United States,* page 79; CLEAR AND PRESENT DANGER RULE, page 57.

Significance The bad tendency test, like the clear and present danger test, proceeds from the search for some formula to solve the problem of balancing individual freedom against the rights of society. Both tests have been used by the Supreme Court over the years, with results determined by the nature of the times and the ideas of the justices. In the years from 1948 to 1952, known as the "era of McCarthyism," the bad tendency rule prevailed against accused subversives. More liberal majorities on the Court have since rejected the bad tendency rule in favor of the clear and present danger doctrine.

Bill of Attainder A legislative act that declares the guilt of an individual and metes out punishment without a judicial trial. The state legislatures and Congress are forbidden to pass such acts by Article I, sections 9 and 10 of the Constitution. *See United States v. Lovett,* page 88.

Significance A legislative body may not exercise the judicial function of ascertaining guilt and pronouncing sentence. Rather, the legislature is limited to passing general laws, with specific applications left to the courts. This is an important ingredient of the separation of powers and of freedom itself.

Bill of Rights The first ten amendments to the United States Constitution. Bills of rights, sometimes called declarations of rights, are also found in all state constitutions. They contain a listing of the rights a person enjoys that cannot be infringed upon by the government. Many important rights, such as trial by jury and the guarantee of habeas corpus, are stated in other parts of the United States Constitution. All bills of rights contain provisions designed to protect the freedom of expression, the rights of property, and the rights of persons accused of crime.

Significance Bills of rights are restrictions on government rather than on individuals or private groups. History teaches that unchecked governmental powers lead to the decay of freedom. A bill of rights provides the legal mechanism through which the individual can challenge the oppressive acts of governmental officials in courts of law. Without guarantees for individual freedom, democracy would become meaningless and unworkable. Some state bills of rights antedate the federal Bill of Rights. The federal Bill of Rights was added to the Constitution as a condition for its ratification, on the insistence of people who feared a strong central government. While these rights were intended to restrain only the national government, since 1925 the Supreme Court has gradually extended them as restraints upon state action through the due process clause of the Fourteenth Amendment.

Censorship   The curbing of ideas either in speech or in writing *before* they are expressed. Accountability *after* expression is provided by laws regulating libel and slander, obscenity, incitement to crime, contempt of court, or seditious utterance. Except in time of war or other national emergency, any prior restraint upon freedom of speech or of the press is forbidden. *See Near v. Minnesota,* page 84; *Freedman v. Maryland,* page 80; *Roth v. United States,* page 86.

    Significance   The rights of freedom of speech or of the press would be meaningless if prior censorship could be exercised. While a person must bear the consequences of any expression, no governmental official may determine in advance what may be said or written. The Supreme Court has made an exception in the case of motion pictures, holding that a city may require submission of films to a censor (*Times Film Corporation v. Chicago,* 365 U.S. 43 [1961]), provided prompt judicial review is available (*Freedman v. Maryland,* 380 U.S. 51 [1965]).

Civil Disobedience   Refusal to obey a law, usually on the ground that the law is morally reprehensible. Recent examples of civil disobedience include Negro refusals to obey segregation laws and the actions of anti-Vietnam war groups in refusing to honor draft regulations. Civil disobedience ordinarily takes the form of nonviolent resistance to law-enforcement efforts, aimed at arousing public opinion against the law.

    Significance   Civil disobedience is to be distinguished from direct or revolutionary attacks upon constituted authority. An individual or group practicing civil disobedience seeks to call attention to a situation considered unjust and willingly suffers community ostracism and imprisonment for such disobedience.

Civil Liberties   Those liberties usually spelled out in a bill of rights or a constitution that guarantee the protection of persons, opinions, and property from the arbitrary interference of governmental officials. Restraints may be placed upon the exercise of these liberties only when they are abused by individuals or groups and when the public welfare requires them.

    Significance   Civil liberties are basic to a free society as contrasted with a totalitarian society, which makes no such guarantees. They are a restraint upon the government rather than upon individuals. Civil liberties may be distinguished from "civil rights" in that the latter is generally understood to refer to positive policies of government to protect individuals from arbitrary treatment both by government and by other individuals. However, the terms are often used interchangeably.

Civil Rights   Positive acts of government designed to protect persons against arbitrary or discriminatory treatment by government or individuals. Civil rights guarantees are sometimes written into constitutions, but frequently take the form of statutes. Though the term is often used interchangeably with "civil liberties," the latter generally refers to negative restraints upon government as found in bills of rights. The term "civil rights" is also to be distinguished from "political rights," which generally refers to the rights to participate in the management of government through such practices as voting. Civil rights have taken on special importance since the Civil War, as Congress and state and local legislatures have endeavored to secure equal treatment for Negroes.

Significance   Since 1940, there have been extensive attempts by government at all levels to secure civil rights for Negroes and other minorities in such areas as employment, housing, and public facilities. Traditional constitutional civil liberty provisions have not always proved workable to meet the challenges of private and governmental discrimination against minority groups. The precise role and extent of governmental action to secure civil rights remains a controversial question. Examples of civil rights legislation include the Civil Rights Acts of 1957, 1960, and 1964, and the civil rights laws enacted in many states and local communities.

Civil Rights Organizations   Groups organized to promote observance of the Bill of Rights and related constitutional provisions. These include organizations concerned with Negro civil rights as well as those with broader interests and goals. The major Negro civil rights groups include the National Association for the Advancement of Colored People (NAACP), which concerns itself mainly with legislative and legal matters; the National Urban League, which concentrates on economic improvement for the Negro; and the Congress of Racial Equality (CORE), the Southern Christian Leadership Conference (SCLC), and the Student Non-Violent Coordinating Committee (SNCC), which concentrate on mass demonstrations, boycotts, and sit-ins. Among the leading general civil rights and liberties groups are the American Civil Liberties Union (ACLU), the National Council of Churches of Christ, most labor unions, and ethnically oriented groups such as the American Jewish Congress.

Significance   Civil rights organizations differ from most American pressure groups in that they are not primarily concerned with promoting the economic interests of their members. While Negro rights groups have compelled public attention, organizations like the ACLU support court tests and in other ways protect First Amendment freedoms of expression and the rights of persons accused of crime. Few organizations are blatantly anti-civil rights, although the Ku Klux Klan, the Black Muslims, and certain right-wing extremist groups oppose the efforts of civil rights organizations.

Clear and Present Danger Rule   A test used by the Supreme Court to measure the permissible bounds of free speech. The test was formulated by Justice Oliver Wendell Holmes in *Schenck v. United States,* 249 U.S. 47 (1919): "The question in every case is whether the words are used in circumstances and are of such a nature as to create a clear and present danger that they will bring about substantive evils that Congress has a right to prevent. It is a question of proximity and degree." The application of this test has varied a good deal since 1919. *See* BAD TENDENCY RULE, page 55; *Schenck v. United States,* page 87.

Significance   Freedom of speech is not absolute, particularly when its exercise has a close relationship to some unlawful act, such as the violent overthrow of the government. Yet, the relationship between mere speech or the advocacy of a doctrine and the performance of an illegal act is not easy to determine. As Justice Holmes put it, one could not falsely shout "Fire!" in a crowded theatre and claim one's right to do so as an element of free speech. The clear and present danger rule is one attempt to establish a criterion for the protection of the individual's right to speak in light of society's right to protection.

Confession   An admission of guilt by one accused of a crime. *See Ashcraft v. Tennessee,* page 78; *Miranda v. Arizona,* page 82.

Significance   A confession must be voluntary and not induced by force, "third-degree" methods, prolonged interrogation, threats, psychological coercion, or promise of leniency. A confession exacted by any illegal means is not admissible in a trial and may result in the release of the accused. A confession must be corroborated with evidence that a crime has actually been committed. This prevents the conviction of deranged persons who confess to crimes they have not committed. The courts have been strict in demanding proof that a confession was made voluntarily and, preferably, in the presence of counsel.

Conscientious Objector   A person who refuses to render military service because of religious training and belief. While the right to religious freedom does not extend to refusal to serve in the military service, Congress has, as an act of grace, authorized noncombatant service or exemption from military service for conscientious objectors. The law does not exempt persons who oppose military service because of "political, sociological, or philosophical views or a merely personal moral code." *See* SELECTIVE SERVICE, page 350.

Significance   A person does not have the right to refuse military duty. A high regard for those whose beliefs make them unable to participate in a war effort has led Congress to this policy of leniency. In effect, Congress gives such people preferred treatment when it excuses them from actual combat, instead of penalizing them by requiring them to do other service. Whether or not a person is a true conscientious objector and not a "draft dodger" is a question to be determined by draft boards and, at times, the courts. In 1965, the Supreme Court held in *United States v. Seeger,* 380 U.S. 128, that persons without formal or traditional religious affiliation or belief could qualify as conscientious objectors if their beliefs occupy "a place parallel to that filled by the God of those admittedly qualifying for the exemption. . . ."

Conspiracy   Any agreement between two or more persons to commit an unlawful act. Conspiracy is a crime under numerous criminal statutes; in the realm of business and labor activities the law forbids conspiracies in restraint of trade. The most prominent conspiracy provision in the field of civil liberties is that found in the Smith Act of 1940, which makes it a crime to conspire to teach, advocate, or organize groups that advocate the overthrow of government by force.

Significance   Conspiracy laws are designed to punish persons who participate in the planning of a criminal act. In the areas of speech, press, and association, conspiracy laws pose the danger that persons who do not have actual plans to do evil may be punished for foolish conjecture.

Cruel and Unusual Punishment   Any lingering torture, mutilation, or degrading treatment, or any sentence too severe for the offense committed. The Eighth Amendment to the Constitution forbids such punishment, leaving the scope of the ban to be determined by the courts.

Significance   The idea of humane treatment for criminals is a relatively modern concept, which holds that even the undesirable elements of the community should have their individual dignity preserved. Whether a particular punishment is cruel depends upon community standards as determined by the courts. Changing attitudes are reflected by Supreme Court decisions holding as cruel and unusual punishment the deprivation of citizenship for wartime desertion (*Trop v. Dulles,* 356 U.S. 86 [1958]) and a state law making it a crime to be addicted to the use of narcotics (*Robinson v. California,* 370 U.S. 660 [1962]).

De Facto Segregation   The existence of racially segregated facilities that are, however, not required by law (*de jure*). De facto segregation refers especially to the school system in typical northern communities, in which neighborhood racial patterns lead "in fact" to predominantly Negro and white schools similar to those in the South that, in the past, were segregated by law.

Significance   De facto segregation in northern schools has led to mass-protest demonstrations and to violence in some large cities. Negro groups have demanded integrated schools, charging that segregation results from housing discrimination and from deliberate policies of school officials. White parents often resist integration efforts, demanding retention of neighborhood schools. Some school districts have tried to integrate schools by "bussing" children to distant schools or by a variety of school mixing plans. The massive ghettos of New York, Chicago and Los Angeles, however, make it virtually impossible to integrate schools on any large scale.

Double Jeopardy   The guarantee in the Fifth Amendment to the Constitution that one may not be twice put in jeopardy of life or limb for the same offense. Thus, a person who has been tried may not be tried again for the same crime. The guarantee does not, however, apply to trials by both the national government and a state, or by two different states for offenses growing out of a single criminal act. Trial following a mistrial is not double jeopardy unless the prosecution has deliberately forced a mistrial in order to get better evidence or a more favorable jury. *See Bartkus v. Illinois,* page 78.

Significance   Although considerable confusion exists as to what constitutes double jeopardy in specific instances, this guarantee does afford protection against continual harassment of accused persons. Also, the courts and the accused are spared endless costs and time-consuming litigation.

Due Process of Law   Protection against arbitrary deprivation of life, liberty, or property. The Fifth and Fourteenth Amendments forbid the national and state governments, respectively, to deny any person his life, liberty, or property without due process of law. While no precise definition of this term has ever been made, it establishes the principle of limited government. Two types of due process—procedural and substantive—have emerged in the course of litigation. Though used sparingly in recent years, substantive due process has been used by the judiciary to strike down legislative and executive acts that are arbitrary or lacking in reasonableness, or that cover subject matter beyond the reach of government. Procedural due process was defined by Daniel Webster as procedure "which hears before it condemns, which proceeds upon inquiry, and renders judgment only after trial." The Supreme Court, in a long series of cases, has marked out the general meaning of the phrase so as to forbid any procedure that is shocking to the conscience or that makes impossible a fair and enlightened system of justice for a civilized people. *See Moore v. Dempsey,* page 84; *Palko v. Connecticut,* page 85.

Significance   Protection against arbitrary treatment is basic to the American system of government. Due process functions both as a limitation on public officials and as a power in the hands of the judiciary, which has wide latitude in applying it. Judges can determine whether a law bears a reasonable relationship to a proper governmental function and whether the procedure used, particularly in criminal cases, is fair and reasonable.

Eminent Domain   The power inherent in all governments to take over private property, provided that it is taken for a public purpose and that just compensation is awarded. Disputes as to purpose or price are generally settled in the courts.

Significance   The right to own and use private property is high in the American scheme of values. Yet, without the power of eminent domain, projects that benefit many persons, such as slum clearance or highway projects, would be impossible. Individual rights, however, are recognized by the provision for equitable compensation.

Equal Protection of the Law   A requirement of the Fourteenth Amendment that state laws may not arbitrarily discriminate against persons. Identical treatment is not required. Classification of persons is permitted provided that the classification is reasonable and bears some relationship to the end sought. Hence, taxation in accordance with ability to pay has been held to be a reasonable classification, whereas classification according to color or religion has been held to bear no reasonable relationship to the functions of government. Current interest in the application of equal protection centers on the desegregation of races in public facilities and on inequality in state legislative apportionment. Though the Constitution does not contain a similar restriction on the national government, the courts have read the equal protection concept into the meaning of the due process clause of the Fifth Amendment. *See Brown v. Board of Education of Topeka,* page 79; *Bolling v. Sharpe,* page 79.

Significance   Equal protection of the law emanates from the democratic concepts of the equality of men under the law and their right to equality of opportunity. Arbitrary or irrelevant barriers to full enjoyment of rights are forbidden. Although the prohibition does not extend to private discrimination, both the national and many state governments have acted to forbid private discrimination against persons based on color, creed, or national origin.

Equal Rights A term used to describe the movement to equalize the rights of men and women. Traditionally in American law, women have not enjoyed the same rights as men. State laws vary widely, although many are protective of women rather than directly discriminatory. Women's suffrage has led to a gradual narrowing of legal differences.

Significance The equal rights movement achieved two major victories in the 1960s—the passage of the Equal Pay Act of 1963, which requires equal pay for men and women doing similar work; and the Civil Rights Act of 1964, which forbids discrimination against women in hiring and other personnel policies. An equal rights constitutional amendment proposal to prohibit all discrimination based on sex has received increasing support in Congress.

Ex Post Facto Law A criminal law that is retroactive and that has an adverse effect upon one accused of a crime. Thus, an ex post facto law is one that makes an act a crime that was not a crime when it was committed, that increases the penalty for a crime after its commission, or that changes the rules of evidence so as to make conviction easier. Neither the state nor the national governments may enact such laws under provisions of Article I, sections 9 and 10 of the Constitution. The prohibition does not extend to civil laws or to laws favorable to an accused person.

Significance The ex post facto prohibition emphasizes that each individual is free to do those things not specifically forbidden by existing law without fear of future punishment. This is pertinent to the concept of a government of laws and not of men, for it prevents abuse of power by governmental officials, who might otherwise retrospectively apply new laws for vindictive purposes.

Fair Employment Practices Laws Laws that forbid private and/or public employers, labor unions, or employment agencies to discriminate in hiring or in other personnel policies on the grounds of race, color, creed, or national origin. Twenty-nine states have enacted such laws. In the Civil Rights Act of 1964, Congress provided for equal employment opportunities in businesses and labor unions engaged in interstate commerce. Equal treatment for women is also required by the Act. *See* EQUAL EMPLOYMENT OPPORTUNITY COMMISSION, page 76.

Significance Fair employment laws represent positive governmental action in the field of private rights, in contrast to the traditional concept of civil liberties as a restraint against government. Both the national and state laws stress education and conciliation, although several state laws provide criminal sanctions. The national law encourages state action in this field.

Fifth Amendment A part of the Bill of Rights that imposes a number of restrictions on the national government with respect to the rights of persons accused of crime. It provides for indictment by grand jury, protection against double jeopardy and self-incrimination, and forbids denial of life, liberty, or property without due process of law. In addition, the Fifth Amendment prohibits the taking of property without just compensation. *See* GRAND JURY, page 211; DOUBLE JEOPARDY, page 59; SELF-INCRIMINATION, page 72; DUE PROCESS, page 60; EMINENT DOMAIN, page 60; IMMUNITY, page 65.

Significance   Together with the Fourth, Sixth, and Eighth Amendments, and with provisions in the Constitution relative to habeas corpus, ex post facto laws, and bills of attainder, the Fifth Amendment is a significant source of liberty. The Amendment has come into contemporary prominence because of the self-incrimination clause. Persons refusing to testify before congressional committees have frequently "taken the Fifth," a shorthand phrase for claiming the privilege against self-incrimination.

Fourteenth Amendment   A post-Civil War Amendment (1868) that defines citizenship, restricts the powers of the states in their relations with their inhabitants, requires reduction of a state's representation in Congress for denials of suffrage, disqualifies former office-holders who participated in the rebellion, and invalidates any war debts of rebellious states. The most important provisions are those that forbid a state to deprive any person of life, liberty, or property without due process of law, or deny to any person the equal protection of the law. *See Palko v. Connecticut,* page 85.

Significance   The due process clause and the equal protection clause have been prominent in constitutional disputes for many years. Both have made possible federal intervention against alleged state encroachment on the rights of the people. For a time, the due process clause was used mainly to limit the states in the exercise of their taxing and police powers in business regulation. Since 1925, the due process clause has been interpreted by the courts to forbid state denials of First Amendment freedoms as well as of essential procedural rights found in the Fourth, Fifth, Sixth, and Eighth Amendments. The equal protection clause has been invoked to restrain racial segregation practices and to maintain fair legislative apportionment by state governments.

Freedom of Assembly   The right of the people to congregate for the discussion of public questions and to organize into political parties or pressure groups for the purpose of influencing public policy. The right of assembly does not authorize meetings designed to accomplish an illegal purpose or those that lead to a breach of the peace or resistance to lawful authority. Freedom of assembly is guaranteed by the First Amendment and by state constitutions. In addition, the Supreme Court has ruled that the due process clause of the Fourteenth Amendment protects the individual's freedom of assembly against infringement by state governments. *See Hague v. CIO,* page 81.

Significance   In a democratic society, the people must have the right to meet freely in peaceable assemblage to consider public questions. This right is closely related to those of freedom of speech and of petition. All act as a restraint upon legislators and other public officials. The peace and civil rights protest movements of the 1960s have put the right of assembly to severe tests because of the potentials for violence in civil disobedience.

Freedom of Association   The right to organize for political, religious, or other social purposes. The Constitution makes no mention of freedom of association, but it is implicit in guarantees of freedom of speech, assembly, and religion. *See NAACP v. Alabama,* page 84.

Significance   The American people are noted for being organization-minded; many Americans belong to several organizations. The right to associate has received much attention because of laws passed to curtail the activities and rights of alleged subversive organizations and their members. Such laws have been attacked in some quarters as imputing guilt by association, since members of a group may not necessarily subscribe to all its beliefs or actions. Persons do not, however, have the right to organize in order to accomplish illegal aims. Another problem is that some southern states have attempted to impede the activities of civil rights groups promoting desegregation. The courts have not, however, permitted any limitations to be placed upon lawful groups. The right to associate is recognized as essential in a democratic society since, generally, an individual can accomplish more with a group than by acting alone.

Freedom of the Press   The right to publish and disseminate information without prior restraint, subject to penalties for abuse of the right. Abuses include libel, obscenity, incitement to crime, contempt of court, or sedition. Freedom of the press is protected by the First and Fourteenth Amendments to the Constitution and by all state constitutions. Major contemporary problems have involved censorship of books and movies for alleged obscenity, restraints on Communist publications, and the difficulty of safeguarding both freedom of the press and a fair trial. *See Near v. Minnesota,* page 84; *New York Times v. Sullivan,* page 85.

Significance   A free press is essential to a free society, particularly as it relates to the dissemination of political information. The Supreme Court has narrowly restricted any efforts at political censorship and has permitted wide latitude to criticize public officials. In dealing with obscenity, the courts have had difficulty in developing a formula to identify this abuse. The conflict between a free press and a fair trial involves a clash between two essential rights. The problem arises from the difficulty of holding a trial free from bias when press, radio, and television publicize details of the crime and the trial. The Supreme Court has held, for example, that television may not be used in notorious trials because of its adverse effect on parties to the trial (*Estes v. Texas,* 381 U.S. 532 [1965]). Both law enforcement officials and the press seek guidelines that will preserve the people's right in both fair trials and freedom of the press.

Freedom of Religion   Freedom of worship and religious practice. The national government under the First Amendment, and the states under their constitutions and the Fourteenth Amendment, may not abridge this right of worship. Any religious practice that is contrary to public peace or morality may be outlawed, such as snake-handling or polygamy. *See* SEPARATION OF CHURCH AND STATE, page 73; *Jehovah's Witnesses Cases,* page 82.

Significance   In a nation with such diversity of religious groups, the free exercise of religion and the separation of church and state are essential. This was foremost in the minds of the Founding Fathers who provided that there be no religious test for public office. Religious freedom is the first item in the Bill of Rights, reflecting the need for freedom of conscience in a free society. Any interference of state with church or of church with state constitutes a danger to both. The free exercise of religion has not proved to be as controversial a matter in American life as has the concept of the separation of church and state.

Freedom of Speech   The right to speak without prior restraint, subject to penalties for abuse of the right. Abuses include slander, obscenity, incitement to crime, contempt of court, or sedition. By virtue of the First and Fourteenth Amendments and state bills of rights, neither the national government nor the states may abridge freedom of speech. *See* FREEDOM OF THE PRESS, page 63; BAD TENDENCY RULE, page 55; CLEAR AND PRESENT DANGER RULE, page 57.

Significance   Freedom is impossible without the right to disseminate ideas. Generally, the courts have treated the guarantee liberally. In recent years, problems have arisen with regard to the advocacy of Communist doctrine. The courts have distinguished between mere advocacy of abstract doctrine and conspiratorial advocacy. In placing limitations on freedom of speech, the courts have attempted to apply such concepts as "clear and present danger" to determine whether a given situation justifies restriction.

Guilt by Association   Attribution of criminal or wrongful behavior or beliefs to a person because of the people or groups with whom he associates. *See Adler v. Board of Education,* page 77; *Scales v. United States,* page 87; FREEDOM OF ASSOCIATION, page 63.

Significance   Guilt by association is a denial of the concept underlying American justice that guilt is personal and that an individual should not suffer any disabilities because of conduct or ideas attributed to his associates. The problem relates to those who lose their jobs or suffer other penalties as a result of membership in an alleged subversive or unpopular group. The issue is whether mere membership or association proves agreement with all the tenets of the group. The Supreme Court has sustained the power of national, state, and local governments to impose disabilities upon members of particular groups or exponents of certain ideas. The Court has noted that people are often judged by the company they keep and this factor may properly be considered in determining loyalty (*Adler v. Board of Education,* 342 U.S. 485 [1952]). Guilt by association should not be confused with conviction for conspiracy to commit a crime, which involves actual and deliberate participation in the planning of a wrongful act.

Habeas Corpus   A court order directing an official who has a person in custody to bring the prisoner to court and to show cause for his detention. The Constitution guarantees the right to a writ of habeas corpus, but Congress may suspend it in cases of rebellion or invasion (Art. I, sec. 9). Though President Lincoln suspended the writ on his own volition, Congress subsequently affirmed his action. A number of state constitutions absolutely forbid its suspension.

Significance   Habeas corpus is generally considered to be the most important guarantee of liberty, in that it prevents arbitrary arrest and imprisonment—the fearful knock at the door and the disappearance of the seized person. A prisoner must be released unless sufficient cause to detain him can be shown. Habeas corpus may also be used by persons serving sentences in state and federal prisons to reopen their cases on the ground of illegal detention because of rights denied before or during their trials.

Immunity   A privilege granted to a person that exempts him from prosecution for any self-incriminating testimony given by him before a court, grand jury, or investigating committee. Immunity involves an enforced waiver of the constitutional right against self-incrimination, so that an individual can be compelled to give testimony or be punished for contempt. No evidence revealed by a witness who has been granted immunity may be used against him in any criminal prosecution, state or federal, or subject him to any penalty by either level of government (*Murphy v. Waterfront Commission*, 378 U.S. 52 [1964]). Many states and the national government make provisions for the granting of immunity to witnesses. *See* SELF-INCRIMINATION, page 72; *Malloy v. Hogan*, page 83; IMMUNITY ACT OF 1954, page 91.
Significance   A grant of immunity is designed to compel testimony from persons who refuse to answer questions on the ground that their answers would tend to incriminate them and subject them to prosecution. Some legal scholars question the propriety of this procedure because it forces an individual to waive a constitutional right. Immunity will not be granted unless the information likely to be secured is of great public importance. Care must be taken not to make immunity a loophole for notorious criminals to escape punishment.

Involuntary Servitude   Slavery, peonage, or forcing a person to work to fulfill a contract or to work out a debt. The Thirteenth Amendment provides that neither slavery nor involuntary servitude, except in punishment for crime, may exist anywhere in the United States. Certain types of employment are not covered by the prohibition when the public safety is jeopardized, as in the case of policemen, firemen, seamen, and train crews. *See Pollock v. Williams*, page 86.
Significance   Though aimed primarily at putting an end to slavery, the Thirteenth Amendment serves as a guarantee of free and voluntary labor, which may be threatened by situations less drastic than outright slavery. Congress has supplemented this Amendment by passage of the Antipeonage Act of 1867, which is still vigorously enforced to protect debtors.

Libel and Slander   Defamation of character, written in the case of libel, and oral in the case of slander. Both include statements that expose a person to hatred, contempt, or ridicule, or that injure his reputation by imputing to him a criminal act, or that harm him in his trade or profession. Libel and slander usually involve suits for civil damages, but they may also be punished under criminal laws. Libel is generally considered more serious than slander because the written word is more durable than a passing remark. The reputation of those involved, the nature of the audience, and the conditions under which the words were written or spoken may prove pertinent in a suit for damages. Truth of a statement is generally an absolute defense. *See New York Times v. Sullivan,* page 85.

Significance   Libel and slander are limitations on the freedom of speech and press, and many state constitutions expressly make this distinction. Libel and slander do not apply to comment made about public officials or newsworthy people unless malicious intent is proved, since such comments are considered to be in the public interest (*New York Times v. Sullivan,* 376 U.S. 255 [1964]). Major recent problems concern: (1) the harm done to private reputations by legislative or executive officials who enjoy immunity from suit for remarks made in the line of duty; (2) whether remarks made on radio and television are libel or slander (for example, do oral remarks made on these mediums have the impact of the printed word?); and (3) "group libel" laws, which make it illegal to impugn the reputation of an entire minority group.

Loyalty Oath   An oath that requires an individual to disavow or abjure certain beliefs and associations. Such oaths were exacted during the Revolutionary War, the Civil War, and the "red scare" of the 1920s. Recent loyalty oaths, inspired by the cold war, generally require persons to swear that they do not advocate the violent overthrow of government nor belong to any organization so advocating. Loyalty oaths are generally required of public employees, teachers, attorneys, defense workers, and recipients of governmental benefits. The courts have generally upheld impositions of loyalty oaths unless the oath did not excuse those whose associations were innocent of wrongful intent, or if the oath was totally unrelated to any governmental purpose. *See Garner v. Board of Public Works,* page 80.

Significance   Few people object to taking an ordinary oath of allegiance declaring loyalty to the United States and swearing to uphold the Constitution. However, loyalty or "test" oaths have met numerous objections based largely on the reversal of the presumption of innocence, since an individual may be considered disloyal unless he swears that he is not. It is also charged that such oaths abridge freedom of speech and assembly by the discretion vested in the imposer of the oath to determine suitable beliefs and asscciations. Moreover, many doubt the utility of oaths as a weapon against subversives who would undoubtedly swear falsely to the oath. The major utility of loyalty oaths lies in making the oath taker aware of possible illegal activities or associations and in bringing perjury charges against those who swear falsely.

Loyalty-Security Programs   Programs carried on by national and state governments to rid the public service of disloyal persons or persons suspected of being security risks. The national government's loyalty program had its inception in 1947 when President Truman ordered that governmental employees be dismissed if grounds existed to doubt their loyalty. President Eisenhower extended the program to include all "security risks"—disloyal as well as generally untrustworthy people. The programs have also been applied to the armed forces, defense plants, maritime workers, and other government-connected activities. Appeal procedures are provided for discharged persons but do not always permit confrontation with informers. An individual, however, has no right to a government job and the programs have resulted in numerous dismissals. In the states, similar programs have been undertaken, although most states have limited their loyalty requirements to the taking of a loyalty oath. *See* ATTORNEY GENERAL'S LIST, page 54.

Significance   Few people insist that disloyal persons should work for the government. Many people, however, have protested the procedures used in the loyalty-security programs, preferring normal police work to uncover dangerous persons. The use of unidentified informers raises much criticism. Many persons are concerned with the effects on the morale of governmental employees who are subject to investigation of all their activities and beliefs. Loyalty-security programs will undoubtedly be part of the American scene as long as the international situation continues to be dangerous.

Magna Carta   The Great Charter of freedom granted in 1215 by King John of England on demand of his barons.

Significance   The source for many of the basic freedoms found in American law are traceable to the Magna Carta. Among these are trial by a jury of one's peers and the guarantee that no person shall lose his life, liberty, or property except by due process of law.

McCarthyism   Unsubstantiated accusations of disloyalty, and abuse of legislative investigatory power, that engender fear over real or imagined threats to the security of the nation. The term was derived in the early 1950s from the actions of Senator Joseph R. McCarthy of Wisconsin who made repeated charges against public officials and private individuals under the protection of his senatorial immunity.

Significance   McCarthyism was a post-World War II phenomenon that fed on the fears generated by the cold war between the United States and the Soviet Union. The period was marked by loyalty-security investigations into the lives of public employees, surveillance of scientists and teachers, the imposition of loyalty oaths, and passage of anti-Communist legislation. Many vestiges of the period remain. McCarthyism utilizes the catchwords of "loyalty" and "security" as justification for limitations on civil liberties. Ultraconservative groups use similar tactics to fight social reform. McCarthyism fosters suspicion among neighbors, distrust of public officials, and the idea of "guilt by association."

Natural Rights   An underlying assumption of the American political creed that men are endowed by their Creator with certain rights that may not be abridged by government. *See* NATURAL LAW, page 11.

Significance   The Judaeo-Christian doctrine, as embodied in the American creed, assumes the inviolability of man's basic rights, as contrasted with the forces of absolutism, which assert that man has only such rights as the government decides to give him. The doctrine of natural rights assumes that man had his rights in a "state of nature" and creates government to protect those rights.

Ninth Amendment   A part of the Bill of Rights that reads, "The enumeration in the Constitution, of certain rights, shall not be construed to deny or disparage others retained by the people." This provision reaffirms the tradition of the natural rights philosophy, supported by those who feared that a listing of rights in the Bill of Rights might be interpreted to mean that no other rights were held by the people.

Significance   The "other" rights that the people retain have not been extensively defined nor has the Ninth Amendment been prominently used in litigation. In the case of *Mitchell v. United States,* 313 U.S. 80 (1941), the Supreme Court noted that the Amendment protected the right to political activity by the people. In *Griswold v. Connecticut,* 381 U.S. 479 (1965), the Court struck down a law that forbade counseling married couples to use contraceptives as an invasion of the right of privacy protected by the First and Ninth Amendments.

Petition   A request to a public official that seeks to correct a wrong or to influence public policy. The First Amendment guarantees to the people the right to "petition the government for a redress of grievances." This provision, like all provisions of the First Amendment, is applicable to the states through the Fourteenth Amendment, although most state constitutions contain a similar provision. The right of petition, closely related to freedoms of speech, press, and assembly, is generally exercised through letter writing to public officials and through pressure group activity.

Significance   It is vital in a free society that persons be able to call the attention of their representatives to their grievances. In this way, government can remain continually responsive to the people and can be made aware of their opinions at times other than at elections. The right of petition is most effectively exercised through the lobbying activities of interest groups and by mass demonstrations and picketing by groups having limited access to the political power structure.

Police Power   The power inherent in state governments to protect the health, safety, morals, and welfare of the people. In the area of civil rights and liberties, a lawful exercise of the police power may justify abridgment of personal or property rights. For example, through use of the police power, a state may destroy property that endangers public health or may limit freedom of speech or assembly when the public safety is jeopardized. *See* POLICE POWER, page 37.

Significance   The police power rests on the assumption that rights are not absolute. The extent of the power is generally determined by the courts when they are faced with concrete situations in which the police power comes into conflict with personal liberties. In a typical civil liberty–police power case, the courts must strike a balance between the needs of society and the rights of the individual.

Political Right   The right to participate in the management of government and to influence public policy. Typical political rights include the rights to vote, to form a political party, and to participate in pressure group activity.

Significance   Political rights are essential for the operations of a free government. Citizens must be given the opportunity not only to speak out on public issues but to take positive action to influence or control the government. So long as these rights remain inviolate, regardless of the party in power, dictatorship cannot take hold. Any group denied these rights is left with the sole recourse of violent revolution to accomplish its goals. In recent years, emphasis has been placed on securing political rights for Negroes and other minority groups who may be denied access to the polls. Limitations, however, have been placed upon the political activities of subversive groups who seek to eliminate such rights.

Privilege   An advantage or opportunity granted to an individual or a group to which it has no right. The courts have held, for example, that governmental employment is a privilege and not a right. The government may establish reasonable qualifications or demands before it grants a privilege, such as a loyalty oath or other demonstration of fitness or reliability.

Significance   An individual may lose a privilege under procedures and circumstances that would not be permissible if a right were abridged. Hence, a person could be discharged from public service on suspicion of disloyalty without a trial, but he could not be punished for disloyalty by fine or imprisonment without the constitutional safeguards accorded accused persons. Similarly, the threat of "withholding of benefits" in place of criminal sanctions is used to secure compliance with governmental programs in such areas as agriculture and welfare.

Procedural Rights   Protection against arbitrary actions by public officials. Under American constitutional law, no person may be deprived of his life, liberty, or property or of any other right guaranteed him, except under well-defined procedures, including a fair hearing before a judicial tribunal. American procedural rights are generally considered to be those listed in the Bill of Rights, particularly in the Fourth through the Eighth Amendments. *Procedural* rights are to be distinguished from *substantive* rights. The latter include those elements that are considered to be of the very essence of freedom, such as freedom of speech, whereas the former are concerned with the methods by which rights are protected. *See* DUE PROCESS OF LAW, page 60.

Significance   A crucial difference between a free society and an authoritarian society lies in the procedures afforded citizens to protect them against arbitrary treatment. Under American law, one may not be tried and condemned except in conformity with due process of law, and any errors in procedure may render a conviction void.

Quartering of Soldiers   A prohibition found in the Third Amendment against housing soldiers in private homes during time of peace without consent of the owner. In wartime, quartering of soldiers may be done under conditions prescribed by law.

Significance   The Third Amendment was a reaction against the practice of the British, during the colonial era, of quartering soldiers in private homes.

This has never been done in the United States, and no cases have arisen concerning this provision. It is one of the elements of civilian control over the military.

Religious Test   A requirement that one profess belief in a particular religious faith or in a Supreme Being as a condition to holding public office. Article VI of the Constitution prohibits such tests. Several state constitutions contain a requirement that public officials profess a belief in God, but in 1961 the Supreme Court held such a Maryland provision unconstitutional (*Torcaso v. Watkins,* 367 U.S. 488). *See* SEPARATION OF CHURCH AND STATE, page 73.

Significance   The prohibition against religious tests for office is a necessary component of the separation of church and state. Until the election of John F. Kennedy, a Catholic, to the presidency in 1960, there appeared to be an "unofficial" religious test for the office of President, since it was widely believed that a non-Protestant could not be elected. Kennedy's victory and the Supreme Court decision in the Maryland case have contributed to the effectiveness of the religious test prohibition.

Restrictive Covenant   A clause entered in deeds to protect the value of properties by restricting their uses. Some restrictive covenants prohibit the sale of property to Negroes or other minority groups.

Significance   Individuals do not violate any provisions of the United States Constitution by entering into restrictive covenant agreements. The Supreme Court, however, has held (*Shelley v. Kramer,* 334 U.S. 1 [1948]) that racially restrictive covenants cannot be enforced in the courts, since such action would constitute governmental support of discrimination contrary to the equal protection clause of the Fourteenth Amendment. Some state and local governments prohibit by law private agreements that discriminate against the property rights of minority groups.

Right to Bear Arms   The guarantee in the Second Amendment of the right to keep weapons, recognizing that "A well regulated militia [is] necessary to the security of a free state." Similar provisions are found in many state constitutions. The keeping and use of arms, however, is extensively regulated. Possession of certain types of weapons, such as machine guns or sawed-off shotguns, is prohibited, and registration of some weapons is required.

Significance   In practice, this Amendment has been of little importance. It is, however, an implicit recognition of the right of revolution, stemming from the idea that a tyrant could not be overthrown if the people were denied the means. In addition, this guarantee was included in the Bill of Rights to assure the states that the national government would not disarm the state militias. The assassination of President John F. Kennedy in 1963 aroused nation-wide concern over the ease of securing firearms and produced pressures for national legislation to control their purchase and use.

Right to Counsel   The guarantee in the Sixth Amendment to the Constitution that a defendant in a criminal case have the assistance of an attorney. The Supreme Court has ruled that the national government (*Johnson v. Zerbst,*

304 U.S. 458 [1938]) and state governments (*Gideon v. Wainwright*, 372 U.S. 335 [1963]) must furnish counsel for indigent defendants. An accused must be permitted to confer with counsel prior to interrogation by the police. He may waive his right to counsel, but the waiver must be an intelligent one in which the defendant recognizes the consequences of his action. *See Gideon v. Wainwright*, page 80; *Miranda v. Arizona*, page 83.

Significance   Right to counsel is based on the assumption that the average person is unable to understand the intricacies of the law or to know the full extent of his rights. In the *Gideon* case, the Court sought to overcome the advantages of those able to afford counsel by providing "equal justice for the poor." The Supreme Court's insistence that indigent defendants be furnished counsel has led to extensive use of the public defender system.

Search and Seizure   Methods by which police officers gather evidence and make arrests. The Fourth Amendment prohibits "unreasonable" searches and seizures. Under ordinary or "reasonable" circumstances, a search warrant must be secured from a judge, commissioner, or magistrate. This is a written order issued under oath; it describes the place to be searched and the person or things to be seized. A warrant is not essential if it can be shown that time or circumstances did not reasonably permit securing it. Evidence gathered through illegal or unreasonable means is not admissible in federal trials nor, under the Fourteenth Amendment, in state trials (*Weeks v. United States*, 232 U.S. 383 [1914]; *Mapp v. Ohio*, 367 U.S. 643 [1961]). *See Mapp v. Ohio*, page 83; WIRETAPPING, page 75; ARREST WARRANT, page 200.

Significance   The Fourth Amendment has proved to be one of the more troublesome provisions of the Bill of Rights. What constitutes an "unreasonable" search and seizure? No precise definition can be made and the courts have treated the issue on a case-to-case basis, considering all the circumstances involved. The most serious contemporary problem is the reasonableness of search through wiretapping and other electronic devices. Evidence that is obtained through an unreasonable search and seizure is inadmissible on the ground that it constitutes self-incrimination—forcing the accused to reveal what he has a right to conceal.

Sedition   Actions that incite rebellion or discontent against duly established government. Espionage, sabotage, or attempts to overthrow the government constitute sedition, as does advocacy by publication or speech to accomplish these goals. The Sedition Acts of 1798 and 1918 put severe limitations on mere criticism of the government. Recent sedition legislation has been aimed at outlawing Communist conspiracies and advocacy of doctrines aimed at overthrow of government by force. *See* ALIEN AND SEDITION LAWS, page 88; SMITH ACT, page 89; INTERNAL SECURITY ACT, page 91; COMMUNIST CONTROL ACT, page 91; *Dennis v. United States*, page 79.

Significance   Though closely akin to treason, sedition does not require the precise standard of proof that the Constitution requires for treason convictions. Few people question the legality or wisdom of outlawing and punishing seditious *actions*. Punishment for seditious *speech*, however, resulted in severe restrictions on nonconformists in post-Revolutionary America and during

World War I. The Supreme Court has sustained convictions of Communists but has drawn a distinction between mere advocacy of abstract doctrine and conspiracy to advocate concrete action (*Yates v. United States,* 354 U.S. 298 [1957]). A law that makes mere criticism of government a crime makes free government impossible, since one may criticize and be loyal at the same time.

Segregation   The separation of the white and colored races in public and private facilities. Laws requiring the segregation of the races (Jim Crow laws) have been or are still on the statute books of several states. In 1896, the Supreme Court upheld such laws under the "separate but equal" doctrine whereby the Negro could be segregated if he were provided with equal facilities (*Plessy v. Ferguson,* 163 U.S. 537). Under this doctrine, a wide pattern of segregation developed in schools, transportation, recreation, and housing. Beginning in the 1940s, the Supreme Court began to weaken the separate but equal doctrine by insisting that the facilities provided for Negroes, particularly in education, be equal, indeed. Finally, in 1954, the Supreme Court struck down the separate but equal formula, holding that segregation based on color denied the equal protection of the laws (*Brown v. Board of Education of Topeka,* 347 U.S. 483). *See Plessy v. Ferguson,* page 86; *Brown v. Board of Education of Topeka,* page 79; CIVIL RIGHTS ACTS, pages 89-90.
    Significance   Segregation has been part of the pattern of life in the seventeen southern states and the District of Columbia. The Supreme Court's 1954 decision has simultaneously strained and improved the status of the American Negro. Since 1954, integration has proceeded at various speeds and, in some states, little progress has been made. In certain areas, integration has precipitated violence. Since 1954, however, with the law no longer permitting separate treatment, the Negro has sought to make the ruling a reality by such actions as "sit-ins" in restaurants, "kneel-ins" at churches, and "wade-ins" at public beaches, and by marches and mass demonstrations. Moreover, Congress has passed civil rights measures in 1957, 1960, 1964, and 1965, to increase Negro political and civil rights. Southern states have sought to resist integration by various evasive schemes but few have found favor in the courts. Unofficial patterns of segregation still exist on a wide scale in both the North and the South and are likely to continue for many years.

Self-incrimination   Testimony by a person that reveals facts that may result in a criminal prosecution against him. The Fifth Amendment of the Constitution provides that no person "shall be compelled in any criminal case to be a witness against himself." Though originally applied to persons on trial, the concept has been extended to cover testimony before legislative committees or executive agencies. A person may not refuse to testify in order to protect another person, nor because his answers might bring disgrace upon himself. The guarantee extends only to testimony that might involve the person himself in a criminal prosecution. A person who has been given immunity or a pardon, or who has already been convicted of the particular offense (so that he may not be tried again), may not refuse to testify. No unfavorable inferences may be drawn from a refusal to testify. The Fifth Amendment guarantee against self-incrimination applies with equal force to both state and federal proceedings

(*Malloy v. Hogan,* 378 U.S. 1 [1964]). *See Malloy v. Hogan,* page 83;
Miranda v. Arizona, page 83; IMMUNITY, page 65.

Significance   In a criminal case, the burden of proof is on the prosecution. The right against self-incrimination is designed to prevent the shifting
of the burden to the defendant by forcing him to reveal incriminating facts.
It also prevents the use of torture or inquisitorial procedures to coerce confessions, as well as the use of evidence illegally obtained. A major problem
involves the question of whether the witness has waived his right by answering
questions directly or indirectly related to a matter that might incriminate
him. Once the witness begins to answer a line of questions he may have un-
knowingly waived the right; for this reason, many witnesses have refused to
answer any questions. This has been particularly true in congressional investigations into subversion and racketeering. A person, however, may be found in
contempt if he uses the right as a mere dodge and refuses to answer proper
questions. While one may not suffer any legal penalty for invoking the Fifth
Amendment, loss of reputation or employment may result. The protection
against self-incrimination is one of the hallmarks of a free society, but, refusal
to testify by "taking the Fifth" in legislative investigations often arouses widespread indignation.

Separation of Church and State   A basic principle of American government
that prohibits the mingling of church and state. The principle rests on the
First Amendment clause forbidding the passage of any law "respecting an establishment of religion." In a series of controversial cases, the Supreme Court
has held that the state must be committed to a position of neutrality and may
neither advance nor retard religion. No public funds may be expended on
behalf of any church nor may the government favor one church over another.
Public schools may not be used for sectarian religious observances and official
requirements for Bible reading or prayer recitals are forbidden. Laws that
have a predominantly secular effect, such as public bus transportation for
parochial schools or Sunday closing laws, have been upheld. The permissible
extent of public aid to church related schools remains, however, unresolved. *See
Everson v. Board of Education of Ewing Township,* page 80; *School District
of Abington Township v. Schempp,* page 87; *Zorach v. Clauson,* page 88;
ELEMENTARY AND SECONDARY EDUCATION ACT, page 311.

Significance   The principle of the separation of church and state is most
controversial when applied to the role of religion in the public schools and to
the use of public funds for parochial schools. The Supreme Court has supported Thomas Jefferson's idea that the establishment clause was intended to
erect "a wall of separation between church and state" toward the end that
official governmental support not be placed behind the tenets of any orthodoxy
and that public institutions not become embroiled in sectarian controversy.

Seventh Amendment   A part of the Bill of Rights that guarantees the
preservation of the right to a jury trial in a suit at common law where the
value in controversy exceeds $20. It also provides that facts tried by the jury
may not be re-examined in any court except in accordance with common law
rules.

Significance   The Seventh Amendment is a rarely litigated item that applies only to cases in which Congress permits common law rules to be used. It does not apply to cases arising out of statutory law nor in equity proceedings. The Seventh Amendment is an example of a portion of the Bill of Rights that is not made applicable to the states by the Fourteenth Amendment, since it involves no right that is basic to fairness or that is so important as to be ranked as fundamental.

Sixth Amendment   A part of the Bill of Rights that stipulates the basic requirements of procedural due process in federal criminal trials. These include a speedy and public trial, an impartial jury, trial in the area where the crime was committed, notice of the charges, the right to confront witnesses and to obtain favorable witnesses, and the right to counsel. See TRIAL, page 224; JURY, page 214; VENUE, page 226; WITNESS, page 226; RIGHT TO COUNSEL, page 70.

Significance   The brief but highly important Sixth Amendment sums up the essential procedures of a fair and impartial trial. An improper denial of any of these ingredients may be sufficient to void a conviction.

State Action   The abridgment of individual rights by state or local governmental agencies, laws, or officials, which is forbidden by the Fourteenth Amendment to the Constitution. Invasions of individual rights by private individuals are not within the purview of the Amendment. For example, a law imposing racial segregation is state action, whereas an individual's discriminatory act does not violate the Fourteenth Amendment, although the individual action may be forbidden by statute. See FOURTEENTH AMENDMENT, page 62; *Smith v. Allwright,* page 123.

Significance   The state action concept has been crucial to the legal assault on racial segregation. Discrimination based on segregation ordinances or on official support by elected officials or police officers has been held by the courts to be state action. Judicial enforcement of racially restrictive real-estate covenants has been likewise prohibited as state action. The major contemporary problem is whether private discrimination becomes state action if an individual seeks governmental support to protect his private interests. The present tests of state action appear to be whether the public interest is strong enough to transform private actions into matters of state concern, and the degree of official involvement in the discriminatory act.

Substantive Rights   Constitutional guarantees essential for personal liberty. These generally include those rights listed in the First, Thirteenth, and Fourteenth Amendments—freedoms of speech, press, religion, assembly, and petition, freedom from involuntary servitude, and the right to equal protection of the law. *Substantive* rights are to be distinguished from *procedural* rights, which are concerned with the manner in which the substantive rights are protected, as by due process and fair trial.

Significance   No precise listing of substantive rights is possible; they include those personal liberties essential to a free society. No person can be considered free if he does not have liberty to express himself in speech, press, or prayer, or if he is arbitrarily discriminated against. Necessary limitations, however, may be placed on substantive rights. Thus, one may be confined to jail or have his speech limited, but only in accordance with due process of law.

Treason   A disloyal act, which, as defined by Article III, section 3 of the Constitution, "shall consist only in levying war against [the United States], or in adhering to their enemies, giving them aid and comfort." The Constitution further provides that one may not be convicted of treason "unless on the testimony of two witnesses to the same overt act, or on confession in open court."

Significance   Treason is the only crime precisely defined in the Constitution as a safeguard against irresponsible charges for this most serious of crimes. Levying war or adhering to enemies of the United States are the only grounds for bringing a prosecution and, unless the suspect confesses, two witnesses must testify that they saw him commit the act. Acts of disloyalty that do not fall within the constitutional definition may be prosecuted under sedition laws. Communist subversive activities are not considered as treason since we are not, technically, at war with Communist states. Many state constitutions contain treason provisions, but it is questionable whether one could commit treason against a state and not against the United States. John Brown, hanged in 1859 for his raid on Harpers Ferry, Virginia, is believed to be the only person executed in this country for treason against a state. Treason trials have not been numerous and no one has been executed for treason by the national government.

Wiretapping   The use of listening devices to intercept telephone messages. The term is generally applied to any electronic device used to intercept private conversations. Congress, in 1934, forbade the interception of telephone messages without the consent of the sender. Evidence so secured is excluded from federal trials but not from all state trials, and the rule with regard to the use of other listening devices is not clear.

Significance   Technological refinements of electronic listening devices has vastly complicated traditional rules of search and seizure. Though intercepted telephone messages may not be used as evidence in federal trials, the Supreme Court has refused to enjoin a state from doing so. Most states, however, follow the federal rule. It appears that other electronic devices may be used, provided no invasion of property takes place, as when conversations are overheard by sensitive listening devices placed outside a home. In spite of the federal law on telephone taps, it is widely recognized that wiretapping is done by law enforcement agencies at all levels, with an apparent distinction being drawn between listening and using the information as evidence. Legislation has been introduced in Congress and in several states to permit wiretapping in such cases as subversion or kidnaping but no useful formula has been discovered whereby the innocent may be protected. A few states permit wiretapping with court approval.

IMPORTANT AGENCIES

Civil Rights Commission   Established by the federal Civil Rights Act of 1957 as a bipartisan commission of six members to investigate the broad area of civil rights. The Commission has conducted investigations and published reports on such matters as voting rights, education, housing, employment, and the administration of justice. The Civil Rights Act of 1964 strengthened the Commission's investigatory power and established it as a national clearing house for civil rights information.

Significance   The Commission has uncovered evidence of abuses of civil rights in all areas of its investigations. Its findings and recommendations played a vital role in the enactment of the Civil Rights Acts of 1960, 1964, and 1965.

Community Relations Service   Established by the Civil Rights Act of 1964 in the Department of Commerce to help communities resolve civil rights problems. The Service is headed by a Director appointed for a four-year term by the President with Senate consent. The facilities of the Service are made available either upon request or through its own initiative. It is directed by law to seek the cooperation of state and local agencies and to carry on its work without publicity.

Significance   The Community Relations Service is patterned after the human relations or community relations agencies found in numerous state and local governments that make available conciliatory services to temper dangerous community tensions. The Service was placed in the Department of Commerce to win the confidence of local businessmen. Though its activities do not receive publicity, indications are that the Service has been involved in a large number of cases.

Department of Justice   Has four divisions that are particularly concerned with civil liberty matters. The Federal Bureau of Investigation (FBI) investigates, and the Criminal Division prosecutes violations of federal laws. The Internal Security Division enforces all criminal laws relating to subversive activities. These include prosecutions for treason or sedition, and prosecutions under the Atomic Energy Act, the Smith Act, and the Internal Security Act. It also conducts cases before the Subversive Activities Control Board and handles matters relating to security requirements for government employees. Finally, the Civil Rights Division is responsible for the enforcement of all statutes affecting civil rights, including the Civil Rights Acts, antipeonage laws, election frauds, and obstructions of justice. It also investigates complaints brought by persons claiming deprivations of their civil rights. *See* DEPARTMENT OF JUSTICE, page 227.

Significance   The Department of Justice is playing an increasingly large role in the field of civil liberties. The Internal Security and Civil Rights divisions underscore the national government's concern in these two areas in recent years and the expansion of activity against subversion on the one hand and in defense of Negro rights on the other. The roles of the FBI and the Criminal Division have been enlarged, too, as the scope of federal law enforcement grows.

Equal Employment Opportunity Commission (EEOC)   Established by the Civil Rights Act of 1964 to investigate and conciliate disputes involving discrimination because of race or sex by employers, unions and employment agencies. EEOC consists of five members appointed for five year terms by the President with Senate consent. EEOC stresses confidential persuasion and conciliation to achieve its objectives, but may refer matters to the Attorney General for legal action. Action by state fair employment agencies is encouraged by the Act.

Significance   The EEOC represents a major victory for civil rights proponents who had sought fair employment practice legislation from Congress for many years. For some years, discrimination had already been forbidden by executive order in governmental employment and in private companies filling governmental contracts. While almost thirty states have established fair employment commissions with varying degrees of enforcement power, the EEOC represents a national commitment to equality of opportunity throughout the nation in both public and private employment.

Subversive Activities Control Board   An independent agency established in 1950 under the Internal Security Act. The Board is composed of five members appointed by the President, with the consent of the Senate, for five-year terms. Its major function is to conduct hearings, upon the request of the Attorney General, to determine whether an organization is a Communist action, front, or infiltrated group subject to the registration requirements of the Internal Security Act. It also considers petitions from registered organizations to have their names removed from the list of Communist organizations. *See* INTERNAL SECURITY ACT, page 91.

Significance   The Subversive Activities Control Board was established by Congress to gather evidence that would identify subversive groups. The Board has ordered a few organizations to register, including the Communist party, and the Supreme Court upheld the order with regard to the party (*Communist Party v. Subversive Activities Control Board,* 367 U.S. 1 [1961]). Since no person registered for the Communist party, however, the Board ordered party leaders to register as individual members, as provided by law. This order was declared invalid by the Supreme Court as an invasion of the right against self-incrimination (*Albertson v. Subversive Activities Control Board,* 382 U.S. 70 [1965]).

IMPORTANT CASES

Adler v. Board of Education, 342 U.S. 485 (1952): Established that a state has the right to remove a public employee from his job if the employee belongs to an organization advocating violent overthrow of the government.

Significance   Many persons viewed the *Adler* decision as endorsing guilt by association, since the Court indicated that persons are often known by the company they keep. The Court held that inquiries into such associations were valid to determine a person's fitness for public service. In related cases, the Court upheld discharges of public employees for refusing to answer questions asked by their employers about their political affiliations, on the ground that such questions may be relevant to an employee's fitness (for example, *Lerner v. Casey,* 357 U.S. 468 [1958]). It held, however, that a public employee may not be discharged solely for invoking his right against self-incrimination before an investigating committee, since he would then be penalized for exercising a constitutional right (*Slochower v. Board of Higher Education*, 350 U.S. 551 [1956]). The Court's view is that no one has a *right* to public employment and that the schools, in particular, should be kept free from subversive influences. An employee, however, may not arbitrarily be discharged.

Albertson v. Subversive Activities Control Board, 382 U.S. 70 (1965): Struck down as a violation of the privilege against self-incrimination a requirement under the Internal Security Act of 1950 that individuals register as members of the Communist party. In 1961, in *Communist Party v. Subversive Activities Control Board*, 376 U.S. 1, the Court upheld provisions of the law requiring the registration of organizations found by the Subversive Activities Control Board to be controlled by a foreign power. No one subsequently registered for the party. In the *Albertson* case, the Court ruled that a party member could not be compelled to register because of laws, such as the Smith Act, that penalize such membership.

Significance   The *Albertson* case climaxed a fifteen-year effort by the Justice Department and the Subversive Activities Control Board to enforce the registration provisions of the Internal Security Act. Unless the government can find a party member willing to register without raising the issue of self-incrimination, the registration provision of the Act will remain nonenforceable.

Ashcraft v. Tennessee, 322 U.S. 143 (1944): Ruled that a confession obtained from a suspect after prolonged interrogation under hot lights by a relay of officers is not admissible in a state trial. Such coercive methods to obtain confessions violate the Fourteenth Amendment.

Significance   Earlier, in *Brown v. Mississippi,* 297 U.S. 278 (1936), the Court announced for the first time that a confession extracted through brutality and torture violated the Fourteenth Amendment. In the *Ashcraft* case, the Court extended this rule to confessions acquired as a result of psychological rather than physical maltreatment. The Court has since examined carefully convictions based on confessions in order to ensure that the confessions have been wholly voluntary.

Barron v. Baltimore, 7 Peters 243 (1833): Held that the Bill of Rights limits only the national government and not the state governments.

Significance   This decision is still operative today although its impact has been greatly modified in practice through interpretations of the Fourteenth Amendment that make state and local government infringement of civil liberties subject to Supreme Court review. The Court has incorporated most of the provisions of the Bill of Rights into the due process clause of the Fourteenth Amendment.

Bartkus v. Illinois, 355 U.S. 281 (1958): Denied a claim of double jeopardy appealed from a conviction in a state court for bank robbery following acquittal by a federal court for the same bank robbery.

Significance   This case underscores the rule that double jeopardy refers only to repeated trials on the same charge by the same jurisdiction. A person may, therefore, be tried by both the national and state courts for a single offense.

Bolling v. Sharpe, 347 U.S. 497 (1954): Declared, in one of the school segregation cases, that segregation in the public schools of the District of Columbia violated the due process clause of the Fifth Amendment.

Significance   The Constitution contains no requirement that the national government afford "equal protection of the laws." The "equal protection" clause is found in the Fourteenth Amendment and is a limitation on the states. Nevertheless, the Court held that segregation of the races by the national government is an arbitrary denial of liberty without due process of law.

Brown v. Board of Education of Topeka, 347 U.S. 483 (1954); 349 U.S. 294 (1955): Established in a major decision that segregation of the races in public schools violates the equal protection clause of the Fourteenth Amendment. The Supreme Court in 1954 overruled the "separate but equal" doctrine that had been in effect since 1896, noting that "Separate educational facilities are inherently unequal." In 1955, the Court ordered desegregation to proceed "with all deliberate speed," leaving it to the federal district courts to determine implementations of the ruling in specific cases brought before them.

Significance   This decision ranks among the most important in American constitutional history. Extensive desegregation of schools has occurred, sometimes with violent results. Other segregation practices have also been declared unconstitutional following this decision. The *Brown* case created a crisis in national-state relations and helped spur the Negro protest movement. The decision initiated a social revolution, since supported by major national Civil Rights Acts and by state and local legislation.

Dennis v. United States, 341 U.S. 494 (1951): Sustained, in a major decision, the conviction of eleven top Communist party leaders for conspiring to teach and to advocate the violent overthrow of the government. The decision upheld the Smith Act of 1940.

Significance   The *Dennis* case attracted wide notice because of the sharp conflict between freedom of speech guaranteed by the First Amendment and the indictment against the Communist leaders for advocating their doctrine. The Supreme Court narrowed the interpretation of the clear and present danger rule by holding that in the interest of self-preservation it was not essential for the government to wait until the conspiracy ripened into action. This decision led to numerous prosecutions of other Communist leaders. In 1957, however, in *Yates v. United States,* 354 U.S. 298, the Supreme Court modified its ruling in the *Dennis* case by holding that a distinction must be drawn between urging people to *believe* in something and urging people to *do* something. In the *Yates* case, the Court found that the defendants were merely preaching Communist doctrine in the abstract and were not teaching or advocating unlawful conduct. The *Yates* case has restored the clear and present danger rule to some extent and has made it more difficult for the government to prosecute Communists without proving some measure of concrete action to overthrow the government by force.

Everson v. Board of Education of Ewing Township, 330 U.S. 1 (1947): Decided that it is not a violation of the First Amendment's establishment of religion clause for a state to pay for the transportation of children to parochial schools. The Court found this to be a benefit to the children rather than an aid to the church.

Significance   This case was the first major test of the establishment of religion clause. In its decision, the Court emphasized that the First Amendment was designed to "erect a wall of separation between church and state." Nevertheless, it found that in this instance the wall had not been breached. The *Everson* case serves as a precedent supporting a variety of state and federal aid programs to parochial schools.

Freedman v. Maryland, 380 U.S. 51 (1965): Held that motion picture censorship is permissible provided that the procedure followed assures prompt judicial review of the censor's decision. By this decision, the Court affirmed its ruling in *Times Film Corporation v. Chicago,* 365 U.S. 43 (1961) that initial submission of a motion picture to a censoring board may be required, but it held that the board's decision could not be final.

Significance   The Freedman case raised motion pictures to a level more closely approximating the protection from prior restraint that other forms of expression have than was previously the case. In 1952, movies had been brought within the protection of the First and Fourteenth Amendments' guarantees of freedom of speech and press (*Burstyn v. Wilson,* 343 U.S. 495). Films still do not enjoy, however, the same degree of freedom as books, since, under the *Times Film* rule, some form of prior submission to a censor is permitted. In the *Freedman* ruling, the Court sought to promote adequate safeguards against undue inhibition of lawful expression, but was not willing to forbid censorship of movies altogether.

Garner v. Board of Public Works, 341 U.S. 716 (1951): Sustained a municipal law requiring a non-Communist affidavit and loyalty oath from public employees. The Court took the view that loyalty was a reasonable requirement for public employment, notwithstanding limitations that the law might place upon the freedom of speech and association of such employees.

Significance   The Court has upheld numerous state and local laws requiring loyalty oaths of public employees and school teachers. The Court has insisted, however, that the oaths be interpreted to mean that the person knew that any organizations to which he belonged had illegal aims (*Wieman v. Updegraff,* 344 U.S. 183 [1952]), and that the oaths not be unduly vague (*Baggett v. Bullitt,* 377 U.S. 360 [1964]). Further, the Court has held that a state may not require a loyalty oath of individuals in order to get general public benefits, such as tax exemptions (*Speiser v. Randall,* 357 U.S. 513 [1958]).

Gideon v. Wainwright, 372 U.S. 335 (1963): A landmark ruling that state courts are required by the due process clause of the Fourteenth Amendment to provide counsel to indigent defendants in criminal cases. This had been required in *federal* criminal trials since the 1938 decision in *Johnson v. Zerbst,* 304 U.S. 458, but state courts were required to furnish counsel to needy defendants only in capital cases (*Powell v. Alabama,* 287 U.S. 45 [1932]) or when special circumstances, such as youth, mental incompetence, or inexperience, necessitated the furnishing of counsel to assure a fair trial (*Betts v. Brady,* 316 U.S. 455 [1942]). In *Gideon,* the Court held that defense by counsel is a fundamental right available to all regardless of wealth or status.

Significance   The *Gideon* case was a major step in the nationalization of the Bill of Rights through the Fourteenth Amendment, because it applied to state cases the guarantee of the assistance of counsel found in the Sixth Amendment. The case was also a forerunner of nation-wide concern with equal justice for the poor. The *Gideon* decision not only overcame an illogical distinction between federal and state criminal proceedings, but recognized that most defendants lack the knowledge and skill to defend themselves against experienced prosecutors. In 1966 the Court ruled that a person has a right to counsel while he is being interrogated (*Miranda v. Arizona,* 384 U.S. 436).

Gitlow v. New York, 268 U.S. 652 (1925): Established, in a landmark case, that the freedoms of speech and press are protected against state impairment by the due process clause of the Fourteenth Amendment. Nevertheless, in this case, the Court upheld a conviction for publishing and circulating materials advocating the overthrow of government by force.

Significance   Prior to this decision, the Court had consistently held that the Fourteenth Amendment did not incorporate any part of the Bill of Rights. Since the *Gitlow* decision, the Court has applied the entire First Amendment, as well as most other portions of the Bill of Rights, to the states under the due process clause of the Fourteenth Amendment. The impact of this decision has been an increasing involvement of the national government in the protection of the people against abuse of their liberties by the states.

Hague v. CIO, 307 U.S. 496 (1939): Declared unconstitutional under the Fourteenth Amendment an ordinance of Jersey City, N.J., that required permission to hold a meeting in or upon public streets, parks, or buildings. Under the ordinance, the officials of Jersey City had molested union organizers of the CIO and had denied them permission to hold meetings or to circulate handbills.

Significance   The *Hague* case established that the right to assemble applies not merely to meetings of private groups but to public meetings in public places. The Court has, in other cases, frowned upon any prior restraints by governmental officials upon public meetings unless some reasonable standards are established for the granting of permits to meet. These standards must in some way be related to the health, safety, and welfare of the people. For example, one might legally be required to secure a permit in order to hold a parade (*Cox v. New Hampshire,* 312 U.S. 569 [1941]).

Heart of Atlanta Motel v. United States, 379 U.S. 241 (1964): Upheld the constitutionality of Title II of the Civil Rights Act of 1964, a provision barring discrimination in restaurants, hotels, and other places of public accommodation, on the ground that it is a valid exercise of the power to regulate interstate commerce. In 1883, the Supreme Court struck down a similar federal law (*Civil Rights Cases,* 109 U.S. 3) on the ground that private acts of discrimination could not be forbidden by the national government. In the *Heart of Atlanta* case and in its companion case, *Katzenbach v. McClung,* 379 U.S. 294 (1964), the Court found ample power in the commerce clause for the national government to prohibit discrimination against persons in accommodations that serve substantial numbers of interstate travelers or that rely upon interstate commerce for a substantial part of their supplies and materials.

Significance   The *Heart of Atlanta Motel* case underscored the determination of the Supreme Court to accord Congress the necessary constitutional tools to meet the crisis in racial discrimination. Many scholars believe that Congress has power under the Fourteenth Amendment to deter discrimination in privately owned public accommodations but, because of the 1883 *Civil Rights Cases,* considerable doubt existed. The commerce power has long been used by Congress to enact social welfare legislation and to control individual behavior.

Hurtado v. California, 110 U.S. 516 (1884): Established that a state is not required by the due process clause of the Fourteenth Amendment to provide for indictment by grand jury in felony cases. Indictment by information is consistent with fair procedure.

Significance   This was the first major test of the meaning of the due-process clause of the Fourteenth Amendment. In this case, the Court made it clear that the Fourteenth Amendment did not make the Bill of Rights applicable to the states, and that merely because indictment by grand jury is required by the Fifth Amendment, the states are not thereby bound. While the Supreme Court has made most provisions of the Bill of Rights that relate to criminal procedures binding on the states, the *Hurtado* rule still applies. Few states use the grand jury today.

Jehovah's Witnesses Cases   Involved, in a series of cases, the religious sect known as Jehovah's Witnesses, testing the scope of religious freedom under the First and Fourteenth Amendments. Among the various decisions were those that held unconstitutional: (1) laws requiring prior official approval to solicit funds for religious purposes (*Cantwell v. Connecticut,* 310 U.S. 296 [1940]); (2) laws levying license taxes on peddlers of religious tracts (*Murdock v. Pennsylvania,* 319 U.S. 105 [1943]); (3) laws prohibiting door-to-door distribution of religious handbills (*Martin v. Struthers,* 319 U.S. 141 [1943]); (4) laws requiring official approval to hold public-worship meetings in public parks (*Niemotko v. Maryland,* 340 U.S. 268 [1951]); and (5) an official requirement that children be compelled to salute the flag contrary to their religious beliefs (*West Virginia State Board of Education v. Barnette,* 319 U.S. 624 [1943]). On the other hand, the Court has held that the sect may not under the guise of religious freedom: (1) hold a parade without permission (*Cox v. New Hampshire,* 312 U.S. 569 [1941]); (2) have a young child sell magazines on a street corner late at night, contrary to state child-welfare laws (*Prince v. Massachusetts,* 321 U.S. 158 [1944]); or (3) create a breach of peace in the course of a public meeting (*Chaplinsky v. New Hampshire,* 315 U.S. 568 [1942]).

Significance   Through these and other cases, Jehovah's Witnesses have forced the courts to consider the constitutional scope of, and limitations on, the practice of religion. For the most part, the Supreme Court has been sympathetic with the proselytizing activities of the sect except when their actions were in conflict with reasonable measures designed to protect the public welfare.

McNabb v. United States, 318 U.S. 332 (1943): Held that the federal courts may not convict a person of a crime on the basis of a confession secured while he was unlawfully detained. The Court ruled that a prisoner must be taken before a judicial officer for arraignment without delay.

Significance   The *McNabb* rule prohibits police officials from unduly detaining a suspect in order to secure a confession. The Court reaffirmed this in *Mallory v. United States,* 354 U.S. 449 (1957), which involved the release of a confessed criminal because of a delay in arraignment. This led to demands from some members of Congress that the rule be changed to permit use of legally secured evidence regardless of such delay, but no law has been enacted. The McNabb-Mallory rule does not apply in state courts, but the cases have had an impact on police and judicial behavior.

Malloy v. Hogan, 378 U.S. 1 (1964): Held that protection against self-incrimination found in the Fifth Amendment to the Constitution applies to the states through the Fourteenth Amendment in the same manner that it limits the national government.

Significance   The *Malloy* case overturned a long-standing ruling that states were not bound by the Fifth Amendment's guarantee against self-incrimination (*Twining v. New Jersey,* 211 U.S. 78 [1908], reaffirmed in *Adamson v. California,* 332 U.S. 46 [1947]). The ruling was part of a pattern of the 1960s, in which the Supreme Court largely abolished the double standard between federal and state criminal procedures. Formerly, state procedures were held to violate the Constitution only when they were shockingly unjust.

Mapp v. Ohio, 367 U.S. 643 (1961): Ruled that a state may not use illegally seized evidence in criminal trials. This decision overruled *Wolf v. Colorado,* 338 U.S. 25 (1949), which held that a state could use evidence secured through an illegal search and seizure.

Significance   Prior to the *Mapp* decision, about half the states admitted illegally seized evidence in criminal trials, although in federal criminal trials such evidence is not admissible (*Weeks v. United States,* 232 U.S. 383 [1914]). In *Mapp v. Ohio,* the Court declared that the *Wolf* rule made the constitutional protection against unlawful search and seizure meaningless. The *Mapp* decision is a major example of national supervision of state criminal procedures through the Fourteenth Amendment, and of the Supreme Court's continuing nationalization of the Bill of Rights so as to equalize the rights of accused persons in state and federal criminal trials. In 1965, the Court held that the *Mapp* rule would not be applied retroactively to persons serving sentences who were convicted under the *Wolf* rule (*Linkletter v. Walker,* 381 U.S. 618).

Miranda v. Arizona, 384 U.S. 436 (1966): A major ruling on criminal procedure to secure the privilege against self-incrimination. The Court held that "Prior to any questioning, the person must be warned that he has a right to remain silent, that any statement he does make may be used against him, and that he has a right to the presence of an attorney, either retained or appointed." The defendant may "knowingly" waive these rights.

Significance   The *Miranda* case followed the highly controversial 1964 decision of *Escobedo v. Illinois,* 378 U.S. 478, which held that when an investigation begins to focus upon an accused, the police must inform him of his right to remain silent and honor his request to consult counsel. The *Miranda* case extended these rights to all accused persons. Police officials generally opposed the rulings as did many citizens who saw them as stumbling blocks to adequate law enforcement. Support came from those who agreed with the Court that criminal law enforcement is more reliable when based on independently secured evidence rather than confessions secured through prolonged interrogation in the absence of counsel.

Moore v. Dempsey, 261 U.S. 86 (1923): Declared that a trial conducted under the influence of a mob, in which public passion dominates the judge, jury, witnesses, and defense counsel, is a denial of due process of law. In this case, the trial of five Negroes was conducted under the duress of a mob, making the outcome a certainty.

Significance   The *Moore* case emphasizes that it is not enough that the mere forms of a trial be observed. The proceedings must be fair and provide the defendant with the full measure of his rights. While the Court is usually concerned with specific aspects of a case, it will, as it did here, insist that the entire proceedings be conducted in an atmosphere that will assure a fair trial.

National Association for the Advancement of Colored People v. Alabama, 357 U.S. 449 (1958): Established that a state may not compel the disclosure of the membership lists of an organization that is pursuing lawful ends, if members are likely to suffer physical, economic, and other hostile reprisals from such disclosure.

Significance   One result of the integration movement in the South has been an effort on the part of some states to harass and impede the activities of the NAACP and other organizations active in behalf of Negro rights. In this case, the Court stressed the importance of the freedom to associate, noting that any interference is subject to close scrutiny.

Near v. Minnesota, 283 U.S. 697 (1931): Defined freedom of the press to mean that the press is to be free from prior restraint or censorship. A state may not, under the due process clause of the Fourteenth Amendment, permanently enjoin a newspaper from being published. If a newspaper abuses its privilege, it may be punished subsequently. The Court held unconstitutional a Minnesota statute that authorized officials to forbid publication of "malicious, scandalous and defamatory" newspapers.

Significance   The *Near* case was the first important decision of the Supreme Court on censorship. The Court admitted that under exceptional circumstances, such as war, a paper might be prevented from publishing, but it stressed that freedom of the press means freedom from governmental censorship or ban. Otherwise, governmental officials would be in a position to suppress news merely, as in the *Near* case, because it was critical of them.

New York Times v. Sullivan, 376 U.S. 254 (1964): Held that a public official could not recover civil libel damages for criticism of his official conduct by a newspaper or other persons. The rule applies even if the criticism is exaggerated or false, unless deliberate malice and reckless disregard for the truth or falsity of the statement can be shown. This principle was extended to suits for criminal libel in *Garrison v. Louisiana,* 379 U.S. 64 (1965).

Significance   The *New York Times* case gives the widest latitude to the freedoms of speech and of the press when they are used to criticize public officials. The Court maintained that the limitation on libel suits was necessary to insure free discussion of public affairs, one of the major purposes of the First Amendment guarantees.

Norris v. Alabama, 294 U.S. 587 (1935): Held, in what is popularly known as the Second Scottsboro case, that Negroes could not be systematically excluded from jury service.

Significance   Under the *Norris* rule, a Negro defendant does not have a right to have members of his race serve on the jury in his trial. Negroes may not, however, deliberately be excluded. In this case, the Court found that no Negroes had ever served on juries in the counties involved and showed that it would look behind the nondiscriminatory wording of the state law to see what the actual practice was with regard to jury selection. Jury discrimination has been a continuing problem leading to reversals of many convictions of Negro defendants and to consideration of corrective national legislation.

Palko v. Connecticut, 302 U.S. 319 (1937): Ruled that the double jeopardy provision of the Fifth Amendment does not apply to the states through the Fourteenth Amendment. In the *Palko* case, the Supreme Court permitted the state to appeal a conviction of a defendant to ask for a more severe sentence.

Significance   The *Palko* case is noteworthy because of the Court's opinion, written by Justice Benjamin N. Cardozo, setting forth the criteria by which the Court determines whether a state violates the rights protected by the due process clause of the Fourteenth Amendment. These include those rights "implicit in the concept of ordered liberty," which are "so rooted in the traditions and conscience of our people as to be ranked as fundamental" or "essential to a fair and enlightened system of justice," or those rights whose denial would be "shocking to the sense of justice of the civilized world." Within this framework, Justice Cardozo indicated that the freedoms of speech, press, religion, and assembly were essential for liberty and hence covered by the Fourteenth Amendment, but that variations in criminal procedures were permissible so long as they violated no fundamental principles of justice. On a case-to-case basis, the Court has marked out the limits of the due process clause, permitting the states, for example, to abolish the grand jury and to hold trial in certain cases without a jury. On the other hand, the Court has forbidden states to conduct unreasonable searches and seizures or to permit cruel and unusual punishment. In the 1960s, the Court has moved toward an equalization of rights for state and federal defendants through incorporation of most of the Bill of Rights provisions into the due process clause of the Fourteenth Amendment.

Plessy v. Ferguson, 163 U.S. 537 (1896): Upheld, in a famous decision, a state law requiring segregation of the races in public transportation. The Court held that under the equal protection clause of the Fourteenth Amendment, a state could provide "separate but equal" facilities to Negroes. This case was overruled in *Brown v. Board of Education of Topeka,* 347 U.S. 483 (1954).

Significance   The *Plessy* case served as justification for the segregation policies of many states until 1954. Although it is no longer effective, the decision demonstrates the great power of the Supreme Court in giving direction to the law. Until the case was overturned, the Court limited itself to considering whether facilities provided to Negroes were indeed equal though separate.

Pollock v. Williams, 322 U.S. 4 (1944): Decided that a state lends support to slavery or peonage, contrary to the Thirteenth Amendment, when it requires that a person must work to discharge a debt or go to jail. The Court held unconstitutional a law that made it a crime to take money in advance and then refuse to perform the required labor. A state may punish fraud but it cannot make failure to work a crime.

Significance   A surprisingly large number of persons appear to be forced into labor because they are ignorant of their rights. The Justice Department gets numerous complaints of involuntary servitude involving persons who are forced to work through indebtedness to their employers. The Court's decision makes clear that it will outlaw practices that are just short of slavery.

Reynolds v. United States, 98 U.S. 145 (1879): Established that religious freedom does not protect a person who commits a crime or an act contrary to accepted public morals. In this case, the Court upheld the enforcement of anti-polygamy laws against Mormons who, prior to 1890, practiced polygamy as a religious doctrine.

Significance   The *Reynolds* case established one of the clearest legal principles involving the free exercise of religion. A person is free to believe and worship as he pleases so long as his conduct violates no laws that validly protect the health, safety, or morals of the community.

Roth v. United States, 354 U.S. 476 (1957): Excluded obscenity from the area of constitutionally protected speech and press. The Court held that the proper standard to determine obscenity is "whether to the average person, applying contemporary community standards, the dominant theme of the material taken as a whole appeals to prurient interest."

Significance   The *Roth* decision was the first effort by the Supreme Court to define obscenity, a matter that has long puzzled American courts. In denying constitutional protection to obscene publications, the Court expressed the view that obscenity was without the "redeeming social importance" of the kinds of speech that the First Amendment is designed to protect. In a companion case,

Alberts v. California, 354 U.S. 476 (1957), the Court applied the same rule to state obscenity laws. Whether or not a particular publication is obscene is determined on a case-to-case basis. In 1964, the Court defined the "community standards" rule of the *Roth* case to mean national rather than local standards (*Jacobellis v. Ohio,* 378 U.S. 184). In 1966, the Court held that the intent of the publisher as evidenced by the nature of the advertising for a publication is an additional factor in determining obscenity (*Ginzburg v. United States,* 383 U.S. 463).

Scales v. United States, 367 U.S. 203 (1961): Sustained that portion of the Smith Act of 1940 that makes it a crime to be a member of an organization that advocates overthrow of the government by force if one knows this to be the purpose of the organization. The Court drew a distinction between active membership and mere membership, noting that active membership in a party that has illegal aims is not constitutionally protected.

Significance   The *Scales* decision strengthened the government's hand in its fight against the Communist party. The Court, however, sought to avoid imputing guilt by mere association, by insisting that the government must prove that an individual was an active participant in illegal activities.

Schenck v. United States, 249 U.S. 47 (1919): Upheld a conviction against Schenck, who had circulated materials urging men to resist the call to military service during World War I. The Court held that this was a justified infringement upon the freedoms of speech and press in view of the wartime emergency.

Significance   The *Schenck* case is noteworthy because of the Court's opinion, written by Justice Oliver Wendell Holmes, which established the clear and present danger doctrine. Justice Holmes wrote that "the question in every case is whether the words used are in such circumstances and are of such a nature as to create a clear and present danger that they will bring about the substantive evils that Congress has a right to prevent." With these words, Justice Holmes provided the formula that has been used in many free speech cases since that time. The *Schenck* case is also noted for the distinction drawn between speech that may be permissible in peacetime but not when the nation is at war.

School District of Abington Township v. Schempp, 374 U.S. 203 (1963): Held devotional Bible reading and/or the recitation of the Lord's Prayer in public schools to be an unconstitutional violation of the establishment clause of the First Amendment as applied to the states through the Fourteenth Amendment. The Court reasoned that while the study of religion could be part of a school curriculum, an organ of government (the public school) could not be used for essentially religious purposes. The Court held that the fact that students could excuse themselves from the devotional exercises was irrelevant, since the exercises in themselves constituted an establishment of religion. "In the relationship between man and religion," said the Court, "the state is firmly committed to a position of neutrality."

Significance   The *Schempp* decision ranks among the most controversial rendered by the Supreme Court. In 1962 in *Engel v. Vitale,* 370 U.S. 421, the

Court struck down a nondenominational prayer written by the New York Board of Regents for public-school recitation on the ground that it was improper for public officials to write or sanction official prayers. The *Schempp* and *Engel* cases led numerous political leaders and citizen groups to demand a constitutional amendment to permit school prayers, although many citizens and church leaders agreed with the Court's interpretation of the establishment clause.

United States v. Lovett, 328 U.S. 303 (1946): Declared unconstitutional as a bill of attainder an act of Congress that named three individuals as ineligible for continued governmental employment, in that the act punished the individuals without judicial trial. *See* BILL OF ATTAINDER, page 55.

Significance   Few cases have arisen in American constitutional history involving bills of attainder. After the Civil War, the Supreme Court found certain laws imposing disabilities upon all persons who participated in the rebellion to be bills of attainder (*Cummings v. Missouri,* 4 Wallace 277, *Ex parte Garland,* 4 Wallace 333 [1867]). Recent legislation designed to keep Communists out of public service has been upheld by the Court on the ground that it established general qualifications for employment rather than naming specific individuals (*Garner v. Board of Public Works,* 341 U.S. 716 [1951]). In *United States v. Brown,* 381 U.S. 437 (1965), however, the Court held that the Landrum-Griffin Labor Act section making it a crime for Communists to hold office or employment in a labor union was a bill of attainder.

Zorach v. Clauson, 343 U.S. 306 (1952): Supported New York's released-time program in public schools, under which students are released from classes to attend religious exercises in their respective churches. The Court found no conflict between this practice and the establishment of religion clause in the First Amendment.

Significance   The teaching of religion in public schools is one of the most controversial questions in public education, going to the heart of the issue of the separation of church and state. The *Zorach* decision attracted wide notice since it followed the Court's decision in *McCollum v. Board of Education,* 333 U.S. 203 (1948), in which the Court declared unconstitutional a program of released time under which children attended religious classes on school grounds. The *Zorach* ruling rested largely on the fact that the religious classes were not held on school property.

IMPORTANT STATUTES

Alien and Sedition Laws   Acts passed in 1798 authorizing the President to deport undesirable aliens and making it a crime to criticize the government or its officials. Through these Acts, the Federalist party sought to silence opposition. About twenty-five persons were jailed or fined for criticizing President John Adams. These Acts were a major reason for the defeat of the Federalist party in the election of 1800. Thomas Jefferson, the winner of that election, pardoned those convicted under the Acts.

Significance   With the exception of these laws, Congress did not find it necessary to pass anti-sedition legislation until World War I. The Alien and

Sedition Laws were undoubtedly unconstitutional, but they were never tested in the Supreme Court. They serve as a reminder that civil rights are under constant threat unless they are zealously guarded by the people. Free government is not possible unless it is understood that one may be loyal to his nation and, at the same time, criticize those who make its policies.

Alien Registration Act of 1940 (Smith Act)   A major sedition law requiring the annual registration of aliens and prohibiting the advocacy of violent overthrow of the government. The major provisions of the Act make it unlawful to teach, advocate, or distribute information advocating the forcible overthrow of government or to knowingly organize or join an organization that so advocates. Other provisions outlaw activities designed to create disloyalty in the armed forces or to encourage participation in a violent revolution or in the assassination of public officials. *See Dennis v. United States,* page 79; *Scales v. United States,* page 87.

Significance   The Smith Act is the first law passed in peacetime since the Alien and Sedition Laws of 1798 that outlaws particular forms of speech and writing. It is also the first act to make it a crime to be a member of an organization; this provision, some critics claim, imputes guilt by association. The advocacy and membership provisions of this Act have been upheld by the Supreme Court (*Dennis v. United States,* 341 U.S. 494 [1951]; *Scales v. United States,* 367 U.S. 203 [1961]). Though the Act does not mention the Communist party by name, and was also intended to apply to Nazi and Fascist groups, it has been applied only against the Communist party leadership.

Civil Rights Acts of 1866, 1870, 1871, and 1875   Laws passed by Congress after the Civil War to guarantee the rights of Negroes. The public-accommodation provisions of the 1875 law were declared unconstitutional by the Supreme Court in the *Civil Rights Cases* (109 U.S. 3 [1883]), as a federal invasion of private rights. Other provisions of these laws were struck down by the courts or repealed by Congress. Today, a few major provisions remain from the Acts of 1866 and 1871. One makes it a federal crime for any person acting under the authority of a state law to deprive another of any rights protected by the Constitution or by laws of the United States. Another authorizes suits for civil damages against state or local officials by persons whose rights are abridged. Others permit actions against persons who conspire to deprive people of their rights.

Significance   The failure of the post-Civil War Acts reflected the general attitude of the time that the national government had a limited role to play in the enforcement of individual rights. The remaining provisions have served occasionally as a weapon in the hands of national officers to restrain state officials who violate the constitutional rights of persons in their charge. Today, as the national government expands its role in the protection of individual rights, particularly in the area of race relations, these laws have taken on new importance.

Civil Rights Act of 1957   The first civil rights law passed by Congress since Reconstruction, designed to secure the right to vote for Negroes. Its major feature empowers the Department of Justice to seek court injunctions against any deprivation of voting rights, and authorizes criminal prosecutions for violations of an injunction. In addition, the Act established a Civil Rights Division, headed by an Assistant Attorney General, in the Department of Justice, and created a six-man bipartisan Civil Rights Commission to investigate civil rights violations and to recommend legislation.

Significance   The Civil Rights Act of 1957 marked a major breakthrough in positive federal action in the field of civil rights. The Act is based on the theory that if the Negro is protected in his voting rights, he will be in a better position to seek reform in other areas of discrimination. It is supplemented by voting provisions in the Civil Rights Acts of 1960 and 1964 and by the Voting Rights Act of 1965.

Civil Rights Act of 1960   A law designed to further secure the right to vote for Negroes and to meet problems arising from racial upheavals in the South. The major provision authorizes federal courts to appoint referees who will help Negroes to register after a voter-denial conviction is obtained under the 1957 Civil Rights Act, and after a court finding of a "pattern or practice" of discrimination against qualified voters. Other provisions: (1) authorize punishment for persons who obstruct any federal court order, such as a school desegregation order, by threats or force; (2) authorize criminal penalties for transportation of explosives for the purpose of bombing a building; (3) require preservation of voting records for twenty-two months, and authorize the Attorney General to inspect the records; (4) provide for schooling of children of armed-forces personnel in the event that a school closes because of an integration dispute.

Significance   Continuing the pattern established in the 1957 Civil Rights Act, Congress sought to strengthen the voting rights of citizens and reached out into other problem areas. The Civil Rights Act of 1964 and the Voting Rights Act of 1965 supplement the Acts of 1957 and 1960.

Civil Rights Act of 1964   A major enactment designed to erase racial discrimination in most areas of American life. Major provisions of the Act: (1) outlaw arbitrary discrimination in voter registration and expedite voting-rights suits; (2) bar discrimination in public accommodations, such as hotels and restaurants, that have a substantial relation to interstate commerce; (3) authorize the national government to bring suits to desegregate public facilities and schools; (4) extend the life and expand the power of the Civil Rights Commission; (5) provide for the withholding of federal funds from programs administered in a discriminatory manner; (6) establish the right to equality in employment opportunities; (7) establish a Community Relations Service to help resolve civil rights problems. The Act forbids discrimination based on race, color, religion, national origin, and, in the case of employment, sex. Techniques for gaining voluntary compliance are stressed in the Act, and the resolution of civil rights problems through state and local action is encouraged. Discrimination in housing is not covered by the law.

Significance   The Civil Rights Act of 1964 is the most far-reaching civil rights legislation since Reconstruction. It was passed after the longest debate in Senate history (eighty-three days) and only after cloture was invoked for the first time to cut off a civil rights filibuster. Compliance with the Act's controversial provisions on public accommodation and equal-employment opportunity has been widespread. Title VI of the Act, which authorizes the cutoff of federal funds to state and local programs practicing discrimination proved to be the most effective provision of the Act. For example, a dramatic jump in southern school integration took place when the national government threatened to withhold federal funds from schools failing to comply with desegregation orders. All agencies receiving federal funds are required to submit assurance of compliance with the 1964 Act. Almost 200 grant-in-aid programs are involved, amounting to fifteen percent of all state and local revenues. The Supreme Court upheld the public-accommodations provisions of the law as a legitimate exercise of the commerce power by Congress (*Heart of Atlanta Motel v. United States,* 379 U.S. 241 [1964]).

Communist Control Act of 1954   An act of Congress that deprives the Communist party of the rights and privileges of other legally organized bodies or political parties and declares it to be a clear and present threat to the security of the United States. The law does not make it a crime to be a Communist.

Significance   The full meaning of the law is not clear. It was passed in Congress with little discussion and has not been vigorously enforced. Many authorities question its constitutionality. The main effect has been to keep the Communist party off the ballot. This is the first time in American history that a party has been denied use of the ballot as a means of gaining adherents to its programs.

Immunity Act of 1954   An act to compel testimony from witnesses who claim self-incrimination when questioned on matters of national security. Either house of Congress, a congressional committee, or a federal district attorney may, after notifying the Attorney General, request a federal district court to grant immunity. Once granted, the witness must testify on those matters covered by the immunity order and may never be prosecuted for any crimes revealed by his testimony in any state or federal court.

Significance   Congress was disturbed by the hundreds of persons who claimed self-incrimination when called to testify on security matters. The law has been used sparingly, since it can result in exemption from punishment for serious crimes. The Supreme Court upheld this act in *Ullmann v. United States,* 350 U.S. 422 (1956).

Internal Security Act of 1950 (McCarran Act)   An act designed to place the Communist party and other totalitarian groups under rigid controls. The Act outlaws any conspiracy, peaceful or violent, that has as its purpose the establishment of a foreign-controlled dictatorship in the United States. A Subversive Activities Control Board has been established to designate Communist "action" groups, "fronts," or Communist "infiltrated" organizations. Once identified, action and front groups must register with the Attorney General, listing their officers and members, financial records, and any printing equipment under their control. Publications of these organizations must be labeled as Communist propaganda. Infiltrated trade unions lose all rights under national labor laws. Individual members of any of these groups may not hold office in a labor union, obtain a passport, or work in any public office, and members of action groups are barred from defense plants. The law also strengthens espionage and sedition laws and immigration requirements and provides for the deportation of Communist aliens. Another provision establishes procedures for detention of suspected saboteurs in an emergency. *See* SUBVERSIVE ACTIVITIES CONTROL BOARD, page 77.

Significance   Many serious constitutional questions are raised by the McCarran Act and, to date, the Supreme Court has upheld only the organizational registration requirement (*Communist Party v. Subversive Activities Control Board,* 367 U.S. 1 [1961]). An order that individual Communist party leaders register was, however, declared invalid by the Supreme Court as an invasion of the right against self-incrimination (*Albertson v. Subversive Activities Control Board,* 382 U.S. 70 [1965]). The Court also struck down the passport provision as a denial of the right to travel (*Aptheker v. Secretary of State,* 378 U.S. 500 [1964]).

Parties, Politics, Pressure Groups, and Elections

Absentee Voting   Provisions of state laws or constitutions that enable qualified voters to cast their ballots in an election without going to the polls on election day. If a person expects to be unable to vote on election day, he obtains a ballot within a specified period preceding the election, marks it, has it notarized, and returns it to the proper official.

Significance   Most states have provisions for absentee voting, although some limit the practice to members of the armed forces. Several million potential voters, because of travel or illness, are unable to vote on election day, but few go to the trouble of securing an absentee ballot. Absentee voters can sometimes affect the outcome of an election, as in 1960, when a late count of absentee ballots in California swung that state's electoral votes from John F. Kennedy to Richard M. Nixon.

Absolute Majority   Any number over fifty percent of the total votes cast by *all* the voters participating in a given election. A *simple* majority, in contrast, is any number over fifty percent of the votes cast on any single issue in an election, even though many voters who go to the polls may not vote on the specific issue. A *plurality* consists of sufficient votes to win an election, but not necessarily a majority. *See* PLURALITY, page 111.

Significance   No federal and only a few state and local elections are conducted with a requirement of an absolute majority. Some states require an absolute majority of all voters participating in any phase of the election to vote "yes" on a question of calling a state constitutional convention or of ratifying an amendment to a state constitution. Hence, failure to vote on the issue is the equivalent of a "no" vote.

At Large   The election of members of a legislative body by the voters of an entire governmental unit rather than from subdivisions thereof. Congressmen at large are elected by the whole electorate of the state when a state legislature fails to redistrict after a decennial census. United States Senators and Electoral College Electors are elected at large in each state. On the local level, members of city commissions are, in some cases, elected at large by the

93

voters of the entire city rather than from wards, especially under the commission and city manager forms.

Significance   Election of representatives at large tends to foster a broader state-wide or city-wide approach to issues rather than the more restrictive "mirroring" of local interests by those chosen from districts or wards. The case against election at large is that representatives so chosen will not respond to the wishes or interests of the voters because of the size, population, and variety of views of the larger electorate. Proponents of election at large claim that it reduces parochialism in politics and makes fuller use of available political talent by allowing several good candidates living in the same area to run for election simultaneously, which is not possible under the district system.

Australian Ballot   A secret ballot prepared, distributed, and tabulated by government officials at public expense.

Significance   For over a century, many American voters were denied a secret ballot. Oral voting and differently colored ballots, prepared by the parties, were used. Extreme pressures could be exerted upon voters who were forced to cast their ballot publicly. Threats of retaliation frequently coerced voters into voting against their choice of candidates. Since 1888, all states have used the Australian ballot. Voting machines are mechanical adaptations of the Australian ballot.

Availability   The qualifications of a potential candidate which are analyzed by his party in making its selection of a nominee. A candidate whom the party believes has the qualities and background to make him a winner is "available."

Significance   The question of availability is especially important in the selection of presidential nominees. Millions of members of each party meet the constitutional and legal requirements for the presidency, but few have the qualifications needed to win. Availability depends on whether the potential nominee has ever alienated a large economic, ethnic, or religious voting group, whether he comes from a key state or strategic section, whether he has demonstrated real vote-getting ability, whether he is too closely identified with one wing or faction in the party, whether he is a good family man—in short, whether his background and his personal and political qualities all appear to add up to victory for the party in the presidential election.

Boss   A political leader who dominates a highly disciplined state or local party organization that tends to monopolize power in its area. Political bosses retain power through patronage disposition, control over nominations, use of "honest" and dishonest graft, and manipulation of voting and elections. Sometimes the term "boss" is used to discredit the successful leader of an opposing party. *See* POLITICAL MACHINE, page 111.

Significance   American politics has proved to be a fertile ground for the growth of political machines and party bosses. This growth stems largely from the decentralization of power in the party system and the apathy of large numbers of voters. Some of the leading party bosses in past years have been Edward J. Flynn of New York's Bronx County, Edward "Boss" Crump of Memphis, Ed Kelly of Chicago, Frank Hague of Jersey City, and Carmine DeSapio of the

Tammany Hall machine in New York City. Political bosses have been equally successful in the countryside and in the big cities. The heyday of the political boss has waned and few remain who are bosses in the old tradition. The direct primary, a better educated electorate, and public welfare programs are among the chief reasons for the demise of "bossism."

Canvassing Boards   Official groups, usually bipartisan, that tabulate the election returns and certify the election of the winners. When the polls close on election day, the returns from each precinct are forwarded to city and county canvassing boards. These consolidate the returns and forward them to the state canvassing authority, which, usually in a few days, certifies the election of the winners. The local group is the county board of supervisors or county board of election. The state canvassing board consists of several ex officio members of the state government, headed by the secretary of state. Each election winner receives a certificate of election from the county or state board.

Significance   Extensive coverage of election returns by newspapers, radio, and television makes the results of most elections known to the public before canvassing boards certify them. In exceptionally close elections, however, the final outcome may turn on the official tabulation and certification. Disputed elections are commonly settled in the courts or through an official recount.

Caucus   A closed meeting of party leaders to select party candidates. In the early days of the Republic, party members in Congress and in the state legislatures selected their party's candidates for national and state office. Presidential candidates were chosen by party caucuses in Congress. Locally, leading members of each party met behind closed doors to select candidates for various local offices. Some local candidates are still nominated by caucus. The term "to caucus" is also commonly used to describe any private meeting of politicians seeking to reach agreement on a course of political action. *See* CAUCUS, page 130.

Significance   Most significant decisions in American politics are officially ratified following agreements reached "in caucus" by political leaders. As a nominating device, "King Caucus" flourished for several decades of early American history. Because Andrew Jackson had been refused nomination for the presidency by the congressional Democratic caucus in 1824, he repudiated the system when he won the office in 1828. By 1835, the legislative caucus as a means of making nominations for public office had almost disappeared. On both national and state levels the nominating caucus was largely replaced by the convention method. Reasons for the demise of the caucus included its: (1) unrepresentative character; (2) violation of the separation of powers theory; (3) use of secret deals and logrolling to manipulate the caucus; and (4) widespread use of the "snap caucus," by which small cliques control the nominating process by not notifying all eligible participants of a caucus meeting.

Challenge   An allegation by a poll watcher that a potential voter is unqualified or that a vote is invalid. Most states provide for a bipartisan group of election judges in each precinct to help decide disputes. An inspector is usually in charge of each precinct and makes the final decision. In some closed-primary states, a voter's party affiliation may be challenged. If he cannot prove his affiliation to the satisfaction of that party's poll watcher, he can be deprived of his vote in the primary. *See* POLL WATCHER, page 113.

Significance   Bipartisan selection of poll watchers and their right to challenge voters and votes are designed to prevent fraud in elections. This builds confidence, not always warranted, in the incorruptibility of the ballot.

Charisma   An attribute of leadership based on personal qualities of the individual. A charismatic leader, typically, has a magnetic personality, a dedication to achieving his objectives, unusual powers of persuasion, and ability to excite and gain the loyalty of supporters. Although a charismatic leader is usually flamboyant, he may have a mystical, withdrawn personality.

Significance   Every candidate for political office seeks to exude some degree of charisma that will set him apart as a leader of men. Charisma has, however, a potentiality for demagoguery and excessive charismatic qualities characterize totalitarian leaders.

Closed Primary   The selection of a party's candidates in an election limited to avowed party members. Voters must declare their party affiliation either when they register or at the primary election. *See* DIRECT PRIMARY, page 99; OPEN PRIMARY, page 109.

Significance   The closed-primary system prevents the "crossover" of registered voters into the other party's primary for the purpose of trying to nominate its weakest candidates or to affect the ideological direction of the other party. Party organizations tend to favor the closed primary because it promotes party regularity and responsibility. Many voters oppose it because it limits their freedom of action to select anew at each primary election the party in which they wish to choose nominees. Independent voters are altogether excluded from participating in the nominating process in closed-primary states. Most states use the closed primary.

Coalition   The fusion of various political elements into a major American party. In multiparty countries, the fusion involves a coalition of a number of individual parties into a working majority. In the United States, however, both major parties combine factions of liberals, moderates, and conservatives.

Significance   The coalition character of American major parties avoids black and white extremes of position that might split the American people into two hostile groups. Conversely, the American system has been criticized on the ground that, because both parties are so similar in their make-up, satisfactory alternatives are not presented to the voters.

Congressional and Senatorial Campaign Committees   House and Senate groups consisting of Republican and Democratic members selected by fellow party members in their respective chambers to organize and to help finance election campaigns. The House Republican Campaign Committee consists of one congressman from each state having Republican representation in the

House. House Democrats use this formula also, but supplement it with women members from some states as selected by the committee chairman. Senate Committees consist of six or seven members selected from the Senate.

Significance   In a presidential election year, each committee may integrate its efforts with those of its national committee, depending upon the "coattail" vote-pulling potential of the party's presidential candidate. In off-year contests, the committees operate more independently. Maintaining permanent staffs, the committees raise funds, furnish speakers, distribute literature, and generally take charge of congressional campaigns. Their efforts may also be integrated with those of state and local committees of their parties.

Convention   A meeting of party delegates at the national, state, or local levels to decide upon party policy and strategy and to nominate candidates for elective office. Each party holds a national convention every four years to nominate its presidential candidate and adopt a platform. In most states, both parties hold county and state conventions annually. Typically, delegates to the county conventions are selected by party voters in precinct elections; delegates to state conventions are selected by county conventions; and delegates to national conventions are selected by state or district conventions, or, in approximately one-third of the states, by voters in presidential primaries. *See* NOMINATION, page 108; NATIONAL CONVENTION, page 107.

Significance   Although state and local conventions have lost most of their nominating power, they continue to serve as the basic policy-makers of the American political parties. Decisions made at national, state, and local conventions give direction to party committees and chairmen in the periods between conventions. On state and local levels, nominating for most elective officers has been taken from conventions and placed under direct primary systems. This has been the result, partly, of increasing democratization of elections and, partly, of convention malpractices that allowed small cliques to dominate them through manipulation. An advantage of the convention system in making policy and deciding nominations is that it tends to force conflicting wings of the party to work out compromises that help hold tenuous intraparty coalitions together.

Corrupt Practices Acts   State and federal laws that seek to limit and regulate the size and sources of contributions and expenditures in political campaigns. Concerning contributions, federal limitations specify: (1) no individual can give more than $5000 each year to any national committee; (2) corporations and labor unions cannot contribute to national committees; (3) national committees may not accept more than $3 million in any one year. Federal regulations of expenditures include: (1) no political committee can spend more than $3 million annually; (2) campaign expenditures may not exceed $25,000 for senatorial candidates and $5000 for House candidates. Federal law also requires full reports of campaign receipts and expenditures. Contributions to and expenditures by state and local political groups are regulated by state laws, which vary considerably. *See* HATCH ACTS, page 124.

Significance   Most corrupt practices legislation now in existence has proved ineffective. Various loopholes exist by which individual and group donors and party committees can circumvent restrictions. Means of avoiding regulations include the subdividing of contributions among family members, the creation of additional "committees," the establishment of business and labor political "education" groups, and a general decentralization of expenditures. The underlying purpose of corrupt practices legislation, to free public officials from being beholden to heavy contributors while serving in office, has not been satisfactorily achieved. State laws are largely concerned with publicizing contributors and amounts received and spent by candidates and committees. This type of legislation has been more successful than attempts to control, limit, and regulate.

Countervailing Theory of Pressure Politics   The concept that in American politics the competition among major business, labor, farm, racial, religious, and other interest groups tends to balance their respective power and influence.
    Significance   The countervailing theory of pressure politics seeks to explain why no single, dominant social group controls the direction of American politics and policies. From this competition of diverse interests, the theory postulates, the public interest tends to emerge.

Credentials Committee   A committee used by political parties in their conventions to determine which delegates may participate. The credentials committee prepares a roll of all delegates entitled to be seated at the convention. Controversy over contested seats arises when rival groups claim to be the official party organization for a county, district, or state. In such cases, the committee makes recommendations to the convention.
    Significance   Recommendations made by the credentials committee to the convention are usually approved without debate or roll call. Conventions have, however, on occasion rejected these recommendations in whole or in part. In national conventions, decisions on seating of delegates from certain states, when two or more rival delegations appear at the convention, may be a decisive factor in the selection of the presidential nominee. As an example, in 1952 at the Republican Convention, rival delegations supporting General Dwight D. Eisenhower and Senator Robert A. Taft arrived from five southern states. The success of the Eisenhower supporters in getting their delegates seated was instrumental in securing the nomination for the General. In recent national conventions, civil rights groups have challenged the seating of southern delegations chosen without Negro participation.

Cumulative Voting   A method of voting in which the individual casts more than one vote in the simultaneous election of several officials, as a means of securing greater representation for minor parties. Each voter is allowed two or more votes, which he can cast for a single candidate or distribute among several. Candidates of minor parties can usually win seats because their supporters concentrate their additional votes for them, whereas major party supporters tend to distribute their votes among several candidates. Cumulative voting is used in electing members of the lower house of the Illinois legislature, with three representatives elected from each district and with each voter casting three votes.

Significance   Cumulative voting is an attempt to provide some direct representation for minority groups. Proponents support it as more accurately representative (and, hence, more democratic) than the two-party system. Opponents point out that it has a tendency to foster a host of splinter parties with the result that, frequently, none is able to gain a majority.

Demagogue   An unscrupulous politician who seeks to win and hold office through emotional appeals to mass prejudices and passions. Half-truths, outright lies, and various means of card-stacking may be used in either subtle or bold-faced attempts to dupe the voters. Typically, a demagogue may try to win support from one group by blaming another for its misfortunes. Another useful demagogic technique is to promise all things to all men.

Significance   Demagogues may thrive in either a dictatorship or a democracy. In the latter, however, because of free speech and press guarantees and frequent elections, the chances of unseating a demagogue are infinitely greater. Generally, the success of American demagogues has been rather short-lived.

Democratic Party   A major American party that evolved out of the Democratic-Republican group supporting Thomas Jefferson. Andrew Jackson, regarded by Democrats as cofounder with Jefferson, changed the name to Democratic party in keeping with his ultrademocratic philosophy. Further development of party principles occurred under the more recent leadership of Woodrow Wilson and Franklin D. Roosevelt. Since 1932, the Democratic party has dominated the American political scene, holding the presidency for all but the eight Eisenhower years (1953-1961) and a majority in Congress for all but four years (1947-1948; 1953-1954). *See* REPUBLICAN PARTY, page 117.

Significance   Many studies show strong Democratic party preference by low-income groups, organized labor, and religious and racial minority groups. In recent years, the Democratic party has generally stood for freer trade, more extensive international commitments, a greater measure of governmental regulation of the economy, and expanded civil rights guarantees. The civil rights issue has cost the party much of its former support from the South. On the issue of states' rights, the party has reversed its early position and, in modern times, has consistently favored expanded national responsibilities. Its policies have generally been more liberal than Republican party policies, although both include a coalition of liberals, moderates, and conservatives. Polls indicate that approximately sixty percent of all registered voters in the United States are Democrats.

Direct Primary   An intraparty election in which the voters select the candidates who will run on a party's ticket in the subsequent general election. Primaries are also used to choose convention delegates and party leaders. In a closed primary, the selection process is limited to avowed party adherents; in an open primary, voters participate regardless of party affiliation or the absence of any. Some state and local governments use nonpartisan primaries to reduce the number of candidates for the general election. Candidates get their names on a primary ballot, typically, through petitions signed by a required number of registered voters. Other means include caucus, preprimary convention, and self-announcement. *See* PRESIDENTIAL PRIMARIES, page 113; CLOSED PRIMARY, page 96; OPEN PRIMARY, page 109; RUNOFF PRIMARY, page 118; *United States v. Classic,* page 123; *Smith v. Allwright,* page 123.

Significance   Since 1900, the direct primary has gradually superseded the convention as a nominating device. All states today use the direct primary system, in one form or another, for some offices. The primary system gives rank and file voters a larger voice in party affairs and enables the voters to get rid of an unpopular but strongly entrenched elected official or party leader. Disadvantages include greater expense both for the candidate and for the taxpayer and, generally, a weakening of party organization and party responsibility.

Disfranchise   Taking away the privilege of voting. Persons may be disfranchised if they lose their citizenship, if they fail to reregister when required, or if they are convicted for certain crimes. Many people are disfranchised temporarily when they move, either within the state or from state to state, until they establish new residence. Voters may also be wholly or partially disfranchised indirectly as a result of dishonesty in ballot counts or through political manipulation, such as gerrymandering. In the South, fear and intimidation fostered by occasional acts of violence have served to keep eligible Negro voters from the polls.

Significance   Each election finds many Americans denied the privilege of voting despite their previous participation. Disfranchisement for loss of citizenship and conviction for crime is infrequent. Much voter disfranchisement would be removed by reducing residence requirements for most elections and eliminating them for presidential contests. Judicial oversight of state redistricting to ensure substantial equality in voting power and increased federal action to prevent disfranchisement because of color or race through the Civil Rights Acts have reduced both indirect and direct disfranchisement.

Electoral College   The presidential electors from each state who meet in their respective state capitals, following their popular election, and cast ballots for President and Vice President. The Electoral College never meets as a national body. The process starts with the nomination of partisan slates of electors by party conventions, primaries, or committees in each state. The number of electors in each state is equal to its number of representatives in both houses of Congress; the Twenty-third Amendment allots three electors for the District of Columbia, making a total electoral vote of 538. In the November presidential election, the slate of electors receiving a plurality of popular votes is elected. The electors usually pledge themselves to vote for their party's candidates for President and Vice President, although the Constitution permits them to use discretion. After casting electoral ballots in their respective state capitals in December, the ballots are counted and certified before a joint session of Congress early in January. The candidates who receive a majority of the electoral votes (270) are certified as President-elect and Vice President-elect. If none receives a majority of the electoral vote, the election of the President is decided by the House of Representatives from among the three highest candidates, with each state having one vote, and that of the Vice President by the Senate from the two highest candidates, with each senator having one vote. Normally, the people of the United States know who has been elected following the popular election in November, and the rest of the process is largely a formality. The rise of political parties that nominate pledged electors has distorted the original intention of the Founding Fathers. They had intended that the electors should be chosen as each state would determine and that they would exercise complete discretion in the selection of the President. *See* TWELFTH AMENDMENT, page 120; ELECTORAL COUNT ACT, page 124; MINORITY PRESIDENT, page 168.

Significance   The Electoral College system has come under severe criticism at times in American history. Several recurring grounds for criticism have been: (1) sometimes candidates with a minority of the popular vote have won election; (2) the machinery has become an anachronism, since the electors no longer actually perform the selecting function envisioned by the Founding Fathers; (3) the unit system under which all of a state's electoral votes go to that party which polls a state-wide plurality is unfair to other candidates and their supporters; and (4) the complicated nature of the entire system tends to confuse voters and complicate the selection process. Proposals for reform include: (1) discarding the Electoral College machinery and placing the election on a direct popular vote on the basis of a nation-wide constituency; (2) eliminating the electors but retaining a state basis for voting, with a plurality needed in a majority of states to win; (3) eliminating the electors but retaining an electoral vote divided in each state at approximately the same ratio as the popular vote (Lodge-Gossett proposal); (4) selection of electors in each state in the same manner as members of the House and Senate are chosen (Mundt-Coudert proposal).

Elite   Persons who exercise a major influence on, or control the making of political, economic, and social decisions. Elites achieve their power position through wealth, family status, caste systems, or intellectual superiority. Elites constitute the "power structure" of local and national communities.

Significance   An elite group may hold power openly and officially or may exercise control over those in authority. On the national level in the United States, no elite group is dominant; on specific issues, however, business, labor, military, and other elites may exercise a decisive influence. In many cities, a business elite constitutes "the establishment" or power structure. Elitism contravenes democratic theory but in practice pervades most institutions.

Favorite Son   A state political leader whose name is placed in nomination for the presidency at a national nominating convention by members of his state's delegation. Usually his nomination is merely a means of honoring him.

Significance   A "favorite son" nominee is seldom given serious consideration by the convention. Delegation members generally vote for their favorite son on the first ballot, especially if a real contest between leading candidates is shaping up. In this way, the delegation can remain noncommittal until after the first ballot gives some indication of the relative strength of leading candidates. At this point, the favorite son will probably withdraw his own nomination and throw his delegation's votes to one of the front-runners. If the recipient of these votes should go on to win the presidency, the favorite son will be in a good bargaining position to obtain a high-level, political appointment or other favors.

Federalist Party   The first American political party, which evolved during the later phases of George Washington's presidency. Its leaders, Alexander Hamilton and John Adams, gained the support of the financial, industrial, and commercial interests for the new party. Many of its members had strongly supported the adoption of the new Constitution and the creation of the federal Union.

Significance   The Federalist party developed national financial and economic programs. These included a protective tariff, an excise tax, the creation of a National Bank, and the assumption of state debts by the national government. To justify the expansion of national powers, the Federalists insisted on a loose interpretation of the Constitution. As a reaction to these policies, Thomas Jefferson and James Madison rallied the small farmers and artisans and the planters of the South into a coalition of Anti-Federalists. In this manner the two-party political system was given birth in the United States. After Jefferson's defeat of the Federalists in the election of 1800, the party began to decline in popularity. In 1816, it disappeared completely from the American scene. Its demise resulted from quarrels among its leaders and from its discredit for both its attempt to silence the opposition through the Alien and Sedition Acts and its failure to support the War of 1812. In 1832, the Whig party evolved as a successor to the Federalists, and, in 1860, the Republican party superseded the Whigs.

Fifteenth Amendment   An amendment to the Constitution, adopted in 1870, that forbids a state to deny a person the right to vote because of race, color, or previous condition of servitude. *See Guinn v. United States,* page 123; *Smith v. Allwright,* page 123.

Significance   Although the Fifteenth Amendment does not give anyone the right to vote, it does prohibit any discrimination because of race or color. Not until recent years has the Negro made significant advances in realizing the goals established by the Amendment. In 1960, for example, the Supreme Court ruled that the racial gerrymandering of Tuskegee, Alabama, so as to exclude all Negro voters from city elections violated the Fifteenth Amendment (*Gomillion v. Lightfoot,* 364 U.S. 339). The Civil Rights Acts of 1957, 1960, 1964, and 1965 were passed by Congress, and the Twenty-fourth Amendment was adopted to aid the Negro in overcoming the various devices used by some southern states to frustrate the purposes of the Fifteenth Amendment.

Filing   The legal act of declaring candidacy for a public elective office. Most states provide that aspirants first circulate candidacy petitions to be signed by a stipulated number of registered voters. The aspirant presents the petitions, and files for candidacy with the appropriate official (secretary of state, county clerk, or city clerk). The candidate may then run against other candidates of his party for the office in a direct primary election to determine which of them will become the party's standard-bearer in the general election. In some states, persons seeking candidacy for local office may file simply by declaring their intentions before an official. In other states, a candidate may file by depositing a sum of money in lieu of petitions, which may be refunded if the candidate polls enough votes. *See* PETITION, page 110.

Significance   Filing is a means by which running for office can be limited to "serious" candidates. A balance must be struck: if the requirements are too difficult, competent, public-spirited citizens may be discouraged from seeking candidacy; if too lenient, a horde of candidates may confuse the voters. In Britain, this problem is met by requiring all candidates to deposit a modest filing fee which is forfeited if the candidate fails to secure a minimum number of votes.

General Election   A state-wide election, usually held shortly after a primary election, to fill state and national offices. States hold national presidential elections every four years, in November, and national congressional elections in the even-numbered years. Typically, states hold state and county general elections every November in even-numbered years, although some states elect some important state officials and judges in general elections held in odd-numbered years, frequently in the spring.

Significance   Voters make their final choice in selecting their public officials in the general election. Such an election is to be distinguished from a primary election, which is a nominating process, and from a special election, which is one called at irregular intervals.

Hare Plan   A system of proportional representation, occasionally used in the United States, that is based on a single, transferable vote. Candidates vie in open competition for a number of elective offices. A quota is established and all candidates obtaining sufficient votes to meet it are declared elected. Surplus votes of winning candidates and the votes of candidates eliminated for low-vote totals are distributed according to the second choices expressed by the voters on their ballots. Votes are transferred in this manner until sufficient candidates have been declared elected to fill all elective seats. *See* PROPORTIONAL REPRESENTATION, page 115.

Significance   The Hare Plan seeks to record the voters' wishes more accurately than can be achieved through the common American elective system of single-member districts, in which all votes not cast for the winning candidate are discarded. Economic and social minority-interest groups are more likely to gain representation under it, giving a broader consensus to the government. The obvious weakness of the Hare Plan, and a characteristic shortcoming of all proportional representation systems, is the difficulty of building in the government a majority that can make decisions. Diverse interest groups often have conflicting views on matters of public policy, and frequently these cannot be reconciled. Government by compromise tends to replace government by majority rule. Only a dozen or so municipalities have adopted the Hare Plan in the United States, many dropping it after a short trial period.

Incumbent   An officeholder seeking re-election.

Significance   An incumbent usually has an advantage in seeking re-election, since he has an established following, is better known to the voters, and has campaign experience. Many states give an advantage to incumbents by permitting their official titles of office to be printed on the ballot. The voter is thus given a choice between a candidate who obviously has had experience in the office and other untried and often unknown persons. Studies have disclosed that incumbents usually win re-election in the United States.

Independent   A voter who disregards party affiliation of candidates running for elective office and casts his ballot for the "best man" or on the basis of issues. Most independents are not party members, but a few retain membership in a party, enabling them to vote in primaries while exercising their own judgment in general elections.

Significance   Although independents are often criticized for not contributing actively to the democratic process through political parties, they are wooed by both major parties. Independent votes are decisive in determining the outcome of many elections, including presidential contests. A large number of independent voters encourages political parties to focus on crucial issues in the campaigns and to act responsibly when elected. Some political analysts question whether there is such a thing as an independent, holding the view that all voters have a predisposition toward one party or the other.

Literacy Test   A suffrage qualification used in less than one-third of the states to determine fitness for voting by means of a reading or "understanding" test. Some southern states require an oral examination of prospective voters who must demonstrate ability to understand and interpret passages from the national or their state constitution. *See* VOTING RIGHTS ACT OF 1965, page 125.

Significance   Literacy tests offer an effective means of discriminating against voters because examining officials have great discretion, especially when the tests are administered orally. In some southern states, for example, Negro college graduates have been disqualified because they failed to interpret constitutional passages to the satisfaction of a white board of examiners. Evidence of discriminatory use of literacy and related tests in six southern states led to passage of the Voting Rights Act of 1965. This Act suspends the use of such tests and authorizes appointment of federal voting examiners to order registration of Negroes in states and voting districts where less than fifty percent of eligible voters are registered. New York's system, generally regarded as nondiscriminatory, consists of a reading and writing test administered through the state educational department to all persons who have not completed sixth-grade school work. A nondiscriminatory, fairly administered literacy test may be a useful qualification for voting, in view of the complexity of issues involved in contemporary elections.

Lobbyist   A person, usually acting as an agent for a pressure group, who seeks to bring about the passage or defeat of legislative bills or to influence their contents. Lobbyists, often called the "Third House" of the legislature, are experts who testify before committees and present important facts on legislative proposals to support their clients' interests. Several states and the national government require the registration of lobbyists and the disclosure of information concerning their employers, their salaries, and the amounts spent to influence legislation. Lobbyists are also active in trying to influence decisions made by executive officials and administrators. *See* REGULATION OF LOBBYING ACT, page 163; *United States v. Harriss,* page 162; PRESSURE GROUP, page 114.

Significance   Lobbyists furnish important factual data to legislators and provide effective representation for organized groups. They are criticized because they use selected facts, often distorted, and are more concerned with particular interests than with the general interest. Except for laws prohibiting bribery and similar criminal offenses, governmental action toward lobbyists has not sought to restrict their activities but to publicize them. Attempts by government to restrict lobbyists and lobbying unduly might be regarded by the courts as an infringement of the First Amendment freedom to petition the government.

Long Ballot   The typical state and local ballot, sometimes called the "bedsheet ballot" or "jungle ballot," which has a large number of offices to be filled, candidates to be selected, and issues to be decided. *See* SHORT BALLOT, page 118.

Significance   The long ballot emerged during the era of Jacksonian Democracy in the 1830s on the theory that the way to expand democracy is to increase the number of elective officials. Today, political scientists question this assumption. They argue that with a smaller number of elective officials, the voter can know the candidates, their qualifications, and the issues of the campaign. The long ballot may enable political machines to retain power because of voter apathy or confusion. The short ballot movement, which started around the turn of the century, has had some success in reducing the length of the ballot in a few states, but the basic problem remains.

Mandate   Popular support for a political program. It occurs in an election by means of a transfer of popular support to a political party and its elected officials. A mandate may be vague or specific, depending upon the clarity with which alternatives are presented to the voters. *See* RESPONSIBLE PARTY SYSTEM, page 117.

Significance   The mandate concept is best implemented where a responsible, well-disciplined party, ready and able to carry out its promised program, exists. The American party system, unlike the British, lacks these qualities and the mandate concept is consequently weakened. Other factors in the American political milieu that weaken the mandate include the separation of powers, bicameralism, and gerrymandering.

Mass Media   The technical means of communication with millions of people, exemplified by television, radio, newspapers, motion pictures, magazines, and periodicals. *See* PROPAGANDA, page 115.

Significance   The mass media of communication have become extremely important to government and politics as a means of informing and influencing millions of citizens. Objectives include the winning of elections, the marshaling of support for or opposition to programs, and the education of the public on major issues. Political scientists, aware of the increasing significance of the mass media in decision-making and of their abuse in totalitarian states, have expressed concern for their effect on the democratic process. The trend in the United States is toward concentration of the ownership of the mass media in fewer hands. The problem of seeking corrections for this situation raises many serious issues, including those concerning the constitutional rights of free expression and property.

Minor Party   A party movement, often based on a single idea or principle, that usually has little influence on elections because its support is either localized or widely scattered. Some observers distinguish it from a third party, a new party based on a protest movement which may influence the outcome of an election. *See* THIRD PARTY, page 120.

Significance   Minor parties have played a significant role in American political life in initiating and successfully publicizing political, economic, and social reforms over a period of years. When a minor party gains a substantial number of adherents to its principle, a major party often incorporates this principle into its own platform so as to gain voter support. The Prohibition party, for example, convinced large numbers of people of the wisdom of prohibition; the Republican party thereupon included a prohibition plank in its platform and, after winning at the polls, instituted prohibition. Minor parties found on the ballot in many states today include the Prohibition, Socialist Labor, and Socialist Workers. Several right-wing conservative and tax reform parties have also appeared on the political scene in recent years.

Multiple-Party System   An electoral system, usually based on proportional representation, that requires a coalition of several parties to form a majority to run the government. Multiple-party systems are typical of continental European democracies. The system can be distinguished from the Anglo-American two-party system, not by the existence of numerous parties, but rather in that many parties seriously compete for, and actually win, seats in the legislature. *See* TWO-PARTY SYSTEM, page 121; PROPORTIONAL REPRESENTATION, page 115.

Significance   Multiple-party systems tend to provide a broader, more diverse representation of the electorate. This strength is, at the same time, a major weakness. Coalition governments, by their very nature, are unstable governments that tend to disintegrate when the parties comprising the coalition have a falling out over a major issue. France, for example, had twenty coalition governments during the period of the Fourth Republic, from 1946 to 1958. The American people have shunned a multiple-party approach to politics by refusing to give substantial support to any but the two major parties. Moreover, the single-member district system, as distinguished from proportional representation, tends to perpetuate the two-party system.

National Chairman   The chairman of a political party's national committee, who is generally chosen by his party's presidential candidate. *See* POLITICAL PARTY, page 111.

Significance   The major responsibility of a national chairman is the management of the national election campaign. Working through the national committee, the chairman may exercise a considerable influence over state and local party organizations, although no formal control mechanism exists. His specific responsibilities include establishing national party headquarters, directing party affairs during and between campaigns, and raising and distributing campaign funds.

National Committee   A standing committee of a national political party established to direct and coordinate party activities during the four-year periods between national party conventions. The Democratic National Committee includes two members, a man and a woman, from each state, from the District of Columbia, and from several territories; the Republican National Committee uses the same formula but adds state chairmen from all states carried by the Republican party in the preceding presidential, gubernatorial, or congressional election. National committeemen and committeewomen are chosen every four years by the various delegations to the national convention. Each committee ratifies the presidential nominee's selection of a national chairman who acts as spokesman for his party. *See* POLITICAL PARTY, page 111.

Significance   Although the national committee appears to top the hierarchical permanent structure of each party, its power and influence are not great. The real locus of power in both party organizations remains at the local and state levels. Each national committee is concerned mainly with the presidential election and points most of its activities toward planning the next campaign. Other important functions include planning the national convention, securing financial contributions, and publicizing the party.

National Convention   A quadrennial meeting held by each major party to select presidential and vice presidential candidates, write a platform, choose a national committee, and conduct party business. Presidential candidates have been nominated by the convention method in every election since 1832. Delegates are apportioned on the basis of state representation with bonuses for states showing voting majorities for the party in preceding elections. Delegates are selected by party conventions or committees in approximately two-thirds of the states and by presidential primaries in one-third of the states. Both parties also accredit delegates from the District of Columbia, Puerto Rico, and the Virgin Islands. The nomination of, and voting on, candidates is conducted by a call of the states in alphabetical order. Democratic party conventions permit state delegations to use the unit rule. Both conventions nominate their candidates by an absolute majority vote. *See* CREDENTIALS COMMITTEE, page 98; FAVORITE SON, page 101; PLATFORM, page 111; PRESIDENTIAL PRIMARIES, page 113; UNIT RULE, page 122.

Significance   Although national party conventions are typified by excitement, both artificial and natural, their responsibilities are extremely important. Most convention efforts and oratory are pointed toward the imminent fall campaign. Despite extensive television coverage in recent years, the national convention remains a puzzling phenomenon for most Americans. Much criticism has been directed at it for its clownish atmosphere, the use of pressure tactics and secret bargains, and the lack of popular participation in the candidate-selection process. Yet conventions seldom ignore public opinion and have chosen many distinguished candidates. Today, conventions remain wholly free from federal regulation.

Nepotism   Granting of political favors to relatives.
    Significance   Nepotism has been carried on by various kinds of public officials on all levels of government throughout American history. It may contribute to efficiency in government if the official's relatives are qualified and cooperative, but it is generally frowned upon by the voting public.

Nineteenth Amendment   An amendment to the Constitution, adopted in 1920, that prohibits any state from denying the right to vote to any citizen because of sex. Wyoming took the initiative, in 1869, in granting suffrage to women, but only a few states followed this lead. Suffragette agitation during the early part of the twentieth century culminated in the Nineteenth Amendment, which was adopted in time for women to participate in the presidential election of 1920.
    Significance   Like the Fifteenth Amendment, the Nineteenth does not grant the right to vote to anyone, but it does restrict the states from discriminating on the basis of sex. Since 1920, there have been no attempts to interfere with the voting rights of women. Some observers believe that the Amendment has had no appreciable effect on elections since "women vote the way their husbands tell them to," but considerable evidence exists to contradict this thesis. Because women voters outnumber eligible male voters today, campaigns have acquired more of a feminine touch, and candidate qualifications now include that of "sex appeal."

Nomination   The official designation of an individual as a candidate for public office. Methods for selecting candidates in the United States have included the rank and file party caucus, legislative and congressional caucuses, the mixed caucus (legislators and party representatives), the party convention, the primary, and petition. Nomination also signifies the first step in the appointment of an executive or judicial official. See AVAILABILITY, page 94; CAUCUS, page 95; CONVENTION, page 97; DIRECT PRIMARY, page 99; PETITION, page 110; NATIONAL CONVENTION, page 107.
    Significance   Today, the direct primary is the most widely used nominating device, being mandatory or optional in all fifty states. The convention system, discredited and largely replaced by the direct primary by 1910, is once again gaining acceptance on the state and local levels. Some disillusionment with the primary system exists, and the convention method is credited with giving greater emphasis to party responsibility and selection of able candidates. The selection of the candidates for the presidency remains in the hands of each party's quadrennial convention.

Nonpartisan Election   An election in which candidates have no party designations and political parties are prohibited from running candidates. Nonpartisan elections are typically used to elect state and local judges and municipal officials. They are often preceded by nonpartisan primaries in which the number of candidates for each office is reduced to two.

Significance   A progressive movement active early in the twentieth century proposed to get rid of corruption by eliminating political parties and partisan elections. Many nonpartisan electoral reforms were introduced, especially on the local levels. Most nonpartisan systems, however, have not produced the anticipated results, since candidates are often identified with parties and parties may seek to influence the election. Political parties have been weakened by severance from their grass roots. At the local level, however, nonpartisan elections have the major advantage of reducing the impact of irrelevant national partisan issues.

Office-Block Ballot   A form of general election ballot in which candidates for elective office are grouped together under the title of each office. The "office block" or "Massachusetts ballot" is in contradistinction to the other common type of ballot, the "party column," or "Indiana ballot," in which all candidates of a particular party are arranged in one column. *See* PARTY-COLUMN BALLOT, page 109.

Significance   The office-block ballot is now used, in some form, in about twenty states. Politicians dislike it because it places more emphasis on the office than on the party and tends to discourage "straight-ticket" voting. Studies have shown that it definitely encourages voters to "split their ticket" in general elections, compared with straight-ticket voting on party column ballots.

Open Primary   A direct primary voting system that permits the voter to choose the party primary in which he wishes to vote without disclosing his party affiliation or allegiance, if any. In an open primary, the voter makes his choice in the privacy of the voting booth. He is still limited, however, to casting votes for candidates of only one party. *See* CLOSED PRIMARY, page 96; DIRECT PRIMARY, page 99.

Significance   Few states use the open primary system. Unlike the closed primary, it permits independents to vote in primaries and does not require public disclosure of party affiliation, regarded as distasteful by many voters. The open primary is criticized because it reduces party responsibility and permits "raiding" by voters of one party who cross over and seek to influence the nomination of candidates of the opposing party.

Party-Column Ballot   A form of general election ballot in which candidates for various offices are arranged in one column under their respective party names and symbols. The "party column" or "Indiana ballot" is in contradistinction to the other common type of ballot, the "office block" or "Massachusetts ballot," in which candidates are grouped under each elective office. *See* OFFICE-BLOCK BALLOT, page 109; STRAIGHT TICKET, page 119.

Significance   The party-column ballot permits voting for all of a party's candidates by marking a single "X" or by pulling a single lever. Some variation of this kind of ballot is used today in about thirty states. Politicians generally prefer the party-column ballot because it simplifies and encourages "straight-ticket" voting. This is particularly true when a party has an exceptionally strong presidential or gubernatorial candidate to head the list of party candidates.

Patronage   The power to make partisan appointments to office or to confer contracts, franchises, honors, or other special favors. Patronage powers are vested primarily in the President, in governors and other state elective officials, in mayors, and in various county officers. Through senatorial courtesy and similar practices, legislators on all levels of government also share in patronage disposition. See SPOILS SYSTEM, page 190; SENATORIAL COURTESY, page 153; MERIT SYSTEM, page 188.

Significance   An era of unrestricted patronage was ushered in on the national level, in 1829, by the Jackson Administration's spoils system. Presidential patronage reached a high water mark during Abraham Lincoln's first term (1861-1864), but began to lose ground progressively after the enactment of the Civil Service Act of 1883 (Pendleton Act). Patronage is often defended as an essential feature of the party system to provide inducements and rewards for party workers. It also enables a chief executive to surround himself with loyal subordinates who support his views and help him redeem his campaign pledges. Antipatronage forces counter these arguments by pointing to the long, disreputable history of the spoils system. Intelligent and well-trained personnel, it is argued, can work effectively with administrations of either party. Today, the county is the major remaining stronghold of the patronage system in the United States.

Petition   A method of placing a candidate's name on a primary or general election ballot by submitting a specified number, or percentage, of signatures of registered voters to an appropriate state or local official for certification. Petitions may also be used to commence the initiative and referendum procedures in several states. See NOMINATION, page 108; DIRECT LEGISLATION, page 136; FILING, page 102.

Significance   The petition requirement to get an aspirant's name placed on a primary ballot is intended to help restrict the election to serious candidates. In general elections, the petition method provides a means for political independents to get their names on the ballot. Petitions frequently become matters of political controversy, involving charges of invalid signatures.

Pivotal States   Those states with large electoral votes that are crucial in winning a presidential election and in which the outcome is doubtful. See ELECTORAL COLLEGE, page 100.

Significance   Each major party usually concentrates its organization, campaign funds, and candidate appearances on the seven most populous states that together comprise 210 of the 270 electoral votes needed to elect a President: California (40), Illinois (26), Michigan (21), New York (43), Ohio (26), Pennsylvania (29), and Texas (25). In most elections, these states have also been given "doubtful" status, adding to the attention given them during campaigns by both parties and their candidates. Popular leaders from pivotal states are also most likely to be nominated as presidential and vice presidential candidates.

Platform   A statement of principles and objectives espoused by a party or a candidate that is used during a campaign to win support from voters. Platforms are, typically, written at national, state, and county party conventions by platform committees and are then adopted by the conventions. *See* NATIONAL CONVENTION, page 107.

Significance   American party platforms consist, for the most part, of generalities and platitudes. They extol the vast accomplishments of their party while indicting the opposition party for its failures. The language used to elaborate subjects on which the party is united, however, is precise and the commitment clear. Party platforms are variously supplemented and modified by candidates and party leaders, but few consider themselves bound by platform commitments when elected.

Plurality   The winning of an election by a candidate who receives more votes than any other candidate but not necessarily a majority of the total vote. *See* ABSOLUTE MAJORITY, page 93.

Significance   Most American electoral laws for national, state, and local elections provide for winning by a plurality vote. Whenever there are more than two strong candidates running for an office, the winner usually secures a plurality rather than a majority vote. An exception is found in the runoff primary system used in several southern states whereby, if no candidate receives a majority vote, a second, runoff election is held between the two highest vote getters.

Political Machine   A well-entrenched party organization headed by a boss or small group of autocratic leaders. Political machines usually operate at the city or county level and occasionally on a state-wide basis. They may use ruthlessly efficient methods in maintaining themselves in power through such techniques as bribery, patronage, "honest graft," control over nominations, and the rigging of elections. Any successful political organization may, however, be dubbed a "machine" by its opponents. *See* BOSS, page 94.

Significance   Political machines have flourished throughout American history, although their number and effectiveness have been reduced in recent years. The direct primary was instituted in the early twentieth century largely as a reform to clean up politics by wresting power from political machines, but new techniques were developed by the bosses to control primaries. A high level of interest, participation, and civic spirit in an aroused community is the best answer to machine politics, but reform movements which incorporate these attributes are often short-lived in their vigor and interest, resulting in a return to power of the machine.

Political Party   A group of individuals having some measure of ideological agreement who organize to win elections, operate government, and determine public policy. A party differs from a pressure group mainly in its basic objective of winning control of the machinery of government. In the United States, political parties are organized on precinct, county, congressional district, state, and national levels, with most decisions made by conventions, chairmen, and committees at the county, state, and national levels. Unlike parties in most countries, power in American political parties is highly decentralized. *See* MANDATE, page 105; MULTIPLE-PARTY SYSTEM, page 106; TWO-PARTY SYSTEM, page 121; DEMOCRATIC PARTY, page 99; REPUBLICAN PARTY, page 117; MINOR PARTY, page 106; THIRD PARTY, page 120.

Significance   Neither of the two major American parties requires ideological conformity as a requirement for participation. In an authoritarian state, a single party, typically requiring rigid adherence to its ideological dogma, is used to develop policies and run the government through dual-party and governmental leadership positions. In multiple-party democratic states, in which each party can compete for a share of political power, individuals join the party that best promotes their economic and social interests. Political parties in the United States: (1) stimulate interest in the political process; (2) publicize political issues; (3) recruit candidates and carry on national, state, and local campaigns; (4) raise finances for political activity; (5) help maintain the honesty of elections; and (6) take responsibility for operating the machinery of government or providing an organized opposition.

Poll   An attempt to uncover public opinion or to forecast an election. Public-opinion polling has developed from the early newspaper straw-vote poll of its subscribers to the personal-interview technique, based on "scientific" quota sampling of the voting population, developed during the 1930s. New polling methods in use today involve probability sampling, in which representative precincts are used as barometers to indicate prevailing opinions. Poll results are checked against the actual voting records of the precincts.

Significance   The best-known polls include those conducted by Dr. George Gallup, Elmo Roper, Lou Harris, A. M. Crossley, and the Princeton Research Service. Most polling interest is directed toward presidential elections, in which pollsters have often accurately predicted voting behavior. In the 1948 presidential election, however, polling groups failed to predict the Truman victory, resulting in considerable public skepticism of polling techniques and suspicion of pollsters' objectives. New techniques, including electronic computers, developed since 1948 have increased predictive accuracy. Polls have also become increasingly significant as a means of keeping elective officials aware of public opinion on important issues, and in the selection of presidential nominees by the major parties. Supporters of polling regard it as a major democratic advance, whereas opponents fear the rigging of polls to influence elections and the restrictions polls may place on policy-makers.

Poll Tax   A special head tax that must be paid as a qualification for voting. The Twenty-fourth Amendment to the Constitution outlawed the poll tax in national, but not state, elections. In 1966, the Supreme Court declared that payment of any poll tax as a condition for voting is unconstitutional (*Harper v. Virginia State Board of Elections*, 383 U.S. 663). *See* TWENTY-FOURTH AMENDMENT, page 121.

Significance   Before the *Harper* decision, a poll-tax requirement in five southern states had reduced the voting participation of both whites and Negroes. The tax worked a greater hardship upon Negroes because of their lower income status and because of unequal enforcement. Prior to the Twenty-fourth Amendment, poll-tax states had turnouts in national elections of only one-half the size of those in states not using the poll tax. In some states, the poll tax was used to maintain the political machines in power because political leaders paid the tax for many of their supporters. In the *Harper* case, the Supreme Court held that a financial requirement for voting denies equal protection of the law.

Poll Watcher   An individual appointed by a political party to be present at a polling place on election day to ensure the honesty of the election. In many states, both major parties have poll watchers present at all polling places during partisan elections. In primary elections, poll watchers may also be appointed to prevent "raiding" by the opposition party. *See* CHALLENGE, page 95.

Significance   Poll watchers can play a significant role in maintaining the honesty of elections, and, in this way, keep American voters from losing confidence in the democratic process. Poll watching is essential when a party challenges an entrenched political machine.

Precinct   The basic unit in the United States in the election process and for party organization. Cities and counties are divided into precinct polling districts, each containing from 200 to 1000 voters and a polling place. In political organization, each party usually elects or appoints a precinct captain or committeeman who functions as a party leader within the precinct. Precinct leaders in the cities may represent their precincts in party ward committees. The precinct also serves for the election or appointment of delegates to city or county party conventions. *See* POLITICAL PARTY, page 111.

Significance   The precinct, being a small voting district, provides easy access to the polls for voters on election days. In politics, the precinct organization of the parties is the key to election success, especially in the metropolitan areas. An effective precinct leader is expected to work tirelessly the year around gaining party converts, getting voters registered, carrying on routine party business, and, most significant for his political future, turning out large majorities for his party on election days.

Presidential Primaries   The election of delegates to a major party's national convention. About one-third of the states hold some form of presidential primary in the weeks or months preceding the conventions; delegates are selected in the other states by political party conventions or committees. Delegates selected in the primaries may or may not be "pledged" to vote for a presidential aspirant. In a few states, delegates are selected by the party organization but are bound to support the candidate designated by the voters in a so-called popularity contest. *See* NATIONAL CONVENTION, page 107; DIRECT PRIMARY, page 99.

Significance   The presidential primary was pioneered by Wisconsin in 1905 and, although by 1916 both parties selected a majority of their national convention delegates by this method, it has since lost considerable ground. The main controversy surrounding the presidential primary concerns the "preferential" problem—that is, should pledged or unpledged delegates be elected. Popular influence is reduced because pledged delegates are under no legal, and little moral, obligation to honor such pledges beyond the first ballot. For this reason and because fewer than one-half the delegates are selected from primary states, the presidential primary has not usually been of great significance in choosing presidential nominees. In 1952, for example, Estes Kefauver won most of the delegates in the preferential primary states but was not selected for the presidential nomination by the Democratic convention; Adlai Stevenson, conversely, did not enter any presidential primaries and yet won the Democratic nomination. Presidential primaries, however, are gaining in significance by eliminating those who lack vote-getting ability and building the stature of those who demonstrate widespread popular support. For example, in 1960, John F. Kennedy won the nomination, and in 1964, Governor Nelson E. Rockefeller withdrew from the race, both largely as a result of their showings in preferential primaries. Supporters of preference primaries argue that they prevent bosses from dominating conventions, build interest for the presidential election, and expand democratic influence. Those who oppose them point out that they are indecisive because voter opinion often is split in many directions, that they prolong the presidential election spectacle until voters get weary, and that only a convention free from voter pledges can reconcile party differences and unite the party behind a candidate. Although popular demands have increased in recent years for a nation-wide preferential primary system, most professional politicians regard such a system as too costly in money, energy, and confusion.

Pressure Group   An organized interest group in which members share common views and objectives and actively carry on programs to influence government officials and policies. Unlike political parties, which seek to win control of and operate the government, pressure groups are mainly interested in determining public policies that directly or indirectly affect their members. Such groups vary considerably in size, wealth, power, and objectives. Their methods, however, are quite similar and include lobbying, electioneering, and propagandizing to influence public opinion. Pressure groups seek to influence decisions in the legislative, executive, and judicial branches. See LOBBYIST, page 104; REGULATION OF LOBBYING ACT, page 163; BUSINESS ORGANIZATIONS, page 258; CIVIL RIGHTS ORGANIZATIONS, page 57; FARM ORGANIZATIONS, page 294; LABOR UNIONS, page 283; VETERANS ORGANIZATIONS, page 308.

Significance   In America's pluralistic society, groups rather than individuals exercise most political influence. The most powerful interest groups are those that have emerged out of the three basic economic areas: agriculture, business, and labor. Other significant groupings that carry on pressure activities include professional societies, women's groups, patriotic and veterans' organizations, and religious and racial groups. Pressure-group efforts are directed toward an identification of their particular interests with the general interest. The countervailing theory of pressure politics holds that the major interest groups, powerful as they may be, tend to counteract and balance each others' power, which keeps any one from exercising a dominant influence. Congress in 1946 sought to regulate the lobbying activities of pressure groups through the Federal Regulation of Lobbying Act. The Act is largely concerned with publicizing lobbying groups and their activities, but its vague and confusing language and the absence of an enforcement agency have encouraged much noncompliance. The enactment of stiffer laws involving extensive regulation of pressure groups and their activities might involve serious questions of constitutionality concerning basic rights of assembly and petition.

Propaganda   Communication aimed at influencing the thinking, emotions, or actions of a group or public. The use of propaganda assumes that changes in men's thinking will prompt changes in their actions. Propaganda is not necessarily true nor false; it is based on a careful selection and manipulation of data. *See* MASS MEDIA, page 105.

Significance   The development of mass media of communication has encouraged the use of propaganda to influence governmental decisions indirectly through public opinion. Government also uses propaganda to cultivate support for its programs and policies and to answer criticisms. Propaganda techniques include the use of simple slogans, the identification of propaganda with local situations, the "straight news" approach, the distortion of facts, appeals to idealism, and the "Big Lie" technique of Adolf Hitler. As a rule, successful mass propaganda must be simple, interesting, credible, consistent, and supported by actual events or experiences. Democracies are characterized by a variety of competing propagandists and their propaganda; dictatorships are maintained by government monopoly of propaganda.

Property Qualification   A qualification for voting that requires the ownership of property, usually real estate. *See* VOTING QUALIFICATIONS, page 122.

Significance   When the Constitution was adopted, voting was generally restricted to white, male property owners. By 1850, most state property qualifications had been eliminated in the democratic reforms that characterized the era of Jacksonian Democracy. Today, six states retain some measure of property qualifications for voting on local bond issues or special assessments.

Proportional Representation (PR)   An electoral system that allocates seats in the legislative body to each party or group approximately equal to its popular voting strength. For example, a minority party that receives five percent of the total vote in an election will win about five percent of the legislative seats. The most commonly used systems of PR are the list system, based on voting by party, and the Hare system, based on voting for individuals using the single transferable vote. *See* HARE PLAN, page 103; MULTIPLE-PARTY SYSTEM, page 106.

Significance   Several American cities, including New York, have experimented with the Hare system to provide some measure of minority representation. Most democratic countries use the continental European PR list system in preference to the Anglo-American, single-member district system. Proponents of PR point out that it provides representation for minority parties, reduces or eliminates machine politics, and is more democratic. Opponents argue that PR tends to proliferate parties, is too complicated for the average voter, and inevitably results in unstable coalition governments.

Public Opinion   An aggregate of individual views, attitudes, or beliefs shared by a significant portion of a community. No single public opinion in the sense of a general will exists; rather, a number of publics hold various opinions on a host of issues. Public opinion can be made known in a democracy through elections, referendums, lobbying and pressure group activities, polls, and by elected representatives who "sound out" grass roots sentiment. See POLL, page 112; MASS MEDIA, page 105; PRESSURE GROUP, page 114.

Significance   A common problem of democracies involves the question of how responsive to public opinion elected representatives should be. Should they, for example, exercise their own best judgment in voting on issues, or should they follow the public opinion positions of their constituents? If the latter, there remain the difficult problems of how to determine the existence of public opinion and how to measure it. Opinion research reveals the existence of a small "attentive public," with the general public unaware of most issues. Although public opinion is a vague concept, most governments recognize its significance in the political process and seek to stimulate and shape it in support of major policies.

Recall   A procedure enabling voters to remove an elected official from office before his term has expired. The required number of valid signatures on petitions results in the calling of a special election. If the majority of voters favor recall, the official is replaced by a successor who is either chosen on the recall ballot or in a subsequent election. Twelve states and numerous local units of government provide for the recall of elected officials.

Significance   The recall enables the voters to hold their public officials continuously responsible. It is used infrequently, but the threat of recall is ever-present, and does not go unnoticed by elected officials. No provision is made for the recall of federal officials.

Registration   Enrolling prospective voters prior to their participation in elections. Under a system of permanent registration, the voter, once qualified, remains on the eligible list until he dies, moves, or fails to vote in several consecutive elections. Periodic registration requires that he enroll at the appropriate local office annually or at fixed intervals. Almost all states now use some form of permanent registration, although in many there is no state-wide application. See VOTING QUALIFICATIONS, page 122.

Significance   Registration permits the orderly enforcement of voting qualifications and helps to maintain the honesty of elections. Permanent registration is more economical and less bothersome to voters than periodic, but it involves the problem of keeping voting lists up-to-date by enrolling new voters and deleting those who die, move, or are otherwise disqualified. Partisan or apathetic administration of these functions can result in fraudulent voting. Under periodic registration, lists are kept relatively up-to-date and vote frauds are discouraged. Periodic registration is most useful in large cities where the mobility of population is high. Under the Voting Rights Act of 1965, federal registrars have enrolled Negroes in southern communities where racial discrimination has foreclosed their registration for many years.

Republican Party   A major American party that emerged in the 1850s as an antislavery party. The Republican party is the successor to two earlier major parties—the Federalist and the Whig. It became firmly established in American politics when its candidate, Abraham Lincoln, won the presidency in 1860 and successfully prosecuted the Civil War. The period from 1860 to 1932 was characterized largely by Republican dominance of the American political scene. *See* DEMOCRATIC PARTY, page 99.

Significance   Studies have shown that Republican support among voters increases as their income and educational levels rise. Traditionally, manufacturing, business, financial, and farming interests have been influential in the party except in the Deep South. The Republican party has consistently advocated individual initiative, free enterprise, fiscal responsibility, and sound-money policies. Its policies have generally been more conservative than Democratic party policies, although both include a coalition of conservatives, moderates, and liberals. Historically, Republicans have favored a high protective tariff and isolationism, although in recent years the party has supported lower tariffs and various American international commitments. It has generally opposed the ideas of the welfare state and big government although it has given support to social welfare programs in recent years.

Residence   A qualification for voting based on domicile. Such laws require that a person live in the state for a specified period of time, commonly one year, although several states in the North and East require only six months and a few in the South demand two years of residence. Additional residence requirements include living within a county and a voting precinct, typically ninety days for the former and thirty days for the latter. *See* VOTING QUALIFICATIONS, page 122; DISFRANCHISE, page 100.

Significance   Residence requirements are intended to prevent the importing of "floaters" to win elections and to ensure that the individual is acquainted with state and local problems and candidates before he becomes eligible. The qualification, however, serves to disfranchise temporarily several million voters as the American people become increasingly mobile. Students of government have recommended the adoption of a constitutional amendment to eliminate or reduce state residence requirements for voting in presidential elections—a change already instituted in several states.

Responsible Party System   A democratic political system in which parties accept full accountability to the voters in developing policy and operating the government. A responsible party requires internal discipline, so that its members give support to its objectives and platform promises. The real test of responsibility is whether the majority party can redeem its pledges to the voters. *See* POLITICAL PARTY, page 111.

Significance   American political parties are fundamentally irresponsible in that they are highly decentralized and lack ideological cohesion. Moreover, the separation of powers, federalism, and sectionalism provide a political milieu not conducive to the growth of responsibility. In contrast, British parties are hierarchically structured, are disciplined through the party-whip system, and effectively translate party promises into government policies. Critics of American parties have suggested a realignment of party wings into a new conservative-liberal two-party system so that both could function more responsibly. Reapportionment of American legislative bodies has helped to overcome the divisive impact of the separation of powers on party responsibility.

Runoff Primary   A nominating system used in eleven southern states, in which a second primary election is held between the top two candidates if the leading candidate in the first primary fails to poll a majority vote. *See* DIRECT PRIMARY, page 99.

Significance   The runoff primary is particularly advantageous in one-party states where winning the primary is tantamount to election. It guarantees that the nominee will have the majority support of the voters rather than a mere pluraliy when three or more candidates are in the running.

Sectionalism   The influence of local or regional loyalties on state or national elections, issues, or party unity.

Significance   Traditionally, national unity has been seriously challenged by sectional cleavage on such vital issues as slavery, civil rights, "free silver," and the tariff. Most deep-rooted sectional loyalties of the early American period have given way, in the course of a century and a half, to nationalizing and unifying forces; but the position of the South on civil rights' issues, for example, remains a major factor of sectional separatism.

Short Ballot   A ballot containing relatively few offices to be filled by election. It is differentiated from the long ballot, which contains numerous elective offices, especially in the executive and judicial branches. Several states, such as New Jersey and Alaska, have reduced the number of state-wide elected executive officials to a governor and lieutenant governor and have considerably cut down the number of judicial elections. The national election ballot is already a "short" one, providing only for the casting of a single vote for President and Vice President, the election of a single representative, and, in two out of three elections, of a senator. The longest ballots, typically, are found on the local government level, especially in the county. *See* LONG BALLOT, page 105.

Significance   During the era of Jacksonian Democracy, the view that "the more numerous the elective offices, the more democratic the system" gained widespread acceptance. In the twentieth century, the short-ballot movement was established to try to reverse this situation. Advocates of the short ballot have called for patterning the state, county, and municipal ballots after the national, by providing for the election of legislators and one or two executive officials, with other executives and judges to be appointive. Underscoring the short-ballot movement is a belief that not only do shorter ballots simplify elections but they also make them more democratic by securing larger and more intelligent voter participation. Opponents adhere to the older doctrines that democracy thrives on numerous elections and that responsibility of office-holders can only be secured with a long ballot.

Single-Member District   An electoral district from which a single legislator is chosen by a plurality vote. The single-member district voting system is used in the United States and Britain, and differs from the multi-member districts typical of continental European electoral systems based on proportional representation. *See* PROPORTIONAL REPRESENTATION, page 115; CUMULATIVE VOTING, page 98; TWO-PARTY SYSTEM, page 121.

Significance   The single-member district is usually regarded as the most influential factor contributing to the development of a two-party system. It provides for elections based on the principle of "winner take all." Minor parties as a result are usually unable to win any share of political power and become parties of principle. Some American states depart from the single-member district principle in holding elections for one house of the legislature, and many cities have instituted multimember systems with at large elections. Other than these exceptions, American elections are based on single-member districts. Supporters of the single-member district principle argue that it avoids confusion, helps guarantee a majority party, and avoids the pitfalls of government by coalition. Those who oppose it point out that the votes of defeated parties and candidates are wasted, that the principle distorts the final election results, and that it fosters a false majority that does not democratically reflect voter sentiment.

Split Ticket   Voting for candidates of two or more parties for different offices. Split-ticket voting is not permitted in primaries. *See* STRAIGHT TICKET, page 119; OFFICE BLOCK BALLOT, page 109.

Significance   Split-ticket voting is encouraged by the "office-block" ballot, which emphasizes individual choice for each office rather than straight-ticket party voting. Some observers regard split-ticket "voting for the best man, not the party" as the most desirable approach to politics. Others oppose it on the grounds that the voter can too easily be fooled by personality and glibness, that issues rather than individuals are most important, and that it tends to weaken party and government responsibility. A frequent result of split-ticket voting is a government in which different parties control the executive and the legislature and in which deadlocks and stalemates are common, with the voters unable to fix responsibility for action or inaction.

State Central Committee   The principal committee of a political party within a state. State central committees are composed of members representing congressional districts, state legislative districts, or counties. *See* POLITICAL PARTY, page 111.

Significance   The state central committee has responsibility for carrying out policy decisions of the party's state convention. During political campaigns the committee makes decisions concerning strategy and the use of party campaign funds. It also may give direction to the party's state chairman, but, typically, has little influence with the party's state legislators or executive officials after they are elected.

Straight Ticket   Voting for all candidates of a single party for all offices. *See* SPLIT TICKET, page 119; PARTY-COLUMN BALLOT, page 109.

Significance   Straight-ticket party voting is encouraged by the use of "party-column" ballots, which require the marking of a single "X" or the pulling of a single lever to vote for all party candidates for all offices. Some observers prefer straight-ticket voting because it reduces the impact of personality, places major emphasis on issues, and promotes party and government responsibility. The case against straight-ticket voting is based on the assumption that intelligent voters should "vote for the man, not the party."

Third Party   A new party, usually comprised of independents and dissidents from the major parties, that, typically, is based on a protest movement and that may rally sufficient voter support to affect a presidential election. Some students of government distinguish a third from a *minor* party, a long-standing party of principle that seldom affects a specific election outcome. *See* MINOR PARTY, page 106.

Significance   Third parties have played an important role in American politics by influencing the adoption of reforms and by keeping the major parties from becoming too similar in their approach to issues, or too indifferent. When a political, economic, or social consensus breaks down, third-party movements have their best opportunity to present voters with a new and different approach. For example, in 1856 the Republican party was a third party that took the initiative away from the Whig party with a forthright antislavery program and replaced it as a major party. Another significant third-party movement was Theodore Roosevelt's "Bull Moose" party, which split the Republican vote and enabled Woodrow Wilson to win in 1912. The Dixiecrat party in 1948 was a sectional third party that failed to influence the election outcome because of a lack of sympathy outside the Deep South for its protest position.

Twelfth Amendment   An amendment to the Constitution, adopted in 1804, that provides for separate ballots to be used by the electors in voting for President and Vice President. Previously, the vice presidency went to the runner-up in the Electoral College vote. The Amendment also reduces the range of choice of the House of Representatives from the five highest to the three highest candidates when none has received an electoral-vote majority. The Senate's choice of Vice President under these circumstances is limited to the two highest candidates. *See* ELECTORAL COLLEGE, page 100.

Significance   The Twelfth Amendment developed out of the confusion in the election of 1800 in which party-pledged electors were chosen for the first time. Since each elector voted for two candidates, the result found Thomas Jefferson, the presidential candidate, tied with his own vice presidential candidate, Aaron Burr. The election was thrown into the House where the lame-duck Federalist party majority finally elected Jefferson President after toying with the idea of electing Burr to embarrass the Jeffersonian Republican party. To avoid such confusion in subsequent elections, the Twelfth Amendment specified that electors "name in their ballots the person voted for as President, and in distinct ballots the person voted for as Vice President." The Amendment adapted the Electoral College to the new political party system, which had not been anticipated by the Founding Fathers.

Twenty-fourth Amendment   An amendment to the Constitution, adopted in 1964, that forbids the levying of a poll tax in primary or general elections for national officials, including the President, Vice-President, and members of Congress. The Amendment does not apply to elections for state or local officials.

Significance   At the time of the ratification of the Twenty-fourth Amendment, only five states levied poll taxes and the Amendment was generally viewed as an attempt to placate growing Negro demands for voting rights. Failure to outlaw poll taxes in state and local elections made the Amendment largely ineffective with the result that Congress, in the 1965 Voting Rights Act, authorized a legal test of all poll taxes. In 1966, the Supreme Court declared that the levying of a poll tax for *any* election is unconstitutional (*Harper v. Virginia State Board of Elections,* 383 U.S. 663).

Twenty-third Amendment   An amendment to the Constitution, adopted in 1961, that enables the people of the District of Columbia to participate in the election of the President. The Twenty-third Amendment allots the District of Columbia three electoral votes. *See* DISTRICT OF COLUMBIA, page 31; ELECTORAL COLLEGE, page 100.

Significance   The Twenty-third Amendment increased the size of the Electoral College to 538 electors, beginning with the 1964 presidential election. Although President Kennedy proposed that voting eligibility in the District be established by ninety days' residence and at the age of eighteen, the Congress, in 1961, prescribed a residence of one year and a minimum voting age of twenty-one. Various groups in the District are continuing their agitation for congressional representation and local self-government.

Two-party System   Division of voter loyalties between two major political parties, resulting in the virtual exclusion of minor parties from sharing in political power. The two-party system is the traditional British system, which has been adopted in many Commonwealth countries and by the United States. *See* SINGLE-MEMBER DISTRICT, page 119; MULTIPLE-PARTY SYSTEM, page 106; THIRD PARTY, page 120.

Significance   The two-party system stems from tradition, the tendency to view problems in terms of black-or-white alternatives, and the use of the single-member district system. The two-party monopoly on governmental power has, on several occasions in American history, been seriously challenged by the rise of a third party. Under a single-member district electoral system, however, the third party cannot compete effectively for political power unless it displaces one of the major parties, as when the Republicans took over the major party status of the Whigs in 1860. Americans support the two-party system because it assures the election of legislative majorities, provides an effective and cohesive opposition, simplifies the role of the voter, and generally provides stability in government. Some opponents of the two-party system, however, charge that it creates artificial legislative majorities, narrows the voter's choice to two alternatives when there may be many, and makes a fetish of stability while denying minority parties and groups representation in the government.

Unit Rule   A rule, applicable in Democratic national conventions, providing that state delegations may cast their total votes in a block for a single presidential candidate. The unit rule is not imposed by the national convention; it is merely recognized when properly invoked by state party authorities. A state delegation may be instructed by the state party convention to use the unit rule, or it may, by a majority vote of its delegates, adopt the procedure. See NATIONAL CONVENTION, page 107.

Significance   Permission to invoke the unit rule in Democratic national conventions reflects the states' rights tradition of the party. It increases the influence of states using the unit rule over those which split their strength among several candidates. Southern state delegations have made effective use of the unit rule in maintaining a significant voice in the selection of Democratic presidential candidates. The Republican party does not recognize the unit rule and permits each delegate to cast his ballot individually.

Voting Qualifications   Requirements that prospective voters must fulfill to become eligible to vote. Qualifications imposed in all of the states include citizenship, age (twenty-one in all but Georgia and Kentucky [eighteen], Alaska [nineteen], and Hawaii [twenty]), and residence (commonly, one year). Special qualifications involving tax payments and literacy are imposed in a minority of the states. Additionally, most states disqualify mental incompetents, prison inmates, election-law violators, and vagrants. According to the Fifteenth and Nineteenth Amendments to the Constitution, no person may be disqualified by a state from voting because of race or sex. See DISFRANCHISE, page 100; LITERACY TEST, page 104; POLL TAX, page 112; REGISTRATION, page 116; RESIDENCE, page 117.

Significance   Fewer than fifty percent of the potential voters actually participate in most elections, and the best turnouts in presidential contests have only slightly exceeded sixty percent. Many potential voters are denied the ballot because of failure to qualify. Suggestions for improving voter participation include: (1) reducing residence requirements for most elections and eliminating them for presidential contests; (2) reducing the voting age to eighteen or nineteen through state action or by federal constitutional amendment; and (3) enforcing the federal Civil Rights Acts of 1957, 1960, 1964, and the Voting Rights Act of 1965 to prevent disfranchisement because of color or race. Although much could be accomplished by such actions, many observers believe that simple inertia and lack of interest by millions of people remain the major difficulties.

IMPORTANT CASES

Gray v. Sanders, 372 U.S. 368 (1963): Ruled that in a given constituency each person's vote must count equally. The case overturned the Georgia "county unit system" for primary elections for state-wide officers whereby the election was decided not by direct popular vote but by a system of county unit votes that discriminated against urban areas.

Significance   The Gray case marked the first explicit application of the "one man, one vote" principle by the Supreme Court. The Court stressed that the concept of political equality found in the Fifteenth, Seventeenth, and Nineteenth Amendments required equality of voting power when all voters are members of the same constituency, as in a state-wide election of a governor or senator.

Guinn v. United States, 238 U.S. 347 (1915): Declared "grandfather clauses" to be unconstitutional under the Fifteenth Amendment. These clauses had been used by many southern states to bestow the franchise upon white voters who had been disfranchised by state tax and literacy requirements intended to keep the Negroes from voting. The grandfather clauses granted the franchise to persons whose ancestors had voted prior to 1867.

Significance   Although the grandfather clause might have appeared to be a means of expanding the electorate, a creditable endeavor, the Court uncovered the subterfuge by recognizing the intent behind it. The decision put the Court on record as regarding any attempt, direct or roundabout, to disfranchise any group because of its color or race as a violation of the Fifteenth Amendment.

Smith v. Allwright, 321 U.S. 649 (1944): Established, finally and conclusively, that the "white primary" was a violation of the Fifteenth Amendment. The case arose over the denial of a ballot to Smith, a Negro resident of Houston, Texas, in the Democratic primary of 1940 for nominating candidates for congressional and state offices. The Court recognized that its earlier decision, allowing the exclusion of Negroes from "private" party primaries, in the case *Grovey v. Townsend,* 295 U.S. 45 (1935), had been "in error." The Court reasoned that the party was actually performing a state function in holding a primary election and was not acting as a private group. Moreover, the Court pointed out that a primary is an integral part of the election process.

Significance   In southern states, nomination in the Democratic primary is usually tantamount to winning the election. By being denied a vote in the primary, Negroes were prevented from effectively participating in the selection of public officials. By invoking the Fifteenth Amendment against a private group (political party), the Court closed a loophole which it had opened with its earlier interpretation. This case stands as an important landmark in the continuing legal battles to ensure voting rights for all. This decision resulted in more vigorous use of other techniques by southern states to keep Negroes from the polls, such as literacy tests and difficult registration procedures.

United States v. Classic, 313 U.S. 299 (1941): Upheld the power of Congress to supervise the holding of state primary congressional elections to ensure the right of the people to vote and to have their ballot counted. Classic, a Commissioner of Elections in Louisiana, was convicted for vote fraud under a federal criminal law prohibiting interference with constitutional rights. The Court based its decision on Article I, Section 4, of the Constitution which establishes the regulatory powers of Congress over congressional elections, holding that the primary is an integral part of the election process.

Significance   The Court's position, that Congress might validly regulate congressional primary elections in the states, overturned its earlier precedent established in *Newberry v. United States,* 256 U.S. 232 (1921). The Court recognized that the "times, places and manner" clause of the Constitution would be meaningless, especially in the one-party states of the South, if it were applied only to general elections and not to the primaries. In 1880, in *Ex parte Siebold,* 100 U.S. 371, the Court had upheld the power of Congress to regulate the conduct of general elections for national office.

IMPORTANT STATUTES

Electoral Count Act   An 1887 act of Congress that provides for settlement of disputes over the election of presidential electors. When more than one set of electors are certified by different authorities of a single state, Congress, voting as two separate houses, decides which to accept. If Congress fails to agree, the electors certified by the governor are accepted. *See* ELECTORAL COL-LEGE, page 100.

Significance   The Electoral Count Act resulted from the great confusion in the election of 1876. Hayes finally won the presidency over Tilden, 185 electoral votes to 184, after 20 contested electoral votes were awarded to Hayes on a strictly partisan basis by an Electoral Commission hastily created by Congress. The establishment of regular procedures is important not only because the outcome of such disputes within one or a few states may affect the outcome of a close presidential election, but also because the effectiveness of the democratic process depends upon the popular acceptance of election results.

Hatch Acts (Political Activities Acts of 1939, 1940)   Two important corrupt practices acts enacted by Congress. The first Hatch Act of 1939 forbids a political committee to spend more than $3 million in any campaign and limits individual contributions to a political committee to $5000. Federal civil service personnel may not be pressured in any way to make political contributions, and they are forbidden to participate actively in politics. The second Hatch Act of 1940 imposed similar restrictions on state and local employees working on projects supported by federal funds. *See* CORRUPT PRACTICES ACTS, page 97; *United Public Workers v. Mitchell,* page 194.

Significance   The Hatch Acts were intended to reduce the increasing influence of heavy campaign funds in winning elections and to free government employees from pressures exerted on them during campaigns by political superiors. The intent of Congress has not been fully realized. The $3 million spending limitation on any party committee has been easily evaded through the creation of additional committees and the decentralization of expenditures in state bodies. The provision that no one individual may contribute more than $5000 to a political committee has been circumvented by making several contributions to different committees and by letting other members of a family make contributions. The section of the law that forbids solicitation of government employees for contributions has been fairly effective, but many make "voluntary" contributions. In general, the Hatch Acts, like most corrupt practices legislation, have proved to be ineffective in correcting the weaknesses in the financing of American political campaigns.

Voting Rights Act of 1965   An act to eliminate restrictions on voting that have been used to discriminate against Negroes. The major provision of the Act automatically suspended the use of literacy or other tests subject to discriminatory manipulation. It authorized the registration of voters by federal registrars in any state or county where such tests were used in the 1964 election and where less than fifty percent of the eligible voters were registered or voted. The states of Alabama, Georgia, Louisiana, Mississippi, South Carolina, Virginia, and parts of North Carolina were mainly affected. Another provision of the Act authorized the Attorney General to bring suit to test the validity of poll taxes in state elections. In 1966, the Supreme Court declared payment of poll taxes as a condition for voting to be unconstitutional (*Harper v. Virginia State Board of Elections,* 383 U.S. 663). Major provisions of the Voting Rights Act of 1965 were upheld by the Supreme Court as a valid exercise of power under the Fifteenth Amendment (*South Carolina v. Katzenbach,* 383 U.S. 301 [1966]).

Significance   The Voting Rights Act was passed in response to dramatic Negro demonstrations during 1965 protesting discrimination in voting registration procedures. The voting provisions in the Civil Rights Acts of 1957, 1960, and 1964 relied upon slow moving judicial procedures to control discriminatory practices and proved ineffective. The Johnson Administration moved swiftly to implement the registration procedures and thousands of Negro voters have been added to the voting rolls. The Act has had a significant impact upon southern and national elections, including the election of numerous Negro officeholders.

Seven

The Legislative Process: Congress and the State Legislatures

Adjournment   To terminate a session of a legislative body. Adjournment sine die means to end the session without definitely fixing a day for reconvening. It is used to end a congressional session officially. Neither house of Congress can adjourn for more than three days without the concurrence of the other. *See* SESSION, page 154.

Significance   Under the Legislative Reorganization Act of 1946, Congress adjourns no later than the last day of July, unless Congress specifically provides otherwise. Under the Constitution, if the two houses of Congress cannot agree on an adjournment day, the President can determine it. This has never occurred.

Advice and Consent   The power vested in the United States Senate by the Constitution (Art. II, sec. 2) to give its advice and consent to the President in treaty-making and appointments. A two-thirds vote of the senators present is required for treaties. Appointments are confirmed by a simple majority vote. The Senate may give its advice through consultations between Senate leaders and the President, by resolutions setting out its position, or by delegating some of its members actually to sit in on the negotiations. *See* CONFIRMATION, page 133; RATIFICATION, page 148; RATIFICATION, page 334.

Significance   Although the Constitution's phraseology seems to associate the Senate with the President throughout the treaty-making process, President Washington, after several attempts to consult with the entire Senate, found it impractical, and initiated the tradition of consulting with the Senate only after a treaty had been negotiated and signed. Since World War II, however, Presidents have increasingly expanded the "advice" role of the Senate by inviting influential senators to participate in the negotiation of the treaty that created the United Nations, several treaties that established military alliances, and other significant treaties. The Senate generally accepts the nominees of the President for high-level positions, but in the case of many presidential appointments within states, the rule of "senatorial courtesy" applies.

Agenda   A list of specific items of business to be considered at a legislative session or at a conference or meeting.

126

Significance   The agenda sets out in itemized form the subjects to be taken up. Hence, by keeping an item off the agenda it can be killed through inaction. In Congress, the House Rules Committee and the Senate Majority Leader exercise considerable control over the agenda in their respective chambers.

Amendment   An action of a legislative body to delete, alter, or revise the language of a bill or an act. Bills in Congress may be amended at any one of a number of stages in the legislative process. Generally, amendments are printed, debated, and voted upon in the same way as a bill. Most laws enacted by Congress are, in fact, amendments to existing laws. *See* AMENDMENT, page 18.

Significance   Through the amending process, a bill may undergo such extreme revision or modification that it loses much of its original character. Often, instead of attempting to kill bills outright, legislators will add amendments to make them innocuous. Legislators may also try to kill bills by attaching amendments that are unacceptable to the majority of their house or the other chamber. Once a bill is enacted into law, it can be amended only through passage of new legislation.

Apportionment   The allocation of legislative seats. The Constitution (Art. I, sec. 2), and the Fourteenth Amendment (sec. 2) provide that representatives shall be apportioned among the several states according to their respective numbers. Under the Apportionment Act of 1929, Congress fixed the number of house seats at 435 and provided that the Census Bureau after each decennial census redistribute the seats among the fifty states, subject to congressional control. Each state, however, is assigned one representative before a population formula is applied. Under the 1960 reapportionment, sixteen states lost, and nine states gained, seats in the House. California led with an increase of eight seats. *See* GERRYMANDERING, page 139; REDISTRICTING, page 149.

Significance   With the mobility of the American people, gross under- or overrepresentation of states in the House is avoided through the "automatic" reapportionment by the Bureau of the Census that follows each ten-year census. Within the states, however, the responsibility for redistricting is then placed upon the majority party in each state legislature.

Appropriation   A legislative grant of money for a specific purpose. First, authorization bills, establishing a specific program, are enacted by Congress. Then, an appropriation bill is usually passed to provide the money to carry out the program. Appropriation bills originate in the House of Representatives by custom; revenue bills must originate in the House under the Constitution. *See* POWER OF THE PURSE, page 146.

Significance   In the American governmental system, no expenditure of public money can be made unless authorized by law. Thus, Congress and the state legislatures exercise "control over the purse strings"—one of the most important powers of legislative bodies.

Bicameralism   The principle of a two-house legislature, in contrast to unicameralism, or a legislature based on one house. At the Philadelphia convention of 1787, the Founding Fathers adopted a compromise solution for representation in Congress. This "Connecticut Compromise" established a balanced bicameral legislature with one house (House of Representatives) based on population and the second (Senate) based on equality of states. In the states, the Nebraska legislature is the only unicameral legislature. *See* UNICAMERALISM, page 158; CONNECTICUT COMPROMISE, page 20; *Reynolds v. Sims,* page 161.

Significance   A two-house legislature provides opportunity for two different types of representation and response to varying interests, such as population, area, and existing political units. Also, the second house can function in a capacity of revising and correcting mistakes made by the first chamber. Bicameralism is consistent with the principle of checks and balances. All bills must pass both houses before becoming law. Although the Supreme Court has declared that the electoral districts for both houses of state legislatures must be based on population (*Reynolds v. Sims,* 377 U.S. 533 [1964]), the American people continue to support bicameralism.

Biennial Session   A regular meeting of a legislature held every two years. Thirty-one state legislatures convene in regular session once every two years, while nineteen meet annually. In biennial session states, typically, legislatures hold their sessions in the odd-numbered years. *See* SESSION, page 154.

Significance   The biennial session was established for the state legislatures by state constitution framers early in our nation's history, partly from a desire to save money, and partly because of suspicions that if the legislature convened too frequently it might engage in mischievous doings. Biennial sessions have proved inadequate to meet the vast number of complex problems facing state governments today and frequent special sessions are necessary.

Bill   A proposed law. Most legislative proposals before Congress are in the form of bills. Members of the House officially "introduce" bills by dropping them into a "hopper"; in the Senate, bills are introduced by verbal anouncement. All bills introduced during a two-year congressional term are designated "HR" in the House and "S" in the Senate, with consecutive numbers assigned in the order in which they are introduced in each chamber. Each bill must have three readings in each house, be approved by a majority vote in each house, and, normally, be signed by the President to become law. A bill passed in one house is called an "engrossed bill," and the final authoritative copy of a bill passed by both houses and signed by their presiding officers is called an "enrolled bill." Public bills deal with matters of general concern and may become public laws. Private bills are concerned with individual matters and become private laws if approved. *See* PRIVATE BILL, page 147; READINGS, page 148.

Significance   Thousands of bills are introduced into every Congress. They are drawn up by pressure groups, interested citizens, congressional committees, individual congressmen, and by members of the executive branch. Only members of Congress, however, can introduce bills in their respective chambers. The great majority of these bills are killed because the committees in each house do not act upon them.

Bill Drafting   The process of formulating legislative proposals. Congress and many state legislatures have staff agencies to aid members in this process. In Congress, members seeking assistance in study and research have access to a Legislative Reference Service in the Library of Congress. Aid in drawing up bills is supplied by legislative counsel. *See* LEGISLATIVE REFERENCE SERVICE, page 160.

Significance   Bills must be drafted with precision. If enacted, the courts may refuse to sanction their enforcement if they are drawn in vague language that allows enforcement officers to exercise too much discretion.

Bloc   Members of a legislative body, not necessarily of the same party, who have common aims or goals. Some examples include the "farm bloc," "high tariff bloc," "silver bloc," and the "anti-civil rights bloc." *See* FARM BLOC, page 138.

Significance   Bloc voting in Congress and in state legislatures is a means by which the interests of a segment of the population can be effectively represented. It is basically a bipartisan approach. The danger inherent in voting blocs results from their narrow positions on specific issues; for thus rivalry is intensified and the legislative body may be split into warring factions. Bloc voting tends to reduce party responsibility.

Calendar   An agenda or list that contains the names of bills to be considered before committees or in either chamber of the legislature. When a standing committee of the House of Representatives reports out a bill it is placed on one of the five possible calendars: *Consent* (noncontroversial bills), *Discharge* (discharge petitions), *House* (nonfiscal public bills), *Private* (private bills), and *Union* (appropriation and revenue bills). In the Senate, all bills reported out go on a single calendar, although nonlegislative matters (treaties and confirmations) are placed on the *Executive* calendar.

Significance   The placement of a bill on a calendar is no guarantee that the bill will be considered by that chamber. Decisions as to which bills will be debated and voted on are made in the House by the Rules Committee and by the House party leaders, and in the Senate by the Majority Leader. In the Senate, the Minority Leader is consulted frequently in order to ensure unanimous consent agreement to consider bills. Many bills are killed because they are still on the calendars at the end of a two-year Congress.

Calendar Wednesday   A procedure of the House of Representatives whereby Wednesdays may be used to call the roll of the standing committees for the purpose of bringing up any of their bills for consideration from the House or the Union Calendars. General debate on each bill called up in this way is limited to two hours. Calendar Wednesday is not observed during the last two weeks of a session and, by a two-thirds vote, may be suspended any Wednesday, which usually is the case. *See* CALENDAR, page 129.

Significance   Calendar Wednesday is a device by which the committee chairmen in the House of Representatives can, when the rule is operative, bypass the Rules Committee and place a controversial bill before the House for debate and a vote. The frequent suspension of Calendar Wednesday testifies to the power of the House leadership to control the legislative process.

Caucus   A meeting of party members in one of the houses of a legislative body for the purpose of making decisions on selections of party leaders and on legislative business. Republicans in Congress prefer to call their party meeting a "conference." The term "to caucus" is also commonly used to describe any informal meeting of legislators seeking to reach agreement on a course of legislative action. *See* CAUCUS, page 95.

Significance   The majority caucus in each house makes important decisions regarding the organization of its chamber; these decisions then become official when they are ratified by that house in regular session. In Congress, the Democrats provide for "binding" caucus decisions regarding party stands on bills, with a two-thirds vote of the caucus required. No member is bound, however, if the party position involves a question of constitutional construction or a measure contrary to a pledge given by the member to his constituents. Republicans operate their conference on a majority-vote basis but do not seek to bind their members on voting positions. Some observers have recommended that the role of party caucuses in Congress be strengthened by providing for *binding* decisions on important legislative proposals. This, they suggest, would strengthen the democratic process by making the parties more responsible.

Censure   A power vested in each chamber of a legislative body by which the chamber can discipline its own members. Under the Constitution, "Each house may . . . punish its members for disorderly behavior, and, with the concurrence of two-thirds, expel a member." (Art. I, sec. 5). *See* EXPULSION, page 137.

Significance   Cases of either house censuring a member are rare. It has occurred on a few occasions; the most recent was the Senate's motion to "condemn" Senator Joseph McCarthy of Wisconsin, in 1954. Disciplinary measures can range in severity from adoption of a simple motion of censure to withdrawal of privileges and, in extreme cases, expulsion of a member. A censured legislator suffers the ostracism of his colleagues and loses much of his effectiveness as a legislator.

Census   A decennial enumeration of the total population of the United States, conducted by the Bureau of the Census. The Constitution provides that the population count be used for the purposes of apportioning direct taxes and representatives among the several states (Art. I, sec. 3). After the first census in 1790, new ones have been taken every ten years since. Approximately one-half of the states conduct a mid-decade census along the same lines as the federal census. The Census Bureau also collects data on a wide variety of subjects useful to Congress and the general public on such matters as business, housing, and units of government.

Significance   The American people have become extremely mobile, with considerable shifts in population occurring within the ten-year periods. The flow of population today is toward the West, resulting in a shift of political power in the same direction. After each census, the Census Bureau reapportions the seats in the House of Representatives on the basis of the new population statistics. No direct taxes are now levied by the federal government. States use census figures in apportioning grants and allowances for local governments.

Cloture (or Closure)   Rule 22 in the Senate, under which debate can be limited and a filibuster broken. One-sixth of the Senate membership can initiate action under cloture by petitioning the Senate to close debate on a pending measure. If such a petition is approved by two-thirds of the senators voting, thereafter no senator may speak for more than one hour on the bill being considered. Hence, in a short time the measure will come up for a vote and the attempt of the minority to "talk the bill to death" by filibuster will have been defeated. *See* FILIBUSTER, page 138.

Significance   Cloture safeguards majority rule by limiting the power of the Senate minority to kill bills by parliamentary maneuvers. Since Rule 22 was adopted in 1917, there have been over thirty cloture votes of which only seven have succeeded (Versailles Treaty, 1919; World Court, 1926; Branch Banking, 1927; Prohibition Reorganization, 1927; Communication's Satellite, 1962; Civil Rights, 1964; Voting Rights, 1965). The reluctance of senators to vote cloture stems from pride in the Senate's tradition of freedom of debate as well as from the practical fear of jeopardizing the minority weapon of filibuster, which each senator may some day want to use.

Committee Chairman   The member of the majority party who heads a standing or select legislative committee. In Congress, the chairmen of the twenty House and sixteen Senate standing committees are selected automatically under the rule of seniority. In most state legislatures, the committee chairmen are appointed by the Speaker in the lower house and usually by a committee on committees in the upper chamber. *See* STANDING COMMITTEE, page 156.

Significance   A committee chairman can exercise an almost decisive control over bills assigned to his committee. He determines when and if the committee will meet, which bills it will consider and the order of their consideration, whether public hearings will be held, and the appointment of subcommittees. He may also, depending upon his political acumen and personal relationships, push bills through his committee, guide them through floor debate, and serve as a member of a conference committee. Next to the Speaker of the House and the Majority Leader in the Senate, committee chairmen exercise the greatest influence over the legislative process. Although a committee majority may overrule its chairman, this seldom occurs because of a reluctance to challenge "the establishment."

Committee of the Whole   An informal procedure used by a legislative body to expedite business by resolving the official body into a committee for the consideration of bills and other matters. In Congress, this procedure is used only by the lower house, which becomes "The Committee of the Whole House [of Representatives] on the State of the Union." A temporary chairman is appointed by the Speaker and the formal rules are suspended.

Significance   Most House business is transacted in the Committee of the Whole. Advantages of this procedure include: (1) only 100 members need be present to constitute a quorum; (2) business is expedited through relaxed procedures; (3) time-consuming roll-call votes are not permitted, nor are members' votes put on record; (4) the full House retains control, in that it must act upon all decisions made by the Committee of the Whole.

Committee on Committees   Party committees that determine the assignments of party members to standing committees in the House of Representatives. The Republican Committee on Committees consists of one representative from each state having Republican members in the House. In voting within the Committee on Committees, each member casts the number of votes equal to the number of Republican members his state has in the House. The Democrats in caucus first choose their party's members of the House Ways and Means Committee and this group then determines the party's standing committee assignments. In the Senate, where only one-third of the seats are filled in each biennial election, a Committee on Committees of each party makes the necessary adjustments for each committee. In the state legislatures, committees in the lower house are appointed by the Speaker of the House. In the upper house, the procedure varies: selections may be made by the presiding officer, by the chamber as a whole, or by a committee on committees. *See* STANDING COMMITTEE, page 156.

Significance   Selections of committee personnel made unofficially in these ways are, typically, approved by the respective party caucuses and thence by their respective chambers. The power to assign committee members is significant because it will largely determine the role that an individual legislator will play as well as substantially influence the fate of any bill a committee might consider that session.

Concurrent Resolution   A special measure, designated "H Con Res" or "S Con Res," that requires approval by both houses of Congress but does not need the President's signature. *See* JOINT RESOLUTION, page 143; SIMPLE RESOLUTION, page 155.

Significance   Concurrent resolutions of Congress are used to make or amend joint rules or to express the sentiment of Congress on some issue or event. Their most important use is as a legislative veto over the President's exercise of powers delegated to him by Congress. Examples might include congressional disapproval of presidential reorganization plans or congressional opinion regarding fixing the date for adjournment, creating joint committees, and welcoming official foreign visitors to the United States with special greetings.

Conference Committee   A special joint committee appointed to reconcile differences when a bill passes the two houses of Congress in different forms. A joint conference committee consists of three to nine "managers" appointed by the Speaker of the House and the President of the Senate. Efforts are directed toward a compromise version of the bill, which must be approved by a majority of the managers for each house voting separately. This compromise version, in the form of a "conference report," then goes for approval to each house. It cannot there be amended, and, if rejected by either house, it may go back to conference for further negotiation.

Significance The most important bills frequently end up in conference committees; differences over bills of lesser importance are usually ironed out by securing the agreement of each chamber to the other's amendments. Frequently, great power is wielded by these committees. Many important bills are substantially rewritten in conference or are killed through failure to achieve a compromise agreement. Meetings of the committees are always secret. Their power is reflected in the large number of times that the two houses accept conference reports and enact them into law.

Confirmation The power of a legislative body to approve nominations made to fill executive and judicial positions. Nominations for such offices made by the President must be confirmed by the Senate with a majority vote. Many of the appointments made by the governors in the various states must also be approved by the upper houses of the legislatures. *See* SENATORIAL COURTESY, page 153; APPOINTMENT POWER, page 164.

Significance All federal judges are appointed subject to senatorial confirmation. Most important diplomatic and administrative positions not under civil service or other merit systems also come under senatorial scrutiny. Often a President will confer with the Senate leaders before nominating an individual for a cabinet position, to determine in advance that he is *persona grata* (acceptable). In the case of appointments to federal positions located in the several states, the senior senator of the President's party from the state in which the appointment is to be made actually selects the appointee, thus reversing the constitutional procedure. This is known as "senatorial courtesy."

Congressional Directory A handbook published annually that contains information regarding the organization of Congress and its committees and brief biographical sketches of the senators and representatives.

Significance The Congressional Directory is a useful reference guide for citizens and students of government found in most libraries.

Congressional District A geographical division of a state from which one member of the House of Representatives is elected. *See* GERRYMANDERING, page 139; REDISTRICTING, page 149; *Wesberry v. Sanders,* page 162.

Significance Districts generally are drawn up by the partisan majorities in state legislatures in such a way as to favor their party's candidates in congressional elections (gerrymandering). For many years, Congress provided that state legislatures draw up congressional districts as "compact and contiguous" areas, substantially equal in population; but since 1929, Congress has not specified criteria for redistricting. As a result of the Supreme Court's 1964 decision in *Wesberry v. Sanders,* 376 U.S. 1, that congressional districts must be based on substantial equality of population, Congress has reconsidered the problem of establishing standards.

Congressional Record A verbatim record of the proceedings (debates, speeches, and votes) in both the House and the Senate, printed daily. Members may edit their remarks and speeches before printing, and they also may insert material, called "extension of remarks," that was not actually delivered on the floor of their chamber. *See* EXTENSION OF REMARKS, page 138.

Significance   The *Congressional Record* is a valuable source of data and resource materials for the student of Congress. The inclusion of committee reports enhances its utility. The increasing length and rising costs of the *Record,* however, are matters of concern to economy-minded citizens.

Congressman at Large   A member of the House of Representatives who is elected by the voters of an entire state rather than by those of a specific district. If a state gains seats following a decennial reapportionment and fails to redistrict, the new seats will be filled by election at large. If a state loses seats and fails to redistrict, then all of the state's congressmen will be elected at large, an arrangement that may result in one party's winning all the seats. States with only one member of the House will, of course, always elect that one at large. Decisions concerning redistricting are made by the majority party in the state legislatures. *See* AT LARGE, page 93.

Significance   Election of congressmen at large usually results from a legislative deadlock or the refusal of a court to accept a redistricting plan. Increasing pressures from the courts to redistrict on a population basis after each decennial census, however, have reduced the likelihood of electing congressmen at large.

Constituent   A resident of a legislator's district. The district itself is sometimes referred to as the member's constituency.

Significance   Legislators must act in the capacity of a go-between in the relationship of the average citizen with his national and state governments. Much of a legislator's day must be spent in answering letters, running errands, showing the sights to visitors, and similar activities on behalf of his constituents. Although this keeps a congressman in close contact with the voters, some constituents regard their representatives as errand boys. As a result, the legislator may be overburdened and unable to devote sufficient time to dealing with the important law-making function.

Constituent Power   Participation in the process of making, amending, or revising a constitution. The constituent power of Congress consists of its authority to propose amendments to the United States Constitution by a two-thirds vote of both houses, or to call a national convention for this purpose on petition of two-thirds of the state legislatures. Amendment proposals must be ratified by three-fourths of the state legislatures or by specially elected conventions in three-fourths of the states. In the states, the legislatures are usually empowered to propose specific amendments to their state constitutions. Extensive revisions of state constitutions are generally done by constitutional conventions established solely for that purpose. Ratification of state constitutional changes is vested in the people of the state. *See* AMENDMENT, page 18; CONSTITUTIONAL CONVENTION, page 363.

Significance   Under a system of limited government, the fundamental law found in the constitution provides for the regulated exercise of power by the three branches of government. To the extent that the legislature exercises some considerable powers of a constituent nature, it can affect and change the nature of the limitations placed upon itself as well as those placed upon the other two branches of government.

Contempt of Congress Willful obstruction of the legislative process. Authority is vested in both houses of Congress and in their investigating committees to cite for contempt of Congress any subpoenaed witness who refuses to appear or to give testimony under oath. The Supreme Court has upheld this power by asserting: "It is unquestionably the duty of all citizens to cooperate with the Congress . . . to respond to subpoenas . . . and to testify fully with respect to matters within the province of proper investigation." (*Watkins v. United States*, 354 U.S. 178 [1957]). Contempt citations are referred by the presiding officer of the offended chamber to the Department of Justice for criminal prosecution through the federal courts. *See Watkins v. United States*, page 162; *McGrain v. Daugherty*, page 161; INVESTIGATING COMMITTEE, page 142.

Significance The contempt power of Congress, though it might occasionally be misused, is essential if Congress is to have the authority to conduct meaningful investigations to learn facts on which to base legislative decisions. As currently interpreted by the courts, valid contempt citations may not be issued for refusal of a witness to testify when: (1) the subject under examination is beyond the proper scope of authority of the committee; (2) questions directed to a witness are not pertinent to the subject being investigated; (3) answers of the witness might provide evidence that could be used against him in a criminal case.

Contested Election Controversy over seating competing claimants to a legislative seat or the qualifications of an elected member. Article I, section 5 of the Constitution states: "Each house shall be the judge of the elections, returns, and qualifications of its own members. . . ." State constitutions have similar provisions. When the election of a member is contested, the chamber concerned sets up a committee to conduct an investigation.

Significance The Constitution makes Congress the exclusive judge of the qualifications of its members. The House and the Senate on occasion have refused to seat elected members for reasons other than those related to constitutional qualifications. Examples include the barring of a polygamist in 1900, of a socialist in 1919, and, in 1926, of two senators because they had exceeded lawful campaign expenditures. Similar cases have occurred in several state legislatures.

Deficiency Appropriation A special bill appropriating funds to make up the difference between an agency's appropriation for the fiscal year and the amount deemed necessary to enable it to continue to operate for the full fiscal year. *See* SUPPLEMENTARY APPROPRIATION, page 157.

Significance Deficiency bills become necessary because of miscalculation in the budget process or because of new developments requiring greater activity by the agencies concerned. Unlike regular appropriations, which are made for the next fiscal year, deficiency appropriations are for the same fiscal year in which they are passed.

Delegation of Power   The transfer of authority from one government or branch of government, that has been constitutionally assigned the power, to another branch, or specific agency. Generally, delegations of power have involved the transfer of legislative power by Congress to the President, to an executive department or official, or to independent regulatory commissions. *See Opp Cotton Mills v. Administrator of Wage and Hour Division,* page 194; QUASI-LEGISLATIVE, page 190.

Significance   The tendency of Congress and state legislatures to delegate legislative powers has increased as legislative workloads have become burdensome and highly technical. Involved in all such delegations, however, is the constitutional question of the legality of the transfer. The United States Supreme Court, for example, struck down the National Industrial Recovery Act of 1933 in two significant cases in 1935, holding that Congress could not constitutionally transfer its legislative power to the President or to an executive agency (*Panama Refining Co. v. Ryan,* 293 U.S. 388 [1935]; *Schecter Poultry Corp. v. U.S.,* 295 U.S. 495 [1935]). In another case, the Supreme Court held that Congress may not delegate its constitutional powers to the states (*Knickerbocker Ice Co. v. Stewart,* 253 U.S. 149 [1920]). In the field of foreign affairs, however, the Supreme Court upheld a sizable delegation of power to the President by Congress on the ground that the President has a special responsibility in foreign affairs (*United States v. Curtiss-Wright,* 299 U.S. 304 [1936]). The Supreme Court has also laid down the general rule that, if delegations of legislative power are to be considered valid, Congress must determine the general policies and establish clear standards to guide the President or agency in making detailed applications of the general law.

Dilatory Motion   An irrelevant or nongermane motion in a legislative body to delay or prevent action on a bill.

Significance   Dilatory motions are not allowed under the rules of either house of Congress, but considerable discretion is left to the presiding officers in enforcement of these rules. They are potentially most useful in the hands of the minority to force concessions by disrupting the time schedule of the majority.

Direct Legislation   Electoral devices that enable voters to participate directly in deciding governmental policies. Direct methods include the initiative and the referendum. *See* INITIATIVE, page 141; REFERENDUM, page 149.

Significance   About twenty states authorize the initiative and/or the referendum. The initiative enables the people of a state to circumvent the inaction of their state legislature. The referendum is a means by which the people can "veto" laws passed by their state legislature before they become effective. In both the initiative and the referendum, the legislature cannot repeal the action of the people. There are no provisions for direct legislation in the national government.

Discharge Rule   A procedure by which a bill in the House of Representatives may be forced out of a committee (discharged) that has refused to report it out for consideration by the House. Bills not reported out within thirty days after referral to a committee may be subject to discharge. The discharge motion must be signed by an absolute majority (218) of the House membership. If the motion to discharge the bill carries by a simple majority vote, consideration of the bill then becomes a matter of high privilege. The Rules Committee may be discharged of a bill after it has held it for only seven legislative days. *See* STANDING COMMITTEE, page 156.

Significance   The discharge rule is one means by which the majority of the House can overcome the "minority" power of legislative committees, which can kill bills by refusing to report them out for consideration. It is used only on rare occasions, since members are reluctant to challenge the prerogatives of committees and their chairmen. Similar to the discharge rule is the discharge resolution in the Senate, which may be initiated by an ordinary motion. Many state legislatures also vest discharge powers in the majority of each house.

Division   A method of voting used in a legislative body. Members voting for or against the motion alternately rise, and are counted by the presiding officer. *See* RECORD VOTE, page 149; TELLER VOTE, page 157; VIVA VOCE VOTE, page 158.

Significance   No record is made of how individual members vote in a division or "standing" vote. Division has the advantage of enabling an accurate count to be made without delay. Its disadvantage lies in the way members may successfully hide their vote from their constituents, weakening democratic responsibility.

Executive Session   A meeting of a legislative body or committee that is closed to the public. Executive sessions are used mainly by committees to interrogate witnesses and to vote on reporting out bills.

Significance   Executive sessions permit greater freedom for members to express themselves, knowing they will not be put on record. The main disadvantage is that they may tend to encourage irresponsible action which can be hidden from public view. Although most committee decisions are made in closed sessions in Congress and in state legislatures, frequently the vote of individual members is made available to the public. City commissions and councils and other local policy-determining bodies often make important decisions in executive committee of the whole sessions prior to the public meeting. Thus, in the formal meeting the group may give the impression of consensus and agreement, when, in reality, major battles had already been fought out at the earlier secret session.

Expulsion   The power of a legislative body, usually exercised by each chamber separately, to expel a member as an extreme disciplinary measure. Typical grounds for expulsion include conduct unbecoming a member, disloyalty, and moral turpitude. By Article I, section 5 of the Constitution, each house is empowered to expel a member with the concurrence of two-thirds of the members of that chamber. State constitutions generally vest similar powers in state legislatures. *See* CENSURE, page 130.

Significance   Expulsion is a rarely used power of legislative bodies. Members usually try to reconcile differences and, if absolutely necessary, to mete out punishment in the form of censure or denial of privileges.

Extension of Remarks   Material incorporated into the *Congressional Record* by a member of Congress, although not delivered verbally on the floor of either chamber. Permission to extend remarks is required by the member's house and is ordinarily granted. Material that elaborates on remarks made by the member on the floor follows the text of his speech; other insertions are printed in the appendix. *See* CONGRESSIONAL RECORD, page 133.

Significance   The extension-of-remarks privilege enables a member to record his position on legislative matters even though he had not been able, or did not wish, to do so orally on the floor of his chamber. Many such insertions are aimed at influencing a congressman's constituents and not other members. Some students of Congress criticize the tendency of members of Congress to misuse the extension-of-remarks privilege by inserting irrelevant materials and personal propaganda. Excerpts are often mailed to constituents who may view such materials as officially endorsed by Congress.

Farm Bloc   A group made up of both Democratic and Republican representatives and senators from the farm states, who put aside party differences to pass legislation favorable to the farmers. The creation of this voting bloc in the early part of the twentieth century followed the attempts of the farmers to achieve their aims through the creation of various farmers' parties that had been unsuccessful in challenging the two major parties. *See* BLOC, page 129.

Significance   The farm bloc was for many years one of the most consistent and successful voting alignments in Congress and in most state legislatures largely because of overrepresentation of farm areas. Increasing urban representation is modifying the power of the farm bloc. Moreover, the farm bloc has lost some of its effectiveness because of the failure of farmers and farm organizations to agree on solutions to farm problems.

Filibuster   A parliamentary device used in the United States Senate by which a minority of senators seek to frustrate the will of the majority by literally "talking a bill to death." Senators are proud of their chamber's reputation for being the world's greatest forum for free discussion. Custom and the Senate rules provide for unlimited debate on a motion before it can be brought to a vote. A filibuster is a misuse of this freedom of debate, since full exploration of the merits and demerits of the pending measure is not its objective. Rather, the minority of senators seeks to gain concessions or the withdrawal of the bill by delaying tactics. These include prolonged debate and speeches on relevant and irrelevant topics, parliamentary maneuvers, dilatory motions, and other tricks of the legislative game. The objective of the minority is to delay action on the measure interminably, until the majority is forced by the press of other business to withdraw it from consideration. *See* CLOTURE, page 131.

Significance   Over the years, many important bills have been filibustered to death. Many more have been killed by using the threat of a filibuster to force withdrawal of a bill. Until the enactment of the Civil Rights Act of 1957, the filibuster or threat of it had been used successfully for many years by southern senators to forestall civil rights legislation. Senator Strom Thurmond of South Carolina holds the record for the longest individual filibuster, speaking for more than twenty-four hours against enactment of civil rights legislation in 1957. Filibusters may be defeated by the use of cloture under Rule 22 or by round-the-clock sessions of the Senate.

Franking Privilege   Enables members of Congress to send materials through the mail free by substituting their facsimile signature (frank) for postage. Free mail privileges have also been accorded by Congress to other officials and agencies of the national government.

Significance   The franking privilege provides a means by which members of Congress can keep their constituents informed on issues, voting records, and other business. It is a recognition that the "representative" function of Congress requires that means be provided by which the individual congressman can keep in contact with his constituents.

Freedom of Debate   The right of members of a legislative body in a democratic system of government to freely discuss, deliberate, and act upon matters of policy without fear of legal action. The Constitution (Art. I, sec. 6), provides that "for any speech or debate in either House, they [Senators and Representatives] shall not be questioned in any other place." Utterances that might otherwise be unlawful are privileged, therefore, when made in Congress (*U.S. v. Johnson,* 383 U.S. 169 [1966]). Immunity to suit does not ordinarily apply to statements made outside of Congress. In all cases, however, whether such statements are made in or out of Congress, members can be held to account through the disciplinary powers of their own house. State constitutions generally provide similar immunity for legislators. Freedom of debate is sometimes used to describe the right to speak indefinitely on a pending measure in the United States Senate.

Significance   The purpose of ensuring maximum freedom of debate is to guarantee that decisions made by the legislative body will be freely made after thorough debate. Without such a guarantee, members might become too restricted in their deliberations to do a good job of legislating. On occasion, however, a member can abuse this right by unjustly slurring the reputation of a citizen, who has no recourse in the courts.

Gerrymandering   The drawing of legislative district boundary lines with a view to obtaining partisan or factional advantage. Gerrymandering is engaged in frequently by partisan majorities in state legislatures when they are drawing up congressional and state legislative districts. The objective is to spread the support for one's own party over many districts and to concentrate the support for the other party in few districts. Gerrymandering is possible because of the pattern of consistency in voting behavior of most Americans. *See*

Wesberry v. Sanders, page 162; *Reynolds v. Sims,* page 161; REDISTRICTING, page 149.

Significance   Most redistricting laws enacted by state legislatures show evidence of varying degrees of boundary manipulation for partisan advantage. Gerrymandering resulted in gross overrepresentation of rural areas in the House of Representatives and in most state legislatures. In 1964, the Supreme Court ruled that congressional and state legislative districts should be drawn on a basis of substantial equality of population. Nevertheless, the boundaries of districts that are substantially equal in population may still be drawn to secure partisan advantage, and gerrymandering persists. Thus, a minority of a state's voters may elect a majority of that state's congressional delegation and a majority in both houses of the state legislature.

Hearing   A public session of a committee of a legislative body to obtain information on a proposed law or resolution. In Congress, public hearings are commonly functions of subcommittees, which report their findings to the full committees. The theory behind public hearings is that out of the "combat" between contestants using every ethical means to convince committee members of the wisdom of their positions will emerge the "true facts." The members can then make their decision, much like a judge and jury in a judicial proceeding. The hearings thus serve as a means by which American citizens can "petition" their elected representatives and seek to influence their decision-making. *See* INVESTIGATING COMMITTEE, page 142.

Significance   Most hearings involve only professional lobbyists. Commonly, administration officials are pitted against private lobbyists. In recent years, there has been an increasing tendency for committees to use hearings to try to influence public opinion or executive action, as in the areas of communism, foreign policy, and crime. Public hearings are used extensively and are a valuable legislative aid. All state legislatures also provide for public hearings on important measures.

High Crimes and Misdemeanors   The Constitution provides in Article II, section 4, that the President, Vice President, and all civil officers of the United States are subject to impeachment and removal from office upon conviction for "treason, bribery, or other high crimes and misdemeanors." There has been no attempt to define precisely what acts might constitute high crimes and misdemeanors. Discretion is vested completely in Congress. *See* IMPEACHMENT, page 141.

Significance   In practice, probably based on English historical precedent, the grounds on which impeachment action is taken are usually restricted to unethical conduct and criminal offenses. Congress has not regarded incompetence or political disagreement as grounds for invoking its impeachment powers. Yet, because so much discretion is vested in Congress by the Constitution, the threat of its use may sometimes constitute a potent weapon.

House of Representatives   The lower house of the bicameral Congress, in which representation is based on population. The upper house, the Senate of the United States, is based on the principle of state equality. The House was intended by the Founding Fathers to be the popular chamber of Congress, and it was made larger and more responsive to the public will than the Senate, which was intended to be the more deliberative body. Each state is guaranteed at least one representative. Since 1910, the House has had a permanent membership of 435. The ratio of population to representatives has been steadily increasing until now it is more than 450,000 per representative. The Constitution vests certain powers exclusively in the House. Among them are: (1) the impeachment power; (2) the initiation of revenue bills; (3) the election of a President if no candidate obtains a majority in the Electoral College; (4) the determination of its own rules of procedure; and (5) the discipline of its members. *See* SENATE, page 152.

Significance   Some critics reject the assertion that the House is the more representative of the two houses of Congress. They point out that because many representatives tend to stress local interests, the House may be less responsive to national problems than the Senate. Its unwieldy size, and the power vested in the Rules Committee, often make it less able than the Senate to cope with contemporary legislative problems. Nevertheless, the American voter tends to regard his representative as his most direct contact with the national government.

Impeachment   A formal accusation, rendered by the lower house of a legislative body, that commits an accused civil official for trial in the upper house. Impeachment is, therefore, merely the first step in a two-stage process. In the national government, constitutional authority to *impeach* is vested in the House and the power to *try* impeachment cases rests with the Senate. All civil officers of the United States are subject to impeachment, excluding military officers and members of Congress. The impeachment process begins with the preferring of charges by a representative, followed by referral to either the Judiciary Committee or to a special investigating committee. A simple majority vote of the House is sufficient to impeach. "Articles of impeachment" are drawn up, setting forth the basis for removal. The House appoints managers who prosecute the case in a trial before the Senate. If a President is on trial, the Chief Justice of the United States presides. The procedure during the trial closely resembles that of a court of law. A two-thirds vote of the Senators present is necessary for conviction. The only punishments that may be meted out are removal from office and disqualification from holding any office in the future. Once removed, however, the individual may be tried in a regular court of law if he has committed a criminal act. The President's pardoning power does not apply to impeachment convictions. *See* HIGH CRIMES AND MISDEMEANORS, page 140.

Significance   In the course of American history, only twelve officers have been impeached and only four—all judges—convicted. President Andrew Johnson was acquitted by the margin of a single vote in 1868. Few state officials have been convicted and removed by state legislatures. Occasionally, partisan politics may influence the exercise of the power as was true in the Johnson case and in the removal of several state officials by their legislatures.

Initiative   An electoral device by which interested citizens can propose legislation or constitutional amendments through initiatory petitions signed by the required number of registered voters. The number of signatures varies from five to fifteen percent of the voters in the different states. The proposition is then voted on by the people. Constitutional amendment proposals usually require a greater number of signatures on the petitions. The "direct" initiative involves a vote of the people following the filing of petitions. The "indirect" provides that the proposal, after being filed, be sent to the legislature; if not approved, it then goes before the voters. See DIRECT LEGISLATION, page 136.

Significance   Fewer than one half of the states provide for the initiative in either form. About twenty states permit its use for ordinary laws, and thirteen for constitutional amendments. Only one state, Alaska, has adopted the initiative since 1918. The United States Constitution does not provide for a national initiative, but groups have, from time to time, advocated its adoption.

Investigating Committee   A legislative committee that exercises a fact-finding role as an aid to the law-making process. Investigating committees may compel witnesses to attend and to produce relevant materials. Investigations are conducted by both the regular standing committees and by special committees created for that purpose. The purposes behind investigations include: (1) finding of facts on which to base legislation; (2) discovering or developing of public opinion; (3) overseeing of administrative agencies; (4) uncovering the questionable activities of public officials and private individuals; and (5) sometimes securing personal or partisan political gain. In terms of time, effort, and publicity, the investigatory activities of Congress and of some state legislatures have in recent years rivaled their legislative functions. A legislative body may investigate any subject that is properly within the scope of its legislative powers. See McGrain v. Daugherty, page 161; Watkins v. United States, page 162; WATCHDOG COMMITTEE, page 159.

Significance   Many important topics have been investigated in the over 600 congressional investigations in the nation's history. Some have been mere "fishing expeditions" and others were politically motivated by attempts to embarrass the rival party. Increasingly, Congress has relied on investigations as a means of seeking to regain its position of power vis-à-vis the executive branch, which has steadily gained in relative power during this century. Serious questions have been raised concerning the scope of congressional inquiries, the rights of witnesses who appear before committees, the fairness of procedures, and the extraction of testimony from unwilling witnesses. Congress has sought to deal with some of these problems through the study and correction of procedures and the setting up of a "fair play" guarantee for witnesses. Several presidents have refused to permit executive officials to appear before investigating committees on matters pertaining to national security or executive prerogatives.

Joint Committee   A legislative committee composed of members of both houses. The number appointed to a joint committee is usually divided equally between the two houses, with each member having one vote. On some, such as conference committees, each chamber may determine the size of its membership on the committee, and the two groups vote separately on measures. Joint committees are usually select (special) committees appointed for a specified purpose: typically, to conduct investigations. Congress has created a few standing (permanent) joint committees, such as the Joint Committee on the Economic Report, and the Joint Committee on Atomic Energy.

Significance   Joint committees make it possible for the two houses of a legislative body to work out compromises on bills or mutual problems. They tend to encourage greater cooperation between the two chambers. Some observers have recommended that all standing committees of Congress be joint committees, so that time-consuming duplication of the existing dual-committee system could be eliminated. Supporters of this proposal believe that it would result in quicker and more effective action on most bills and would eliminate the need for two appearances before separate committees by persons wishing to testify for or against a bill. Opponents point out that such a change would eliminate much of the effectiveness of the checks and balances system inherent in a bicameral legislative body.

Joint Resolution   A measure, similar to a bill, that must be approved in both chambers and by the executive. In Congress, joint resolutions are designated "H J Res" and "S J Res" and, if passed by a simple majority in both houses, must be signed by the President to become law. The procedure is identical to that used in passing a bill into law except when the joint resolution is used to propose an amendment to the Constitution. Then the President's signature is unnecessary. About half of the state legislatures also employ the joint resolution in enacting laws and proposing constitutional amendments. *See* CONCURRENT RESOLUTION, page 132; SIMPLE RESOLUTION, page 155.

Significance   Joint resolutions are employed by Congress to approve of executive actions in foreign affairs or to take the initiative in foreign policy. They have occasionally proved useful in circumventing the two-thirds vote requirement in the Senate on treaty matters, as in the annexation of Texas and of Hawaii. Joint resolutions are also used for such limited matters as the passing of a single appropriation bill for a designated purpose.

Joint Session   A meeting of the members of both chambers of a legislative body.

Significance   Congress meets in joint session to count the electoral votes and certify the election of the President, and when addressed by the President or a foreign dignitary. A joint session is never used to consider specific bills. Most state legislatures meet in joint session to receive the governor's annual message.

Legislative Council   An interim committee employed by some legislatures between sessions to study state problems and to plan a legislative program. In some states, legislative councils have pursued extensive fact-finding research programs. The councils range in size from five members to the entire legislature. Usually, membership is selected from the two houses of the legislature, but, in several states, the governor is authorized to include representation from the executive branch.

Significance   Legislative councils are a means by which the legislatures of three-fourths of the states have sought to develop leadership and planning facilities staffed by their own members. In this way, dependence on the executive to formulate a comprehensive program for consideration by the legislature is reduced. Moreover, as the workload becomes heavier and more complex, legislatures are becoming more dependent upon well-prepared programs worked out carefully in advance. The fear that power might become too concentrated in the hands of those legislators making up the councils has not been justified in the experience of the states that have adopted the plan.

Logrolling   An arrangement by which two or more members of a legislative body agree in advance to support each other's bills. The technique pertains especially to the trading of votes among legislators in order to gain support for appropriations beneficial to each legislator's home district. See PORK BARREL LEGISLATION, page 145.

Significance   To the extent that logrolling exists, it probably results from the American belief that a representative should seek to "deliver the goods" for his home district. This encourages "horse trading" of votes. Logrolling is inevitable in legislative bodies in which strong party discipline does not prevail.

Majority Floor Leader   The chief spokesman and strategist of the majority party who directs the party's forces in legislative battles. In the House, only the Speaker is considered to be more influential. In the Senate, the Majority Leader is the undisputed leader of his party. Floor leaders seek to carry out decisions of their party's caucus and are aided by party whips. Their counterparts in the other party are the minority floor leaders. Floor leaders are selected by their respective party caucuses. Similar party leadership positions exist in most state legislatures. See WHIP, page 159.

Significance   Much of the success of a floor leader depends on his ability. If he is an able organizer and possesses personal leadership characteristics, he can exercise considerable influence on legislation. In the Senate, he must work closely with the minority leader because much business is transacted through unanimous consent.

Morning Hour   A period reserved in Congress at the start of a legislative day to consider routine business. The Senate sets aside the first two hours of each new legislative day for such matters as committee reports, the introduction of bills and resolutions, and the receipt of presidential messages. In the House, the morning hour is seldom used since most routine business is transacted in the Committee of the Whole.

Significance   The morning hour frees the remainder of the Senate's legislative day for consideration of pending legislation. During the morning hour, Senators may speak on a variety of topics not necessarily related to current business. Senate committees often meet during that chamber's morning hour.

Pair   An understanding reached in advance between two legislators, holding opposing views on a bill, to withhold their votes on a yea-and-nay roll call.

In this way, each is assured that his absence from the chamber during the vote will not affect the outcome. In effect, each member of the pair cancels out the other's vote. A "special" pair applies to one or several votes taken on the same subject. A "general" pair, occasionally used in the Senate, applies to all votes taken over a specified period of time. On a question requiring a two-thirds vote, two members must be "paired for" the measure to balance off one "paired against" it.

Significance   The advantage of pairing lies in the nature of the "gentlemen's agreement" between the two lawmakers. Neither can show up unexpectedly and vote in the roll call without breaking the agreement. Each, in effect, casts a vote by cancelling out the other's vote, although they are not counted in vote totals. Members of Congress frequently find it necessary to be absent from their chamber, and pairing enables them to put their position on bills on record.

Pigeonhole   To kill a bill in committee by putting it aside and not reporting it out for consideration by the chamber. The term relates to the old-time desks in committee rooms of Congress, which had open "pigeonholes" rather than drawers with handles. To pigeonhole a bill means, figuratively, to open the desk and file the bill away and forget it. This usually kills the bill.

Significance   More bills die in committee each congressional session than are rejected by the two houses. The same is true in the state legislatures. Chances for a pigeonholed bill to be enacted into law are slight because members of the chamber are reluctant to use the extraordinary procedures required to discharge bills from committee.

Policy Committee   A party committee in Congress that works with party leaders to formulate plans and strategy. A majority and minority policy committee function in each chamber. With the floor leader, the majority policy committee often determines the order in which measures will be considered. Representation on the policy committees is given to all major regions of the nation and important factions within the party.

Significance   Policy committees have superseded the Democratic and Republican steering committees as the basic party strategy organs. Their importance to the legislative process varies, depending upon the degree of party unity and the personalities and drive of the individuals on the committees. The majority policy committee in the Senate plays a more vital role than its House counterpart because of the power of the House Rules Committee over the agenda.

Pork Barrel Legislation   Appropriations made by a legislative body providing for expenditures of sums of public money on local projects not critically needed. The term is closely related to logrolling, in that members of the legislative body usually do not question each other's pet projects for fear that their own may be voted down. It is frequently a simple matter of *quid pro quo*—that is, "You scratch my back and I'll scratch yours." *See* LOGROLLING, page 144.

Significance   Pork barrel legislation results in the expenditure of large sums of money each year. Basically, the problem relates to the theory of representation. The American representative goes to his legislature or to Congress as the representative of the people of his district rather than of the state or nation. This means that he will be expected by his constituents to perform creditably on their behalf. If he can obtain "pork" (appropriations for local highways, river and harbor construction projects, and so forth) by raiding the pork barrel (the state or national treasury) he is likely to improve his chances for re-election.

Power of the Purse   The historic power of democratic legislative bodies to control the finances of government. The power extends to both revenue and appropriation functions. In the national government, the Constitution specifies that "No money shall be drawn from the Treasury, but in consequence of appropriations made by law." (Art. I, sec. 9). New programs must be twice approved, first, through authorization and, second, through appropriation to finance them. Expenditures by the executive must be validated by the General Accounting Office to ensure that such outlays fall within the limits of appropriations made by Congress. Additional checks are carried on through the "watchdog" oversight committees of Congress. *See* APPROPRIATION, page 127; WATCHDOG COMMITTEE, page 159.

Significance   The "power of the purse" remains a major power of all legislative bodies. The power can be used in an affirmative manner to force positive action by government as well as in a negative way to stop action. The threat of budget cutting is usually enough to elicit cooperation from executive officials. Historically, legislative bodies first succeeded in limiting executive absolutism through control of the purse. One of the major grievances leading to the American Revolution was the taxation of the colonists without their consent.

President Pro Tempore   The temporary presiding officer of the Senate in the absence of the Vice President. He is elected by the Senate, following his nomination by the majority party caucus. He is eligible for the presidency of the United States following the death or disability of the President, Vice President, and Speaker of the House.

Significance   Like the Speaker of the House, the President pro tempore is a partisan officer using his position to aid the program of the majority party. Although the office is usually overshadowed by that of the majority floor leader, it is one of considerable prestige and is usually awarded to the senior member of the majority party.

Previous Question   A motion in a legislative body to cease debate and force a vote on a pending measure. In Congress, the rules permit its use in the House but not in the Senate. The motion itself cannot be debated nor laid on the table. If the motion carries before any debate on the bill has occurred, each side is allowed twenty minutes to present its case. State legislatures use similar rules to limit debate.

Significance   The "previous question" rule in the House makes it possible to avoid unlimited discussion such as occurs during a filibuster in the

Senate. With 435 members in the House, such a rule is necessary to prevent the chamber from bogging down in endless debate. It is also used as a parliamentary device to prevent amendments which might cripple a bill.

Private Bill   Bills introduced into a legislative body that deal with specific matters and individuals rather than with general legislative affairs. In Congress, although the number of private bills was considerably reduced by the Reorganization Act of 1946, thousands are still introduced at each session. The main categories include: (1) immigration and naturalization bills applying to specific individuals; (2) claim bills not subject to administrative resolution; and (3) land bills assigning title to individuals. Private bills are introduced by congressmen who are petitioned by their constituents to right a government-inflicted wrong or to deal with a matter not covered by general statute. If enacted, they become private law and apply only to specific individuals named in the act. All state legislatures allow introduction of private bills. *See* BILL, page 128.

Significance   Many observers believe that it would add considerably to the efficiency of Congress to reduce further the categories of private bills. Their complete elimination is unlikely. Private bills tend to force the legislative body into performing a judicial-like function in determining the merits of particular claims made by individuals. They are time-consuming and detract from the general lawmaking function of Congress as well as of the legislatures in the states. Further use of administrative agencies to handle these matters could lighten the burden of the legislative body.

Quorum   The minimum number of members of a legislative chamber who must be present in order to transact business. The Constitution specifies that "a majority of each [house] shall constitute a quorum to do business." (Art. I, sec. 5). This means 218 in the House and 51 in the Senate. In the House, the quorum for the Committee of the Whole is 100. Typically, state legislatures also require a majority of members to be present for the transaction of business.

Significance   The House frequently escapes the quorum requirement of 218 by dissolving into the Committee of the Whole. Decisions reached, however, must be ratified by the duly constituted House. Both chambers often proceed with fewer than a quorum present unless challenged by a point of order. When this occurs, either the chamber must adjourn or the Sergeant at Arms is instructed to round up the absent members.

Ranking Member   That member of the majority party on a legislative committee who ranks first after the chairman in number of years of continuous service (seniority) on the committee. *See* COMMITTEE CHAIRMAN, page 131; SENIORITY RULE, page 153.

Significance   In Congress, the ranking member automatically succeeds to the chairmanship of a committee if that post is vacated while his party has majority control of that house. The ranking member is often accorded the chairmanship of one of the committee's important subcommittees. Most state legislatures follow the same procedures.

Ranking Minority Member   The minority party member of a legislative committee with the longest continuous service (seniority) on the committee. *See* SENIORITY RULE, page 153.

Significance   In Congress, the ranking minority member succeeds to the chairmanship of the committee when his party wins control of that house. Most state legislatures also follow the rule of seniority. The ranking minority member also provides some leadership for the minority members on the committee.

Ratification   A power vested in a legislative body to approve (or reject) agreements entered into with other states and constitutional amendment proposals. In the states, interstate compacts negotiated by the governors of several states must be approved by the state legislature of each before becoming effective. Amendments proposed to the United States Constitution must be ratified by legislatures or conventions in three-fourths of the states to become effective. Amendments proposed to state constitutions, however, must be ratified by a vote of the people of that state. The term "ratification" is also popularly used to describe the "consent" function of the United States Senate regarding treaties negotiated by the United States with foreign nations, although here the term more properly applies to the role of the President in accepting or rejecting the Senate version of a treaty. *See* RATIFICATION, page 171; RATIFICATION, page 334; AMENDMENT, page 18.

Significance   Ratification gives the legislative body an effective check over agreements entered into with other states and over changes made in the fundamental law. Often, important agreements and amendment proposals are killed by the failure of legislatures to bring them to a vote or by the failure of proponents to secure the necessary extraordinary majority vote.

Readings   The three readings of a bill required at different stages of the legislative process. In Congress, the first reading occurs when the bill is introduced and printed by title in the *Congressional Record*. The second, often a reading in full, takes place when the bill is brought out of committee for consideration before the chamber. The third reading, usually by title only, comes after amendments have been voted on and the bill is up for a final vote. State legislative procedure is similar. *See* BILL, page 128.

Significance   The required three readings of a bill, based on traditional parliamentary law, is expected to ensure careful consideration of all bills and to prevent any from sneaking through almost unnoticed. The procedure is of little significance today in the legislative process of either Congress or the state legislatures. On occasion, full reading of a bill may be demanded, and used, as a delaying tactic.

Recommittal   The action of a legislative body to send a bill back to the committee that had reported it out for consideration. A motion to recommit may instruct the committee to report the bill out again with certain amendments or at a later date. Most motions for recommittal, however, simply call for further study by the committee.

Significance   In most cases, the adoption of a motion to recommit a bill to committee is considered a death blow. Often legislators prefer not to alienate constituents who support a bill by directly voting it down. Recommittal can accomplish the same purpose without giving the appearance of killing the bill.

Record Vote   A "yea or nay" roll-call vote in a legislative body in which each member's vote is required to be recorded. Those members not voting for or against the measure will either be "paired" or "present." In Congress, the Constitution requires a record vote for overriding a presidential veto, and whenever one-fifth of the members demand it. Record votes are not taken in Committee of the Whole. State constitutions also require record votes on important measures before the state legislatures. *See* DIVISION, page 137; TELLER VOTE, page 157; VIVA VOCE VOTE, page 158.
    Significance   In Congress, a roll-call vote is demanded on almost all important bills. In a representative system of government it is essential that the voters have an opportunity to examine a legislator's voting record. In the House of Representatives, a record vote is frequently used as a delaying tactic to allow time for absent members to participate in the vote. Some state legislatures have installed electronic voting devices so that a complete record of the vote can be made instantaneously.

Redistricting   The action of a state legislature or other body in redrawing legislative electoral district lines following a new population census. After each decennial federal census, congressional seats are reapportioned among the fifty states. In each state that gains or loses seats, the state legislature usually draws up new districts. Additionally, state legislatures are required by most state constitutions to redraw district boundary lines for electing state representatives and senators to the legislatures following each federal census. *See* GERRYMANDERING, page 139; *Baker v. Carr,* page 160; *Reynolds v. Sims,* page 161; *Wesberry v. Sanders,* page 162.
    Significance   Redistricting decisions, typically, are made by partisan majorities in the legislatures, and the partisan nature of the undertaking is usually reflected in the final results, called gerrymandering. In the past, large cities were underrepresented and rural areas tended to be grossly overrepresented because of state legislative refusals to redistrict or to redistrict on a population basis. Since 1962, federal and state court rulings have required that districts be drawn on a basis of substantial equality of population. This new pattern of redistricting has radically altered the distribution of political power in American legislative bodies in favor of urban and suburban interests.

Referendum   An electoral device, available in twenty-two states, by which voters can "veto" a bill passed by a legislature. Emergency and financial bills are commonly excluded from referendum action. In states providing for the referendum, bills passed by the legislature do not take effect for a specified period (usually ninety days), during which the bill may be suspended by obtaining the required number of voters' signatures on petitions (usually five percent of total votes cast in a preceding election). A suspended bill is voted upon by the electorate and, if disapproved by a majority, is killed. The *constitutional referendum* gives voters an opportunity to approve or reject amendments or revisions of state constitutions. Many state and local governments may also use the *optional* or *advisory referendum,* by which a legislative body may voluntarily refer a measure to the voters for an expression of popular sentiment. *See* DIRECT DEMOCRACY, page 7; DIRECT LEGISLATION, page 136.

Significance   The referendum was adopted by many states in the early part of the twentieth century as an ultrademocratic weapon to check the objectionable enactments of the legislatures. It is not intended for regular use, but rather remains a "gun behind the door," by means of which the people hold a continuing veto power. The referendum has been used infrequently in most states that provide for it. Supporters of the referendum regard it as a useful check on ill-considered or dangerous actions by the legislature and as an expansion of democracy. Those who oppose it regard it as an unnecessary check on representative government that weakens legislative responsibility, gives great power to organized groups, and provides for the making of decisions on complex or technical issues by the average citizen who may be incapable of voting intelligently on them.

Refer to Committee   The sending of a bill that has been introduced into one of the houses of a legislative body to a standing committee. In Congress, public bills are assigned to committees by the parliamentarian under the scrutiny of the presiding officer in each house. Private bills are usually referred to the committee requested by the senator or representative who introduces the bill. *See* STANDING COMMITTEE, page 156.

Significance   Referral of bills to the proper committee is generally a routine matter. Some bills may include subject matter pertinent to several committees. In such cases, the presiding officer in each house may exercise some discretion in assigning bills, which may have a significant effect on whether specific bills are killed in committee or reported out. For example, the Speaker of the House would be likely to refer a bill to a committee favoring such legislation if he personally favored it. In each house, the majority of members can overrule the decision of the presiding officer by removing a bill from one committee's jurisdiction and assigning it to another. This occurs rarely.

Report   The action of a legislative committee in sending out its findings and recommendations to its chamber following consideration of a bill or investigation of some matter. The report explains the reasons for the committee's action. Most committee reports are favorable, but on rare occasions a committee will report out a bill with a recommendation that its parent chamber kill the bill. In any case, many reports are not unanimous, and those members of the committee who dissent may file a minority report. If a bill has been amended in committee, the majority report will provide an explanation for this action. *See* STANDING COMMITTEE, page 156; DISCHARGE RULE, page 137; RULES COMMITTEE, page 151.

Significance   Typically, the great majority of bills introduced each session in most legislative bodies fail to become law because they are not reported out by the various committees to which they have been assigned. Some state legislatures require committees to report out all bills. In the House of Representatives, a committee's refusal to report out a bill for consideration can be overridden only by the rarely used discharge rule, and in the Senate the discharge resolution can be used. Most bills and resolutions reported out with recommendations to the chamber that they be passed are acted on favorably. Recommendations on bills of a controversial political nature are of lesser importance in influencing action in the chamber. In the House, bills reported out by committees are sent first to the Rules Committee, which also has the power to kill bills by refusing to report them out for floor consideration unless they are discharged.

Representative   A member of the House of Representatives in Congress or of the lower house of a state legislature. Representatives are elected for two-year terms and, in keeping with the idea that the lower house is to be the more representative of the two chambers, all members' terms are coterminous. The Constitution provides that a representative must be at least twenty-five years of age, a citizen for seven years, and a resident of the state from which he is elected. Vacancies are filled by special election called by the governor. *See* HOUSE OF REPRESENTATIVES, page 140; SENATOR, page 153.

Significance   In Congress, representatives, also called "congressmen," serve as the most direct contact between the citizen and his government. The two-year term makes it necessary for the representative to keep in touch with his constituents if he wishes to be re-elected. In 1966, President Lyndon B. Johnson proposed a four-year term coterminous with that of the President to alleviate the pressures of constant campaigning and to provide greater continuity. While neither national nor state representatives enjoy the same prestige accorded members of upper chambers, many who have acquired seniority through long service exercise considerable political power.

Resident Commissioner   A delegate elected by the people of a territory to represent them in the House of Representatives. He may speak in the House and serve on committees, but he may not vote. His salary is the same as that of all congressmen. Only Puerto Rico has a resident commissioner.

Significance   Permitting a territory to elect a delegate to Congress demonstrates willingness to prepare the territory for self-governance and possible statehood or independence. Since the people of Puerto Rico are subject to many federal laws, they are entitled to have their interests represented.

Rider   A provision, unlikely to pass on its own merits, added to an important bill so that it will "ride" through the legislative process. Riders become law if the bills to which they are attached are passed. *See* ITEM VETO, page 167.

Significance   In Congress, most riders are attached to appropriations bills, although this procedure is technically banned under the rules of the House and Senate. Opponents of the rider, and the President, are forced to accept the provision if they want the bill to become law. In several states, the governors have been given the item veto power; this permits them to veto only those sections of a bill with which they disagree, allowing the remainder to become law. Such power vested in the President would go far toward meeting the problem of riders.

Rules Committee   A standing committee of the House of Representatives that can provide special rules under which specific bills will be debated, amended, and considered by the House. The Rules Committee functions as a valve or sifting device to control the flow of bills from the committees to the floor for consideration.

Significance   Because more bills are reported out of committees than the House has time to consider, the Rules Committee functions as a legislative traffic-control officer. In this role it can exercise a virtual veto power over bills reported out by other committees. It can, conversely, send out bills to be considered under favorable procedures. If a majority of the Committee favors a bill, their approval will most likely be reflected in the rule specified for consideration of that bill. The Committee may also provide a "gag" rule by which amendments to the bill may be forbidden or limited to specified areas. Because of these powers, the Rules Committee exercises almost absolute power over legislation in the House. Under the House procedure, a bill can be pulled out of the Rules Committee after seven days by means of a discharge petition signed by a majority of House members. This method has not proved satisfactory because of a reluctance of congressmen to challenge committee leadership and prerogatives. In 1961, the membership of the Rules Committee was enlarged by three to a total of fifteen. This was an attempt to offset the conservative control of the Committee by the addition of liberals who would help to prevent the Committee from sitting on some of the major presidential legislative proposals. In January 1965, under pressure from the Johnson Administration, the House authorized the Speaker to recognize a member of a standing committee to move consideration of one of its bills which the Rules Committee has held for twenty-one days. Nevertheless, the Rules Committee remains one of the most powerful in the House today.

Select Committee   A legislative committee established for a limited time period and for a special purpose. Select committees may be created by either house or may include members from both houses (joint committee).

Significance   Select committees are given assignments that do not fall within the jurisdiction of any standing committee, or that the latter may prefer not to carry on. Most special committees have been given investigative duties, although others have been assigned supervisory, housekeeping, and co-ordination responsibilities. The Legislative Reorganization Act of 1946 reduced the need for select committees by placing responsibility for investigations in the standing committees.

Senate   The upper house of the United States Congress and of forty-nine state legislatures. Representation in the United States Senate is based on the principle of state equality, and the Constitution specifies that no state may be deprived of its equal representation in the Senate without its consent. The Senate is comprised of one hundred Senators from fifty states. Most state senates have fewer than fifty members. The Vice President is the presiding officer of the Senate; in the state legislatures, the lieutenant governor normally presides. In the absence of a presiding officer, a president pro tempore elected from the membership assumes that role. *See* HOUSE OF REPRESENTATIVES, page 140.

Significance   Contrary to popular myth, many observers regard the

Senate as being more responsive to national interests than the House because it tends to respond to the needs of the nation rather than to localized interests. Aside from lawmaking and representational functions, the Senate is also vested with special powers, including the power to try impeachments and to give advice and consent to treaties and appointments. If no candidate for the vice presidency receives a majority of the electoral vote, the Senate then elects the Vice President from the two candidates with the highest electoral votes. State senates, too, exercise special powers, such as confirmation of appointments and trial of impeached officials.

Senator A member of the United States Senate or of the upper house in state legislatures. United States senators have been directly elected by the people of their respective states since the adoption of the Seventeenth Amendment in 1913. The term of office is six years, with one-third of the Senate seats up for election every two years. Vacancies are usually filled by appointment by the state's governor, although the legislature may provide for a special election. The Constitution provides that a senator must be at least thirty years of age, a citizen for nine years, and a resident of the state from which he is elected. In the state legislatures, senators are in all cases elected by the people, usually for four years. *See* REPRESENTATIVE, page 151; SEVENTEENTH AMENDMENT, page 155.

Significance In Congress, senators generally are regarded as more capable and as having greater prestige than their colleagues in the lower house. Many representatives aspire to achieve election to the Senate. Most senators represent more constituents than do House members, and the smaller size of the chamber makes possible more thorough deliberation on measures. In state legislatures, the average senator represents more constituents than does a member of the lower house and usually exercises considerable power in state matters.

Senatorial Courtesy An unwritten agreement among senators that requires the President to confer with the senator or senators of his party from a state before he makes a nomination to fill a federal office in that state. The Senate will almost invariably reject a presidential nominee when the senator involved raises a personal objection. When neither senator of a state is of the President's party, the President is apt to consult state party leaders. *See* CONFIRMATION, page 133.

Significance Senatorial courtesy has resulted in the transferring from the President to senators of his party the patronage distribution within a state. This means that such senators normally choose the appointees and give their names to the President. Federal positions affected by senatorial courtesy include judges, district attorneys, customs officials, postmasters, and field service officials of most important agencies. Presidents may reject senatorial recommendations, but this rarely occurs.

Seniority Rule A custom nearly always followed in both houses of Congress of awarding chairmanships of committees to the majority party member who has the longest number of years of continuous service on the committee. Each party, majority and minority alike, strictly lists its members on the various committees according to the seniority rule. When a high-ranking member leaves the committee, all members of that party move up one notch on the seniority list. Most state legislatures follow the seniority rule. *See* COMMITTEE CHAIRMAN, page 131; RANKING MEMBER, page 147.

Significance   The seniority rule has been a source of much controversy inside and outside Congress. Supporters of seniority argue that: (1) it guarantees chairmen will have had long experience in committee matters; (2) it avoids intrigues, conflicts, and deadlocks within the party organizations which would inevitably occur whenever a new chairman was chosen; (3) it makes possible the rise to positions of importance of the congressmen from small states; and (4) it has produced men of ability and stature in the chairmanships of the important committees. Opponents of seniority argue that: (1) it tends to hold back men of ability while often it moves mediocre men steadily ahead; (2) it requires nothing more of a man than that he continue living and getting re-elected; (3) it tends to favor the stagnant, one-party voting areas of the nation over the two-party competitive areas which reflect changes in public opinion; and (4) it reduces party responsibility by filling most key power positions in both houses with members from the conservative wings of either party. Likelihood of changing the seniority rule is remote. Denial of seniority rights may occur as a result of campaign defections. In January 1965, for example, the House Democratic caucus denied seniority rights to two southern members who had supported Republican presidential candidate Barry Goldwater.

Session   The period during which a legislative body assembles and carries on its regular business. Each Congress has two regular sessions based on the requirement in the Constitution that Congress assemble at least once each year. In addition, Congress may be summoned into special session by the President. The first session of a Congress usually begins on January 3 of odd-numbered years, with the start of the terms of all representatives and one-third of the senators. The second session begins on January 3 of even-numbered years. The Congress that assembled in January 1967, for example, was the Ninetieth Congress, first session. Adjournment is left up to Congress, although the Constitution provides that if the two houses cannot agree on a date, the President may adjourn them at his discretion. No President has exercised this authority. In the states, most legislatures convene in regular session every two years, although nineteen have regular annual sessions. Most state constitutions limit the length of legislative sessions either by specifying the number of days or by cutting off pay and allowances for legislators after a certain date. *See* SPECIAL SESSION, page 155; TWENTIETH AMENDMENT, page 157.

Significance   To cope with the many complex problems of modern society, a legislative body must be in session regularly and not only at widely separated intervals. Because the Constitution leaves sessions pretty much up to the discretion of Congress, this problem does not exist in the national government. In most of the states, however, sessions are generally short and infrequent. Constitutional revision is needed in most states to free the legislatures from restrictions that date back more than a century.

Seventeenth Amendment An amendment to the Constitution, adopted in 1913, that provides for the direct election of United States senators. The amendment changes those sections of Article I that authorized senators to be chosen by the legislatures of the states. It also provides that, when a vacancy occurs, the legislature may authorize the governor to make a temporary appointment until an election can be held. Most legislatures have so authorized their governors. *See* SENATOR, page 153.

Significance Prior to the adoption of the Seventeenth Amendment, selection of senators frequently resulted in lengthy distractions from normal state legislative business. Deadlocks in the selection process often kept states unrepresented in the Senate for many months. Although popular election is no guarantee of fitness, most observers believe that senatorial abilities, stature, and responsiveness to the public will, have all tended to increase since 1913.

Simple Resolution A measure adopted by one chamber of a legislative body. It does not require approval either by the other house or by the President. Simple resolutions are designated either "H Res" or "S Res." *See* CONCURRENT RESOLUTION, page 132; JOINT RESOLUTION, page 143.

Significance Simple resolutions do not have the force of law. They are usually adopted for the purpose of making or amending rules of procedure. In Congress, one chamber may adopt a resolution to express its sentiment on a current issue or to give advice to the President on foreign policy or other areas of executive responsibility.

Speaker of the House The presiding officer in the House of Representatives and in the lower chamber of state legislatures. His election by the House is a formality that follows his selection by the majority party caucus. As a member of the House, the Speaker may engage in debate and vote on measures.

Significance The Speaker is the most powerful and influential member of the House. As presiding officer, he recognizes members wishing to speak, interprets and applies the rules, and decides questions of order. Although he can be overruled by the House itself, this rarely occurs. He appoints select and conference committees and refers bills to committee. His real importance lies in the fact that, in exercising all of the foregoing powers, the Speaker may use discretion and political acumen. He is thus placed in a strategic position whereby he can influence the passage or rejection of bills at almost every stage in the legislative process in the House. As the leader of the majority party in the House, the Speaker also exercises considerable power in shaping and implementing party decisions on pending legislation. Most Speakers have been men of ability, stature, and tact, able to provide the kind of leadership needed by the majority party. The role and powers of speakers in the various state legislatures are analogous to those of the Speaker in the House of Representatives, and they have the additional power to appoint members of standing committees.

Special Session An extraordinary session of a legislative body convoked, usually, on the initiative of a chief executive. The Constitution grants power to the President to summon Congress or either house into session "on extraor-

dinary occasions" (Art. II, sec. 3). Although the House has never been called
into special session, the Senate has been convoked to act upon executive appointments or treaties. In all fifty states, the governors are empowered to call
special sessions of the legislatures. In several states, a stipulated number of
legislators may petition the governor to call the legislature into session. In a
few others, the legislature can call itself into special session.

Significance   Congress when called into special session possesses full
constitutional power to legislate. In about one-half of the states, legislatures
convened in special sessions are similarly free to act, whereas in the other half
they are limited to acting upon what the governor specifies in his call. Special
sessions may be useful in meeting a sudden crisis or new problem. A chief
executive can use the call of a special session as a political weapon to focus
public attention on an issue and pressure the legislative body to consider it.
Although executive officials may summon legislative bodies into special sessions,
they cannot exercise appreciable control over legislative action or inaction once
the body convenes.

Standing Committee   A regular committee of a legislative body that considers bills within a subject area. In Congress, there are twenty House and
sixteen Senate standing committees. House committees range in size from nine
to fifty members and Senate committees from seven to twenty-seven members.
Representatives are normally assigned to only one standing committee, senators
to two. In the House, the leading standing committees include Rules, Ways
and Means, Appropriations, Foreign Affairs, Commerce, and Agriculture. In
the Senate, influential committees include Foreign Relations, Appropriations,
Finance, Judiciary, Armed Services, and Banking and Currency. The majority
party in each house holds a majority vote on each committee and the chairmanship. Positions of importance on the committees are determined under the
rule of seniority. *See* COMMITTEE CHAIRMAN, page 131; COMMITTEE ON COM-
MITTEES, page 132; SENIORITY RULE, page 153.

Significance   The standing committee system operates on the principle
of specialization secured through a division of labor. Members of Congress
usually respect the decisions and recommendations made by the standing committees on pending legislation. Thus, the fate of most bills is decided in committee rather than on the floors of the two chambers. This great power led Woodrow Wilson to describe American government as "government by the standing
committees of Congress."

Statute (Act)   A law enacted by Congress or by a state legislature. Simple,
concurrent, and joint resolutions adopted by Congress are not considered statutes. Statutes take the form of public and private laws and are numbered consecutively in each session of Congress. *See* BILL, page 128; CODE, page 203.

Significance   All acts of Congress are published first in the form of
"slip laws" and are bound after each session in the *Statutes at Large of the
United States*. Those applicable today can be found in the *United States Code*,
which is revised every six years and supplemented annually. The *Code* is organized on a subject matter basis. State laws are published but not codified
regularly.

Supplementary Appropriation   An appropriation of public money authorized by a legislative body after the regular appropriation bills have been enacted. It differs from a deficiency appropriation in that it is passed prior to the fiscal period in which it will be spent. *See* DEFICIENCY APPROPRIATION, page 135.

Significance   Supplementary appropriations are useful in correcting miscalculations in the budget process, in meeting new problems, and in reacting to changes in public opinion.

Suspension of Rules   A time-saving procedure used by a legislative body to bring a measure to a vote. In the House of Representatives, a motion to "suspend the rules and pass the bill" requires a two-thirds vote of members present for passage. Debate on the bill is limited to forty minutes and no amendments are permitted.

Significance   Because of the size of the House, a means by which debate can be closed and a measure brought to a vote quickly is necessary to the flow of business. The Senate, with its rules for unlimited debate, can obtain these results only through unanimous consent.

Teller Vote   An unrecorded vote in which the members of a legislative body are counted as they file past tellers. In Congress, the House, but not the Senate, uses teller votes, which can be demanded by one fifth of a quorum (forty-four in the House, twenty in Committee of the Whole). When a teller vote is called, two tellers, one for and one against, stand in front of the Speaker's desk and count the votes as the members file past. The Speaker then announces the results, but individual votes are not announced. *See* DIVISION, page 137; RECORD VOTE, page 149; VIVA VOCE VOTE, page 158.

Significance   A teller vote offers a means of securing an accurate vote quickly. By not recording the individual congressman's vote, however, his accountability to his constituents is weakened.

Twentieth Amendment   An amendment to the Constitution, adopted in 1933, that provides that a new Congress elected in November of even-numbered years will convene on January 3 of the following year. Prior to its adoption, a newly elected Congress did not convene in regular session until December of the following year—a lapse of thirteen months. The old Congress, meanwhile, with many members who had failed to win re-election ("lame ducks"), met in perfunctory session for four months following the election. The Amendment also changed the presidential term to start a month and one half earlier, on January 20 instead of on March 4. *See* TWENTIETH AMENDMENT, page 174.

Significance   The Twentieth Amendment provides for more democracy and greater efficiency. By reducing the interim period between an election and the assumption of office by newly elected members of Congress, the people's mandate may be more quickly and accurately realized. By changing the President's term to start at an earlier date, a new President has the opportunity to present his legislative and budgetary programs to a new Congress. Some observers, including former Presidents, have suggested that the interim period be reduced still further so as to enable a new Congress and President to come to grips with pressing problems of government at an even earlier date.

Unanimous Consent   A time-saving procedure, also known as "without objection," used by a legislative body to adopt noncontroversial motions, amendments, and bills without submitting them to a vote. Both houses of Congress use the procedure to expedite business. In the House, an objection from a single member results in the tabling of the bill or motion for two weeks.

Significance   Unanimous consent can be useful in rapidly disposing of a host of minor matters cluttering up a legislature's docket. By expediting noncontroversial measures, more time is made available for dealing with crucial issues.

Unicameralism   The principle of a one-house legislature, as contrasted with bicameralism, a legislature based on two houses. One state legislature —Nebraska's—is unicameral, as are local governmental policy-determining bodies, such as county boards, city councils, township boards, and school boards. See BICAMERALISM, page 127.

Significance   The merits of unicameralism include: (1) greater economy and efficiency of operation; (2) greater prestige, which attracts outstanding citizens; (3) elimination of deadlocks resulting from rivalry and friction between two houses; (4) elimination of the need for conference committees; and (5) more accurate fixing of responsibility of elected representatives by the public. Arguments against unicameralism include: (1) hasty, careless, ill-considered legislation may result; (2) special interest lobbies can concentrate their influence more effectively against one house; (3) one house may be more susceptible to aroused popular passions and other democratic excesses; and (4) control over a one-house legislature may be focussed in a single major interest group or in a small geographical area.

Vice President   The presiding officer of the United States Senate. Under the Constitution, the Vice President is primarily a legislative official, but in modern times he has been assigned executive responsibilities by the President. See VICE PRESIDENT, page 175.

Significance   Unlike the Speaker of the House, the President of the Senate is not the chosen leader of the majority party in the Senate, nor is he a member of the Senate. He cannot speak from the floor on issues and, as presiding officer, he must not show his partisanship. He can cast a vote only in case of a tie. Although the Vice President's powers are negligible, he may, as some have, exercise considerable influence in the Senate's decision-making by reason of his ability and personal powers of persuasion. Also, if he is a leader of high standing in the majority party of the Senate, his potential influence is increased. In recent years, a succession of Vice Presidents selected from the Senate—John N. Garner, Harry S. Truman, Alben W. Barkley, Richard M. Nixon, Lyndon B. Johnson and Hubert H. Humphrey—have proved to be valuable liaison agents between the President and the Senate.

Viva Voce Vote   A voice vote in a legislative chamber in which the presiding officer determines the outcome from the volume of response from those for and against the measure. See DIVISION, page 137; RECORD VOTE, page 149; TELLER VOTE, page 157.

Significance   Viva voce votes on important measures are often challenged because it is difficult to determine voice volume with precision. Much discretion can be exercised by the presiding officer if left unchallenged. Its main advantage lies in the speed with which it permits great quantities of business to be transacted. A defect of this procedure is that individual votes are not recorded.

Watchdog Committee   A committee established by a legislative body for the purpose of overseeing the administration of the laws. In Congress prior to 1946, each house created a number of select committees to perform this oversight function. In the Legislative Reorganization Act of 1946, Congress vested the "watchdog" responsibility in the standing committees, each responsible for overseeing the execution of laws within its jurisdiction. *See* INVESTIGATING COMMITTEE, page 142.

Significance   In its report in 1946 that led to the Reorganization Act, the Joint Committee stated: "Without effective legislative oversight of the activities of the vast executive branch, the line of democracy wears thin." The Committee recommended "a continuous review of the agencies administering laws originally reported by the committees." The Government Operations Committees of the House and the Senate have been given the special responsibility of "studying the operation of government activities at all levels with a view to determining its economy and efficiency." Congressional oversight can be distinguished from congressional investigations in that the former is more a continuing scrutiny of executive operations, whereas the latter involves a more intense digging for facts within a limited problem area.

Ways and Means Committee   A standing committee of the House of Representatives to which all bills for raising revenue are referred. Its twenty-five members study tax and tariff bills and make recommendations to the full House. Occasionally, the Committee itself writes new tax measures.

Significance   The Ways and Means Committee is usually regarded as second in importance only to the House Rules Committee. Democratic members of the Committee are chosen by the Democratic caucus. These members then assign the Democratic members to all other House committees, subject to caucus approval. Republican members do not exercise this power. When the Ways and Means Committee holds public hearings on tax and tariff measures, large numbers of citizens and lobbyists testify before the Committee, reflecting the importance of the revenue raising function.

Whip   An assistant floor leader who aids the majority or minority leaders of each party in each house of Congress. Whips are selected in party caucuses, usually on the recommendation of the floor leaders. Each whip in the House appoints several assistants to aid him, whereas the Senate whips are aided by the secretaries to their respective party policy committees. *See* MAJORITY FLOOR LEADER, page 144.

Significance   The duties of the whips include: (1) canvassing fellow party members so as to inform party leaders of the number of votes which can be counted on; (2) taking action to bring full voting power of their party to bear on key issues; (3) acting for the floor leaders when they are absent from the chamber. On crucial issues, when close votes are anticipated, much depends on the party organization and the effectiveness of the whips' operations.

IMPORTANT AGENCIES

Legislative Reference Service   A staff agency of Congress established to provide research data to aid members of Congress in their legislative duties. It was established in the Library of Congress in 1914 and has been progressively strengthened to include a professional staff of specialists in a variety of fields of legislative interest. Each year, studies, statistics, and charts are furnished to congressmen and committees in response to thousands of inquiries. Many state legislatures have created similar staff facilities.

Significance   The creation and expansion of the Legislative Reference Service have resulted somewhat from the reluctance of Congress to be dependent upon "experts" in the executive branch for information. The Service not only performs essential staff functions but, because of the nature of its work, has a considerable effect on the end product of legislation.

Library of Congress   The national library of the United States, which serves the entire national government and state and local governments as well as the public. The Library of Congress was created in 1800 by Congress and is headed by the Librarian of Congress, who is appointed by the President with Senate approval. Two important divisions of the Library are the Copyright Office and the Legislative Reference Service.

Significance   The Library of Congress is particularly useful to Congress and the executive branch because it is a vast storehouse of official records and documents. Much legislation involves extensive studies and research, and the role of the Library has grown as governmental activities have increased and grown more complex.

IMPORTANT CASES

Baker v. Carr, 369 U.S. 186 (1962): Ruled, in an epic Supreme Court decision, that federal courts have jurisdiction over lawsuits challenging the apportionment of legislative districts, on the ground that malapportioned districts may violate the equal protection clause of the Fourteenth Amendment. The case had the effect of overturning *Colegrove v. Green,* 328 U.S. 549 (1946) in which the Court held that the issue of malapportioned legislative districts was a political question and relief should be sought through the political process. The *Baker* case involved a suit to compel the Tennessee legislature to redistrict state legislative districts on a population basis, a provision of the Tennessee Constitution that the legislature had ignored for over sixty years.

Significance   Many state legislatures had long refused to provide for equitable apportionment for state legislative and congressional election districts. The *Baker* decision reflected the new view of the Court's majority that it is unrealistic to seek to achieve a fair system of representation through the ballot box, since state legislators often maintain themselves in power through gerrymandering and refusals to redistrict. The *Baker* case led to a plethora of challenges to districting patterns in most states. Subsequently, the Supreme Court ruled that in state-wide primary elections for United States senators and state executive officers, each person's vote must count equally (*Gray v. Sanders,* 372 U.S. 368 [1963]), that congressional districts must be substantially equal in population (*Wesberry v. Sanders,* 376 U.S. 1 [1964]), and, that both houses of a bicameral state legislature must be apportioned on a population basis (*Reynolds v. Sims,* 377 U.S. 533 [1964]). These and later decisions have affirmed that the basic constitutional principle of voting equality can mean only one thing—"one person, one vote."

McGrain v. Daugherty, 273 U.S. 135 (1927): Decided that Congress has the right to compel testimony from private individuals as an aid to its power to pass laws. This investigation arose out of the Teapot Dome scandal involving bribery and other illegal acts by public officials. The Court held that Congress could subpoena a private individual as well as a public official when this action is pertinent to a proper legislative function.

Significance   The *McGrain* case established the constitutional basis for legislative investigations along with the power to compel testimony and production of papers and other materials. So long as an investigation has a legislative purpose, the courts will not inquire further into the motives of Congress.

Pacific States Telephone and Telegraph Co. v. Oregon, 223 U.S. 118 (1912): Involved the question of whether the initiative and referendum provisions of the Oregon Constitution destroy the republican form of government guaranteed to all states by the United States Constitution in Article IV, section 4. The Court held it to be a political question not open to judicial inquiry.

Significance   Although no provision is made by the Constitution for direct action by the people in the lawmaking process, the Court, in effect, here recognized that the states may validly adopt such measures. About one-third of the states and numerous cities have adopted the initiative and referendum, most of them during the first two decades of the twentieth century.

Reynolds v. Sims, 377 U.S. 533 (1964): A landmark decision that under the equal protection clause of the Fourteenth Amendment both houses of a bicameral state legislature must be apportioned on the basis of population. The Court rejected the "federal analogy" that, like Congress, a state legislature could have one house based on a factor other than population. It held that political subdivisions in states are not sovereign entities (on which equal representation of states in the Senate is predicated). Since both houses of a legislature must agree to enact legislation, representation on factors other than population dilutes the vote of citizens living in heavily populated areas. "Legislators represent people, not trees or acres," said the Court, and an apportionment scheme cannot discriminate on the basis of residence any more than it can on the basis of race or economic status.

Significance   *Reynolds v. Sims* is among the most important decisions in American history, overcoming years of inaction by legislative bodies on the representation problem. It transformed the American political scene by ending dominance of state legislatures by rural minorities in favor of the urban majorities. It also has had a direct impact on national politics, since state legislatures draw congressional district lines. Efforts to overturn the decision by constitutional amendment failed. In the *Reynolds* case and subsequent decisions, the Court has not insisted on absolute equality of representation, permitting "substantial" equality of representation. But the "one man, one vote" principle remains firm.

United States v. Harriss, 347 U.S. 612 (1954): Upheld the constitutionality of the Federal Regulation of Lobbying Act of 1946 against charges that it violates due process, freedom of speech and press, and freedom of petition.

Significance   The Court narrowly construed the application of the Lobbying Act by holding that it applies only to lobbyists who directly seek to influence members of Congress concerning pending or proposed federal legislation. Lobbyists who seek to influence federal legislation indirectly through public opinion do not fall within the scope of "lobbying activities" regulated by the Act. The Court emphasized that the intention of the Lobbying Act was to enable Congress to discover "who is being hired, who is putting up the money, and how much." This is information that Congress is entitled to know.

Watkins v. United States, 354 U.S. 178 (1957): Established that a person may refuse to answer a question put to him by an investigating committee of Congress if the question is not pertinent to the inquiry. The Court upheld Watkins' refusal to answer questions of the House Committee on Un-American Activities regarding certain persons who had at one time been members of the Communist party. For refusing to answer, Watkins was cited for contempt of Congress. The Court reversed his conviction on the ground that the Committee had failed to demonstrate that the questions were pertinent.

Significance   Many rights guaranteed in the Constitution apply to congressional investigations as well as to judicial proceedings. In the same way that an individual is entitled to know the precise charges against him when charged with a crime, so he is entitled to know how any particular question asked of him at a legislative investigation pertains to the matter under investigation. Congress may not conduct a "fishing expedition" in the hopes of uncovering information. This case illustrates one of the limitations on the investigatory powers of Congress.

Wesberry v. Sanders, 376 U.S. 1 (1964): Held that congressional districts must be substantially equal in population. The Court based its ruling on Article I, section 2, of the Constitution, which provides that the House of Representatives shall be chosen "by the People of the several States." While mathematical precision is impossible, said the Court, the Constitution requires that, as nearly as practicable, each man's vote in a congressional election is to be worth as much as any other man's vote.

Significance   The *Wesberry* case provided the legal basis for ending overrepresentation of rural areas in the House of Representatives. For example, in a recent Congress, a representative from one district represented eight times as many constitutents as another representative. This kind of disparity resulted from redistricting patterns established by state legislatures that were themselves malapportioned in favor of rural minorities.

IMPORTANT STATUTES

Legislative Reorganization Act of 1946   An act to strengthen Congress in its organization and operations. The Act was based on the studies of a bipartisan joint committee that was charged with recommending plans "with a view toward strengthening Congress, simplifying its operations, improving its relations with other branches of the United States Government, and enabling it to meet its responsibilities under the Constitution." The Act provided for structural and procedural changes, including: (1) reducing the number of committees; (2) strengthening the operations of the committees; (3) providing for a legislative budget system; (4) reducing the workload of Congress; (5) increasing the professional assistance available to each member of Congress; (6) increasing congressional salaries and fringe benefits; and (7) regulating lobbying activities.

Significance   Committee functioning has been definitely strengthened as a result of the Act, although the number of subcommittees has been increased. Claims legislation has been reduced, but many minor matters remain under congressional responsibility. The legislative budget proposal proved unworkable and was discarded. Lobbying has been brought under a measure of public and congressional oversight. Congressional salaries have since been increased to $30,000. Staff assistance has been improved in quantity and quality. Two persistent problems—the seniority system in committee organization and the filibuster in the Senate—were excluded from any consideration by the joint committee. New reorganization proposals are under study in Congress to adapt the legislative branch to contemporary conditions.

Regulation of Lobbying Act (Title III, Legislative Reorganization Act of 1946)   The first attempt by Congress to control interest groups, lobbyists, and lobbying activities through legislation. The act provides for a minimum of *regulation* and a maximum of *publicity*. Specific provisions include: (1) persons or organizations receiving money to be used principally to influence passage or defeat of legislation before Congress must register; (2) persons or groups registering must, under oath, give their name and address, employer, salary, amount and purpose of expenses, and duration of employment; (3) each registered lobbyist must report quarterly full information on his activities, which are then published in the *Congressional Record;* and (4) severe penalties are prescribed, ranging up to a $10,000 fine and a five-year prison term, and including a three-year ban against further lobbying. *See United States v. Harriss,* page 162.

Significance   The Lobbying Act has been criticized on the ground that its language is confusing and vague, resulting in much noncompliance. No enforcement agency has been created by Congress. The public generally has ignored the publicity given in quarterly reports. It is doubtful whether the Act has had any appreciable effect on lobbyists or their activities. Congress must be careful in enacting lobby-control legislation to avoid regulations that might abridge freedom of speech, press, or petition.

Eight

The Executive: Office and Powers

Amnesty   Power exercised by the President to grant a blanket pardon to all members of a group who have violated national law. Amnesties have also been occasionally granted by Congress. *See* PARDON, page 168.

Significance   Amnesties have been used generally to absolve groups from legal accountability for political offenses. For example, President Thomas Jefferson granted a general amnesty to all persons convicted under the Alien and Sedition Acts. The best known amnesties in American history were those granted by Presidents Abraham Lincoln and Andrew Johnson to all Confederates who had participated in rebellion against the United States. An attempt by Congress to limit the effect of Johnson's amnesty proclamation was found by the United States Supreme Court to be an invalid interference with the President's constitutional pardoning powers (*Ex parte Garland,* 4 Wall. 333 [1867]).

Appointment Power   The authority vested in a public official to fill a vacancy in a governmental office or position. The appointment power is usually shared by the chief executive, who nominates the candidate, with the legislative body, which confirms the appointee. In the national government, the President possesses the full appointing power for some positions but must obtain the Senate's "advice and consent" for others. Positions filled by presidential appointment include those in the executive branch, the federal judiciary, commissioned officers in the armed forces, and members of the independent regulatory commissions. Governors and most mayors share a limited appointment power with their state senate and city council, respectively. The President and governors may make recess appointments between Senate sessions. *See* CONFIRMATION, page 133; RECESS APPOINTMENT, page 171; REMOVAL POWER, page 172.

Significance   The appointment power permits an executive to select persons sympathetic to the policies of his administration. Through patronage appointments, he may control his political party. The key difference in executive authority between the President and most governors, and between a "strong" and a "weak" mayor, lies in the substantial appointing power of the former in each case. The trend at all levels of government, however, is toward reducing the executive appointing power in favor of merit selection.

Budget Message   The receipt and expenditure estimates recommended by the President for the next fiscal year. In January of each legislative session, the President sends his annual budget message to Congress as required by the Budget and Accounting Act of 1921. Unlike the State of the Union message, which precedes it, the budget message is not usually delivered in person by the President but is sent to Congress in writing to be read to each chamber by its clerk. Many governors, especially of those states that have undergone recent reorganization, also deliver or send to the legislature annual or biennial budget messages. *See* BUDGET AND ACCOUNTING ACT OF 1921, page 254.

Significance   The importance of the budget message is that it places responsibility for the initiation of the financial plan for government on the executive. Legislative bodies begin their consideration of financial matters only after the budget message, with its detailed itemization of fiscal recommendations, has been laid before them. Although Congress or a state legislature is free to modify or reject the proposals found in a budget message, its size and specificity tend to reduce legislative discretion. The executive may also use his budget message as a means of arousing public support for certain programs, even though immediate enactment is unlikely.

Cabinet   An advisory group selected by the President to aid him in making decisions. President Washington instituted the Cabinet idea when he began regularly to call together the heads of the four executive departments and the Vice President to consult with him on matters of policy. The Cabinet today remains an informal group, with its membership determined by tradition and presidential discretion. By custom, the heads of the major departments (State; Treasury; Defense; Justice; Post Office; Interior; Agriculture; Commerce; Labor; Health, Education, and Welfare; Housing and Urban Development; and Transportation) are members of the Cabinet, and the President may also invite the Vice President and other officials to sit in on Cabinet meetings.

Significance   The Cabinet may be a highly influential or relatively insignificant staff agency, whichever the President decides to make it. The members of the Cabinet individually are often far more influential in advising the President than is the Cabinet as a body. Some Presidents, such as James Buchanan and Warren G. Harding, placed great reliance on their Cabinets; others, such as Woodrow Wilson and both Theodore and Franklin D. Roosevelt, assigned their Cabinets an insignificant role. Abraham Lincoln is reported to have summarily rejected a unanimous vote of his Cabinet, an act that illustrates the advisory nature of Cabinet decisions. In making Cabinet appointments, Presidents, typically, seek to obtain broad geographic and interest group representation and to give some representation to the different political wings of their party. To promote bipartisanship, especially during periods of national crisis, Presidents have appointed members of the opposition party to Cabinet posts. For these reasons, Presidents usually prefer to seek advice elsewhere and to confine Cabinet meetings to general discussions of Administration policy.

Chief Legislator   The role of the President in influencing the making of laws. Constitutional powers available to the President to affect legislation include the recommending of legislative programs through messages to the Congress, the veto, and some control over sessions. Informal methods of influencing legislation include the President's personal contacts with congressional leaders, his use of patronage, his ability to arouse public opinion in support of his program, his efforts to influence the election of congressmen sympathetic to his views, and the continuing efforts of executive officials acting as a "presidential lobby" before congressional committees. In addition, the President's legislative powers include the issuing of rules and executive orders having the effect of law under powers delegated to him by the Constitution or by Congress.

Significance   An evaluation of a President's administration is based considerably upon his success or failure in his role as chief legislator. Presidents who have initiated broad legislative programs and successfully pushed them through Congress, using a variety of constitutional and informal political methods and weapons, are generally classified as "strong" presidents; those who have failed to provide effective legislative leadership, through unwillingness or inability, have generally been relegated to the category of "weak" Presidents. Congress, because of its size and diffusion of interests, lacks the means of formulating broad legislative programs and of enacting them into law without the continuing leadership and goading of the President and his aides.

Chief of State   The role of the President as ceremonial head of the government of the United States. Duties of the chief of state include greeting foreign dignitaries, acting as host at state dinners, throwing out the first baseball at the start of the season, and bestowing honors.

Significance   The President serves in a dual capacity as chief of state and as chief executive. In most countries, these roles are split, as in Britain where the Queen is the ceremonial head of state and the Prime Minister and Cabinet head the government and formulate policies. Many students of government believe that the role of chief of state detracts from the ability of the President to give sufficient time and energy to his many other, significant responsibilities. His role as chief of state, however, has blended with his political and executive roles, enabling him to stand as a symbol of national unity, especially during crises.

Economic Message   The annual Economic Report submitted each January by the President to Congress, as required by the Employment Act of 1946. The economic message is concerned with employment levels, production, purchasing power, trends of the nation's economy, and recommendations to Congress on maintaining or improving economic activity. The Economic Report is prepared by the President's Council of Economic Advisers, comprised of three leading economists. A joint congressional Committee on the Economic Report, of seven members from each house, studies the message and makes recommendations for implementing it. See EMPLOYMENT ACT OF 1946, page 277; COUNCIL OF ECONOMIC ADVISERS, page 270.

Significance   The President's annual economic message reflects an acceptance by the national government of responsibility for maintaining stability in the nation's economy through monetary and fiscal policies. Like other messages, it adds to the President's role as chief legislator by enabling him to initiate and recommend legislative programs and to give them nation-wide publicity through the message technique.

Emergency Powers   Powers exercised during a period of crisis by the national government, or those powers conferred by Congress upon the President for a limited period of time. The President's exercise of inherent powers in the field of foreign affairs provides an additional source of power during emergencies. *See* INHERENT POWERS, page 326; *Youngstown Sheet and Tube Co. v. Sawyer,* page 178.

Significance   The Constitution does not recognize the need for additional national powers during an emergency. The Supreme Court has made this clear in stating that "emergency does not create power" (*Home Building and Loan Association v. Blaisdell,* 290 U.S. 398 [1934]). Yet, emergencies have helped to develop the use of otherwise dormant powers and the novel application of ordinary powers.

Executive Agreement   An international agreement, reached by the President with foreign heads of state, that does not require senatorial approval. Such agreements are concluded under the President's constitutional power as commander in chief and his general authority in foreign relations, or under power delegated to him by Congress. *See* EXECUTIVE AGREEMENT, page 323.

Significance   Executive agreements contribute to the President's position of leadership in foreign affairs. Quick, decisive action can be taken during a crisis without having to follow the difficult and time-consuming route of treaty-making. Secrecy can be maintained through executive agreements when open debate in the Senate would be dangerous or provocative. Moreover, by possessing the executive agreement alternative, the President is placed in a better bargaining position with Congress on foreign policy matters.

Executive Order   A rule or regulation, issued by the President, a governor, or some administrative authority, that has the effect of law. Executive orders are used to implement and give administrative effect to provisions of the Constitution, to treaties, and to statutes. They may be used to create or modify the organization or procedures of administrative agencies or may have general applicability as law. Under the national Administrative Procedure Act of 1946, all executive orders must be published in the *Federal Register. See* QUASI-LEGISLATIVE, page 190; DELEGATION OF POWER, page 136.

Significance   The use of executive orders has greatly increased in recent years as a result of the growing tendency of legislative bodies to delegate discretionary powers to the executive branch by statute. This trend will likely continue as government continues to concern itself with highly complex and technical matters in its regulatory and promotional functions. The increasing use of executive orders to implement statutes contributes to the importance of the executive's role as chief legislator.

Item Veto   The power exercised by the governor in all but a few states to veto sections or items of an appropriation bill while signing the remainder of the bill into law. Governors in several states can reduce appropriation items and in two states may veto sections of nonfinancial bills. The legislature may override the vetoed items. The President does not exercise the item veto power. *See* VETO, page 174; RIDER, page 151.

Significance   It is often suggested that the item veto power be given to the President. Many constitutional amendments to this effect have been introduced into the House and Senate, but none has passed. Congress might delegate a limited item veto to the President by inserting such a provision into each appropriation bill. The item veto power is consistent with growing executive responsibility in fiscal affairs. With it, the executive is able to curtail riders, reduce pork barrel legislation, and generally fight legislative extravagance. Those who oppose the item veto regard it as a serious impairment of legislative authority and as an unwarranted increase in executive powers.

Minority President   An elected President who has received fewer than fifty percent of the total *popular* votes cast for all candidates although obtaining a majority of the *electoral* votes. A winning candidate is most likely to be a minority president when there are several fairly strong minor party candidates in the presidential contest. *See* ELECTORAL COLLEGE, page 100.

Significance   Many American Presidents have been "minority presidents," including Abraham Lincoln, Woodrow Wilson, Harry Truman, and John F. Kennedy. Two Presidents, Rutherford B. Hayes in 1876 and Benjamin Harrison in 1888, won election even though in each case their major opponent polled more popular votes than they. So long as more than two candidates run for the office, there is always the possibility of electing a minority president.

Pardon   The granting of a release from the punishment or legal consequences of a crime by the proper executive authority before or after conviction. An "absolute pardon" restores the individual to the position he enjoyed prior to his alleged commission of a crime. A "conditional pardon" requires that certain obligations be met before the pardon becomes effective. The President exercises the complete pardoning power for federal offenses except for convictions in impeachment cases. Pardons are administered for the President by the Office of the Pardon Attorney in the Department of Justice. Thirty states entrust the governor with the full authority for granting pardons. In the remainder, the governor typically shares the power with a pardon board or with the state senate. Pardons are granted usually to provide a remedy for mistakes made in convictions or to release offenders who have been properly rehabilitated. Executives also have the power to grant *reprieves,* which postpone the execution of a sentence for humanitarian reasons or to await new evidence. *See* AMNESTY, page 164; *Ex parte Grossman,* page 176.

Significance   The President's pardoning power extends to all offenses against the United States, including contempt of Congress or of a federal court (*Ex parte Grossman,* 267 U.S. 87 [1925]). Most governors regard the pardoning power as among their most bothersome and distasteful tasks. Relatives and friends of offenders besiege governors with applications and pressures for pardons. The trend in the states is toward vesting greater responsibility in recommending or deciding pardons in full-time boards staffed by correctional experts.

Pocket Veto   A special veto power exercised at the end of a legislative session whereby bills not signed by a chief executive die after a specified time. Under the Constitution, if the President holds a bill for ten days without signing or vetoing it, the bill becomes law if Congress is in session, and is pocket vetoed if Congress adjourns during the ten days. In about one-third of the states, the governors exercise a similar pocket veto power if they do not approve the measure during a stated period after legislative adjournment. This period varies in these states from three to thirty days. *See* VETO, page 174.

Significance   The pocket veto provides a chief executive with a major legislative power. Unlike the ordinary veto, which is merely suspensive in nature and can be overridden, the pocket veto is absolute. Whereas the regular veto requires an explanation from the chief executive, the pocket veto does not, although Presidents usually defend their position in Memorandums of Disapproval. Most significantly, the pocket veto is available at the crucial period at the end of the legislative session when large numbers of bills are enacted in a last-minute legislative rush. In some states, it is the practice of the legislature to recess rather than adjourn when work is completed. It then reassembles briefly before the pocket veto becomes effective and thereby prevents its use by the governor.

President   The chief executive of the United States and the key official in the American system of government. The Constitution in Article II vests the complete executive power in the President. The President is elected every four years through the Electoral College machinery, and is eligible under the Twenty-second Amendment to one additional term. His chief official advisers are found in the Executive Office of the President and in the Cabinet. The President exercises a broad array of powers, some provided by the Constitution, some based on custom and tradition, some delegated to him by Congress, and others that are simply inherent in the nature of his office. Foremost are those broad and largely undefined powers that he exercises in his role as chief of foreign policy. These include the leadership of the armed forces, the recognition of foreign states and governments, the conduct of diplomacy, the making of international agreements and treaties with the Senate's approval, the initiation of new foreign programs, and the providing of leadership for the United States and the free world. In his role of chief administrator, the President exercises broad appointing and removal powers, directs and supervises the operations of the executive branch, directs the formulation of the annual budget, and sees that the laws are faithfully executed. As chief legislator, the President initiates comprehensive legislative programs, delivers regular and special messages to Congress, summons Congress into special sessions, wields a broad veto power, and influences the course of much legislation in his relations with legislative leaders and by arousing public opinion to support his programs. As chief of party, the President dispenses patronage, influences the direction and nature of party policies, provides leadership to his party's delegation in both houses of Congress, and generally influences and determines party actions and policies. In his role as chief of state, the President maintains relations with other nations and performs numerous ceremonial functions in the United States. The prestige of his office contributes much to the effectiveness of the President in his many roles. His easy access to the mass media of communication aids him in molding public opinion. His many sources of information keep him well-informed on the complex problems facing the nation. *See* ELECTORAL COLLEGE, page 100; CHIEF LEGISLATOR, page 165; CHIEF OF STATE, page 166; STEWARDSHIP THEORY, page 173.

Significance   The office of President has been shaped by the experiences of the various Presidents who have held the office during American history. Much has depended upon the personalities of the individual Presidents, their political, economic, and social philosophies, and their conceptions of the office itself. Often, the man and the office have been shaped by the temper of his time, quiet and peaceful or hectic and crisis-filled. Some Presidents, such as William H. Taft and Calvin Coolidge, have viewed the presidency largely in terms of administration and law enforcement. Others, like Abraham Lincoln, Woodrow Wilson, and the two Roosevelts, have regarded the presidency as a position that allows and demands strong leadership and the exercise of broad, undefined powers, whenever they are necessary for the security and well-being of the country. The former group has been labeled as "weak," the latter as "strong," Presidents. All indications are that the nation is moving in the direction of stronger executive leadership, toward what has often been called "presidential government."

President-Elect   The candidate selected by the Electoral College to be the next President. Following the November popular election, the winning candidate is unofficially called the "President-designate" until the electors are able to ratify the people's choice. Under the Twentieth Amendment, the President-elect is sworn into office at noon on the twentieth day of January, and if the President-elect fails to qualify at that time, the Vice President-elect then acts as President until a President qualifies. If the President-elect dies, the Vice President-elect is then sworn in as President. *See* TWENTIETH AMENDMENT, page 174.

Significance   The status of President-elect is an important one because it enables the new chief executive to prepare for his assumption of the duties and responsibilities of the office. From the November election until the inauguration on January 20, the President-elect may meet periodically with the outgoing President to be briefed on special continuing problems, especially those in the foreign affairs field. The President-elect may also begin unofficially to select his top appointees, prepare some of his legislative messages, study the new budget which he inherits, and make other preparatory efforts.

Presidential Succession   The Constitution, in Article II, section 1, stipulates that "In case of the removal of the President from office, or of his death, resignation, or inability to discharge the powers and duties of the said office, the same shall devolve on the Vice-President. . . ." Congress is empowered by the same section of Article II to provide for the officer to act as President in case both the President and Vice President are unable to serve. Congress has from time to time provided by statute for the line of succession, with the present order based on the Presidential Succession Act of 1947. This law provides for succession by the Speaker of the House, President pro tempore of the Senate, and members of the Cabinet, with the Secretary of State first in line. Cabinet members serve only until a Speaker or President pro tempore is available. In addition, the Twentieth Amendment provides that the Vice President-elect shall become President if the President-elect is unable to assume office on inauguration day. *See* PRESIDENTIAL SUCCESSION ACT, page 178; VICE PRESIDENT, page 175.

   Significance   Eight Vice Presidents have succeeded to the office of President as a result of the deaths of Presidents in American history. No President, however, has resigned, been removed, or been incapacitated to the extent of turning the office over to the Vice President. The question of disability has arisen on several occasions, but the Constitution makes no provision for making such a determination other than for the disabled President to step down voluntarily. As a result of serious illnesses suffered by President Dwight Eisenhower, attempts were made to establish a statutory remedy to this problem, but to no avail. Following his second illness, Eisenhower entered into a pact in 1958 with Vice President Richard Nixon, which provided that the Vice President could determine presidential inability if the President were unable to communicate with the Vice President. Presidents John F. Kennedy and Lyndon B. Johnson entered into similar agreements with their Vice Presidents. The knotty problem of determining inability led Congress in 1965 to propose a constitutional amendment that spells out procedures for determining presidential disability, that would permit the Vice President to become Acting President under certain conditions, and that provides for filling a vacancy in the office of the Vice President.

Ratification   The approval by the President of the version of a treaty that has received Senate consent by a two-thirds vote. Ratification may involve the problem of whether a President will accept amendments and reservations to the treaty affixed by the Senate, which might entail reopening of negotiations with other signatory nations. *See* RATIFICATION, page 334.

   Significance   Ordinarily, presidential ratification of a treaty requires the exchange of ratification documents with other signatories to the treaty and an official proclamation putting the treaty into effect. When significant amendments or reservations are made by the Senate, the President must decide whether to try to gain their acceptance by the other parties to the treaty or to drop the matter, which kills the treaty as far as the United States is concerned. For example, when President Wilson refused to accept crippling reservations to the Versailles Treaty in 1919, this action contributed to the eventual defeat of the Treaty and the refusal of the United States to join the League of Nations. By leaving the last word with the President so far as American approval of treaties is concerned, the ratification power serves to enhance his role in foreign affairs.

Recess Appointment   An appointment of a federal official made by the President to fill a vacancy while the Senate is not in session. To prevent the President from postponing appointments until the Senate has adjourned, Congress has by statute prohibited the payment of salary to an officer appointed to fill a vacancy that existed but was not filled while the Senate was still in session.

Recess appointments expire at the end of the next congressional session unless the Senate has confirmed the appointed official by a majority vote. Most state constitutions provide for recess appointments by the governors.

Significance   Recess appointments have often been a matter of contention between the President and the Senate. The provision denying salary to an official who was given a recess appointment, although the position became vacant while the Senate was in session, is an obvious attempt to limit the President's use of recess appointments to circumvent the Senate's approval. Presidents usually refrain from straining relations with the Senate by not giving recess appointments to highly controversial persons or to those previously rejected by the Senate. In the states, recess appointments may be more contentious because of the typical lack of harmony between governors and state senates, and because such appointments are often for long durations owing to the sizable interims between legislative sessions.

Recognition   The power exercised exclusively by the President to establish diplomatic relations with foreign states. Recognition powers are vested in the President by the Constitution, which grants him the power in Article II, section 2 to send and receive ambassadors. See RECOGNITION, page 334.

Significance   The President's recognition power is particularly significant because it involves the ability to refuse to recognize a new state or government as well as to grant recognition. Thus, the act of accrediting foreign diplomats, perhaps intended to be a mere ceremonial function, has become a significant discretionary power in the day-to-day conduct of foreign relations. In deciding whether or not to recognize a new state or government, the President may be influenced by his advisers, by Congress, and by public opinion, but the final decision is his alone. Important recognition controversies in American history have involved the question of whether revolutionary regimes, or states created by conquest, should be recognized. In the case of Communist China, for example, the President faces a dilemma: should he recognize the Communist regime and thereby help stabilize it with some degree of international respectability or, should he refuse to recognize it and hope thereby to hasten its collapse? Also involved is the question of whether the President considers it advantageous to maintain direct communication with and observation of the regime. Presidents have used their own discretion in such cases and no consistent American recognition policy has been developed.

Removal Power   The authority of an executive official to dismiss appointed officials from office. Although the Constitution is silent on the subject, the President has from the beginning exercised the power to remove executive and administrative officials. As a general rule, all officials appointed by the President serve at his pleasure. Federal judges, however, have life tenure, on good behavior, while members of "independent commissions," and merit system employees can be removed only for cause. The removal power of state governors generally compares unfavorably with that of the President because of the number of elective officials in most states and the sharing of the governor's removal power, in many states, by the state senate. See Myers v. United States, page 177; Humphrey's Executor [Rathbun] v. United States, page 177.

Significance   The ability of the President to get the vast national administration to follow his leadership and direction depends to a considerable degree on his authority to dismiss those who disobey his orders, are unsympathetic toward his program, or neglect their duties. Unless the President can surround himself with loyal subordinates who will strive to carry out his program, the system of democratic accountability, focused in the President as the only elected executive official, breaks down. Congress has, on occasion, sought by statute to gain a share of the power to remove executive officials, but the matter was finally decided by the Supreme Court in favor of unrestricted presidential removal power (*Myers v. United States*, 272 U.S. 52 [1926]). This decision, however, was modified by the Supreme Court in holding that members of independent regulatory commissions can be dismissed by the President only for cause as specified by Congress (*Humphrey's Executor [Rathbun] v. United States*, 295 U.S. 602 [1935]). In the states, the recent trend has been toward strengthening and expanding the governors' removal powers.

State of the Union Message   An annual message to Congress in which the President proposes his legislative program. It is based on the constitutional directive that the President "shall from time to time give to the Congress information of the state of the Union, and recommend to their consideration such measures as he shall judge necessary and expedient. . . ." (Art. II, sec. 3). Although the President may choose his time for the message, it has become customary to transmit it at the beginning of a legislative session. *See* CHIEF LEGISLATOR, page 165.

Significance   The importance of the State of the Union message lies primarily in its placing the initiative for developing a broad, comprehensive legislative program in the hands of the President. At the opening of a new legislative session, members of Congress busy themselves with routine organizational matters and minor legislative proposals until the President presents them with his legislative program. In his message, the President discusses the major problems facing the nation and recommends statutory solutions. His message is followed up in subsequent months by scores of bills drawn up in the executive departments and introduced in Congress by "administration" congressmen. Over the past three decades, all Presidents have delivered their State of the Union messages in person. Radio and television have greatly increased the importance of these messages, and the President now speaks not only to Congress but to the American people and, in a sense, to the world as well. It offers him an opportunity to dramatize his policies and objectives and to gain support for them by arousing public opinion.

Stewardship Theory   The view of presidential powers that holds that the President has not only the right but the duty to do anything needed to safeguard the nation and to protect the American people, unless such action is specifically forbidden by the Constitution. The stewardship theory is usually ascribed to Theodore Roosevelt.

Significance   The stewardship theory is one of several conceptions of the President's powers that has contributed to the shaping of that office. Strong presidents have often acted on the stewardship assumption without theorizing.

The theory is closely related to the doctrine of inherent powers. President Taft and others rejected the stewardship view and emphasized the contractual and limiting nature of our constitutional system.

Twentieth Amendment   The "lame duck" Amendment to the Constitution, adopted in 1933, which changed the date for beginning the presidential and vice-presidential terms from March 4 to January 20, and that for beginning congressional terms from March 4 to January 3. Other provisions are: (1) if the President-elect dies before taking office, the Vice President-elect shall become President; (2) if a President-elect has not been chosen or fails to qualify by January 20, the Vice President-elect shall act as President until a President is chosen; (3) if neither qualifies, then Congress shall decide who shall act as President until a President or Vice President qualifies; and (4) if the election of the President and Vice President is thrown into the House and the Senate and a candidate dies, Congress shall determine by law what shall be done. *See* TWENTIETH AMENDMENT, page 157; PRESIDENT-ELECT, page 170.

Significance   The Twentieth Amendment reduced the "lame duck" period for the outgoing President, enabling the newly elected President more quickly to usher in a new administration with its new policies. The change reflects a disposition to make the office more responsive to democratic influences and enables a newly elected President to proceed to develop his policies and programs with little delay. The provisions in the Amendment regarding the inability of the President-elect and Vice President-elect to serve are designed to close a gap in the original Constitution, which failed to provide for these eventualities.

Twenty-second Amendment   An amendment to the Constitution, adopted in 1951, limiting presidential tenure to two terms for an individual. A Vice President who succeeds to the office may serve as long as ten years as President, provided he has not served more than two years of the uncompleted term of his predecessor. The incumbent President, Harry S. Truman, was excluded from the limitations of the Amendment, but he chose not to run for a third term.

Significance   The Twenty-second Amendment was proposed by the Republican-controlled Eightieth Congress in reaction to the four terms of Franklin Roosevelt. Roosevelt had shattered the strong "no-third-term" tradition started by Washington and followed until 1940. The Amendment was also a reaction to the growth of executive power that had resulted from war and depression crises and reflected a yearning to return to the "normalcy" of congressional domination of weak presidents. Supporters of the Amendment defend it as a useful safeguard against the dangers of executive tyranny and self-perpetuation in power. Opponents argue that it tends to reduce further a second-term President's already weak position as political leader and exhibits a fundamental distrust of the democratic process.

Veto   A legislative power vested in a chief executive to return a bill unsigned to the legislative body with reasons for his objections. The Constitution provides that every bill that passes the House and the Senate must be sent to the President before it becomes law. When the President receives a bill, he may:

(1) sign it, whereupon it becomes law; (2) not sign it, whereupon it becomes law after ten congressional working days; (3) veto it, and send it back to the house of its origin; or (4) not sign it, whereupon if Congress adjourns within ten days the bill is killed (pocket veto). The President vetoes a bill by writing "veto" (I forbid) across the face of the bill; he then sends it back to Congress with a message setting forth his objections. Congress may amend the bill according to the President's demands and then repass it, or it may reject the President's objection and override the veto by repassing the bill with a two-thirds roll-call vote in each house. Governors, too, exercise the veto power and, in all but a few states, may veto items of appropriation bills—a power denied to the President. In the states, the number of votes needed to override a gubernatorial veto varies from a simple majority in each house to a two-thirds vote of all members elected to the legislature. *See* ITEM VETO, page 167; POCKET VETO, page 169.

Significance   Presidents employed the veto power infrequently and with great caution until the post-Civil War administration of Andrew Johnson. Since 1865, the veto power has been used with increasing vigor by most presidents; Grover Cleveland with 414 regular and pocket vetoes, and Franklin Roosevelt, with 631, have been its most persistent users. The scope of the veto power has also expanded since 1865. The earlier view that the veto should be used to block unconstitutional or technically imperfect laws has been supplemented by its employment to express disapproval of any kind. Although the veto is merely suspensive in effect, few vetoes are overridden by Congress, since if one-third plus one of the members of *either* house support the President's view, the veto prevails. The *threat* of the veto can also be used effectively by a chief executive to shape and change legislation while it is still in the hands of the legislature.

Vice President   The constitutional officer assigned to preside over the Senate and to assume the presidency in case of the death, resignation, removal, or disability of the President. The Vice President is elected on the same ballot with the President and, if no candidate receives a majority of the electoral vote, the Senate chooses from the two candidates with the highest number of electoral votes. Although President of the Senate, the Vice President is not considered to be a member, participating only informally, if at all, in its deliberations, and voting only when a tie occurs. *See* VICE PRESIDENT, page 158; PRESIDENTIAL SUCCESSION, page 170.

Significance   During most of American history, the vice presidency has been regarded as an insignificant office and as a political graveyard to be avoided by promising politicians. The low repute of this potentially significant office perhaps results mainly from the method of selecting vice-presidential candidates—to balance the party ticket or to reward or appease party wings. Recent Presidents have sought to make more effective use of their Vice Presidents as intermediaries between the President and Congress and as roving ambassadors of good will in foreign affairs. Vice Presidents customarily attend Cabinet meetings, and Presidents Eisenhower, Kennedy, and Johnson assigned their Vice Presidents additional responsibilities in the executive branch. The trend is toward developing the office into an assistant presidency. Eight Vice

Presidents have succeeded to the office of President upon the death of the President, thereby leaving the office of Vice President vacant. In addition, seven Vice Presidents died in office and one (John C. Calhoun, 1832) resigned. A constitutional amendment proposed in 1965 would permit the President with the consent of Congress to appoint a Vice President when the office is vacant.

IMPORTANT AGENCIES

Executive Office of the President   The top staff agencies that give the President help and advice in carrying out his major duties. President Franklin D. Roosevelt established the Executive Office by executive order under the Reorganization Act of 1939. The components of the Executive Office of the President have changed over the years and today include the Bureau of the Budget, the White House Office, the National Security Council, the Council of Economic Advisers, the National Aeronautics and Space Council, the Office of Economic Opportunity, the Office of Emergency Planning, the Office of Science and Technology, and the Office of the Special Representative for Trade Negotiations.

Significance   The objective in the creation of the Executive Office was to provide the President with a "general staff" to give him the help needed to direct the far-flung activities of the executive branch. The President has been hampered, however, by the refusal of Congress to place some key agencies within the Executive Office, such as the Civil Service Commission and the General Accounting Office. All indications point to a growth in the importance of the Executive Office as the President's tasks become more extensive and complex and he is forced to place increasing dependence upon his staff. The White House Office in particular contains the close confidential advisers whom the President leans on for day-to-day operations of the executive branch.

Secret Service   A law-enforcement division of the Treasury Department, which has full responsibility for protecting the life and security of the President and his family. The Secret Service also performs security functions concerned with treasury matters.

Significance   Like the "G-men" of the FBI, the "T-men" of the Treasury Department are carefully selected, rigorously trained, and devoted to duty. Each year, Secret Service agents check out thousands of "crank" and threatening letters sent to the President and investigate numerous threats made against the life of the President or members of his family. Whenever the President travels at home or abroad, all security arrangements are handled by the Secret Service, with the cooperation of the police of the area or country which the President is visiting. Following the assassination of President John F. Kennedy and the Warren Commission Report on the assassination, the Secret Service force was increased and closer cooperation with the FBI in safeguarding the President was undertaken.

IMPORTANT CASES

Ex parte Grossman, 267 U.S. 87 (1925): Upheld a pardon granted by the President to Grossman, who had been convicted of contempt of Court. It was alleged that the independence of the judiciary depends upon the authority of judges to try without jury individuals who violate court orders, and to sentence them for contempt of court free from interference by other departments of government. The Court rejected this argument and upheld the President, holding that he "can reprieve or pardon all offenses after their commission, either before trial, during trial or after trial, by individuals, or by classes, conditionally or absolutely, and this without modification or regulation by Congress."

Significance   The effect of the *Grossman* case was to extend the President's pardoning power to all federal cases regardless of which branch of government is involved. Only conviction of a public official through impeachment proceedings is beyond the President's pardoning power.

Humphrey's Executor [Rathbun] v. United States, 295 U.S. 602 (1935): Upheld the provisions of the Federal Trade Commission Act providing that members of the Commission may be removed from office only for causes specified in the Act. President Roosevelt had removed Humphrey for political reasons, and in this case, decided after Humphrey's death, the Court held that Congress clearly had the authority to limit the President's removal power to instances of "inefficiency, neglect of duty, or malfeasance in office." The Court pointed out that the broad removal powers accorded to the President in *Myers v. United States,* 272 U.S. 52 (1926), pertained only to purely executive officers, whereas members of the Federal Trade Commission exercise legislative and judicial powers as well. *See Myers* case, page 177.

Significance   The *Humphrey* case emphasized the distinction between independent regulatory commissions, such as the FPC, the FTC, the SEC, and the ICC, and agencies of the executive branch. The Court, in recognizing the validity of statutory requirements for tenure of commissioners, cited the character of their work, the need to develop expertness through experience, the legislative intention to keep them free from political domination or control, and the threefold nature of their duties—administrative, quasi-legislative, quasi-judicial.

Mississippi v. Johnson, 4 Wallace 475 (1867): Rejected an attempt by the State of Mississippi to enjoin President Johnson from enforcing the Reconstruction Acts of 1867. The Court held that the President cannot be restrained by injunction from carrying out his official duties of a political nature, such as the enforcement of an act of Congress.

Significance   The decision enhanced the position of the President under the separation of powers by freeing him from judicial interference with his law-enforcement duties. Laws alleged to be unconstitutional may be struck down by the courts only after the President has begun to enforce them.

Myers v. United States, 272 U.S. 52 (1926): Upheld the President's removal from office of a postmaster without securing the approval of the Senate to the removal. The Court held that Congress cannot limit the President's power to remove executive officials, and the provisions of a law of 1876 requiring the Senate's concurrence in presidential removals was held to be unconstitutional. *See Humphrey's* case, page 177.

Significance   The *Myers* case, with the Court's majority speaking through Chief Justice (former President) Taft, asserted a broad presidential removal power that had been in some doubt during much of American history. In *Humphrey's Executor* [*Rathbun*] *v. United States,* 295 U.S. 602 (1935), however, the Court upheld the power of Congress to limit the President's authority to remove members of the independent regulatory commissions.

Youngstown Sheet and Tube Co. v. Sawyer, 343 U.S. 579 (1952): Struck down the President's Executive Order that had authorized seizure of steel mills and their operation by the national government. President Harry S. Truman acted under his inherent power as chief executive and commander in chief to safeguard the nation's security during the Korean War, when a strike in the steel mills threatened the supply of weapons. The Court held that the President has no authority under the Constitution to seize private property unless Congress authorizes the seizure, and that the Constitution does not permit the President to legislate.

Significance   The immediate result of the *Youngstown* case was the return of the steel mills by the government to their private owners and the resumption of the strike by the United Steelworkers Union. More fundamentally, the case established for the first time that limits exist in the exercise of the President's inherent powers in seeking to safeguard the security of the nation. It reaffirmed the inviolability of private property rights under the Fifth Amendment, and the exercise of legislative powers only by Congress.

IMPORTANT STATUTES

Presidential Succession Act   An act that provides for the line of succession to the presidency beyond the Vice President, in the following order: Speaker of the House, President pro tempore of the Senate, the Secretaries of State, Treasury, and Defense, the Attorney General, the Postmaster General, and the Secretaries of Interior, Agriculture, Commerce, and Labor. Of these, only those meeting the qualifications of the Office of President are eligible, and they must first resign from their positions to accept the presidency.

Significance   The Presidential Succession Act of 1947 changed the old line of succession under which Cabinet officials in the above order followed the Vice President. The Speaker of the House is in a preferred position under the Act, not only because he is first in line after the Vice President, but because the line of succession is unlikely to go beyond him. Under the Act, Cabinet members serve only until a Speaker or President pro tempore qualifies to succeed to the presidency. The Act was supported by those who believed that it would be more democratic to place two leaders of Congress in the first two succession slots. Some students of government, however, have opposed the change, holding that the prestige and ability needed for the presidency are more likely to be found in the Secretary of State or Secretary of the Treasury than in the congressional leadership.

Nine

Public Administration: Organization and Personnel

Administration   The procedure by which laws are enforced and public policy is carried out. *Public* administration, as distinguished from private or business administration, is largely the function of the executive branch of government. It carries out the policies established by the legislative branch subject to the oversight and review of both the legislative and judicial branches. Administration is the art or science of managing public affairs with emphasis on such factors as organization, personnel, and finance. *Significance*   All organizations are faced with the problem of efficient administration. Public administration, however, is increasingly complex because of the tremendous range of responsibilities that modern government has undertaken, the need for organizing and directing millions of employees, and the problem of controlling the expenditure of billions of dollars. The traditional view that administration and policy formation are separate has given way to recognition of the policy-making aspects inherent in administration. This recognition is buttressed by the assignment of rule-making and adjudicating functions to many agencies. In recent years, much scholarly attention has been paid to developing sound principles and practices of administration in order to ensure the responsibility and accountability of administrative personnel to the people.

Administrative Order   A directive, issued by an administrative agency, that has the force of law. An order is generally distinguished from a "rule" or "regulation" in that an order is specifically directed to an individual or group to correct infractions of a rule. An example would be an order of the National Labor Relations Board to a union or an employer to cease violation of a labor practice that the Board had declared to be unfair. Orders are issued after a hearing conducted by the agency which resembles the procedures of a court of law. Appeals may be brought to the regular courts. Orders of federal agencies are published in the *Federal Register*. See HEARING EXAMINER, page 186; *Opp* case, page 194; ADMINISTRATIVE PROCEDURE ACT, page 195. *Significance*   Administrative orders are part of the over-all development of the administrative process. Legislative bodies have vested control over complex economic and social problems in various administrative agencies that have been granted broad powers to prescribe rules and regulations and to enforce these rules through orders. In this way, the legislature is saved the impossible job of determining in advance all the aspects of complex matters, and the courts are freed from deciding disputes over technical subjects in which they lack competence. The administrative agency can develop the necessary expertness to handle specialized cases. An increasing number of businesses and individuals are subject to administrative orders.

Administrative Reorganization   The reform of administrative agencies and procedures to improve efficiency, economy, and responsibility. Reorganization movements have generally had as their major purposes the concentration of authority and accountability by: (1) integrating agencies with similar functions to eliminate overlapping and waste; (2) fixing responsibility in some hierarchical arrangement; (3) establishing advisory and centralized housekeeping agencies to aid the chief administrator; (4) eliminating multiheaded boards or commissions and elective officers engaged in purely administrative work; and (5) improving personnel, budget, and auditing procedures. *See* REORGANIZATION ACT, page 196.

Significance   The twentieth century has witnessed increased interest and activity in administrative reorganization at all levels of American government. It has resulted in increased authority for the President, governors, and mayors, the shortening of the ballot, and the adoption of the council-manager plan at the municipal level. Official reorganization studies are continuously carried on, and the President and some governors have been given authority to reshuffle agencies. Budgetary and personnel practices have been improved. Reorganization movements frequently meet resistance from legislatures that fear executive power, from interest groups that seek to protect the position of agencies serving them, and from agency personnel who fear loss of status.

Auxiliary Agency   A governmental unit that services other governmental agencies. Typical auxiliary agencies include central purchasing, personnel, and accounting. They perform what is sometimes called housekeeping or technical services. *See* CIVIL SERVICE COMMISSION, page 193; GENERAL SERVICES ADMINISTRATION, page 193.

Significance   Auxiliary agencies not only provide a centralized and less expensive means of dispensing technical services; they also give the department head or the chief executive an important control mechanism. For example, while it is possible for each agency to do its own hiring or purchasing, improved administration generally results from the assignment of such functions to centralized auxiliary units.

Board   A group of persons, usually three or more, who are charged with responsibility for directing a particular governmental function. The term "commission" is frequently used interchangeably with board.

Significance   Multiheaded versus singleheaded directorship is one of the most controversial problems of administrative organization. Both forms are found at all levels of government. It is generally agreed that a board is more desirable than one man when the agency has quasi-legislative and quasi-judicial functions, particularly in the area of regulation of the economy. Then, a board permits the use of bipartisan personnel for controversial matters and, where terms of board members overlap, continuity of policy. A board makes it difficult, however, to fix responsibility, and conflict may develop within the board itself. A single head makes for well-defined responsibility and unity of purpose. Administrative experts recommend the single director for purely administrative tasks, but boards or commissions are frequently used for this purpose. A compromise proposal that has found favor is to retain plural bodies for regulatory and adjudicatory functions but to assign administrative responsibility to the chairman of the board. This has been done, for example, in the Federal Trade Commission and the Civil Service Commission.

Bureau   A major working unit of a department or agency. Bureaus are generally assigned specific functions and their heads are responsible to the head of the entire department. Well-known examples include the Federal Bureau of Investigation (FBI) in the Department of Justice and the Census Bureau in the Department of Commerce. Bureaus are usually subdivided into various divisions, branches, or sections, each with responsibility for specialized activities.
    Significance   While the nomenclature assigned to various parts of an agency is not uniform, it is considered useful for the development of scientific principles of administrative organization. The Hoover Commission, which studied the organization of the federal executive branch, and the "little Hoover commissions" in the states, suggested a standard nomenclature for all administrative units. In this way, responsibility is more clearly fixed within a major department and persons working within a department better understand their roles.

Bureaucracy   Any administrative system, especially of governmental agencies, that carries out policy on a day-to-day basis, that uses standardized procedures, and that is based on a specialization of duties. Bureaucracy also connotes a system wherein excessive growth of administrative agencies is accompanied by concentration of power in administrative officials, excessive red tape, dedication to routine, and resistance to change. The term, "the bureaucracy," is often used simply to designate the administrative or executive branch of government.
    Significance   All modern governments have extensive administrative units. The problem in a democracy is to keep governmental employees responsive to the law and to the elected representatives of the people. Safeguards against the development of irresponsible bureaucracy include congressional oversight of administrative agencies through investigations and the power of the purse, presidential direction of the administration, and judicial review of administrative actions. The increased growth and power of administrative agencies makes imperative strong control over their actions, lest administrative officials obstruct rather than further the policies established by the people's representatives.

Career Service   A professionalized civil service wherein employment is based on merit, opportunity is afforded for advancement, and guarantees are

provided against arbitrary dismissal. *See* MERIT SYSTEM, page 188; FEDERAL
SERVICE ENTRANCE EXAMINATION, page 185; ROGERS ACT, page 344.

Significance   Employment by merit has made large inroads on the spoils
system, with stress now placed on a career service that emphasizes the opportunity to spend a satisfying lifetime in government service and to reach positions
of honor and prestige. In recent years, the national government and some
states have attempted to recruit talented college graduates for governmental
careers. In the federal civil service, major opportunities are made available to
those college graduates who pass the Federal Service Entrance Examination
and the Management Internship Examination. The concept of a career service
has also been successfully applied in the Foreign Service, which has its own
personnel system.

Cease and Desist Order   An administrative order directed to an individual,
firm, or labor union to refrain from violating the law or the rules and regulations established by an administrative agency. *See* ADMINISTRATIVE ORDER, page
179.

Significance   The cease and desist order has become the major instrument of economic regulation through administrative agencies. The power was
first given to the Interstate Commerce Commission and subsequently to most
independent regulatory commissions, state and national. Violation of a cease
and desist order may result in prosecution or in the loss of benefits that the
agency administers, such as a license to do business.

Centralized Purchasing   Vesting authority in one agency to purchase and
handle supplies and materials for governmental agencies. This is now done for
the national government by the General Services Administration, and the practice has been adopted by most states and many local units of government. *See*
GENERAL SERVICES ADMINISTRATION, page 193.

Significance   Centralized purchasing has replaced the system whereby
each department or agency purchases its own supplies. The advantages include
savings through large purchases, standardization of equipment and record keeping, reduction of possibilities of corruption, and centralization of responsibility.
The major disadvantage is that standardized purchases may not meet specialized
needs of specific agencies, but this problem can be solved by mutual arrangements or by exempting certain items from central purchase.

Certification of Eligibles   The practice by which a civil service commission
provides a hiring officer of an agency with the names of persons who have
qualified for a position. This is usually done in accordance with the ranking
of individuals on test scores. The practice in most jurisdictions is to certify the
top three names, often called the "rule of three."

Significance   Certification is the initial step in the hiring process. The
rule of three is designed to give the hiring officer a chance to weigh intangible
factors, such as personality, in making a final decision. In some jurisdictions,
only the name at the top of the list may be certified, while in others, five or
more are required. Personnel experts differ over what constitutes the best practice. Certification rules may be further complicated by limiting certain positions

to veterans or by the availability of two or more suitable lists from which a position might be filled. A person whose name is certified but is not selected is returned to the eligible list.

Civil Service A collective term for most persons employed by government who are not members of the military services. It is more generally understood to apply to all those who gain governmental employment through a merit system, more correctly called the "classified civil service." Elective officials and high ranking policy-making officers who are appointed by elected officials, and members of the judiciary are not considered to be civil servants. *See* MERIT SYSTEM, page 188.

Significance The civil service has gained prestige in recent years. The merit system in particular has made substantial headway in the national government and in some states and cities. Most county and township governments, however, still retain the spoils system. Marked interest has arisen in professionalizing civil service employment and in applying sound principles of personnel management. In the United States, civil servants are restricted in the scope of their political activities and, though permitted to join labor organizations, may not strike. One of the essential ingredients of modern civil service is the loyalty of the civil servants to whatever administration is in power.

Classified Service Positions of governmental employment that are under the jurisdiction of a civil service commission and that are filled by merit. Congress has permitted some agencies to establish their own personnel systems outside the classified service, such as the Foreign Service, TVA, FBI, and CIA. *See* SCHEDULES A, B, AND C, page 190.

Significance Under federal law, the President may exempt certain positions from the classified service. This includes top-ranking administrators as well as persons holding confidential or highly technical positions. In the states, exemptions may be determined by statute or by a civil service agency. It is generally left to the latter to determine which classified positions will be filled by competitive exam and which by noncompetitive exam, or which are exempt from examination. The latter categories include technical or top-ranking positions and positions for which there is no suitable examination procedure, such as laborers or part-time employees.

Decentralization An administrative concept applied by large organizations or departments in assigning decision-making responsibility to subunits on a geographical or subject matter basis. Decentralization usually takes the form of field-service operations or division of tasks through specialization. *See* FIELD SERVICE, page 185.

Significance It is impossible for the head of a large department to make every decision concerning the operations or services of a particular agency. Decentralization encourages responsible participation by lesser officials and permits adaptation to local needs. Major policy decisions, however, should be made by top officials.

Delegation of Authority The assignment of decision-making responsibility to subordinate officials. The heads of large agencies find it essential to delegate some of their authority to others, but this must be done within clearly defined standards, subject to review by the head.

Significance   In establishing a public agency, Congress often assigns a wide range of power to the agency head. He, in turn, must delegate some of his authority if he is to maintain adequate control over the agency and not have to handle every detail alone. Successful administration requires that delegations of authority be made ungrudgingly and that authority be commensurate with responsibility. Many top officials overburden themselves out of fear of losing power or fear that others will make the wrong decisions. Proper delegation of authority, under standards of policy established at the top, enables the settlement of many matters at lower levels of the administrative hierarchy. Personnel and administrative experts point out that departmental morale is improved by delegation of authority, through giving others a sense of participation.

Department   A major administrative unit with responsibility for the conduct of a broad area of government operations. In the national government, the departments are headed by officers who comprise the President's Cabinet. These departments include State, Treasury, Defense, Justice, Commerce, Labor, Agriculture, Interior, Post Office, Health, Education, and Welfare, Housing and Urban Development, and Transportation. State and local governments also departmentalize major functions. Departments are generally subdivided into bureaus, divisions, sections, and other units. (For specific departments, *see* Index.)

Significance   Most of the work of government is conducted through major departments. Departmental status generally indicates a permanent interest on the part of the government to promote a particular function. The Departments of the Army, Navy, and Air Force retain the title but have been incorporated into the Department of Defense. A number of major functions are vested in agencies outside the regular departments, such as independent regulatory commissions and corporations, in order to remove them from direct presidential supervision. Many administrative authorities feel that all functions should be assigned to one of the major departments to prevent diffusion of responsibility.

Ex Officio   A Latin term for "by virtue of office." Many persons hold a position on a board or agency by virtue of their holding some other related position. For example, a governor, typically, is a member of numerous state boards and commissions by virtue of his position as governor.

Significance   The ex officio principle is designed to involve important officials in the decisions of major agencies. It serves to coordinate the efforts of related agencies and to strengthen responsibility.

Federal Register   A United States Government publication initiated by the Federal Register Act of 1935, which requires that presidential proclamations, reorganization plans, and executive orders be published. The Administrative Procedure Act of 1946 requires every public agency to publish a statement of its organization, authority, methods of operation, and statements of general policy in the *Federal Register*. Notice of proposed rules and regulations and administrative orders resulting from the adjudicatory functions of the agency must also be published. The *Federal Register* is published five times each week. The documents are codified in the *Code of Federal Regulations* (CFR). Some states have similar publications.

Significance   The increasing growth of executive orders and administrative rules and regulations makes the *Federal Register* one of the most important and widely read government publications. Prior to its publication, the citizen and business interests in particular had no way of knowing what and how new rules applied to them. Publication of proposed rules and regulations assures interested parties an opportunity to be heard prior to their enforcement.

Federal Service Entrance Examination   A federal civil service examination open to college juniors, seniors, and graduates with broad educational backgrounds who are interested in securing junior management positions in federal service upon graduation from college. The examination tests general intelligence and aptitudes to find promising career servants who can move into management positions in the future. Persons who take the examination may take an additional examination called the Management Internship Examination which, if passed, offers greater opportunities.

Significance   Unlike most civil service examinations, which test specific skills, the Federal Service Entrance Examination is part of the government's effort to attract persons who possess qualities essential for supervisory and administrative positions. Many college graduates ineligible to take examinations for specific skills may quality under this program. A few states have similar examinations.

Field Service   Decentralized administration typified by local or regional branch offices of a federal or state agency. Operations, personnel, and finance are under the control of the central office in Washington, D.C., or the state capital.

Significance   Most governmental work is conducted through field offices. Only about ten percent of federal employees work in Washington, D.C.; the remaining ninety percent are assigned to field-service offices around the nation and abroad. Field–headquarters relationships pose a continuing problem for sound administration in securing coordination of activity and responsibility. Field offices provide the citizen with close-to-home services and make possible the settlement of most problems where they arise.

Functional Consolidation   Combining several administrative units that do related work into one major department. *See* FUNCTIONAL CONSOLIDATION, page 367; ADMINISTRATIVE REORGANIZATION, page 180.

Significance   Functional consolidation is a basic principle of administrative organization. The tendency of legislative bodies to create new agencies to meet new problems results often in diffusion of responsibility and the existence of too many agencies for the chief executive to direct and control effectively. Administrative experts suggest that, on the state level, all agencies should be consolidated into from ten to twenty departments. Both the New Jersey Constitution of 1947 and the Michigan Constitution of 1963 place a limitation of twenty departments in the executive branch. The Hoover Commission suggested, in 1949, that some 1800 federal agencies could logically be consolidated into twenty-two major departments.

Government Corporation   An agency of government that administers a business enterprise. The corporation form is used when an activity is primarily commercial in nature, produces revenue for its continued existence, and requires greater flexibility than Congress normally permits regular departments. Corporations are used at the national level for such enterprises as electric power distribution (Tennessee Valley Authority) and insuring of bank deposits (Federal Deposit Insurance Corporation). At the state level, corporations (often called "authorities") operate airports, turnpikes, and harbors, the best known being the Port of New York Authority.

Significance   The corporation device enables government to operate diverse business services with flexibility similar to private enterprise. Prior to 1945, Congress permitted corporations a great degree of independence, but the Government Corporation Control Act of 1945 subjects them to budgetary and auditing controls and to civil service laws. Corporations are generally run by a board of directors and many are attached to one of the major departments for administrative purposes. The problem of how to balance a corporation's need for flexibility with the democratic requirements of legislative and executive controls remains.

Hearing   Adjudication by an administrative or regulatory agency of alleged violations of laws or of rules and regulations administered by it. Hearings are also held to give interested parties an opportunity to be heard prior to the promulgation of a rule. *See* HEARING EXAMINER, page 186; QUASI-JUDICIAL, page 189; HEARING, page 211.

Significance   Hearings may be initiated by the agency itself or by any aggrieved party. They are conducted in a manner similar to, but less formal than, a court of law, under rules established by the Administrative Procedure Act of 1946. Decisions result in the issuance of administrative orders having the force of law. Appeals may be made to the courts, which generally limit themselves to a review of the overall fairness of the hearing and to whether the record substantiates the findings of the agency. The quasi-judicial power of agencies is one of the major administrative developments of the twentieth century. The requirement of a hearing prior to the promulgation of a rule permits parties likely to be affected by a rule to have a part in its formulation.

Hearing Examiner   An official who conducts hearings for a regulatory agency and makes recommendations to the heads of the agency on issuance of administrative orders. Under the Administrative Procedure Act of 1946, hearing examiners are appointed under civil service rules, are protected against arbitrary dismissal and loss of salary, and may not be assigned administrative duties. *See* QUASI-JUDICIAL, page 189; ADMINISTRATIVE PROCEDURE ACT, page 195.

Significance   Hearing examiners were created in response to the pre-1946 concern that regulatory agencies were both prosecutor and judge of those accused of violating their rules. By giving a degree of independence to hearing examiners, Congress sought to overcome the major weaknesses of administrative adjudication of private rights. Decisions of hearing examiners are presented to the agency heads who may hear appeals from the examiner's recommendations. If no appeal is made from the examiner's recommendations, the decision is final.

Hoover Commission   A commission appointed in 1947 to study the organization of the executive branch. The group of twelve persons (four appointed by the President, four by the President pro tempore of the Senate, and four by the Speaker of the House), known as the Commission on Organization of the Executive Branch, was headed by former President Herbert Hoover. It filed its report in 1949. A second Hoover Commission, similarly appointed in 1953, was charged with the function of suggesting which federal functions might be discontinued. *See* REORGANIZATION ACT, page 196.

Significance   The first Hoover Commission submitted a voluminous but highly regarded series of reports and made almost 300 specific recommendations, approximately seventy percent of which have been adopted. Basically, the Commission proposed greater consolidation of agencies, greater authority and assistance for the President, and improved budget, personnel, and administrative procedures. The Commission inspired the creation of "little Hoover commissions" in about half the states, many of which have met with some success. The second Hoover Commission's concern with policy matters rather than organization has limited the influence of its report.

Independent Agency   A federal agency that is not part of the twelve executive departments. The term may include independent regulatory commissions, but is generally used to describe agencies which perform service rather than regulatory functions. Examples of independent agencies are the Civil Service Commission, the Veterans Administration, and the General Services Administration. Many independent agencies are organized like regular departments and are headed by persons responsible to the President. Others take the form of boards or commissions, such as the Tariff Commission and the Atomic Energy Commission.

Significance   A large number of agencies have independent status. Some do not fit into any particular major department and others service all departments. In other cases, Congress has wanted to keep a tighter rein on an agency than departmental status would permit or has responded to the pressures of interest groups which seek autonomy for a given function. A few have been given independent status to shield them from partisan politics, as in the cases of the Tariff Commission and the Atomic Energy Commission. Terms of officials frequently overlap to avoid control by any one President, and the removal power of the President may be limited. The existence of large numbers of independent agencies complicates the organizational pattern and lines of responsibility of the executive branch.

Independent Regulatory Commission   An agency outside the major executive departments charged with the regulation of important aspects of the economy. The Commissions are the Interstate Commerce Commission, Federal Trade Commission, Federal Power Commission, Securities and Exchange Commission, Federal Communications Commission, National Labor Relations Board, Civil Aeronautics Board, Federal Reserve Board, and Federal Maritime Commission. All of these agencies are empowered to establish rules for the particular industries they regulate and to prosecute violators. All are multi-headed, with five or seven members, except for the eleven-member Interstate Commerce Commission. (For specific commissions, *see* Index.)

Significance   The independent regulatory commissions possess vast authority to determine individual and property rights. They have been established because of the sheer complexity of modern economic problems and the desirability of having agencies that could develop expertness and continuity of policy with regard to these problems. Neither Congress nor the courts have the talent or the time. The agencies are independent of the President in order that their legislative and adjudicatory functions are removed from partisan politics. Though members of the commissions are appointed by the President with the Senate's consent, they may be removed only for cause. Terms of office are lengthy and overlapping in order to avoid dominance by the appointees of one President. No more than a majority of commissioners may be of one party. Problems arise from the tendency of commissions to become captives of the industries they are supposed to regulate, since many officials are necessarily drawn from the regulated industries. Further, the independence of the commissions may result in policies that are contrary to those of the party in power. These commissions have often been called "the headless fourth branch" of government, because of their peculiar place in the organization of the government and lack of continuing supervision from the President or Congress.

Line and Staff   An administrative concept that categorizes the work of an agency as an operating or advisory function. The line carries out legislative programs and deals directly with the people. The executive departments such as Agriculture or Labor are typical line departments. The staff serves in an advisory capacity, aiding the chief executive and the line officials through such activities as planning, coordinating, and budgeting. The Bureau of the Budget is a major staff agency of the federal government. See AUXILIARY AGENCY, page 180.

Significance   The distinction between line and staff prescribes the division of labor in large organizations. The distinction is, however, by no means a precise one. Line officials may engage in staff or advisory work, as members of the Cabinet generally do, and some staff agencies may engage in operating tasks, as some budgeting or planning offices do.

Merit System   The selection, retention, and promotion of government employees on the basis of demonstrated fitness. Though the term is often used interchangeably with "civil service," the merit system emphasizes positive programs of sound personnel management rather than the mere placing of restraints upon the spoils system. See CIVIL SERVICE, page 183; CLASSIFIED SERVICE, page 183.

Significance   The merit system has not been universally adopted in the

United States, particularly when viewed as a thoroughgoing personnel program. While much headway has been made at the national level, much remains to be done on the state and local levels, particularly in counties and townships. Originally, the concept of civil service was limited to keeping unfit persons out of government service. The merit system represents a more positive approach looking toward the development of a career service and toward in-service training, position classification, pay standardization, and retirement programs.

Organization   The arrangement of persons for the most effective achievement of a purpose or objective. Public administration experts are concerned with the problem of the best way to organize the government or a particular agency to eliminate friction and to best accomplish the task assigned. This involves decisions as to the nature of line, staff, and auxiliary agencies, the location of responsibility, and the over-all coordination of efforts. Activities may be organized according to major purpose (for example, the Department of Agriculture), process or skills (central purchasing), area (fire and police protection), or clientele (Veterans Administration). The use of a single head or a board is another concern of organization. *See* ADMINISTRATIVE REORGANIZATION, page 180.

Significance   Organizational concepts and techniques are mainly the concern of administrative specialists but are also important to all citizens who seek to understand the nature of administrative organization and problems of reorganization. All agencies contain all or some of the organizational patterns, and one is rarely used to the exclusion of others. Much depends on the purposes to be served and, in government in particular, on the desires and influence of legislative bodies and pressure groups.

Position Classification   The grouping of government employment positions on the basis of duties, responsibilities, and qualifications. A position is classified in accordance with the nature of the job rather than the person holding the position. *See* MERIT SYSTEM, page 188.

Significance   Position classification is regarded as an essential ingredient of a sound merit system. The benefits include: (1) simplification of recruitment and selection of personnel through administration of similar tests for similar positions; (2) equal pay for equal work, an important goal of public personnel administration and essential for high morale; (3) well-defined lines of responsibility for the individual worker and top management; (4) clear avenues of promotion and transfer. The over-all objective of position classification is equitable treatment of government employees, which benefits both the employee and the public. It is necessary, however, that classification schemes be reviewed from time to time, lest they act as a straitjacket on effective administration, and optimum utilization of employees. Position classification is used in the national government and in several state and local governments.

Quasi-judicial   Powers exercised by administrative agencies that have the characteristics of a judicial act. Independent regulatory commissions as well as other administrative agencies exercise quasi-judicial powers when they conduct hearings and make decisions having the force of law. *See* HEARING, page 186.

Significance   Under the doctrine of the separation of powers, only courts and judges may exercise judicial power. The highly technical nature of modern economic regulation has necessitated the delegation of "quasi-" (Latin for "seemingly" or "resembling") judicial power to expert administrators. For example, Congress has empowered the Federal Trade Commission to determine what constitutes an unfair trade practice. Concern over the inherent violation of the separation of powers led to the passage of the Administrative Procedure Act of 1946, which requires the use of hearing examiners, more judicial-like procedures, and expands the power of judicial review of administrative adjudications.

Quasi-legislative   Rule-making powers, exercised by administrative agencies, that have the characteristics of a legislative act. Numerous administrative agencies are authorized to issue rules and regulations having the force of law. These include not only the independent regulatory commissions but a host of other agencies, such as the Department of Agriculture, which issues rules relative to crop quotas and other agricultural practices. *See* ADMINISTRATIVE ORDER, page 179.

Significance   Under the doctrine of the separation of powers, all legislative power is vested in the legislative body. Congress and the state legislatures, however, cannot legislate in sufficient detail to cover the problems which arise in a complex society. Thus, the legislature delegates power to administrative agencies to "fill in the details" under the standards established by the legislature. The Administrative Procedure Act of 1946 requires administrative agencies to give notice and hold hearings on proposed rules and regulations and to publish all rules and regulations in the *Federal Register*. Congress retains a check on "quasi-" (Latin for "seemingly" or "resembling") legislation by being able to change the basic law of the agency. The courts, too, maintain a check over abuse of powers delegated to agencies. A substantial number of rules that govern the individual originate in administrative agencies rather than in the legislature.

Schedules A, B, and C   Three classes of positions in the federal service that are filled without the usual competitive examinations. Schedule A positions are those for which no practical examination is possible, such as federal attorneys. Schedule B positions are filled by noncompetitive examination, which includes a survey and evaluation of a candidate's experience and qualifications. Schedule C includes positions of a confidential and policy-making character. *See* CLASSIFIED SERVICE, page 183.

Significance   Schedules A, B, and C give flexibility to civil service rules, since it is impracticable to fill all jobs by competitive examination. The Civil Service Commission determines which positions fall into these schedules. The most controversial classification is Schedule C, since it is possible to utilize this classification in order to increase patronage appointments and to remove career servants. Yet, it is recognized that the President should have a number of confidential and policy-making positions that he can fill as he wishes.

Secretary   The title of most of the heads of the major executive departments in the national government and a few major state officials. *See* DEPARTMENT, page 184; CABINET, page 165.

   Significance   The secretaries of the executive departments are part of the President's Cabinet, and serve at the pleasure of the President. They are the legal and administrative heads of their departments and have broad powers over expenditures and personnel. Several have quasi-legislative and quasi-judicial powers. They set the tone with which a department operates and act as advisers to the President. Generally, they are chosen more for their political acumen and acceptability than for their training in the subject area of the department. State government secretaries may have similar powers and duties but are generally elected. The title is most commonly used in the states for the office of secretary of state.

Separation from Service   Termination of employment in the classified service. Separation may be voluntary, as by resignation, or may be the result of retirement laws, a reduction in force, or disciplinary action for conduct unbecoming a public employee. *See* TENURE, page 192.

   Significance   A public employee may resign at any time without prejudice. Liberal retirement allowances are provided for those who serve twenty years in the federal service. When a reduction in force is ordered because of a cut in appropriations or a lessened need for employees, as after a war or crisis period, due weight is given to such factors as seniority, performance, and veterans' preference. Dismissal from service is permitted "for such causes as will promote the efficiency of said service," and procedures are established by law. Contrary to popular assumption, civil servants may be, and are, dismissed without elaborate procedures. Basically, the head of an agency may hire and fire employees. In order to avoid dismissal for racial, religious, or political reasons, the department head must inform the employee in writing of the causes for his dismissal and give him an opportunity to respond. No hearings are held unless the employee is a veteran and appeals his case to the Civil Service Commission. Those in sensitive positions may also be discharged as "security risks" and all government employees are given security checks. Similar procedures are followed in many states, while, in others, more formal appeal procedures, to a commission or court, are in effect.

Span of Control   An administrative concept concerned with the number of agencies or subordinates that one person can supervise effectively. Experts have different opinions about what constitutes a manageable span of control, but most agree that no person can direct more than twenty agencies or persons.

   Significance   The President and almost all governors have too many agencies under their supervision. The same is true for many persons with top-level jobs in government. Most reorganization plans reduce the span of control by drawing many functions into as few departments as possible. In this way, a hierarchy of responsibility can be developed in which no supervisor has more than a few persons reporting directly to him.

Spoils System   The award of government jobs to political supporters and friends. The term derives from the expression, "to the victor belongs the spoils."

The spoils system is generally associated with President Andrew Jackson. *See* PATRONAGE, page 110.

Significance   The spoils system is usually defended on the grounds that it is essential for the maintenance of a party system, since people are not likely to work for a party without some reward, and that victorious candidates should have as employees those who are loyal to them and to their policies. President Jackson took the view that government work is so simple that anyone could handle it and that rotation in office is necessary and healthy for vigorous administration. Few people today consider government work simple, but many still support the principle of rotation in office, since civil service tenure may result in an administration having unsympathetic employees. Though the merit system has made large inroads on the spoils system, vestiges of the spoils system remain at the local governmental level and many federal jobs are still filled by patronage.

Tenure   The right to hold a position or office free from arbitrary dismissal. Public employees in the classified service achieve tenure after serving a probationary period. *See* SEPARATION FROM SERVICE, page 191.

Significance   Tenure is essential to the operation of a merit system of employment. It encourages freedom of thought and action on the part of the employee and frees him from fear of dismissal for purely personal, political, or arbitrary reasons. Safeguards have been established by law to assure tenure for government employees who are in the classified service.

United States Government Organization Manual   The official organization handbook of the three branches of the federal government. It lists all federal departments and agencies with detailed descriptions of their powers, duties, and activities. The *Manual* is published annually in July.

Significance   The *Manual* is a useful resource for students of government and citizens generally. It includes major agencies of government, various units within the agencies, lists of governmental publications, and charts of the more complex agencies. A list of agencies that have been discontinued in recent years is also provided. Similar information about state agencies can be found in state manuals.

Unity of Command   An administrative concept that no person should be subject to the orders of more than one superior. It is related to the idea of "chain of command," which is common to the military services.

Significance   Unity of command is difficult to put into practice in the public service because of the variety of tasks that government undertakes and the large number of persons employed. The problem is most acute in areas of technical specialization, where a clash may occur between general administrators and the specialists. Informal chains of command may develop in an agency when subordinate individuals command more respect than the actual head. Government agencies also may be independent of the chief executive and more responsive to the legislature or a pressure group. To achieve unity of command, agencies with similar functions should be integrated, a hierarchical arrangement of responsibility established, and authority for final decisions vested in one individual to avoid irresponsibility and confusion.

Veterans' Preference   Special consideration given to veterans in various aspects of the civil service. These include: (1) the addition of five points to the test scores of veterans, ten points to disabled veterans; (2) the waiver of age, physical, and education requirements in some instances; (3) the limitation of competition for some positions to veterans; (4) the provision for special rights with regard to layoffs and dismissals; (5) the extension of veterans' preference to wives, widows, and mothers of disabled or deceased veterans. These preferences are provided by almost all civil service jurisdictions in the United States.

Significance   Veterans' preference has resulted in filling a majority of civil service positions with veterans. These special considerations are based on the idea that the country owes a debt to the veteran, and veterans' preference is vigorously supported by veterans' interest groups. Yet, personnel experts view veterans' preference as a derogation of the merit principle and an obstacle to qualified nonveterans seeking a government career.

IMPORTANT AGENCIES

Civil Service Commission   The central personnel agency of the national government, established in 1883. It is composed of three members appointed to six-year terms by the President with the Senate's consent. Its principal activities include the recruitment, examination, and preparation of eligible lists of prospective governmental employees. The Commission also administers a variety of laws pertaining to governmental employees with regard to veterans' preference, classification, security checks, political activity, retirement, and insurance programs.

Significance   The Civil Service Commission is largely concerned with providing leadership in federal personnel administration by establishing standards of good practice and stimulating improvements in personnel methods in the operating agencies. The Commission has ten regional offices in major cities. Day-to-day personnel matters are handled in individual departments and agencies, with the Commission playing a policy-making and supervisory role. Though conflicts often arise between the various governmental agencies and the Commission over personnel policies, the Commission has managed to maintain a strong, independent position in the executive branch. Civil service commissions are also found in most states and in many local units of government.

General Services Administration   An independent agency established in 1949 to centralize purchasing and property and records management for the national government. The General Services Administration, headed by an Administrator appointed by the President with Senate approval, is assigned responsibility for the procurement, supply, and transportation of property and services for the executive agencies, the acquisition and management of federally owned or leased property, disposal of surplus property, and records management.

Significance   The General Services Administration gathers under one agency a number of functions formerly performed by separate units. The General Services Administration was created upon the suggestion of the Hoover Commission, which noted the need for centralized purchasing and property management in order to avoid waste and duplication in the world-wide operations of the national government. In addition to its service activities, the General Services Administration publishes the *Statutes at Large,* the *Federal Register,* and the *United States Government Organization Manual.*

IMPORTANT CASES

Opp Cotton Mills v. Administrator of Wage and Hour Division, 312 U.S. 126 (1941): Declared that the provisions of the Fair Labor Standards Act of 1938 authorizing an administrative determination of minimum wages in a particular industry do not constitute an unconstitutional delegation of legislative power.

Significance   The *Opp* case was one of the last in a long series of cases which challenged the right of Congress to vest rule-making power in an administrative agency. The Court pointed out that in a complex society Congress could not be expected to fill in the details of all public policies. So long as a standard is established within which the administrative agency must operate, the delegation of authority is permissible. The Court noted further that the Constitution does not demand the impossible and Congress could not be expected to set every wage rate, railroad rate, or every other rule which a business must follow. The *Opp* case put an end to the delegation of power issue in American constitutional law.

Railroad Comm'n of Texas v. Rowan and Nichols Oil Co., 311 U.S. 570 (1941): Refused to overturn a ruling of the Railroad Commission relating to the amount of oil that could be taken from wells in Texas. The Court noted that the issue was too complex for judges to determine and that the Commission's order must stand in the absence of a showing that it was based on insubstantial evidence.

Significance   In this case, as in numerous others challenging specific rulings of state and national administrative agencies, the Court has taken the view that administrative decisions stand if they are supported by "substantial evidence." Otherwise, the Court would be substituting its judgment for that of an expert administrative agency. Congress, in the Administrative Procedure Act of 1946, has supported the Court's stand by providing that the scope of judicial review of administrative rulings be limited to determining relevant questions of law and by approving the substantial evidence rule.

United Public Workers v. Mitchell, 330 U.S. 75 (1947): Ruled that Congress may prohibit federal employees from participating in political activities. The Court upheld the Hatch Act of 1939, which authorizes the removal of a person from civil service employment for his taking an "active part in political management or political campaigns."

Significance   The Court found no invasion of the constitutional rights of public employees in the Hatch Act. In another case, the Court applied this ruling to state government employees working on projects financed by federal grants-in-aid (*Oklahoma v. United States Civil Service Commission,* 330 U.S. 127 [1947]). Critics of these rulings claim that they bar millions of persons from active participation in the democratic process. The Court, however, agreed with Congress that the Hatch Act contributes to the efficiency of the public service and prevents the growth of bureaucratic political machines.

IMPORTANT STATUTES

Administrative Procedure Act of 1946   A major law governing the procedures of regulatory agencies and providing for standards of judicial review of administrative determinations. The Act requires that every agency publicize its operations, give advance notice of proposed rules, and permit persons to testify, to be accompanied by counsel, and to cross-examine witnesses. The Act provides further that the same official may not act as both prosecutor and judge and that persons may appeal decisions of these agencies to the courts. The courts are authorized to set aside any agency ruling that is arbitrary or unsupported by substantial evidence.

Significance   The Administrative Procedure Act was passed in response to growing criticism of the lack of procedural safeguards in administrative legislation and adjudication. Since so many private rights are now affected by administrative agencies, Congress sought to regulate the internal procedures by which rights are determined and to provide broad standards for judicial review.

Pendleton Act (Civil Service Act of 1883)   This law, as amended over the years, forms the basis for the personnel policies of the national government. The law established the principle of employment on the basis of open, competitive examinations, and created a Civil Service Commission to administer the personnel service. The Pendleton Act extended the merit principle to only ten percent of national employees, but later laws and executive orders have extended coverage to more than ninety percent of employees.

Significance   The Pendleton Act was a direct result of the assassination of President James Garfield by a disappointed office seeker. The Act brought to a close the period of Jacksonian spoils which made governmental employment a reward for political activity. The Pendleton Act turned the tide in favor of employment by merit, which, despite occasional lapses, has spread to all levels of government.

Ramspeck Act (Civil Service Act of 1940)   Authorizes the President to place, by executive order, nearly all federal positions under the civil service system. Exemptions include those positions filled by presidential appointment requiring the Senate's approval, and certain special agencies, such as the Tennessee Valley Authority and the Federal Bureau of Investigation, which have merit systems of their own.

Significance   The Ramspeck Act is considered to be the culmination of the civil service reforms initiated in 1883 by the Pendleton Act. Presidents since 1940 have used this authority to broaden the coverage of the civil service laws. As a result, most national government positions are covered. At first, this power was used to "freeze" political appointees into their positions, but the net effect has been to strengthen civil service in the United States.

Reorganization Act of 1949   A grant of power to the President to reorganize the executive branch of the government. Plans for reorganization must be submitted to Congress, and either house may veto the proposal within sixty days. The Reorganization Act has been extended several times since 1949.

Significance   A vast enterprise needs continuing reorganization to ensure efficiency of operation. The Reorganization Act places the initiative in the hands of the President who bears major responsibility for administration. The veto in the hands of Congress prevents any reshuffling that may threaten the status of any "pet" agencies of members of Congress or major pressure groups. A substantial portion of the recommendations of the Hoover Commission have been put into effect through procedures established by the Reorganization Act.

Ten

The Judicial Process: Courts and Law Enforcement

Activism versus Self-restraint   Two approaches to judicial decision-making in the American political system. Activists hold that a judge should use his position to promote desirable social ends. Proponents of self-restraint counter that in deciding cases a judge should defer to the legislative and executive branches, which are politically responsible to the voters, and not indulge his personal philosophy. Both schools of thought recognize the policy-making nature of judicial decisions on major social questions, but they differ on how that power should be used.

Significance   The activism versus self-restraint dichotomy is most clearly evidenced on the United States Supreme Court. Justice Hugo L. Black is the leading spokesman for the activists and Justice John M. Harlan for the restrainers. This division underscores the policy-making role of the Supreme Court in its decisions on questions of broad policy that are framed in legal terms. Most observers take the view that judges cannot help but inject their personal views into decisions and that one is apt to accept or reject the Court's role depending upon how it affects the outcome of particular cases. For example, during the New Deal period of the 1930s, liberals opposed the "activism" of the Court in striking down social welfare programs, whereas many of these same liberals today favor Court "activism" on behalf of civil rights.

Administrative Law   That branch of law that creates administrative agencies, establishes their methods of procedure, and determines the scope of judicial review of agency practices and actions. The term also describes the rules and regulations made by administrative agencies. Administrative law deals with rate-making, operating rules, the rights of persons and companies regulated by administrative agencies, and the power of the courts to review. *See* ADMINISTRATIVE PROCEDURE ACT, page 195.

Significance   The widespread use of administrative agencies to regulate important aspects of economic and social life results in their producing a great flow of law governing individual conduct. Correspondingly, a body of law controlling the operations of administrative agencies to assure fair procedures that protect the rights of persons affected by these operations has evolved.

197

Increasingly, more people are affected by administrative rules than by legislative statutes.

Admiralty Jurisdiction   Authority vested in federal courts to hear cases involving shipping and commerce on the high seas and on the navigable waters of the United States. It is a highly technical body of law based on tradition, congressional statutes, and international law. Typical cases involve maritime contracts, collisions, and crimes committed on vessels. *See* JURISDICTION, page 214; NAVIGABLE WATERS, page 264.

Significance   The federal courts have exclusive jurisdiction over admiralty and maritime cases as provided in Article III, section 2, of the Constitution. This assures maintenance of national supremacy over foreign and interstate commerce over water routes.

Advisory Opinion   An opinion given by a court, though no actual case or controversy is before it, on the constitutionality or legal effect of a law. No advisory opinions are rendered by federal judges. Eleven states, however, do authorize the highest state court to give such opinions upon the request of the legislature or governor. An advisory opinion is not binding except in the state of Colorado.

Significance   The advisory opinion avoids the confusion that might result from a declaration of unconstitutionality after a law has been in effect for a long period of time. Such an opinion serves as a guide to the legislature, particularly when a statute appears to break new ground, and to governors in deciding whether to sign or veto legislation. When rendering an advisory opinion, however, a court lacks the benefit of opposing arguments by adverse parties.

Amicus Curiae   A legal term meaning "friend of the court." As *amicus curiae,* individuals or groups not parties to a lawsuit may aid or influence the court in reaching its decision. The court may at its discretion give permission to or request persons to appear as *amicus curiae.* Often, a party will seek to appear as *amicus curiae* when the decision in the case will affect his rights as well as the rights of those directly involved. In some states, a friend of the court is permanently attached to a court to help it reach decisions in cases involving minors, divorce, or criminal offenders.

Significance   Many lawsuits have implications reaching far beyond the interests of the litigants involved in the case. For example, in a case involving civil rights, several interest groups may seek permission to testify or file documents to demonstrate to the court the implications of the case. The federal government, acting through the Solicitor General, frequently exercises its right to appear as *amicus* before the Supreme Court on matters involving federal policies.

Appeal   Taking a case from a lower court to a higher tribunal by the losing party. The term also identifies those types of cases brought to the United States Supreme Court as a matter of right; these include cases from federal courts and highest state courts when state or federal laws are declared in conflict with the Constitution or a treaty. Such cases are brought to the Supreme Court "on appeal." An appeal is generally a complex and costly process. Simplified provisions are made for filing of appeals *in forma pauperis* by indigent appellants in criminal cases. *See* APPELLATE JURISDICTION, page 199.

Significance   An ordinary appeal is designed to serve as a check upon any errors committed in lower tribunals. When the Supreme Court reviews cases "on appeal," it ensures that controversial questions of constitutionality and national supremacy are decided in the highest court in the land. The Court may, however, decide that the issue lacks significance and simply dismiss it.

Appellate Jurisdiction   Authority of a court to review decisions of an inferior court. In the federal court system, the courts of appeals and the Supreme Court have power to review decisions of district courts and other tribunals. All states have courts of appellate jurisdiction to review decisions of lower state courts. The losing party in a lawsuit generally has the right to appeal the decision to an appellate court. *See* JURISDICTION, page 214.

Significance   Courts of appellate jurisdiction serve as a check upon errors of law or fact that might arise in the course of trials in lower courts. They also serve to give the losing party a second chance to win his case. The scope of appellate jurisdiction, that is, the types of cases and questions that may be appealed, is determined by rules of procedure established by the courts or by the legislative body.

Arbitration   A method of settling a dispute whereby the parties to the dispute select the arbitrators and agree to accept their decision as binding. A number of states authorize arbitration and make decisions enforceable by the courts. *See* ARBITRATION, page 279; ARBITRATION, page 317.

Significance   Arbitration provides an informal forum for settlement of disputes, saves the time and expense of court action, and relieves the burden of crowded court dockets. Technical matters can be arbitrated by experts in the field of the dispute. The American Arbitration Association, a private organization, provides a panel of available arbitrators.

Arraignment   A stage in criminal proceedings in which the accused is brought before the court to hear the formal charges against him as prepared by a grand jury or prosecutor. The accused is then asked to plead guilty or not guilty. The Supreme Court has ruled that there must be no unnecessary delay between arrest and arraignment. A confession or other evidence obtained as a result of such delay will be barred as evidence (*Mallory v. United States,* 354 U.S. 449 [1957]). *See McNabb v. United States,* page 83.

Significance   A major factor in fair criminal procedure is that the accused be informed of the charges against him so that he can prepare his defense. Speedy arraignment acts as a safeguard against arbitrary arrest, prolonged detention, and unsavory police tactics. Police officials across the country argue that too stringent application of the *Mallory* rule handicaps law enforcement.

Arrest Warrant   An order issued in writing by a court or magistrate authorizing the detainment of a person. The Fourth Amendment to the Constitution specifies that such warrants are to be issued only upon "probable cause" supported by oath, describing the person to be seized. All state constitutions have similar provisions. *See* SEARCH AND SEIZURE, page 71.

Significance   This guarantee has the effect of protecting persons against overzealous officers. Arrests may be made without a warrant if the law officers have "probable cause" for making the arrest. For example, an officer who witnesses a crime need not secure a warrant. Whether an arrest has been properly made is a matter for judicial determination. An arbitrary arrest may void any subsequent conviction.

Attorney General   The head of the Department of Justice and a member of the President's Cabinet. He serves as legal advisor to the President and to all agencies of the executive branch and is the chief law-enforcement officer of the United States. The Attorney General directs the work of federal district attorneys, United States Marshals, and federal penal institutions. Criminal investigations and the conduct of lawsuits involving the United States fall under his charge. An attorney general is also found in each of the states, where he is frequently an elected official. He, too, serves as legal advisor and law-enforcement officer. *See* DEPARTMENT OF JUSTICE, page 227; ATTORNEY GENERAL, page 357.

Significance   The office of Attorney General is one of the most powerful in government. His opinions on legal matters, published as *Opinions of Attorney General,* have the force of law unless overturned by a court. The emphasis given to enforcement of particular laws, such as antitrust or civil rights laws, rests largely in the discretion of the Attorney General. At the national level, broad discretion is vested in the Attorney General in the areas of immigration, citizenship, and subversion.

Bail   Funds provided as assurance that a person will appear in court at the proper time. Bail is permitted after arrest and before trial, as well as after conviction pending appeal or sentencing. Bail is usually denied in capital cases. The Eighth Amendment to the Constitution forbids excessive bail; wide discretion is left the courts to determine the amount in relation to the severity of the offense, the record and resources of the defendant, and the likelihood of his reappearing in court. A defendant may appeal a denial of release on bail or the amount of the bail.

Significance   Bail rests on the theory that one is innocent until proved guilty and should not have punishment inflicted by unnecessary internment until guilt is established. Bail permits a defendant freedom to prepare his case before trial and to continue his normal work and family life. Since the poor have difficulty raising bail, many jurisdictions now release defendants on their own recognizance when it appears likely that the defendant will not flee to avoid prosecution.

Blue-ribbon Jury   A system of jury selection that uses specially competent jurors to try difficult, complex, or important cases. Such juries are impaneled upon request of a party to the suit with the consent of the presiding judge. This method of juror selection contrasts with the ordinary, random selection of jurors from voting or tax lists to represent a cross section of the community. The use of the blue-ribbon jury has been approved by the Supreme Court (*Fay v. New York,* 332 U.S. 463 [1947]). *See* PANEL, page 218.

Significance   Blue-ribbon juries represent an attempt to meet the objection that many jurors are incompetent to try complex cases. In widely publicized cases, it may be difficult to get an unbiased jury and the blue-ribbon jury may serve to speed the administration of justice. Some, however, see it as an attempt to exclude all but the "best citizens" from jury duty.

Capital Punishment   The death penalty for conviction of a serious crime, such as murder, rape, kidnaping, or treason. Electrocution is the most commonly used method of execution; lethal gas and hanging are also employed. In Utah, the condemned person may choose to be hanged or shot. Eleven states bar or severely restrict the imposition of capital punishment: Alaska, Hawaii, Delaware, Maine, Michigan, Minnesota, New York, North Dakota, Oregon, Rhode Island, and Wisconsin; Puerto Rico and the Virgin Islands do likewise. Several states have reinstated the death penalty after having once voted to abolish it. In some states, the death penalty is mandatory for certain crimes while in others the jury may recommend life imprisonment instead of the death penalty.

Significance   Capital punishment has long been debated on both moral and legalistic grounds. Many authorities question its utility as a deterrent to crime, while others abhor it for religious or moral reasons. In recent years, legislation has been frequently introduced in Congress and in numerous states to abolish the death penalty. The number of executions has decreased in recent years, due in part to the reluctance of judges and juries to assign the death penalty. In the decade of 1930-1939, 1666 persons were executed; 716, in the decade 1950-1959.

Certiorari   An order issued by a higher court to a lower court to send up the record of a case for review. Most cases reach the United States Supreme Court through the writ of certiorari, as authorized by the Judiciary Act of 1925. The writ is issued at the discretion of the Court when at least four of the nine justices feel that the case should be reviewed.

Significance   Though it is commonly assumed that anyone may bring his case to the Supreme Court, only a limited number of cases may be appealed as a matter of right. In all other cases, the party must petition the Court to issue a writ of certiorari. Because of the press of work, fewer than fifteen percent of petitions for certiorari are granted, thereby leaving the lower court decision as final. Only cases of importance reaching far beyond the interests of the particular parties to the suit tend to be heard. Often, the Court limits its grant of certiorari to specific questions rather than reviewing all elements of the trial or of lower court decisions.

Challenge   Objection to having a prospective juror serve on a jury. A juror may be challenged by either party. A challenge may be either for "cause" or "peremptory." An unlimited number of challenges may be made for cause with approval of the presiding judge. Peremptory challenges, for which no reason need be given, are limited to a specific number, which varies from state to state, and depends upon the nature of the offense involved. For crimes punishable by death, as many as forty peremptory challenges may be allowed; as few as five may be permitted for minor offenses. *See* JURY, page 214.

Significance   Both parties to a case are entitled to a trial by an impartial jury. The challenge permits counsel to remove prospective jurors who show bias or who, for any reason, appear unfit to sit in judgment. The limit placed on peremptory challenges prevents unreasonable delay in filling the jury panel.

Charge   A statement by the judge to the jury at the conclusion of a trial to aid the jury in reaching its verdict. The judge instructs the jury in the law governing the case and reviews the evidence. The authority of the judge to comment on the facts of a case, as distinguished from the law involved, varies from state to state; federal judges have wide latitude. *See* JURY, page 214.

Significance   The charge to the jury serves to refresh the minds of the jurors, particularly after a lengthy trial. It is for the jury to weigh the truth or falsity of the evidence, but the jury is bound by the law as interpreted by the judge. If the judge is careless in his charge or demonstrates bias, the case may be overturned by a higher court. Nevertheless, the charge to the jury may play a major role in the verdict which the jury eventually reaches.

Chief Justice   The highest judicial officer of the United States or of a state. The Chief Justice of the United States is appointed for a life term by the President with the consent of the Senate. He presides over sessions of the United States Supreme Court, assigns the writing of opinions, and performs a variety of administrative duties as head of the federal court system. In the states, the chief justices are chosen in a variety of ways—appointment, election, seniority—usually for a limited term. Their duties are similar to the Chief Justice of the United States, although in many states they lack control over lower court administrative matters.

Significance   Aside from administrative duties and a slightly higher salary, chief justices have no more power than other members of highest courts in deciding cases. The position does carry considerable prestige, however, and the chief justice may be in a position to use his post as presiding officer to influence the course of decision-making.

Circuit Court   A general trial court in the states, sometimes called a district court or a superior court. In many states, the court serves several counties and the judges go on "circuit" from one county to another according to a schedule. In most states, the judges of these courts are elected by the voters of a particular county or circuit, with terms varying from two to six years. These are courts of "original jurisdiction," where important civil and criminal cases begin, trials are held, and juries are frequently used. Cases from minor courts, such as justices of the peace or municipal courts, may be appealed to the circuit court. From circuit courts, cases may be appealed to higher state courts.

Significance   For most people, the circuit court represents their main contact with the judicial branch of the government. This includes not only parties to a suit but witnesses and jurors as well. Hence, it is vital that trial courts be efficiently administered in order to maintain respect for the law. Competent judges and juries and simplified procedures, frequently lacking in these courts, are goals of proponents of state judicial reform.

Civil Law   The code regulating conduct between private persons. It is to be distinguished from criminal law, which regulates individual conduct and is enforced by the government. Under civil law, the government provides the forum for the settlement of disputes between private parties in such matters as contracts, domestic relations, business relations, and auto accidents. The government may be plaintiff or defendant in a civil suit but, in a criminal case, the government is always the prosecutor. Most civil cases in both state and federal courts are tried without jury. Where juries are used, some states authorize trial by a jury of fewer than twelve persons, and decision by less than unanimous vote. *See* CRIMINAL LAW, page 207.

Significance   Civil law provides stability in private arrangements. Thus, a person who enters into a legal contract can seek the aid of the civil law and the courts to enforce the contract. Civil law provides a substitute for private duels as a means of settling private disputes. The government not only provides an impartial tribunal but will see that any judgment reached (a money award, for example) is enforced.

Code   A compilation of laws in force, classified according to subject matter. Federal laws currently in force are collected in the *United States Code,* which is kept up to date with annual supplements and is revised every six years. Many states have collected and classified their statutes, including pertinent judicial decisions, under the title *Compiled Laws. See* STATUTE, page 156.

Significance   Without a code, one would have to search through the annual statute books for laws relating to a particular subject. Codes collect all related laws under a subject heading for easy reference use. The failure of some states to keep their codes up-to-date works a hardship on professional legal personnel and laymen alike who want to know "what the law is."

Common Law   Judge-made law that originated in England from decisions shaped according to prevailing custom. Decisions were reapplied to similar situations and, thus, gradually became common to the nation. Common law forms the basis of legal procedures in American states, except in Louisiana, where certain French legal traditions are preserved. There is no federal common law, since the national government is one of delegated powers; however, federal judges apply state common law in cases involving citizens of different states, where there is no applicable federal statute. A statute overrides the common law, but many statutes are based upon the common law and are interpreted according to the common law tradition. *See* EQUITY, page 209; *Erie Railroad v. Tompkins,* page 229.

Significance   Many important matters, such as the idea of a twelve-man jury, are part of the common law. Reliance on precedents (previous judicial decisions) in determining legal rights and duties characterizes the common law tradition. The common law permits judges great flexibility to adjust the law to community needs, thereby enhancing judicial power.

Conciliation   A method by which a third party attempts to settle a controversy between disputants outside the courtroom. It is similar to arbitration, except that the decision is not binding upon the parties nor enforceable in court. A number of large cities have established a conciliation branch in their judicial structure.

Significance   Conciliation looks toward less formal proceedings for settlement of disputes in the hope of easing the burden on courts and lessening expenses for litigants. Conciliation has proved to be particularly effective in divorce proceedings and labor disputes.

Concurrent Jurisdiction   Authority vested in two or more courts to hear cases involving the same subject matter. The term is generally used to indicate those instances in which both federal and state courts may hear the same kind of case. For example, the Congress has conferred concurrent jurisdiction upon state and federal courts in suits between citizens of different states where the amount in controversy exceeds $10,000. The parties to such a suit may choose to have their case heard in either a federal or state court. Suits involving less than $10,000 must be heard in state courts. *See* JURISDICTION, page 214.

Significance   Concurrent jurisdiction may serve to ease the burden on a court if a certain type of case tends to crowd the court dockets. For example, auto accidents between citizens of different states have become quite common. By sharing this kind of case with state courts, federal courts have been freed to handle other federal cases.

Concurring Opinion   An opinion of one or more judges, usually of an appellate court, that supports the conclusions of a majority of the court but offers different reasons for reaching that conclusion. Concurring opinions are quite common in the United States Supreme Court. *See* DISSENTING OPINION, page 208.

Significance   A concurring opinion is of no legal force or effect. Yet, by offering alternative approaches to the interpretation or application of the law, it frequently serves as a guidepost for future decisions. Thus, a concurring opinion may become the majority view of the court in the future. A concurring opinion signed by a substantial minority of a court or several concurring opinions may reduce the impact of the precedent.

Constitutional Court   A federal court established under the provisions of Article III. Constitutional courts are limited to the jurisdiction conferred by Article III and their judges are protected as to tenure and compensation. These are to be distinguished from "legislative courts," which are created by Congress under its delegated powers. The major constitutional courts are the district courts, courts of appeals, and the Supreme Court. Congress has conferred constitutional status upon certain specialized courts, such as the Court of Claims, the Customs Court, and the Court of Customs and Patent Appeals. *See* LEGISLATIVE COURT, page 215.

Significance Constitutional courts enjoy a greater degree of independence than do legislative courts. Congress has somewhat confused the distinction by conferring constitutional status upon judges of certain specialized or legislative courts while not giving these courts jurisdiction under Article III. In effect, constitutional status today refers mainly to the selection and tenure of judges.

Constitutional Law Law that involves interpretation and application of the Constitution. It is concerned largely with defining the extent and limits of governmental power and the rights of individuals. Final decision as to the meaning of the Constitution is in the hands of the United States Supreme Court. In the case of state constitutions, the highest court of the state renders final decisions, with appeal possible to the United States Supreme Court if conflict with the national Constitution, laws, or treaties can be shown.
Significance Constitutional law represents the highest law, and the Constitution, as interpreted by the Court, is the supreme law of the land. American constitutional law is noted for its flexibility, with the judiciary acting to maintain its vitality to meet changing social and economic conditions. Typically, constitutional law involves interpretation of such vague phrases as "interstate commerce" or "due process of law." Judges wield their greatest power when they are called upon to interpret the Constitution.

Contempt of Court Disobedience of a court order, or any action that operates to impair the authority of a court or to interfere with its proper functioning. Contempt may be civil or criminal. Civil contempt involves a refusal to honor a court judgment in a civil case. Criminal contempt involves any interference with court proceedings. Both may be punished by fine or imprisonment or both. Usually, contempt is punished summarily (without trial), when it is committed in the presence of the court.
Significance If a court order is to have any meaning, the court must have power to enforce its order and to punish disobedience. Similarly, judges need authority to maintain order in their courtrooms so that justice may be served. The power to punish criminal contempt may be abused when a judge too hastily censures overemotional lawyers or observers. More serious is the conflict with freedom of speech and press that may arise when a judge cites a person for contempt for verbal or published remarks made outside the courtroom that, in his view, obstructs the administration of justice.

Coroner A county official who investigates deaths that occur by violent means and certifies the cause of deaths unattended by a physician. In the case of violent death, the coroner may conduct an investigation, called an "inquest," to determine if death resulted from a criminal act. A jury of six persons hears evidence presented by the county prosecutor. If the verdict is death by criminal act, the coroner may order the arrest of suspected persons. Most coroners are elected, although a number of states have substituted an appointed medical examiner to perform the duties of the coroner and have transferred his inquest function to the prosecutor.
Significance Most students of government oppose the election of coro-

ners. The office requires extensive medical knowledge as well as knowledge of criminal investigation and judicial proceedings. Often, the coroner is a layman with no medical or legal training; in some cases, he is an undertaker who may profit personally from his position. The trend is toward the appointment of physicians as medical examiners, the abolishment of the coroner's jury, and the use of the prosecutor for the legal aspects of the office.

Court of Appeals   In the national court system, the appellate court below the Supreme Court. A few states also have an intermediate court of appeals, although in Kentucky, Maryland, and New York, the highest state court is called the Court of Appeals. On the national level, there are eleven courts of appeal. The country is divided into eleven "circuits" including the District of Columbia. Prior to 1948, these courts were known as the Circuit Courts of Appeals. The United States Courts of Appeals have only appellate jurisdiction, being empowered to hear appeals from the district courts in their particular circuit and to hear appeals from decisions of independent regulatory commissions, such as the Federal Trade Commission or Interstate Commerce Commission. Each court normally hears cases in panels of three judges but, on occasion, a full court of nine judges will sit. All judges are appointed for life by the President with the Senate's consent.

Significance   In most appeals, decisions of the courts of appeals are final, since few cases reach the Supreme Court. Hence, judges of those courts wield considerable power and influence in American law. Review of decisions of independent regulatory commissions gives the Washington, D.C. circuit, in particular, an important role in development of administrative law.

Court of Claims   A court established in 1855 to hear claims of private individuals against the government for breach of contract, for injuries caused by negligent behavior of government employees, or for recovery of other claims, such as back pay. It also determines claims referred by Congress and the executive departments. The Court of Claims has five judges who sit "en banc" (together) in Washington, D.C. Any awards made by the Court cannot be paid unless Congress appropriates the money, which it usually does. Its decisions may be appealed to the Supreme Court by writ of certiorari. Since 1953, it has held the status of a constitutional court, and its judges are appointed for life by the President with the Senate's consent.

Significance   The national government may not be sued without its consent, but it would be grossly inefficient if Congress had to consider each claim. The Court of Claims relieves Congress of much of this burden. In most instances, its decisions are final since the Supreme Court rarely accepts a case from the Court of Claims.

Court of Customs and Patent Appeals   A court established by Congress in 1909 which reviews appeals from decisions of the Customs Court, the Patent Office, and the Tariff Commission. The Court has five judges who sit "en banc" (together) in Washington, D.C. They are appointed for life terms by the President with consent of the Senate. Congress designated it a constitutional court in 1958. Decisions may be appealed to the Supreme Court by writ of certiorari.

Significance   A large body of specialized law has been developed in the subject areas assigned to the Court of Customs and Patent Appeals. The expertness developed by this court takes an immense burden from the regular federal courts.

Court of Military Appeals   A court established by Congress in 1950 to review court-martial decisions. Composed of three civilian judges appointed for fifteen years by the President with consent of the Senate, the court is judicially independent but is part of the Department of Defense for administrative purposes. The court is obligated to review decisions affecting top military personnel, as well as those imposing the death penalty; it has discretion to review certain other cases upon petition, such as bad conduct discharges or those involving lengthy prison terms. The court applies military law, a special body of rules developed by Congress, rather than ordinary federal criminal law. Appeals may be made to the Supreme Court by writ of certiorari. *See* COURT-MARTIAL, page 346.

Significance   Military service for millions of Americans has caused great concern over the standards and procedures of military justice. The Uniform Code of Military Justice, passed by Congress in 1950, attempts to strengthen rights of persons in court-martial proceedings while meeting the needs of military discipline. The Court of Military Appeals is part of this reform effort. By requiring that its judges be civilians and by permitting appeal to the Supreme Court, Congress has assured civilian control over military justice.

Criminal Law   The code that regulates the conduct of individuals, defines crimes, and provides punishment for violations. In criminal cases, the government is always the prosecutor, since all crimes are against public order. The major body of criminal law is enacted by states although the list of federal crimes is growing. Criminal law falls into two categories, felonies and misdemeanors, the former being the more serious. *See* CIVIL LAW, page 203.

Significance   Criminal law reflects the mores of society and protects the public against wrongdoing. Laws that define criminal acts must be clear so that people are put on notice as to what they may or may not do. Violators are prosecuted under procedures established by the Constitution or other law to assure fair treatment. Government prosecution and punishment for crime serves as a civilized substitute for personal vengeance.

Customs Court   A special court established by Congress in 1926 to decide disputes that arise over tariff laws and duties levied on imported goods. The Court consists of nine judges appointed for life terms by the President with the Senate's consent. It sits in divisions at principal ports of entry, with its main office in New York City. In 1956, the Customs Court was given constitutional status by the Congress. Its decisions may be appealed to the Court of Customs and Patent Appeals.

Significance   The Customs Court relieves regular courts of the burden of hearing the many disputes arising over classifications and valuations placed by customs officers on imported goods. The court has developed the competence necessary to deal with the problems raised by the increased volume of international trade.

Declaratory Judgment   A court procedure used to declare the rights of parties under a contract, will, or other dispute, before any damage occurs. It is a method of preventive justice contrary to the traditional procedure of suing for damages after the damage results. The national government (since the enactment of the Declaratory Judgments Act of 1934) and most of the states permit the use of this procedure.
    Significance   Declaratory judgments are relatively new in law, reflecting the view that the power of the courts should be made available to prevent the doing of a wrong as well as to redress a wrong. They differ from advisory opinions in that the parties must have an actual controversy in which loss or injury is likely to occur. Expensive legal entanglements are often forestalled.

Dissenting Opinion   An opinion of one or more judges, usually of an appellate court, that disagrees with the decision reached by a majority of the court. Such opinions are frequently presented on the United States Supreme Court. *See* CONCURRING OPINION, page 204.
    Significance   A dissenting opinion has no legal force. Ofttimes, however, a dissenting view has eventually become the law. If a court is sharply divided —for example, a five–four vote on the Supreme Court—a dissenting opinion may weaken the force of the majority view.

District Attorney   A county official, elected in all but six states for two or four year terms, who represents the state in prosecutions against violators of criminal laws. In some states, he is called the county attorney, county prosecutor, or, simply prosecutor. Prosecutions for the national government are handled by United States Attorneys. District attorneys also conduct proceedings before grand juries. In states where grand juries are not used, the district attorney brings charges in the form of an information. In addition, the district attorney acts as legal advisor to the county and represents the county in lawsuits.
    Significance   District attorneys wield great power in local government. Decisions of whether to prosecute alleged violators are within their discretionary powers, often conditioned by their political ambitions. Their recommendations to the court regarding bail or sentences are generally given serious consideration. The office has been used as a political steppingstone by many young attorneys. The conduct of the office may well depend upon the political climate of a given county, resulting in an uneven application of criminal law within the state.

District Court   The federal court of "original jurisdiction," where most federal cases begin. It is the only federal court where trials are held, juries are used, and witnesses are called. Both criminal and civil cases arising under federal law are heard. Each state has at least one district court; a few have as many as four. District courts are also found in Washington, D.C., and the territories of Puerto Rico, Guam, the Virgin Islands, and the Panama Canal Zone. Each court has from one to twenty-four judges, depending on the volume of business, but each judge holds court separately. Certain cases are heard by a three-judge panel. All judges are appointed for life terms by the President with the Senate's consent except those serving in territorial courts who have eight year terms.

Significance   The bulk of judicial work in federal courts is conducted by the district courts. About 100,000 cases a year are tried, mostly civil cases involving such matters as admiralty law, bankruptcy proceedings, torts, civil rights, and postal laws. A small proportion of cases are appealed to courts of appeals and a few reach the Supreme Court. Thus, for most people, contact with federal justice is limited to district courts.

Diversity of Citizenship   Lawsuits involving citizens of different states. The Constitution (Art. III, sec. 2) confers jurisdiction in such cases on the federal courts, which, generally, apply relevant state law. Congress has conferred exclusive jurisdiction on state courts for suits between citizens of different states if the amount in controversy is less than $10,000, and concurrent jurisdiction if more than $10,000 is involved. *See Erie Railroad v. Tompkins,* page 229; JURISDICTION, page 214.

Significance   A very complicated body of law has developed in diversity of citizenship cases. Originally, the purpose of the constitutional provision was to prevent bias by state courts against out-of-state litigants. Today, federal court dockets are filled with such cases, due to the increasing mobility and interrelationships of the American people. Automobile accidents between citizens of different states, for example, can be cause for a federal case. Congressional action giving state courts jurisdiction over diversity of citizenship cases is aimed at reducing pressures on the federal courts. In turn, the federal courts have tried to cut the number of these cases by applying relevant state law, so that litigants will not "shop around" for more favorable treatment under federal law.

Eleventh Amendment   An amendment to the Constitution, adopted in 1798, that provides that federal courts do not have authority to hear cases brought against a state by an individual citizen of another state or of a foreign state. The Amendment overruled a decision of the Supreme Court in *Chisholm v. Georgia,* 2 Dallas 419 (1793), which had upheld the right of a citizen of one state to sue another state in federal court.

Significance   Although Article III did confer jurisdiction upon federal courts to hear cases between a state and citizens of other states, the states were alarmed by the *Chisholm* decision, which denied the necessity for the state's consent to be sued. The states feared the possibility of many suits against them for defaulting on their debts, as well as the loss of "states' rights." The Eleventh Amendment applies only to suits against the state itself; a suit may be brought against an officer of the state.

Equity   A branch of law that provides a remedy where the common law does not apply. The common law is concerned largely with granting of damages after a wrongful action. Equity is designed to provide justice where damages may come too late to be meaningful. In an equity case, the court may order that something be done (specific performance) or forbid certain actions (injunction). In a typical case the court may order a person to fulfill a contract or forbid a union to go on strike under certain conditions. Equity procedures are less formal than regular court procedures and juries are seldom used. *See* COMMON LAW, page 203; INJUNCTION, page 212.

Significance   Equity is a legal inheritance from England that grew out of petitions to the king to redress wrongs for which the law provided no remedy. It was based largely on abstract principles of justice, but has developed its own body of rules and precedents. A few states have separate courts for equity proceedings, sometimes called chancery. The courts have a wide area of choice in equity cases to provide solutions to impending conflicts. Irreparable damages are thereby avoided.

Ex Parte   A judicial proceeding by or for one party without contest by an adverse party. In an ex parte proceeding, there may be no adverse party, or a possible adverse party has had no notice of the case. The term "in re" is sometimes used in place of ex parte.

Significance   Individuals frequently bring actions in their own behalf seeking the aid of the court. A typical ex parte proceeding may be one brought by a prisoner seeking a writ of habeas corpus. Such cases are reported under the name of the person bringing the suit preceded by the term "ex parte": *Ex parte Milligan,* for example.

Felony   A serious crime punishable by death or by imprisonment in a penitentiary for a year or more. The precise character of a felony varies from state to state and is defined by law. Less serious violations of law are called misdemeanors. Felonies generally include murder, arson, robbery, aggravated assault, and forgery. *See* MISDEMEANOR, page 217.

Significance   Persons accused of felonies are accorded the full protection of constitutional guarantees, such as indictment by grand jury or information, and trial by jury. Misdemeanors are generally tried by "summary process," without indictment or trial by jury. Minor state courts rarely have jurisdiction to try felonies, which are usually heard by district or circuit courts. On the national level, felonies are tried in the district courts.

Five-to-Four Decision   A decision of the United States Supreme Court in which the justices divide sharply over the decision or interpretation of the Constitution or law. Such decisions tend to attract wide notice and it is sometimes said that one justice, in effect, decided the case.

Significance   Many important cases have been decided by a five–four vote. When constitutional questions are involved, as happened frequently during the New Deal period in the 1930s, a five–four decision emphasizes a philosophical division on the Court over political, social, and economic questions. Since so close a vote casts serious doubt upon the durability of the decision, scholars have suggested that a minimum of six or seven, or even all nine justices must agree when a law is declared unconstitutional.

Grand Jury   A body of from twelve to twenty-three members who hear evidence presented by the prosecuting attorney against persons accused of a serious crime, and decide whether or not to present a "true bill" that "indicts" the accused. If indicted, the accused will be bound over for trial; if not, he goes free. The Fifth Amendment requires that this be done for any capital or infamous crime, generally those for which death or imprisonment may result. Unlike a petit or trial jury, a grand jury does not determine guilt or innocence but only whether the evidence warrants bringing the accused to trial; it meets in secret and decides by a majority rather than a unanimous vote. The grand jury may also conduct investigations on its own when a prosecutor is lax or when official misconduct is suspected. In such cases, any resulting accusation is called a "presentment." The grand jury exercises vast powers under the common law, being empowered to subpoena witnesses and records and to compel testimony under oath. More than half of the states have abolished or limited grand jury indictment to capital cases, replacing it with the "information" that permits the prosecutor alone to bring charges. *See* INDICTMENT, page 211; INFORMATION, page 212; *Hurtado v. California,* page 82.

   Significance   The grand jury procedure is time-consuming and expensive and the grand jury tends to follow the dictates of the prosecutor. It has been abolished in England, its place of origin, as well as in many states. The grand jury, however, serves as a protection against overzealous prosecutors and as a watchdog against official wrongdoing. It originated with the idea that before an individual could be subjected by capricious prosecutors to the costs and humiliation of a public trial, sufficient evidence to justify such action must be shown and be acceptable to a majority of a grand jury.

Hearing   In an equity case, a hearing is a trial. In a criminal case, a hearing is an examination of the accused to determine if he should be held for trial; this is generally referred to as a "preliminary hearing" or "preliminary examination." If a preliminary hearing is held in an equity case, it is called an interlocutory hearing. *See* HEARING, page 186.

   Significance   The term "hearing" has a technical meaning in law. Whereas in an equity case it is technically the trial of the case, in a criminal proceeding, the hearing is not a trial to determine guilt or innocence but a procedure to protect the accused from unwarranted detention.

Indeterminate Sentence   A sentence of imprisonment with minimum and maximum limits set by the court or by statute. Once the prisoner serves the minimum sentence, he may be released upon approval of a parole board or a special commission. This is the procedure now used in most states in place of the fixed sentence. *See* PAROLE, page 218.

   Significance   The indeterminate sentence reflects present policy to reform and rehabilitate criminals rather than to exact revenge for wrongdoing. It provides hope to the prisoner of early release for good behavior and demonstration of fitness to return to society.

Indictment   The formal accusation, drawn up by the prosecutor and brought by a grand jury, charging a person with the commission of a crime. *See* GRAND JURY, page 211.

Significance   Indictment is a procedure to avoid arbitrary accusations and to inform the accused of the precise charges against him so that he can prepare his defense. A faulty or vague indictment justifies dismissal of the case. The cumbersome nature of this procedure, however, has resulted in its widespread replacement by the "information."

Information   An accusation made under oath by a prosecuting attorney before a court, charging a person with a crime. Though regularly used for minor offenses, more than half the states have substituted the information for indictment by grand jury in serious cases as well. The national government is making increased use of the information for noncapital offenses.

Significance   The trend has definitely been in the direction of substituting the information for the grand jury indictment. Thus, the prosecuting attorney bypasses the grand jury and final determination of whether the evidence justifies a trial is placed in the hands of the judge. Use of the information instead of the grand jury results from considerations of both efficiency and economy.

Injunction   An order issued by a court in an equity proceeding to compel or restrain the performance of an act by an individual or government official. A "mandatory" injunction demands that something be done, although the term "injunction" generally refers to a restraining order. Violation of an injunction constitutes contempt of court, punishable by fine or imprisonment. *See* WRIT, page 226; EQUITY, page 209; INJUNCTION, page 282.

Significance   The injunction prevents irreparable damage to an individual's personal or property rights through the power of courts to issue orders without the necessity of a lawsuit after damages are done. Judges enjoy a great deal of discretion to determine the scope of an injunction.

Intermediate Court   A court of appeals below the level of the highest court. It is found in about one-fourth of the states, mainly those with large populations. In about half the states, county courts function as intermediate courts as well as trial courts by hearing cases *de novo* (a new trial) appealed from decisions of municipal and justice of the peace courts. In both cases, "intermediate" refers to the fact that these courts exercise appellate jurisdiction with further appeal possible to a higher court.

Significance   The use of the term "intermediate" reflects the great variety in court organization, structure, and jurisdiction, found in the several states. Intermediate courts of appeals serve to lighten the burden on state supreme courts and provide at least one appeal from decisions of minor courts.

Judicial Council   An investigative and advisory agency composed of judges, lawyers, and laymen to promote efficient administration in state courts. Councils are used in about three-fourths of the states. Though their composition and authority vary from state to state, they are generally charged with collecting statistics on court operations and recommending changes in court organization, court procedure, assignment of judges, and other matters to improve the handling of court business. *See* ADMINISTRATIVE OFFICE, page 227.

Significance   Little attention has been paid to the efficient administration of court business compared with the amount of concern over the outcome of particular cases. The judicial council is a relatively recent innovation, recognizing the importance of applying sound administrative techniques to the operations of courts. The judicial council acts as a unifying force to counteract the decentralization of most state court systems and the independence of locally elected judges. On the national level, the Administrative Office of the United States Courts performs duties similar to those of a judicial council.

Judicial Review   The power of the courts to declare acts of the legislative and executive branches unconstitutional. All courts, both state and national, may exercise this authority, though final decision is usually made by the highest state or federal court. Though the United States Constitution is silent on this matter, the Supreme Court asserted the power of judicial review in the famous case of *Marbury v. Madison,* 1 Cranch 137 (1803). Judicial review is based on the assumptions that the Constitution is the supreme law, that acts contrary to the Constitution are void, and that the judiciary is the guardian of the Constitution. *See* CONSTITUTIONAL LAW, page 205; SUPREME COURT, page 222; *Ashwander v. TVA,* page 228; *Eakin v. Raub,* page 229; *Marbury v. Madison,* page 230.
　　Significance   Judicial review is one of the basic principles of the American system of government. It places in the judiciary, and the Supreme Court in particular, vast power to determine the meaning of the Constitution and to act as final arbiter over questions involving the power of governmental officials at both the state and national levels. Several hundred state laws and about eighty federal laws have been declared unconstitutional by the Supreme Court. Though this number is small compared with the total number of laws passed, a declaration of unconstitutionality may deter a long line of similar legislation. Courts are reluctant to exercise this vast power, since due respect must be accorded the other branches of government and since the Constitution is susceptible to varying interpretations. A court decision on the Constitution can be changed only by amending the Constitution or by a change of view by the court itself. The exercise of judicial review invariably generates widespread comment from those dissatisfied with the decision, particularly when the court is divided in its decision. Throughout American history, courts have played a major role in the development of public policy by the exercise of this power. Since 1937, the Supreme Court has used considerable self-restraint in exercising the power of judicial review over federal actions, but has used the power extensively to nullify state actions, particularly in civil liberty and apportionment cases.

Judiciary   A collective term for courts and judges. In the United States, the judiciary is divided into the national and state judiciary. Each is independent of the other with the exception that the United States Supreme Court may, under special circumstances involving federal questions, review a state court decision. Jurisdiction of particular courts or judges is determined by either the national or state constitutions and laws.
　　Significance   An independent judiciary, coequal with the legislative and

executive branches, is one of the cornerstones of the American system of government. The judiciary protects the people against excessive exercise of power by the legislature and executive and provides an impartial forum for the settlement of civil and criminal cases.

Jurisdiction   Authority vested in a court to hear and decide a case. The term literally means power "to say the law." The jurisdiction of national courts is controlled by the Constitution and by Congress. State court jurisdiction is similarly determined by state constitutions and statutes. Jurisdiction may be assigned according to such factors as the amount of money involved or the type of offense. Courts may exercise original or appellate jurisdiction, or both. *See* ADMIRALTY JURISDICTION, page 198; APPELLATE JURISDICTION, page 199; CONCURRENT JURISDICTION, page 204; DIVERSITY OF CITIZENSHIP, page 209; ORIGINAL JURISDICTION, page 217; *Ex parte McCardle,* page 229.

Significance   Lawsuits must be brought to the court that has authority "to say the law" in such a case. A case brought to the wrong court will either not be heard or be overruled by an appellate court. It is common practice in lawsuits for the attorney to show immediately that the court has authority to hear the case. The separate jurisdiction of state and national courts helps preserve the federal system, since each government maintains control over the application of its law. Within any court system, specialized jurisdiction tends to promote expertness in the courts.

Jury   An impartial body that sits in judgment on charges brought in either criminal or civil cases. A trial jury is also known as a petit jury to distinguish it from a grand jury. Under the common law, a trial jury must consist of twelve persons and their decision must be unanimous. The national government and many states authorize trial by less than twelve in certain cases and a decision by less than a unanimous vote. Jury trials may be waived by the accused. Generally, the jury is the judge of the facts, though some states permit the jury to determine the law and the punishment as well as the facts. The jury must be impartial and no specific class of persons may be deliberately and systematically excluded from jury service. Trial by jury is required by Article III, section 2, and by the Sixth and Seventh Amendments, of the United States Constitution. *See Norris v. Alabama,* page 85; PANEL, page 218; CHALLENGE, page 201; CHARGE, page 202; BLUE-RIBBON JURY, page 200.

Significance   The right to be judged by a jury of one's peers is a longstanding tradition of the common law. The competence of the average jury and the motivations which may lead it to a particular verdict are frequently questioned. Yet, the jury system brings the common sense of the community to bear upon the laws of the state or nation. It permits the citizen to participate in the administration of justice and gives the people more confidence in the application of the law.

Justice of the Peace   A judicial officer empowered to try minor civil and criminal cases, such as traffic violations or breaches of peace. In some areas, he conducts preliminary hearings to determine whether a person should be held for trial in a higher court. The justice of the peace is usually elected in rural areas and small towns for a two-year term. He is generally paid through fees. *See* MAGISTRATE, page 216.

Significance   The office of justice of the peace has been under attack in recent years. Not many justices are learned in the law, although a few states require a law degree. The fee system, it is charged, leads to corruption and biased judgment. Supporters argue that the justice of the peace provides an inexpensive method of dispensing justice in petty cases. In many urban areas, the office of justice of the peace is being replaced by municipal courts.

Justiciable Question   A dispute that can be settled through the exercise of judicial power. For a controversy to be justiciable: (1) it must be an actual case, not a trumped-up suit; (2) the person bringing the suit must have a direct interest at stake and have standing to sue; (3) the case must be ripe for adjudication, other remedies having been exhausted; and (4) the court must have jurisdiction over the subject. A question may be ruled "political" rather than justiciable if the court believes that the other branches of the government are better equipped or constitutionally responsible to handle the matter. *See* JURISDICTION, page 214; POLITICAL QUESTION, page 218; *Frothingham v. Mellon*, page 230.

Significance   The rules regarding justiciable questions help preserve the separation of powers by confining courts to their proper functions. While a court may exercise considerable discretion to determine justiciability, careful adherence to the rules assures that courts will not become embroiled in issues over which they lack competence or that will weaken the judiciary vis-à-vis the other branches. The wide use of "class actions" has somewhat altered the rule of standing to sue by permitting a person not solely liable to sustain a direct injury to bring a suit on behalf of himself and others similarly situated. This has enabled the courts in recent years to entertain several important issues, such as integration and legislative apportionment, involving questions in which litigants did not have an interest beyond that of the general public.

Law   A rule of conduct prescribed by or accepted by the governing authority of a state and enforced by courts. The law may derive from the constitution, legislative acts, and administrative rules, or may develop through custom, as have common law and equity. The law controls relations among men, and between men and their government. Penalties are imposed for violation of law. *See* ADMINISTRATIVE LAW, page 197; CIVIL LAW, page 203; COMMON LAW, page 203; CONSTITUTIONAL LAW, page 205; CRIMINAL LAW, page 207; EQUITY, page 209; INTERNATIONAL LAW, page 327; ORDINANCE, page 372.

Significance   Democracy is distinguished from totalitarian government largely in terms of the place of law in society. A totalitarian system operates under the whim of the rulers. In a free society, law provides advance notice of what legally is right and wrong. Conflicts are resolved by application of pre-existing rules. Law must emanate from and be enforced only by duly constituted authority.

Legislative Court   A court established by Congress under its delegated powers rather than under the authority granted in Article III. The judges of legislative courts need not have life tenure, may be assigned nonjudicial functions, and have only that jurisdiction that Congress assigns. For example, the Territorial Courts of Guam, Virgin Islands, and the Panama Canal Zone were created under congressional power to govern the territories. The judges have limited terms, and the courts have regular federal jurisdiction as well as jurisdiction over matters that ordinarily belong in state courts. Another example is the Court of Military Appeals, created under the power to make rules for the armed forces. *See* CONSTITUTIONAL COURT, page 204.

Significance   By establishing legislative courts, Congress provides flexibility to the court system and relieves the regular courts and Congress, itself, of some burdens. The Court of Claims, the Customs Court, and the Court of Customs and Patent Appeals, originally established as legislative courts, have been granted constitutional status by Congress and judges of these courts now enjoy life tenure.

Magistrate   A minor judicial officer, usually elected in urban areas, with jurisdiction over traffic violations, minor criminal offenses, and civil suits involving small amounts of money. Magistrates may also conduct preliminary hearings in serious criminal cases and commit the offender for trial in a higher court. In some areas, the magistrate court is called a police court, and its authority is similar to that of a justice of the peace serving in a rural area. Juries, though rarely used in magistrate courts, may consist of only six jurors. *See* JUSTICE OF THE PEACE, page 214.

Significance   Magistrate courts have been established to handle the large number of cases which arise in urban communities. Unlike the justice of the peace, a magistrate is usually paid a salary rather than a fee per case. The magistrate can dispose of large numbers of petty offenses, thereby relieving the burden on higher courts and facilitating matters for offenders. Increasingly, cities are turning to specialized courts, such as traffic courts and domestic relations courts, to handle the large volume of work.

Mandamus   An order issued by a court to compel performance of an act. A writ of mandamus may be issued to an individual or corporation as well as to a public official. In the case of public officers, a writ will be issued only to compel performance of a "ministerial" act—one that the officer has a clear legal duty to perform. If he has discretion to determine whether he will perform an act, the court will not order him to do so. *See* WRIT, page 226.

Significance   The authority of the court may be brought to bear upon anyone who fails to perform an act that someone has a legal right to expect. Thus, a contract must be fulfilled as agreed upon, or a court order will be issued. Similarly, a public officer who refuses to issue a license to someone authorized to have one may be ordered to do so by the court. Failure to obey the court order is contempt of court.

Marshal   An official of the federal Department of Justice attached to each federal district court. The duties of United States Marshals correspond to those of sheriffs in county governments. They make arrests in federal criminal cases, keep accused persons in custody, secure jurors, serve legal papers, keep order in the courtroom, and execute orders and decisions of the court. Marshals are appointed by the President subject to the Senate's confirmation, for four-year terms.

Significance   Marshals are part of the executive, not the judicial branch, and perform federal police duties. Although the job is not quite as glamorous as portrayed on television westerns, modern day United States Marshals perform important functions in enforcement of federal law. Deputy marshals are also attached to most district courts. United States Marshals have played a prominent role in the enforcement of federal court orders in major desegregation crises.

Misdemeanor   A minor criminal offense. The precise nature of a misdemeanor varies from state to state where it is defined by law. It may include such offenses as traffic violations, petty theft, disorderly conduct, and gambling. Punishment is usually limited to light jail terms or fines. Minor courts such as justices of the peace or municipal courts usually hear such cases without a jury. *See* FELONY, page 210.

Significance   Most violations of law are misdemeanors and constitute the bulk of judicial business in the United States. Many such cases are handled by "summary process," without indictment or trial, and are settled by payment of a fine. Misdemeanors are to be distinguished from "felonies," which are more serious violations of law, requiring more formalized proceedings in arrests and trials.

Missouri Plan   A method of selecting state judges, used in six states, which combines both appointment and election. In Missouri, judges of the Supreme Court, of courts of appeals, and of courts in St. Louis and Kansas City are appointed by the governor from a list of three names prepared by a commission composed of lawyers and laymen. The judge serves one year and then stands for election on the basis of his record. There is no opposition candidate. If the voters approve, he serves for six to twelve years, depending on the court. If he is defeated, the procedure is started anew. Other communities in the state may come under the plan if the voters approve. A similar plan exists in California, where, however, the governor nominates the candidate subject to approval of, rather than from a list prepared by, the commission.

Significance   The issue of appointment versus election of judges is one of the "great debates" of American politics. The Missouri Plan has been hailed as a satisfactory compromise in that it retains power in the electorate while freeing the judges from the necessity of campaigning for office.

Obiter Dictum   A statement in a court opinion on an issue not precisely involved in the case. Since such statements are not relevant to the conclusions reached in the decision, they are not binding as precedents.

Significance   Obiter dicta provide clues to the thinking of the court on issues related to the case at hand and may influence the decisions of the court in similar cases.

Original Jurisdiction   The authority of a court to hear a case in the first instance. Generally, courts of original jurisdiction are minor courts or trial courts. They are to be distinguished from courts of appellate jurisdiction, which hear cases on appeal from courts of original jurisdiction. A court that is primarily appellate may have some original jurisdiction. The United States Supreme Court, for example, has original jurisdiction over suits involving ambassadors and those to which a state is a party. See JURISDICTION, page 214.

Significance   Original jurisdiction is often "final" jurisdiction, since few cases are heard on appeal by higher courts. Even if a case is appealed, the determination of the facts in the case by the judge or jury in the court of original jurisdiction is generally considered to be final, with questions of law heard by the appellate court.

Panel   The list of persons summoned for jury duty. A trial jury is "impaneled" when the parties to the case have agreed to the selection of the jurors from the panel. Panels are selected in a variety of ways in different states by jury commissioners or county or township clerks or other officials. Names are usually selected from voting or taxpayer list. See JURY, page 214; BLUE-RIBBON JURY, page 200.

Significance   The major problem in selecting jury panels is to assure fair trials by impaneling representative cross sections of the community. State laws frequently exempt public employees, professional persons, and those who will suffer financial hardship while serving. As a result of these exemptions, it is often difficult to get a representative panel to enable an accused person to be tried by a jury of his peers. No persons may be systematically excluded from jury panels because of race, religion, or color.

Parole   Release from prison prior to the expiration of a sentence. The release is based on the good behavior of the prisoner, who may be returned to prison if he violates the conditions of his parole. In the national government, paroles are administered through the Department of Justice by the Board of Parole, consisting of eight members appointed by the President. In the states, paroles are generally administered by parole boards or by the governors.

Significance   The possibility of parole encourages prisoners to be on their good behavior and to demonstrate fitness to return to a normal life. The parole system illustrates that modern penology emphasizes rehabilitation rather than punishment. A major criticism of parole practice is that parole boards are often composed of political appointees rather than properly qualified persons. Well-qualified parole officers who supervise the parolee while he is out of prison are vital for successful parole administration.

Political Question   A doctrine enunciated by the Supreme Court holding that certain constitutional issues cannot be decided by the courts but are to be decided by the executive or legislative branches. The doctrine has generally been invoked when the issue would place the courts in serious conflict with other branches, involve the courts in political controversies, or raise serious enforcement problems. Examples of "political questions" include presidential power to recognize foreign governments, congressional power to determine whether constitutional amendments have been ratified within a reasonable time, and congressional and presidential power to determine whether states have a republican form of government. *See Luther v. Borden,* page 42; *Baker v. Carr,* page 160.

Significance   The doctrine of the political question is a self-imposed restraint on the Court's power of judicial review. Thus, it is for the Court to decide which issues are "political" and which are "justiciable." Few cases have involved "political questions," and it is impossible to predict with certainty what issues will be considered to be "political." Much depends upon the political climate of the day and the viewpoint of the majority of the Supreme Court.

Precedent   A court ruling bearing upon subsequent legal decisions in similar cases. Judges rely upon precedents in deciding cases. The common law is based primarily upon reasoning from precedents. *See* COMMON LAW, page 203; *Stare Decisis,* page 221.

Significance   Legal disputes in the United States are fought out largely over the application of precedents to a particular controversy. A lawyer will try to convince the court that the precedents serve to prove his case. Judges, in turn, must decide between competing precedents in reaching a decision. If a precedent appears to be unreasonable or unjust, a court may specifically overrule it and establish a new precedent.

Probate Court   A court, used in about one-half the states, with jurisdiction over wills, estates, guardians, and minors. Probate courts are found at the county level; in states without separate probate courts, such matters are handled by regular county courts. In some areas, probate courts are called surrogate courts. Much of the work connected with probate courts is administrative in nature, concerned largely with proper handling of minors and estates by guardians and administrators. Juries are rarely used. Probate judges are generally elected.

Significance   Probating, or proving, the authenticity of a will and the subsequent administration of an estate are important elements of American law, reflecting concern with property rights. The rights of minors, too, are zealously protected. Probate courts exist, in the main, to help people rather than to punish wrongdoers. One major problem is that separate probate courts tend to proliferate an already complicated court system in the states. In a more simplified court system, probate duties would be assigned to regular courts within an integrated system.

Probation   Suspension of the sentence of a person convicted of a crime, permitting him to remain free, subject to good behavior. Persons on probation are subject to supervision by an agent of the court. If the person's conduct justifies it, he will be released from probation after a period of time determined by the court. Failure to observe the terms of probation subjects him to possible imprisonment.

Significance   Imprisonment may do more harm than good to numerous offenders. Probation permits the offender to demonstrate to the court that he can become a good citizen. This technique has been particularly effective with juvenile delinquents. A competent probation office staff is essential for successful administration of probation.

Public Defender   An official whose duty it is to act as attorney for persons accused of crime who are unable to secure their own counsel. Since the Supreme Court ruling in *Gideon v. Wainwright,* 372 U.S. 335 (1963) that indigent defendants must be furnished counsel, many state and local governments have established public defender systems. *See* RIGHT TO COUNSEL, page 70.

Significance   The use of a public defender is considered to be superior to the more common practice of assignment of counsel by the court or by a private legal aid association. Assigned counsel not only vary in ability but in willingness to devote attention to the defendant's interests. Moreover, private counsel frequently lack the resources available to the public prosecutor. The public defender tends to equalize the differences between the public prosecutor and the defendant by assuring the latter adequate counsel regardless of his financial resources. In short, the public defender system is designed to assure greater "justice for the poor."

Referee   A person, ordinarily an attorney, appointed by the court to conduct a hearing on a particular matter and to report to the court. In federal courts, referees are used often in bankruptcy proceedings to collect information and to present it to the court for final disposition of the case. Under the 1960 Civil Rights Act, the federal courts were authorized to appoint voting referees to help qualified Negroes to register to vote in areas where a pattern or practice of discrimination existed.

Significance   The referee relieves the judge of attention to routine matters or matters of detail. Preliminary consideration is given to questions which eventually require judicial decision. This is particularly useful when accounting or administrative detail is involved, as in a bankruptcy case.

Sheriff   The chief law enforcement officer of a county, an elective position in all the states except Rhode Island. His duties pertain to both civil and criminal actions. In addition to general law enforcement, the sheriff, as an officer of the court, serves papers, enforces orders, maintains the jail, and collects taxes, with particular functions varying from state to state. In many jurisdictions, the sheriff is paid through fees for each job performed rather than on a regular salary basis. Law-enforcement activities are generally limited to areas outside cities and to patrol on county highways.

Significance   The office of sheriff has had a long history, dating back to ninth-century, Anglo-Saxon England. Though the office has declined in power and prestige, it remains strongly entrenched as part of American law enforcement. In many areas, the office has proved to be highly lucrative because of the fee system, but it rarely excels as a police agency. With the growth of population in suburban areas, sheriff's offices are faced with increased responsibilities which untrained sheriffs and appointed deputies are not able to meet. Critics advocate the substitution of a professional, county-wide police system.

Small Claims Court   A court found in many large cities to expedite minor cases at low cost. Disputes over such issues as fuel or grocery bills or wages are quickly settled by a judge.

Significance   Thousands of small claims are settled each year in small claims courts without cluttering the dockets of regular courts and without need for the parties to hire attorneys or go to other great expense. Where small claims courts are not found, such cases are generally heard by justices of the the peace who receive a fee for their service.

Solicitor General   An important official in the Department of Justice who conducts cases on behalf of the United States before the Supreme Court. In addition, his approval is necessary before any appeal may be taken on behalf of the federal government to any appellate court.

Significance   As chief counsel for the national government, the Solicitor General's conduct of cases may decide the fate of many important programs. As supervisor of appeals, he is in a position to affect the administration of federal criminal and civil law by determining which issues or cases are worthy of appeal. His decisions and the general conduct of his office may be important keys to the policies of the administration in power in Washington, as reflected in the types of cases in which appeals are brought and in the arguments made before the Supreme Court.

Stare Decisis   A legal term meaning "let the decision stand." It is an important element of the common law whereby a decision applies in similar cases and is binding upon lower courts. Precedents thus established stand until overruled. *See* PRECEDENT, page 219.

Significance   The rule of stare decisis lends stability to the law and to legal arrangements among individuals. Thus lawyers, judges, and the public at large, are bound by what has gone before unless compelling reasons call for establishing new precedents.

Statute of Limitations   A state or federal legislative act that establishes a time limit within which lawsuits may be brought, judgments enforced, or crimes prosecuted. The time limit varies among different jurisdictions and with the nature of the case, although for certain major offenses, such as murder, no limits are placed on prosecution.

Significance   Statutes of limitations prevent endless harassment of individuals by other persons or by the government. Though certain violations of law may go unchallenged, it is considered desirable that at some point, the threat of prosecution be ended.

Statutory Construction   Judicial interpretation of legislative enactments. The application of a statute is not always clear from the words of the statute. Judges seek "legislative intent" by consulting legislative committee hearings, floor debates, and legislative journals. If these sources do not reveal the legislature's objectives, the court must then discern the meaning of the law.

Significance   Statutory construction is one of the most difficult tasks of the judiciary. In a complicated society, most laws can be stated only in the most general terms, with specific application to wide varieties of situations left to judges as disputes arise. While the legislative history of an act may produce needed information, it often fails to reveal how the legislature intended the law to fit a specific situation. It is this lack of clarity that often leads to lawsuits. Legislative bodies may deliberately leave statutes vague so that details can be worked out by judges on a case-by-case basis. The net effect of statutory interpretation is to strengthen greatly the power of the courts.

Subpoena   An order of a court, grand jury, legislative body or committee, or of any duly authorized administrative agency, compelling the attendance of a witness. A *subpoena duces tecum* requires the witness to produce specific documents. Failure to honor a subpoena may subject the person to prosecution for contempt.

Significance   Public agencies could not properly perform their functions without the power of subpoena. Persons called may refuse to testify or to reveal certain documents if they validly claim that such action may result in self-incrimination. The power of subpoena is of special importance in judicial proceedings, in which both sides of a case have the right to compel testimony of witnesses.

Summons   A complaint made by an individual or a police officer and signed by a judicial officer requiring a person to appear in court to answer charges made against him.

Significance   The summons is usually the first step in civil suits or minor criminal cases, which gives formal notice to the defendant of the charges made against him. In serious criminal matters, charges are made through indictment by grand jury or through a prosecutor's information. The summons satisfies the requirement that a person not be brought to trial without formal complaint and proper notice of the charges against him.

Supreme Court   The court of last resort in the federal and in most state judicial systems. In a few states, the highest court is called by another title. The Supreme Court of the United States is composed of the Chief Justice of the United States and eight associate justices. The number of justices is established by Congress; it has varied from five to ten, but has been set at nine since 1869. Cases are decided by majority vote. The Supreme Court is the only court specifically provided for in the Constitution, and its original jurisdiction is set therein to include cases affecting ambassadors, public ministers and consuls, and those to which a state is a party. Its appellate jurisdiction is determined by Congress. Certain cases involving federal questions may be appealed to the Supreme Court from the highest state court. With the exception of certain specified cases involving questions of constitutionality, the Supreme Court determines which cases it will hear through the writ of certiorari. The Court sits from October to June and its decisions are reported in the *United States Reports*. State supreme courts vary in size and jurisdiction in accordance with state constitutions and laws but, except for cases that may be brought to the United States Supreme Court, they are the courts of last resort in each state. Justices of the United States Supreme Court are appointed by the President, with the Senate's consent, for life terms, subject to impeachment. Most state supreme court judges are elected. The United States Supreme Court, and some state supreme courts, oversee their respective court systems in matters of procedure and administration. *See* ACTIVISM VERSUS SELF-RESTRAINT, page 197; JUDICIAL REVIEW, page 213; UNITED STATES REPORTS, page 225; *Ashwander v. TVA*, page 228.

Significance   Courts of last resort, particularly the Supreme Court of the United States, wield tremendous power and play a major role in the development of public policy. In the final analysis, these courts determine the meaning of the Constitution and of statutes, the scope of legislative and executive power, and the scope of their own power. Decisions as to the meaning of constitutional phrases have lasting impact, unless overruled by the court itself (as in the segregation cases) or overturned by constitutional amendment (as in the case of the income tax). Decisions are binding upon all lower courts, assuring uniformity of judgments. Because of the importance of the questions that, typically, reach it, the United States Supreme Court has often been involved in major economic, political, and social controversies. Appointments to the Court are watched with avid interest to ascertain in which way the new justices may influence the interpretation of the Constitution and laws.

Supreme Court Packing Plan   A proposal made in 1937 by President Franklin D. Roosevelt that the President be authorized to appoint an additional justice of the Supreme Court for each justice over the age of seventy who did not retire after ten years of service. The maximum number of appointments was to have been six, thereby possibly increasing the size of the Supreme Court from nine to fifteen. The President claimed that this plan would increase the efficiency of the Court, but it was defeated in the Congress on the ground that Roosevelt was trying to "pack" the court to overcome unfavorable decisions on New Deal programs.

Significance   The idea of packing the court so as to affect the nature of decisions is not novel in American history. The size of the Court was altered on six different occasions by Congress, either to prevent appointments by a President or to affect decisions. These instances, plus the Roosevelt plan, point up the significance of the Supreme Court in the formulation of public policy. The plan met with strong resistance from members of the Court and Congress as well as from the public at large, demonstrating general support for the Court as an institution that should not be tampered with. In the course of the debate, the Court reversed its previous position, handing down new interpretations of the Constitution that gave free rein to the New Deal. It is said that President Roosevelt "lost the battle but won the war."

Taxpayer's Suit   A suit brought by a taxpayer to prevent the expenditure of public funds for a given purpose. Such suits are permissible in most of the states but not in federal courts. *See Frothingham v. Mellon*, page 230.

Significance   The taxpayer suit is based on the theory that each taxpayer has an interest in how public funds are spent, regardless of the amount of his contribution. Such suits are not heard in federal courts because the Supreme Court has held that no taxpayer has a sufficient personal interest in the vast expenditures of federal funds (*Frothingham v. Mellon*, 262 U.S. 447 [1923]).

Territorial Court   A court established by Congress in a territory of the United States. Congress has established district courts in Guam, Puerto Rico, the Virgin Islands, and the Panama Canal Zone, under its power to govern the territories, and has authorized minor courts in some cases. With the exception of Puerto Rico, the federal district courts of the territories also hear cases ordinarily heard in state courts. Judges of all territorial courts are appointed for eight-year terms. *See* LEGISLATIVE COURT, page 215.

Significance   Residents of Guam, Puerto Rico, and the Virgin Islands are citizens of the United States. Though statehood is not in the offing, Congress has provided these areas with regular district courts, thereby establishing the American legal tradition and recognizing the basic rights of the inhabitants.

Tort   A wrongful act involving injury to persons, property, or reputation, but excluding breach of contract. The injured party may bring suit against the wrongdoer. This is an important and often used branch of law. A major tort problem concerns the responsibility of governmental units for torts committed by government employees against individuals.

Significance   Tort law serves as a substitute for private duels and assures that for most wrongs there will be a remedy. The issue of the tort liability of government has not been definitely resolved. Generally, no one may sue the government without consent. Many states and the national government have authorized suits for certain kinds of torts. At the municipal level, the law varies from state to state, but as a general rule, municipalities are not responsible for torts committed by their employees when they are engaged in purely "governmental" functions. There may, however, be liability for torts committed in the course of "proprietary" functions (such as gas supply, transportation, and other businesslike functions). The Federal Tort Claims Act of 1946 permits claims of $1,000 or less against the national government to be settled by administrative officials.

Trial   The examination of a civil or criminal action in accordance with the law of the land before a judge who has jurisdiction. A trial must be public, conducted fairly before an impartial judge, and, in the case of criminal trials, started without unreasonable delay. *See Moore v. Dempsey,* page 84; SIXTH AMENDMENT, page 74.

Significance   A speedy, impartial, and public trial conducted in conformity with established procedures of the law is one of the major hallmarks of a free and civilized people. Knowledge that disputes will be settled in this manner gives the people confidence in the law and makes unnecessary private feuds for settlement of grievances. American trial procedures give adequate opportunity to each side to present its case for examination by the judge or jury.

Unified Court System   An integrated state-wide or area-wide court system, organized into divisions for more efficient distribution of case load and judges. A chief judge, aided by a judicial council or business manager, supervises the operations of the courts, shifts judges about to meet case load demands, and, through collection of significant data, promotes the efficient administration of justice.

Significance   Most proponents of judicial reform endorse the unified court plan. Most state and local court systems are organized on a geographic basis, with many types of cases heard in each jurisdiction by the same judge. The unified plan, its proponents claim, will encourage specialization among judges, relieve the situation in which some court dockets are crowded while others are not filled, and promote uniformity in decision-making. Over-all supervision by a chief judge will result in more efficient use of manpower and money, and expedite the business of the courts.

United States Attorney   A federal official whose principal function is to prosecute violations of federal law. A United States Attorney is assigned to each district in which a federal district court is located. He is appointed for a four-year term by the President with the Senate's consent, and is under general supervision of the Department of Justice and the Attorney General of the United States.

Significance   The functions of the United States Attorney underscore the divided nature of American law enforcement. Though he may cooperate with local law enforcement officials, he is responsible only for violations of federal law. The position is frequently a step toward appointment to the federal judiciary.

United States Commissioner   An official of a federal district court, appointed by the judge for a four-year term, who holds preliminary hearings in criminal cases. Commissioners issue arrest warrants, determine if the accused shall be held for the grand jury, and may set bail.

Significance   Commissioners relieve regular judges of routine and preliminary matters, thereby freeing the judge for full-time attention to his major trial duties. Where district courts serve a large area or an entire state, commissioners serving in various locations in the district make it unnecessary to bring federal law violators to the seat of the district court immediately.

United States Reports   The official record of cases heard and disposed of by the United States Supreme Court, including the full opinions of the justices. The volumes are issued at the conclusion of the term of the Court but opinions are available in "advance sheets" prior to issuance of the volumes. Two or three volumes of the *Reports* may emerge each year, depending on the volume of business and length of opinions. The volumes are numbered consecutively but, prior to 1874, at which time the *Reports* totaled ninety volumes, they were identified by the names of the official court reporters. These include: Dallas, Cranch, Wheaton, Peters, Howard, Black, and Wallace. Thus, a case cited as 1 Cranch 137 (1803), means that the case, decided in 1803, can be found on page 137 of the first volume compiled by Cranch. Since 1874, the volumes are simply numbered, beginning with 91. A case cited as 345 U.S. 123 (1953) will be found on page 123 of volume 345 of the *United States Reports,* and was decided in 1953. All recorded legal decisions in any court may be found in similar fashion by locating the title, volume, and page of the *Report* in which it is given. Reports are available from federal courts of appeals (*Federal Reporter*), district courts (*Federal Supplement*), and highest state courts which are identified by the name of the state, for example, 156

Michigan 124. Commercial companies also put out volumes reporting these cases: *the Supreme Court* reporter (cited as 57 Sup. Ct. 234) and the *Lawyers' Edition* (cited as 57 L. Ed. 234).

Significance   The reports of cases are available for use by lawyers, legal scholars, and all citizens. The report of Supreme Court cases, in particular, provides some of the best material available on American political and legal thought and practice. Major social and political issues are apt to find their way to the Supreme Court and the opinions are important social documents.

Venue   The county or district in which a prosecution is brought for trial and from which jurors are chosen. Venue refers to a particular area, not to the court that has jurisdiction.

Significance   Under American law, trials are held in the area in which the wrong is done. The Sixth Amendment to the Constitution provides that, in federal criminal prosecutions, trials are to be held in the state and district in which the crime was committed. Similar provisions are found in state constitutions. This gives the defendant the benefit of a court and a jury familiar with the problems and people of the area. A defendant may, however, ask for a "change of venue," a transfer of the trial to another locality, on the grounds that the people of the locality are prejudiced against him and that an impartial jury could not be drawn. It is for the judge to determine whether a change of venue is justified.

Witness   A person who presents information or evidence in a trial or investigation. Under the Sixth Amendment and most state constitutions, a person accused of a crime is entitled to confront the witnesses against him and to compel the attendance of witnesses in his favor. In 1965, the Supreme Court ruled that the right of confrontation of witnesses applies in state trials under the due process clause of the Fourteenth Amendment (*Pointer v. Texas* 380 U.S. 400).

Significance   In a criminal case, the government must permit cross-examination of any witness it uses. If it wishes to conceal the identity of an informant, then that person may not be put on the stand, nor may his testimony be introduced. In addition, the defendant is entitled to see any reports made to the police by a witness, unless the judge rules otherwise. The right to compel the attendance of favorable witnesses is an important corollary to the right of confrontation, and the defendant has the right to government aid to subpoena any reluctant witness. Though these rights are fairly well established in criminal trials, attention in recent years has been directed to the lack of these rights in congressional investigations. In hearings on subversion in particular, criticism has been made of the fact that while persons accused of subversion are usually permitted to testify, they are not permitted to confront and cross-examine accusers nor to compel the attendance of favorable witnesses.

Writ   An order in writing issued by a court ordering the performance of an act or prohibiting some act. A wide variety of writs exist, ranging from orders to appear in court to orders regarding the execution of the court's judgment. *See* CERTIORARI, page 201; INJUNCTION, page 212; MANDAMUS, page 216.

Significance   Courts exercise their power largely through the issuance of writs, which are essential for the orderly progress of judicial functions. The right to enforce a decision is as necessary as the right to hear and decide cases. Failure to honor a writ subjects a person to a fine and/or imprisonment for contempt of court.

IMPORTANT AGENCIES

Administrative Office of the United States Courts   An agency that handles administrative matters for all federal and territorial courts except the Supreme Court. The Office, established in 1939, is headed by a director who is appointed by the Supreme Court. Its functions include supervision of administrative personnel of the courts, the fixing of compensation of such personnel, preparation of the budget for the operations of the court system, and care of court funds, books, equipment, and supplies. The Office also gathers statistics on dockets, and supervises administration of bankruptcy and federal probation.

Significance   The Administrative Office of the United States Courts has established centralized control over court administration. In the past, little attention had been paid to the administrative problems involved in maintaining an effective judiciary. In many of the states, similar duties are carried on by judicial councils. Information on court dockets helps promote efficient administration of justice.

Department of Justice   A major department of the executive branch concerned with the enforcement of federal laws. The Justice Department is headed by the Attorney General who is a member of the President's Cabinet. The Department furnishes legal counsel in cases involving the national government, interprets laws under which other executive agencies operate, supervises federal penal institutions, directs United States Attorneys and Marshals, supervises immigration laws, and directs paroles of federal prisoners. The Department includes the Federal Bureau of Investigation (FBI), which is the major police agency for the national government. *See* DEPARTMENT OF JUSTICE, page 76.

Significance   The Department of Justice maintains a close relationship with all other units of the national government because of its widespread responsibility for law enforcement. Its functions also put it into frequent contact with the judicial branch at all stages of judicial proceedings, from the apprehension of law violaters to their imprisonment and parole. The Department is not, however, a part of the judicial branch, as is sometimes erroneously thought; this would constitute a violation of the separation of powers because it would unite prosecutor and judge.

IMPORTANT CASES

Ableman v. Booth, 21 Howard 506 (1859): Established that a state court may not issue a writ of habeas corpus to a prisoner in federal custody.

Significance   The *Ableman* case underscores the independence of state and federal courts from each other in their proper spheres of authority. No judicial order can have any effect outside the lawful jurisdiction of the court.

Neither the states nor the federal courts can intrude into the domain of the other unless the nature of the case demands the exercise of the supreme federal authority.

Ashwander v. TVA, 297 U.S. 288 (1936): Upheld the right of the TVA to sell surplus electric power. Furthermore, the case is well-known for the concurring opinion by Justice Louis D. Brandeis in which he attempted to sum up the rules that the Court had developed in considering the constitutionality of the acts of the legislative and executive branches. Among these were: (1) The Court will not decide questions of a constitutional nature, unless absolutely essential to dispose of the case. (2) The Court will not pass upon a constitutional question if the case can be disposed of on some other ground. (3) The Court will not formulate a constitutional rule broader than is required by the precise facts of the case. (4) The Court will try to construe a statute so as to avoid ruling on constitutional questions, even if serious doubts exist as to its constitutionality. *See Ashwander v. TVA*, page 299.

   Significance   The Court's self-denying rules, as formulated by Justice Brandeis for handling constitutional issues, have governed its course in recent years. It remains reluctant to rule on the constitutionality of federal legislation, and only a few statutory provisions have been declared unconstitutional since 1937. Through these rules, the Court has sought to avoid controversy with the legislative and executive branches.

Cohens v. Virginia, 6 Wheaton 264 (1821): Ruled that state court decisions are subject to review by the Supreme Court if the case involves a question of federal law, treaties, or the Constitution, even though a state is a party to the suit. An appeal brought to a federal court by a defendant who has been convicted in a state court does not constitute a suit against the state contrary to the Eleventh Amendment.

   Significance   The question of whether the Supreme Court had appellate jurisdiction over cases appealed from state courts was crucial to the development of federal judicial power. Prior to the *Cohens* decision, the Supreme Court held, in *Martin v. Hunter's Lessee,* 1 Wheaton 304 (1816), that it had the right to review state court decisions involving suits between private individuals when a federal question is involved. The *Cohens* decision extended this principle to cases in which a state is a party. In both cases, the Court pointed out that federal jurisdiction is essential to establish uniformity of decision throughout the United States on the interpretation of the Constitution, federal law, or treaties. Otherwise, each state, rather than the national government, would be supreme.

Dred Scott v. Sanford, 19 Howard 393 (1857): Held, in a famous case, that Negroes could not become citizens of the United States nor were they entitled to the rights and privileges of citizenship. The Court also ruled that the Missouri Compromise, which had banned slavery in the territories, was unconstitutional.

   Significance   The *Dred Scott* decision is considered to be one of the most disastrous handed down by the Supreme Court. The Court, itself, was badly divided and muddled in its views. The case failed to resolve the slavery issue and contributed to making inevitable the Civil War conflict. Both the Civil War and the provisions of the Fourteenth Amendment on citizenship were needed to overcome the *Dred Scott* ruling. The *Dred Scott* case is also noted for being the second in which a federal law was declared unconstitutional, following the Supreme Court's exercise of judicial review in *Marbury v. Madison,* 1 Cranch 137 (1803). The crucial role of the Supreme Court in American life and politics is underscored by the *Dred Scott* case.

Eakin v. Raub, 12 S. & R. 330 (1825): Decided by the Supreme Court of the State of Pennsylvania, this case is famous for an opinion by Judge John B. Gibson discussing the power of judicial review. Judge Gibson disagreed with the logic of Chief Justice John Marshall's opinion in *Marbury v. Madison,* 1 Cranch 137 (1803) in which Marshall argued that judges had a special duty to interpret the Constitution and to declare any law in conflict with the Constitution null and void. Judge Gibson argued that the judges had no such duty. Rather, the legislature bore the responsibility for unlawful acts and the people should hold them responsible.

     Significance   Judge Gibson's opinion is the best-known argument by a judge against the principle of judicial review. Although it never overthrew that principle, the position he took is still held by many persons. The student of government may find the complete opinion of Judge Gibson reproduced in many casebooks or textbooks on constitutional law.

Erie Railroad v. Tompkins, 304 U.S. 64 (1938): Ruled that, in diversity of citizenship cases heard in federal courts, the law to be applied is the state law as declared by the state legislature or courts. There is no federal common law.

     Significance   The *Erie* case overruled *Swift v. Tyson,* 16 Peters 1 (1842), which had held that in the absence of a state statute controlling a case, the federal courts could apply their own principles of the common law. After almost a century of confusion resulting from several versions of the common law, particularly in commercial cases, the Court declared in the *Erie* case that the *Tyson* rule was not only incorrect but unconstitutional as well, since there is no general federal common law.

Ex parte McCardle, 7 Wallace 506 (1869): Declared that the Supreme Court may not exercise appellate jurisdiction over a case when Congress prohibits such jurisdiction. This case arose when Congress repealed an 1867 law that had authorized appeals to the Supreme Court in certain cases involving enforcement of the post-Civil War Reconstruction Acts.

     Significance   Congress withdrew jurisdiction from the Supreme Court in this case for fear that the Court would declare the Acts unconstitutional. Nevertheless, the Court dismissed the case on the ground that it lacked jurisdiction. The *McCardle* case demonstrates the veto power of Congress over the appellate jurisdiction of the Supreme Court. The Constitution in Article III, section 2, provides that the Supreme Court has appellate jurisdiction in all cases heard in federal courts "with such exceptions, and under such regulations as the Congress shall make." Congress does not grant appellate power but may make exceptions to its exercise.

Frothingham v. Mellon, 262 U.S. 447 (1923): Held that a taxpayer may not bring suit in a federal court to restrain the expenditure of federal funds. The case involved a protest against a federal grant-in-aid to the states for maternity benefits. *See Massachusetts v. Mellon,* page 42.

Significance   An important element of judicial procedure is that a party to a suit must have standing to sue. That is, a party must be able to show "some direct injury . . . and not merely that he suffers in some indefinite way in common with people generally." Although taxpayer suits are common in state and local courts, the Supreme Court has taken the view that an individual's interest in federal taxation and expenditures is too minute. As a consequence, the *Frothingham* rule frees the federal court docket of taxpayer suits and makes it impossible to challenge federal tax and expenditure legislation.

Marbury v. Madison, 1 Cranch 137 (1803): Struck down, for the first time in American history, an act of Congress as unconstitutional. The Court, speaking through Chief Justice John Marshall, held unconstitutional a portion of the Judiciary Act of 1789 that had added to the original jurisdiction of the Supreme Court, as specified in Article III of the Constitution. The case was essentially a political controversy between the defeated Federalist party and the incoming Jeffersonian party over last-minute Federalist party appointments to the federal courts.

Significance   Few cases have had the impact upon American governmental development of *Marbury v. Madison,* in which Chief Justice Marshall struck a decisive blow for judicial supremacy. Marshall argued that the Constitution was the supreme law, and that judges were bound by their oath and the nature of their positions to act as guardians of the Constitution. Any law in conflict with the Constitution cannot be enforced by the courts. The logic of Marshall's opinion has never been successfully refuted. Although the Constitution fails to mention judicial review, the American people have accepted its exercise by the courts as an integral part of the American constitutional system.

IMPORTANT STATUTES

Judiciary Act of 1789   A law passed by the first Congress to establish the federal court system. The Act determined the organization and jurisdiction of the courts. Over the years, the Judiciary Act has undergone numerous changes, adding and deleting courts, changing jurisdiction of courts, establishing rules of procedure, and providing for a variety of court officers and employees. The last major revision of the law took place in 1948.

Significance   The Judiciary Act of 1789 and its subsequent amendments demonstrate congressional authority over federal court organization, jurisdiction, and procedure. The only constitutional limit placed on Congress is that a Supreme Court must exist with specified original jurisdiction. A portion of the Judiciary Act of 1789 was declared unconstitutional in the famous case of

Marbury v. Madison, 1 Cranch 137 (1803), because, in it, the Congress had unconstitutionally added to the original jurisdiction of the Supreme Court. Changes of significance include the Act of 1891, which established the courts of appeals and the Act of 1925, which gave the Supreme Court discretionary authority to issue writs of certiorari.

Eleven

Finance and Taxation

Ability Theory   The belief that taxes should be based upon the individual's ability to pay, as indicated by income, property, or wealth. *See* PROGRESSIVE TAX, page 245.

Significance   The ability theory is often challenged, particularly by advocates of the benefit theory, who hold that taxes should be paid by those who derive benefits from them. The income tax most nearly approximates the ideal of the ability theory because of its progressive increases in rates as income (and, hence, ability to pay) rises. The federal individual income tax is based on the ability theory, although many exemptions, and other favored treatments, have reduced its progressive nature.

Assessed Valuation   Value assigned to property for tax purposes. The general property tax levied by local governments in the United States is based on the valuation placed upon real estate (land, buildings, and other improvements) and personal property, both tangible (machinery, livestock, merchandise) and intangible (stocks, bonds, bank accounts). The tax paid on property is based on the assessed valuation and the millage or tax rate applied to the assessed value. The assessed valuation is based on a proportion of the actual value of each piece of property assessed within a taxing district, usually thirty to fifty percent of true market value. Assessments can be changed by reappraisals, adjustment of individual inequities by a board of review, adjustment of unequal valuations for different assessment districts by a county or state board of equalization, or by a general revaluation of all assessments within a district. *See* PROPERTY TAX, page 245.

Significance   The assessment of property for tax purposes is a complex process that produces much controversy among taxpayers, many of whom believe their property has been assessed too high or unequally with their neighbor's. The fair assessment of personal property poses the greatest problem because of the difficulty for assessors to find and appraise movable property. When a taxing district crosses assessment boundaries, such as a school district that includes a city and several townships, the danger of disparities in assessed valuation is increased. The key to a fair assessment system may be found in the appointment of professional county-wide or state-wide assessors.

Assessor   A public official who determines the value of real and personal property for purposes of taxation. Assessors are commonly elected in towns, townships, or counties. In some midwestern townships, the supervisor serves as the assessor. About fifteen percent of city assessors are still elected. *See* PROPERTY TAX, page 245.

   Significance   Many students of government challenge the election of assessors. The elective method is unlikely to secure competent assessors, and elected officials may under-assess so as not to antagonize the voters. Critics also charge that the town or township is too small a unit for assessment purposes. Many areas have moved in the direction of appointing assessors on a merit basis and making the county the assessment unit.

Auditor   An official, usually an agent of a legislative body, who checks on the expenditure of appropriated funds to determine that they have been spent for the purposes approved by the legislature in its appropriation acts. The federal auditor, the Comptroller General, is appointed by the President with the Senate's approval; state and local auditors are either appointed, or elected by the voters. *See* COMPTROLLER GENERAL, page 235.

   Significance   Proper auditing of disbursed funds is essential to fiscal responsibility. In many state and local governments, only a preaudit in the form of a spending authorization is required, with no proper postaudit after expenditures to check their validity. In other cases, the same officials who authorize the expenditures are later called upon to check on the authenticity of their own work. Effective auditing procedures require careful examination of the validity of accounts and payments by competent, independent auditors *after* the expenditures have been made by the executive branch.

Banking Systems   The national and state banking systems, which exist side by side in the United States. Congress was not granted the specific power to charter banks, but the power is implied from granted powers that can best be carried on through banks, such as the borrowing and currency powers. Both national and state chartered banks are privately owned financial institutions, which are regulated and have their accounts audited by the respective chartering government. National banks, chartered by the national government since 1863, are supervised by the Comptroller of the Currency in the Treasury Department, and are required to join the Federal Reserve System. Most state banks accept Federal Reserve membership and, thereby, come under a measure of national as well as state regulation. The citizen can usually distinguish between a national and state chartered bank by their names, such as First National Bank or Industrial State Bank. *See* FEDERAL RESERVE SYSTEM, page 240.

   Significance   Federal and state regulation of banks involves such matters as issuance of stock, stockholder liabilities, assets and investments, organization and management, reserves, loans, and depositor security. The public is protected through periodic inspections and audits by examiners, and by deposit insurance, up to $15,000 for each account, guaranteed by the Federal Deposit Insurance Corporation. The dual national-state banking system provides some measure of financial flexibility, although state banks have lost much of their autonomy through membership in the Federal Reserve System.

Benefit Theory   The belief that individuals should be taxed in proportion to the benefits they derive from governmental services. *See* SPECIAL ASSESSMENT, page 247.

Significance   The benefit theory has largely been superseded by the ability theory, which is regarded as more equitable and easier to determine in a complex society in which benefits derived from taxes often go unnoticed. The benefit theory is still applied in special areas where the benefits can be directly or easily assessed. The 1956 Federal Highway Act, for example, provides for financing of the vast interstate highway system with federal gasoline excise taxes levied on highway users. On the local level, special assessments on improvements that benefit the property owner are used extensively.

Board of Review   Public officials charged with the duty of reviewing individual tax assessments on property. The review function is to be distinguished from "equalization," which is the comparison and adjustment of assessments between entire tax-imposing units. The board of review may be elected or composed of local government officials serving ex officio. *See* PROPERTY TAX, page 245.

Significance   Citizens dissatisfied with their property tax may appeal to a board of review. The board's objective is to tax all citizens equitably, according to the value of their property. Most citizens fail to take advantage of their right of review, not wanting to take the time or trouble, or out of fear that their assessment may be raised.

Bond   A certificate of indebtedness, tendered by a borrower to a lender, that constitutes a written obligation for the borrower to repay to the lender the principal plus accrued interest on the loan. A public bond is issued by the national government or by a state or local government as a means of borrowing money for public needs that cannot be financed out of current revenues. *See* BOND, page 257.

Significance   Various types of bonds, such as savings bonds, are issued by the United States government to finance budget deficits and to carry the public debt. State and local governments commonly make use of either serial bond or sinking fund issues to finance new projects. Sinking fund bonds are paid from a separate fund set aside from revenues over a period of time until the bonds are due for payment. Serial bonds, which are becoming more popular than the sinking fund type, come due at different dates over a period of years, with each series paid off by the borrowing authority from current revenues.

Borrowing Power   The authority of a government to finance those expenditures that exceed its income. The Constitution (Art. I, sec. 8) provides Congress with full borrowing power, free from restrictions. Most state constitutions, however, severely limit the authority of state governments to incur indebtedness, permitting state borrowing only when authorized by constitutional amendment or by a vote of the people. Local units of government are restricted by state constitutional or statutory limitations on their borrowing power. *See* DEBT LIMIT, page 236; PUBLIC DEBT, page 246.

Significance   The borrowing power is essential for governments to meet short and long term crises and to finance major projects that cannot be paid for out of current income. The national government, for example, used its borrowing power extensively during World War II and the economic crisis of the 1930s. Deficit spending to counteract economic recessions has become a standard weapon in the arsenal of federal fiscal policy. Most state and local borrowing, conversely, is used to finance major building projects. Some citizens support borrowing for capital improvements as an investment in the future, similar to borrowing by a family to purchase a home. Others view extensive use of the borrowing power as fiscal irresponsibility.

Budget   An estimate of the receipts and expenditures needed by government to carry out its program in some future period, usually a fiscal year. The President is responsible for formulating the national budget under the Budget and Accounting Act of 1921, and governors of most states likewise operate under an "executive budget" system. The budget process begins with the lengthy and detailed process of preparing estimates, followed by a central review in which budget officers hold hearings in which agency officials defend their estimates. Next, the budget is approved by the chief executive and submitted to the legislative body in a "budget message." After study and the holding of hearings by appropriations committees, the budget is enacted as an appropriation act. This is followed by budget execution, the actual spending of the money during the fiscal period by executive officials. The final step is a post-audit check on the validity of expenditures. Some states and cities use a separate capital budget for financing major public works projects, which are often paid for on a long-term bonding or self-liquidating basis. *See* PERFORMANCE BUDGET, page 244; BUDGET AND ACCOUNTING ACT, page 254; BUREAU OF THE BUDGET, page 252.

Significance   A budget is a work plan that gives direction to the execution of government policies. The budget process has undergone a major change in the twentieth century with the adoption of the executive budget to replace the formulation of budgets by legislative committees. The executive budget gives the chief executive—President, governor, or mayor—extensive control over fiscal affairs.

Comptroller General   The federal official responsible for auditing the accounts of all national government agencies. He heads the General Accounting Office (GAO), and is appointed by the President with the Senate's approval for a fifteen-year term. The Comptroller General (pronounced con-troller) also has power to validate all payments to ensure that they fall within the purposes and limits of congressional appropriations acts and to standardize accounting systems of government agencies. He can be removed from office by impeachment or by joint resolution of Congress. *See* GENERAL ACCOUNTING OFFICE, page 252.

Significance   The Comptroller General acts as an agent of Congress in controlling and auditing the budget execution process in the executive branch. Without his approval, money cannot validly be withdrawn from the Treasury. Controversy has developed on occasion when the Comptroller General has been charged with letting his personal views influence the validation of expenditures. For example, President Franklin Roosevelt became involved in many controversies with the Comptroller General because the latter's open hostility to the New Deal was regarded as the reason for his holding up many emergency spending programs. Numerous observers, including the first Hoover Commission, have recommended that the Comptroller General's "preaudit" validation of payments be transferred to an executive official, leaving the Comptroller General with responsibility for a "postaudit." In recent years, the Comptroller General has expanded his operations by sending his GAO investigators abroad to check on foreign aid and other types of overseas spending.

Corporation Income Tax   A national tax levied on corporations, based on their annual net income. The corporation income tax rate in recent years has been a flat twenty-two percent for the first $25,000 of net income and forty-eight percent on all net income over that figure.

Significance   The federal corporation income tax is probably the most complicated tax levied by the national government, resulting from controversy over what constitutes "net income" and "legitimate" expenses for a corporation. It ranks next to the individual income tax in the amount of its annual yield. In recent years, it has produced over $20 billion annually. The tax has been attacked for fostering "double taxation," that is, the taxing of corporation income through the corporation income tax, followed by the taxing of shareholders' dividends through the individual income tax. Others have criticized the corporation income tax for its lenient rates and loopholes.

Debt Limit   A constitutional or statutory limitation upon the ability of a government to incur indebtedness. In the national government, the debt limit is fixed by Congress and can be changed to meet new debt needs. All but a few states, however, are restricted by constitutional provisions that usually limit state indebtedness to a specified figure. Debt limitations on local governments generally take the form of restricting total debt to a percentage of assessed valuation or involve state approval of bond issues. *See* PUBLIC DEBT, page 246.

Significance   Self-imposed statutory debt limits established by legislative bodies, as by Congress, are useful only psychologically, if at all. Over the past three decades, Congress has altered the public debt limit on numerous occasions, raising it to more than $300 billion. On the state and local levels, cumbersome constitutional restrictions have produced many new techniques for evasion. Although debt limits can ordinarily be exceeded by favorable referendum votes in the state and local governments, voter apathy or conservatism has made this increasingly difficult. Devices that have been used to incur indebtedness beyond state or local limits include borrowing by state agencies instead of the state, per se, and borrowing on a self-liquidating basis without state certification of bonds. For example, state toll-road authorities borrow large sums to construct highways, and repay the debt out of income from tolls. Despite efforts to keep debt limited on the national, state, and local levels, new demands for governmental functions and services beyond the means of current income keep debt rising in the United States.

Deficit Financing   A technique of fiscal policy that utilizes government spending beyond income to combat an economic slump. The use of deficit financing to "prime the pump" of the free enterprise economy was popularized by the British economist, John Maynard Keynes, in the 1930s. *See* FISCAL POLICY, page 241; PUBLIC DEBT, page 246.

Significance   The objective of deficit financing is to inject new purchasing power into the economy to stimulate an upturn in economic activity during a period of stagnation resulting from overproduction or underconsumption. Deficit financing is accepted today by most economists and politicians, on the assumption that deficits incurred during economic slumps will be paid off with budget surpluses during periods of prosperity. Conservatives generally oppose it on the grounds that it involves fiscal irresponsibility and is ineffectual, and they usually demand government cutbacks in spending as the best means of stimulating the free economy. The national government used deficit financing extensively during the depression of the 1930s and has employed it to combat four post-World War II recessions.

Deflation   An economic condition in which the price level is decreased and the value of money in terms of purchasing power is consequently increased. Deflation may result from either a decrease in the amount of money and credit available or an oversupply of consumer goods. *See* INFLATION, page 243; MONETARY POLICY, page 244.

Significance   Proponents of stable monetary policies regard deflation and inflation, its opposite, as twin evils to be equally avoided. Deflation is characteristically associated with economic depressions, just as inflation tends to accompany prosperity. Most economists believe that deflation can be prevented or controlled through proper use of monetary policy by the Federal Reserve Board and the Treasury and by the use of fiscal policy, such as deficit financing. A policy of deflation is sometimes adopted by a nation suffering from an adverse balance of payments, with the objective of reducing prices to make exports more attractive to other countries.

Devaluation   A policy undertaken by a nation to reduce the value of its monetary unit in terms of gold or its exchange ratio with other national currencies. The United States devalued the dollar by about fifty-nine percent in 1934 by increasing the price of gold to $35 an ounce, a figure at which it has since remained fixed. *See* GOLD STANDARD, page 242; BALANCE OF PAYMENTS, page 317.

Significance   Although American devaluation of the dollar in 1934 was based largely on domestic reasons, ordinarily the objective of devaluation is to improve a nation's balance of international payments by reducing imports and expanding exports. These results are likely to occur because devaluation increases the cost of foreign products and decreases the cost of domestically produced items in foreign markets. Devaluations are often matched by equal or greater devaluations by competitor states in an effort to maintain their position in international trade. Although successive rounds of devaluations were carried on by many states during the 1930s, the only major devaluations in the postwar era occurred in 1949 when Britain and most sterling bloc countries depreciated their currencies by about thirty percent. In recent years, there has been much speculation over the possible devaluation of the dollar because of the imbalance in the American balance of payments and the resulting outflow of gold. One of the major responsibilities of the International Monetary Fund (IMF) of the United Nations is to try to eliminate competitive unilateral devaluation as an international trade weapon.

Direct Tax   Any tax paid directly to the government by the taxpayer. An indirect tax, such as a sales or excise tax, conversely, is paid to private business persons who then remit it to the government. The Constitution, in Article I, section 9, states: No capitation, or other direct tax shall be laid, unless in proportion to the census or enumeration hereinbefore directed to be taken." This provision means that, for example, the people in a state containing ten percent of the nation's population would pay ten percent of any direct tax levied by the national government. *See Pollock v. Farmers Loan and Trust Co.,* page 253.

Significance   The question of which taxes are direct and therefore to be apportioned according to the population of the states, has been the subject of much legal controversy. In 1796 (*Hylton v. United States,* 3 Dallas 171), the Supreme Court interpreted "direct taxes" to include poll taxes and taxes on land. In 1895 (*Pollock v. Farmers Loan and Trust Co.,* 158 U.S. 601), the Court struck down an income tax as a direct tax that Congress must apportion among the states. This decision was overcome by the Sixteenth Amendment, which granted the Congress the power to tax incomes "without apportionment among the several states, and without regard to any census or enumeration." Congress has generally refused to levy direct taxes, because apportionment involves many administrative complications and because of inequities that would result since tax-paying ability is not divided equally among the people of the fifty states.

Earmarking   Allocation of tax revenues for specific purposes. Earmarking gasoline taxes for highway purposes is the most common example, with about half the states doing so by constitutional provision, and the others by statutory requirement. About half of total state revenue is earmarked for specific purposes, such as highways, education, or welfare.

Significance   Earmarking tax revenues by constitutional provision reduces legislative and executive control over budgeting and finance. Earmarked programs may be adequately financed while other equally deserving public needs go unfilled. It is often easier, however, for the legislature to secure public consent to an earmarked tax, since the people can clearly see the object of the tax.

Equalization   The review and adjustment of tax assessments among taxing districts in the state. The equalization function may be exercised at the county level to adjust assessments among the townships, cities, and other units of the county and, at the state level, to equalize assessments among counties. If property in one area is assessed at fifty percent of value and in another at thirty percent, some adjustment is necessary to equalize the burdens borne by taxpayers. Equalization differs from the local review of assessments in which individual rather than area assessments are reviewed. *See* PROPERTY TAX, page 245.

Significance   One of the characteristics of local government in the United States is the multiplicity of taxing units. This, combined with underassessment by popularly elected assessors, often results in unequal distribution of tax burdens. Equalization reduces inequities among units of government but does not eliminate them or resolve inequities in assessment of individual properties.

Estate Tax   A tax, usually with progressive rates, levied on the property of deceased persons. Estate taxes apply to the total estate, whereas inheritance taxes are levied on the portions of the estate received by the beneficiaries. The national government has regularly levied an estate tax since 1916, and all states except Nevada have an estate or inheritance tax, in most instances, the latter.

Significance   The federal estate and gift taxes together have averaged over $2 billion annually in recent years. The gift tax, having rates nearly as high as the estate tax, is used to plug the loophole by which money was given to relatives and friends before death in order to avoid estate taxes. A high percentage of state death taxes may be offset as a credit against payment of the federal estate tax, which has served as an encouragement for the states to enact such levies. State inheritance taxes are also progressive, with rates increasing sharply as the beneficiary's share rises, and increasing also as the relationship of the beneficiary to the deceased becomes more distant. Estate and inheritance taxes are aimed at preventing excessive concentrations of wealth in a few families.

Excess Profits Tax   A special tax levied during wartime to supplement the corporation income tax. The excess profits tax is calculated on the difference between business earnings in normal years and earnings during the war years when profits soar. An excess profits tax was levied by Congress during World Wars I and II, and during the Korean action from 1951 to 1953. In the last case, the tax was fixed at thirty percent of the excess profits, with the limitation that the combined corporation income tax and excess profits tax should not exceed seventy percent of net income.

Significance   The excess profits tax is designed primarily to recapture abnormal profits and to help finance military expenditures. It also is psychologically motivated to quiet public fears of wartime business profiteering. The opposition of businessmen to the tax, usually quiescent during the war period, has always forced an early repealing of the tax at the war's end.

Excise Tax   A tax levied upon the manufacture, transportation, sale, or consumption of goods within a country or a state. Federal excise taxes are permitted by the Constitution, and such levies have been placed on a variety of consumer goods. The main excise taxes used by the states are sales and use taxes.

Significance   Federal income from excise taxes is exceeded only by the individual and corporation income taxes. The excises on liquor and tobacco provide the greatest yields. State excise taxes, unlike the federal, are often criticized for their regressive character in taxing necessities, with the tax burden falling proportionately heavier on low-income families. Many federal excises were first levied during World War II as emergency income measures, but were continued until 1965 when Congress eliminated some and reduced others.

Federal Reserve Notes   Currency issued by Federal Reserve banks, backed by deposits with the government of discounted commercial paper (such as promissory notes or bills of exchange), government bonds, and gold certificates.

Significance   Federal Reserve notes are the most important kind of currency in circulation in the United States today. A small volume of silver certificates, treasury notes, federal bank notes, and national bank notes still circulate, but, except for the silver certificates, are being slowly retired. Since going off the gold standard in 1934, the United States has had a "managed" currency. Elasticity in the supply of Federal Reserve notes is provided by its commercial paper backing; when borrowing is heavy, more currency can be issued, and when demand for loans shrinks, the issue of currency can be reduced. Gold backing of Federal Reserve notes is fixed by statute at twenty-five percent, but the gold reserve has consistently remained at more than that amount.

Federal Reserve System   The private-public banking regulatory system in the United States, which establishes banking policies and influences the amount of credit available and the currency in circulation. The Federal Reserve System was created by Congress in 1913. It consists of twelve Federal Reserve banks, each located in one of the twelve Federal Reserve districts into which the country is divided, and a central Board of Governors of seven members appointed by the President and confirmed by the Senate. Each of the Federal Reserve banks is headed by a board of nine directors, six of whom are chosen by the member banks in the district and three by the Federal Reserve Board in Washington. Membership in district Federal Reserve banks is required of all national banks and permitted to state banks, and most of the latter have joined. The Federal Reserve banks are actually privately owned "bankers' banks," with all member banks required to hold stock in them. Buying and selling of commercial paper and government securities is carried on through an Open Market Committee. See BOARD OF GOVERNORS, page 251; OPEN MARKET OPERATIONS, page 244; REDISCOUNT, page 246; RESERVE RATIO, page 247; MONETARY POLICY, page 244.

Significance   The Federal Reserve System determines the nation's general monetary and credit policies through decisions made by the Board in Washington, D.C., and by the regional directors. The policies are carried out through the Reserve banks and by the thousands of member banks across the country. The System has played an increasingly significant role in meeting the nation's major economic problems of inflation and recession. In trying to control inflation, the System has tried to carry out "hard" money policies during economic boom periods when inflationary pressures are greatest. In fighting recessions, the System has carried out more liberal monetary and credit policies designed to stimulate investment and purchasing power.

Fiscal Policy   The use by government of its financial powers to influence the nation's economy. Decisions on fiscal policy are made largely by the President and Congress, and are concerned with revenue, expenditure, and debt. John Maynard Keynes, the British economist, was one of the first to develop the theoretical basis and sophisticated applications of fiscal policy in combating economic slumps. *See* MONETARY POLICY, page 244; EMPLOYMENT ACT, page 277.

Significance   Fiscal policy is usually aimed at using governmental financial programs to maintain economic stability by arresting and reversing violent downswings or upswings in the economy. The objective is to maintain a viable economy while steering a middle course between inflation and recession. Fiscal policies available to fight a serious downturn or recession include compensatory (deficit) spending, public works projects, and tax reductions. To combat inflation, reverse policies of reduced government spending, surplus budgets and debt retirement, and increased taxes are called for. Although the application of governmental fiscal policies to effect changes in the nation's economy is generally accepted as a proper function for government, some opposition exists. Most controversy, however, involves conflicts over the choice of specific policies, and arises, particularly, from groups adversely affected.

Fiscal Year   The twelve-month financial period used by a government for record keeping, budgeting, appropriating, revenue collecting, and other aspects of fiscal management. The fiscal year of the national government runs from July 1 to June 30, but some state and local governments use the calendar year from January 1 to December 31, while a few states use a two-year fiscal period.

Significance   It is important for the student of government to differentiate between those statistics that apply to the calendar year and those that apply to the fiscal year. The national government's fiscal year was selected to conform with the flow of governmental actions involved in budgeting and appropriating.

General Welfare Clause   The clause in Article I, section 8 of the Constitution that authorizes Congress to lay and collect taxes to provide for the common defense and general welfare of the United States. *See* SOCIAL SECURITY CASES, page 311.

Significance   The general welfare clause appears to give Congress an unlimited spending power, but it has been a source of constitutional controversy. The issue is whether Congress can spend tax monies only for purposes authorized in other sections of the Constitution, or whether the general welfare clause gives Congress an unlimited power to spend for whatever might contribute to the "common defense and general welfare." The former position has been held by the strict constructionists, the latter by the loose or liberal constructionists. The liberal constructionist view of the interpretation of the general welfare clause has prevailed, and the spending power as such has never been successfully challenged in the courts. The only limitation suggested by the Supreme Court (*United States v. Butler,* 297 U.S. 1 [1936]), was that taxes levied by Congress be spent for *national* welfare and not for the welfare of particular groups. The general welfare clause has enabled the national government to carry on programs in fields not specifically granted to it by the Constitution, as in the social security programs.

Gold Standard   A monetary system in which a nation's currency is backed by gold, has a standard of value measured in gold, and can be exchanged for gold. An international gold standard provides for free convertibility of currencies into gold and the unimpeded movement of gold bullion from one nation to another to pay international debts. The gold standard became universally accepted during the nineteenth and early twentieth centuries; the United States adopted it in 1900. In the world-wide depression of the 1930s, the nations of the world discarded it, with the United States going off the gold standard in 1934. *See* DEVALUATION, page 237.

Significance   The gold standard provided stability in domestic monetary systems, and an "international currency" and self-regulating payments system in international trade and finance, for many years. The severe depression of the 1930s, however, forced the major industrial countries, including the United States, to adopt flexible fiscal and employment policies based on "managed" paper currencies that were incompatible with the gold standard. In discarding the gold standard, Congress provided for calling in gold and gold coin in circulation and fixed the price at $35 for a fine ounce.

Gross National Product (GNP)   A measurement of the total annual output of goods and services of a country expressed in terms of its market value. In the United States, the Department of Commerce gathers such data on a quarterly basis and publishes it as an annual figure.

Significance   The Gross National Product has become a major analytical tool for measuring a nation's economic well-being and for comparing progress in different countries and economic systems. A more accurate picture of economic progress, however, requires analysis of GNP in terms of constant dollars to avoid inflation- or deflation-caused price changes, and measurement of GNP on a per capita basis to determine standards of living. Comparative economic growth rates are based on annual changes of GNP corrected for price changes. GNP in the United States has grown from about $300 billion in 1949 to a figure in excess of $700 billion in 1966.

Income Tax   A tax levied on income received from profits, salaries, rents, interest, dividends, and other sources, less deductions permitted by law. The national government's income tax includes a tax on both individual income and corporation income, with different rates applicable to each. More than thirty states also levy income taxes, most applicable to both individual and corporate income. Many cities, because of increasing resistance to higher property taxes, have adopted an income tax. *See* SIXTEENTH AMENDMENT, page 247; WITHHOLDING TAX, page 251.

Significance   The individual income tax is based on ability to pay and provides for progressive or graduated tax-rate increases as income increases. The federal tax rate currently starts at fourteen percent for the first $2000 in income and increases progressively to a high of seventy percent on taxable income over $200,000. The income tax also permits flexibility in providing greater or lesser yields simply by adjusting a few rates. Its major weakness results from its complicated nature and the successful efforts of various pressure groups to riddle it with exemptions and loopholes. Over forty million persons pay some income tax today, the majority through the payroll withholding system. The individual income tax is the major source of revenue for the national government, producing about twice the receipts of the next most important source, the corporate income tax. The two together provide over eighty percent of total national tax receipts. In the states, the income tax, including individual and corporate, is the third largest source of state revenue. Increased use of income taxes by the states or by local governments is hampered by the extensive pre-emption of the field by the national government and by public opposition to additional taxes on incomes.

Inflation   An economic condition in which the price level is increased and the value of money in terms of purchasing power is consequently decreased. Inflation may result from either an increase in the amount of money and credit available or a decrease in the supply of consumer goods. *See* DEFLATION, page 237; MONETARY POLICY, page 244.

Significance   The traditional definition of inflation—too many dollars chasing too few goods—has been supplemented by the "cost-push" explanation of the phenomenon. This view holds that when typical conditions for inflation do not exist, but inflation does, it is then a product of rising costs of production, or of imperfect competition reflected in "administered prices" whereby business-men reduce production and set artificially high prices. Mass psychological factors may be a significant ingredient of inflation. Most economists believe that serious inflation—an increase in the price level of three percent or more per year—can be prevented through proper use of monetary policy by the Federal Reserve Board and the Treasury, and by fiscal policy, such as providing for surplus budgets and increased taxes. Although the effects of inflation are largely internal, a nation suffering from a serious inflation may jeopardize its foreign markets and suffer consequently from a disequilibrium in its balance of international payments. Within a country, persons living on a fixed income typically suffer most from inflation.

Legal Tender   Any medium of exchange that by law must be accepted in payment of a debt. The Constitution gives the national government full control over the nation's money, and it forbids the states to "make anything but gold and silver coin a tender in payment of debts. . . ." (Art. I, sec. 10). *See* LEGAL TENDER CASES, page 253.

Significance   A major legal controversy developed over the first century of American history as to whether the national government could issue fiat notes not backed by the precious metals as legal tender. A series of cases was climaxed in 1884 by *Juilliard v. Greenman,* 110 U S. 421, in which the Su-preme Court declared that Congress has full power to issue notes as legal tender in the payment of debts. The states for many years authorized state chartered banks to issue notes for circulation as currency, but not as legal tender. Although these issuances did not violate the Constitution, Congress regarded them as a danger to monetary uniformity and stability. In 1865, Congress levied a ten percent tax upon state notes that was sustained by the Supreme Court (*Veazie Bank v. Fenno,* 8 Wallace 533 [1869]), and that drove all state notes out of circulation.

Monetary Policy   A policy that aims at affecting the amount of currency in circulation and the availability of credit. The Federal Reserve Board uses "tight money" monetary policies to restrain and prolong boom periods in the nation's economy and to fight inflation. "Loose money" policies are used to check deflation and to fight recessions by making money and credit more freely available. *See* FISCAL POLICY, page 241; FEDERAL RESERVE SYSTEM, page 240.

Significance   In the post-World War II period, Federal Reserve monetary policies have been employed in fighting recessions and restraining economic booms. The use of such policies must be delicately and expertly handled lest a serious deflationary or inflationary spiral be touched off. In pursuing a tight or hard money policy, the Federal Reserve Board decreases the availability of money and credit by raising member banks' reserve requirements, by raising the rediscount rate, and by selling government securities through its Open Market Committee. The Federal Reserve Board pursues policies exactly the opposite of these when loose or soft money policies are called for. Monetary policy is particularly effective when harmonized with fiscal policies initiated by the President and Congress and aimed at the same objectives.

Open Market Operations   Buying and selling government securities, bills of exchange, and other commercial paper by the Federal Open Market Committee. The Committee is composed of the Board of Governors of the Federal Reserve System and five directors of the Federal Reserve banks chosen annually by the boards of directors.

Significance   The Federal Open Market Committee operations facilitate commerce and business and stabilize credit in the United States. Its functions are particularly useful in implementing the monetary policies determined by the Federal Reserve Board. For example, when inflation threatens, the Committee sells government securities and commercial paper in the open market to restrict the availability of credit; when deflation or recession threatens, the Committee buys so as to make credit more easily available through member banks. The Committee's open-market operations are supplemented by other instruments of monetary policy, such as the fixing of the rediscount rate and the reserve requirements for member banks.

Performance Budget   The drawing up of a plan for anticipated expenditures based on the activities, services, and functions performed by government, rather than allotting funds on the basis of items to be purchased and salaries to be paid by each department and agency. *See* BUDGET, page 235.

Significance   Based on the recommendations of the Hoover Commission, Congress adopted the principle of the performance budget in the Budget and

Accounting Procedures Act of 1950. Since 1951, the Bureau of the Budget has drawn up much of the general budget for the national government on a performance basis. The major advantage of the performance budget is that by detailing how and for what government funds are expended it gives a clearer picture than did the itemization system.

Personal Property Tax   A tax levied on things of value other than real property. Personal property is usually classified as tangible or intangible, the former including valuables of substance, such as business inventories, machinery, jewelry, and household goods, and the latter a right, claim, or interest of value, such as found in bonds, stocks, and bank accounts. *See* ASSESSED VALUATION, page 232.

Significance   Property is usually classified for tax purposes, the tax on personal property being applied at a rate ordinarily lower than that on real property. Personal property tax collection involves considerable administrative work, particularly that of getting the owners to declare their property for tax purposes or, if they do not, of finding it. This becomes an almost hopeless task when levying the tax on intangible properties which can easily be concealed from the assessors' eyes. Often, the value of such intangibles as stocks and bonds exceeds the value of real estate and tangibles, yet the taxes levied upon them depend almost entirely on the personal honesty of the individual taxpayer. Most personal property taxes are levied by local governments and are paid mainly by business and industry.

Progressive Tax   Any tax in which the tax *rates* increase as the amount to be taxed increases. It is the opposite of a regressive tax, in which tax rates remain uniform or decline as the tax base increases. *See* REGRESSIVE TAX, page 247.

Significance   Progressive taxes levied by the national and state governments include the individual and corporate income taxes and the estate and gift taxes. Progressive taxes are based on the principle of ability to pay, as reflected, for example, in the federal individual income tax, in which percentage rates range from fourteen percent on $2000 to seventy percent on income over $200,000. Supporters of progressive taxation regard it as an equitable means of securing necessary government income. Opponents criticize it mainly on the ground that it penalizes initiative and success.

Property Tax   An ad valorem (according to value) tax levied on real or personal, tangible or intangible property. The general property tax is levied by local units of government throughout the country, and most states make limited use of some form of the tax. The tax process includes assessment of property valuations, determination of tax rates (millage), tax computation, and tax collection. To correct injustices, boards of review on the local level adjust inequalities in assessments. Where the taxing jurisdiction crosses political boundaries, central assessment or equalization is provided to avoid geographical inequities. *See* ASSESSED VALUATION, page 232; ASSESSOR, page 233; BOARD OF REVIEW, page 234; EQUALIZATION, page 238.

Significance   The general property tax provides the fiscal foundation for local units of government across the nation. In recent years, it has provided about eighty-five percent of the tax revenue for cities, counties, school districts, towns, townships, villages, and other local units. For many years, the general property tax was the nations major source of revenue, exceeding all state and national levies until the twentieth century's many crises boosted income and sales taxes. The general property tax has come increasingly under attack in recent years because of difficulties and conflicts involved in assessment, equalization, and exemptions. The flexibility of the tax as a source of revenue has nearly reached exhaustion in many localities because of constitutional or statutory limitations, popular rejections of tax increase referendums, and heavy tax loads resulting from failure to find other tax sources.

Public Debt   The total indebtedness, including accrued interest, of a government or of a country, the latter embracing the indebtedness of all its units of government. The public debt of the United States government is usually referred to as the national debt. Whenever expenditures exceed revenue during a fiscal year, the deficit is added to the public debt; when revenue exceeds expenditures, the public debt is reduced by the amount of the surplus. *See* DEBT LIMIT, page 236; DEFICIT FINANCING, page 237.

Significance   Over a period of four decades of frequently unbalanced budgets, the United States has built up a national public debt of huge proportions. The national debt rose from about $16 billion in 1931 to almost $49 billion in 1941, as a result of deficit financing to stimulate the stagnated economy; by 1946, it had risen to $269 billion through the financing of World War II; from that point, it rose to a level of more than $320 billion in 1967 as a result of financing defense programs and combating four postwar recessions. Much controversy has arisen concerning the rapid rise of the national debt in recent years. Some economists view the debt as a useful governmental weapon for stabilizing the economy, adding to it by "pump priming" (deficit spending) during economic downturns, and retiring portions of it through surpluses during periods of prosperity to reduce the threat of inflation. Some students of finance are relatively unconcerned about the size of the debt, pointing out that "we owe it to ourselves," that much of the debt constitutes an investment for the future of the American people, and that the debt has actually grown smaller in recent years if measured on a per capita basis or in relation to national income. The concerned, on the other hand, regard the "owe it to ourselves" argument as specious, and contend that future generations of Americans will suffer from excessive spending, and that the size of the debt threatens not only economic solvency but national security as well. In recent years, state and local debt has increased at a more rapid rate than the national debt.

Rediscount   Credit granted by a Federal Reserve bank to a member bank on negotiable instruments that had already been discounted (a loan with interest subtracted in advance) when the member bank made loans to its customers. *See* FEDERAL RESERVE SYSTEM, page 240.

Significance   The Federal Reserve System uses the rediscount rate as a tool of monetary policy. By lowering the rediscount rate, the Federal Reserve Board can encourage member banks to liquidate their holdings of commercial paper by having the Federal Reserve banks buy them at a discount of their face value. This frees funds of the member banks and enables them to make additional loans to the public, thus stimulating purchasing power and, thereby, the nation's economy. By raising the rediscount rate, the Federal Reserve banks can obtain the opposite result of contracting the availability of credit in the country. Typically, therefore, the rediscount rate is lowered during a recession to stimulate an upturn in the economy (loose money policy), and raised during a boom period when serious inflation threatens (tight money policy).

Regressive Tax   Any tax in which the burden falls relatively more heavily upon the low-income groups than upon the more wealthy taxpayers. It is the opposite of a progressive tax, in which tax rates increase as ability to pay increases. *See* PROGRESSIVE TAX, page 245.

Significance   Regressive taxes are used mainly by the state and local governments and include, for example, the sales tax and the uniform or declining rate income tax. Such taxes take a higher percentage of the total income of low-income groups than of the total income of the high-income groups, even though the rates are uniform. Sales taxes on the necessities of life are probably the most regressive in nature, since a major portion of the expenditures of low-income families are for such commodities.

Regulatory Tax   A tax levied for purposes other than the raising of revenue. A protective tariff is a clear example. More subtle uses of taxing power for nonrevenue regulatory purposes include restricting the marketing of a product (the heavy tax on oleomargarine many years ago to maintain the butter market) or adding to the government's arsenal against illegal or undesirable activities (a tax on gamblers). *See Veazie Bank v. Fenno,* page 254.

Significance   All taxes have a regulatory function even when levied primarily for revenue. The income tax, for example, controls the distribution of wealth and is used to promote specific fiscal policies. With rare exceptions, the courts will not question the motives of the legislature in levying a tax. A regulatory tax may be used to reinforce an existing power of government or to reach a problem for which no direct legislative authority exists. For example, a heavy tax on a commodity may effectively keep it off the market though no power exists to do so directly.

Reserve Ratio   The percentage of liquid assets held by a bank as a reserve for its deposits. The *legal* reserve ratio is that percentage set by government to ensure that banks will maintain a safe proportion of ready cash to meet depositors' demands for their money. Under the Federal Reserve System, the legal reserve requirement is set for the member banks within each district by the Federal Reserve Board of Governors. Reserve requirements for state banks are usually set by law in each state. *See* FEDERAL RESERVE SYSTEM, page 240.

Significance   Legal reserve requirements are set by government to protect the accounts of individual depositors. Through the Federal Reserve System, the government additionally obtains a powerful means of carrying out monetary policy and maintaining stability with flexibility in the monetary system. When deflation or economic recessions threaten, the Federal Reserve Board can free money and credit to stimulate business by lowering the reserve requirements of member banks. When inflation threatens, or it is desirable to restrain an economic boom, the Board reduces the availability of money and credit to business and consumers by raising reserve requirements. Along with its open market operations and its rediscount function, the setting of reserve ratio requirements is a major monetary tool that helps the Board set the general direction and tone of the American economy.

Revolving Fund   An operational fund established for a governmental agency carrying on proprietary (business-type) functions that make the agency financially self-supporting, or nearly so. Income from the agency's operations is not turned in to the Treasury Department but is spent directly by the agency. For example, the Tennessee Valley Authority (TVA) uses its revenue from electric power sales to finance its continuing operations and its expansion programs.

Significance   A revolving fund gives a public business enterprise the financial flexibility to carry out long-range programs. Agencies ordinarily cannot plan operations beyond those approved by Congress in its annual appropriations, and a revolving fund frees the agency from this kind of dependence. The revolving fund principle has been followed especially in federal lending agencies.

Sales Tax   A tax levied upon the sale of commodities, usually paid by the purchaser. The sales tax may apply generally to all commodities or it may be restricted to certain classifications or specific commodities. Typically, the sales tax is levied on retail sales, but in some cases it is imposed on sales by manufacturers and wholesalers as well. Closely related to the sales tax is the "use" tax, which applies to purchases made outside the taxing jurisdiction and is designed to prevent state residents from avoiding the sales tax through out-of-state purchases. Thirty-eight states levy sales taxes of from two to five percent.

Significance   Most of the states that levy a sales tax adopted it during the depression of the 1930s when they were under heavy obligation to meet rising welfare and general governmental costs. The sales tax has become the single most important source of state revenue. Most opposition to the sales tax centers around its regressive character, which places a heavy tax burden upon the low-income groups. Some states have sought to reduce its regressive impact by exempting food, clothing, or other necessities. Support for the sales tax is based on the idea that all citizens should contribute to the support of government and that the sales tax makes this possible because all persons are consumers.

Severance Tax   A tax levied upon natural resources at the time they are taken from the land or water.

Significance   Severance taxes are used by many states for both revenue and conservation purposes. Conservation objectives can be achieved by adjusting tax rates to control the "severing" of timber, minerals, and other resources from the soil. Some states accomplish the same purpose without a severance tax per se, by, for example, exempting timberland from the general property tax until the timber has been harvested.

Sixteenth Amendment   An amendment to the Constitution, adopted in 1913, that grants Congress the power to levy taxes on incomes without apportioning them among the states according to population. The individual and corporation income taxes of the national government are based on the power granted by this Amendment. *See* INCOME TAX, page 242; *Pollock v. Farmers Loan and Trust Co.,* page 253.

Significance   The Sixteenth Amendment resulted from a Supreme Court decision that a federal income tax is a direct tax and, under Article I, section 9, must be apportioned among the states according to population (*Pollock v. Farmers Loan and Trust Co.,* 158 U.S. 601 [1895]). Although a Civil War income tax levy had been upheld by the Supreme Court as an indirect tax, the 1895 decision reversed this view. The controversy, however, continued. The Sixteenth Amendment put aside the question of whether income taxes are direct or indirect by giving Congress blanket power to lay and collect taxes on incomes "from whatever source derived," and without any apportionment or regard to any census. Without this Amendment, income taxes apportioned among the states according to population would have been manifestly unfair and inequitable because of the vast differences in income among the states, and Congress refused to levy such a tax. Since 1913, the individual and corporation income taxes have become the major sources for federal revenue.

Special Assessment   A charge made by a government against a property owner for that part of the cost of public improvements made adjacent to his property that are especially useful or beneficial to his property. Special assessments are different from taxes in that the improvements have been petitioned for by the landowners concerned.

Significance   Special assessments are used mainly by local units of government in providing facilities for homeowners, such as paved streets, sewers, and sidewalks. A portion of the cost of such public improvements is, typically, borne by the local government out of taxes. This is a recognition that the improvements are generally beneficial to the community as well as to the individual landowner. Such projects are financed through special assessment bonds, which are backed by the government's power to assess for public improvements.

Tax Exemption   The privilege granted by a government legally freeing certain types of property, sales, or income from general taxpaying obligations.

Significance   Most of the states have established constitutional or statutory exemption of educational and religious properties from the general property tax. Income from certain national, state, or local bonds may be exempted from taxation, and cooperatives from income tax levies. Most state sales taxes exempt certain classes of commodities. Tax exemptions may be used to encourage activities as well as to recognize that exceptions within general taxpaying categories must be acknowledged in the interest of fairness. Often, tax exemptions may merely illustrate the political power of special interest groups.

Tax Incidence   The point at which the actual burden of paying a tax falls, regardless of whom the tax is formally levied upon. Those taxes in which the

burden cannot be shifted to someone else by the taxpayer are sometimes classified as *direct* taxes; those in which the burden can be passed on are *indirect*
taxes.

Significance   The incidence of almost all taxes that are levied at some
point in the production and consumption of goods is, typically, shifted to consumers through higher prices for commodities. The price of a loaf of bread, for
example, may include scores of national, state, and local taxes that, having
been paid by different farmers, processors, distributors, and retailers, are passed
on to the ultimate consumer. Direct taxes for which the burden cannot ordinarily be shifted include income levies, poll taxes, and taxes on land, although
when the land is rented the owner can shift the burden of his tax to the renter.
The incidence of taxation brings into serious question the fairness of taxes that
are eventually paid by others than those who make the formal tax payments.

Tax Offset   A device used by the national government to induce states to
adopt certain types of taxes or programs by permitting individuals to deduct
such state taxes from the amount of federal tax that they would otherwise pay.

Significance   The tax offset has been used effectively by the national
government to prod the states into adopting such tax programs as unemployment compensation and state inheritance taxes. To induce the states to adopt
unemployment compensation programs, for example, the national government
levies a payroll tax on employers, but permits them to offset ninety percent of
that tax if they contribute to a state unemployment compensation fund. The
effect of this tax offset was to secure a nation-wide, but state administered,
program of unemployment compensation. Some economists regard the tax offset as the best means of inducing all of the states to adopt uniform tax programs
to meet growing revenue needs, with none losing ground in the fierce competition among states to attract and hold industry by means of low taxes.

Tax Sharing   The levying and collecting of a tax by one unit of government, which turns over a certain portion of the tax yield to another unit of
government, according to a formula established by law. *See* STATE AID, page
374.

Significance   Most shared taxes involve state and local governments.
Many state governments, for example, levy and collect sales or income taxes
with a constitutional or statutory requirement that a certain percentage of these
collections be turned over to local government. Common examples of taxes collected by the states and shared with their local governments are motor fuel,
license, income, liquor and cigarette, and sales taxes.

Valuation   The determination of assessments, taxes, charges, rates, or profits
based on an appraisal of the value of the property or service. *See* ASSESSED
VALUATION, page 232.

Significance   In governmental regulatory and taxation functions, the
equitability of the rates or taxes often depends upon the skill and honesty with
which government officials estimate the value of property or services. For
example, the property tax paid by an individual is determined by the assessed
valuation placed on his property by an assessor, as well as by the tax rate

determined by his elected representatives. Rates charged consumers of utility services likewise depend considerably on the valuation placed upon the assets of the public utility in determining a fair profit for its operations. Because valuation cannot be made into a precise scientific or mathematical function, it leads to innumerable controversies over estimated valuations.

Withholding Tax   Provisions of an income or payroll tax system by which the employer deducts a specified percentage from an employee's wage or salary and remits it to the government's tax bureau. Amounts withheld by employers constitute a credit against the employees' total tax liability.

Significance   Under the Current Tax Payment Act of 1943, the national government provides for the payment of federal income taxes through employer-withholding of wages and salaries and the payment of an estimated tax in quarterly installments on income derived from other sources. The individual taxpayer must still file a return by April 15 of each year, at which time he must pay any amount owed over his total withholdings or file a refund claim if his tax is less than his withholdings. The withholding system was adopted by Congress during World War II to help finance the military effort. The main advantages of the system are that it makes tax collections more certain and facilitates payment of taxes through relatively "painless" deductions from paychecks. It also provides the Department of the Treasury with sizable funds coming in regularly during the year. Most opposition has come from employers, who dislike the extensive bookkeeping involved, and from other groups who oppose the singling out of wage and salary incomes for withholding. In recent years, Congress has considered extending the withholding principle to other categories of income, such as interest and dividends.

IMPORTANT AGENCIES

Board of Governors, Federal Reserve System   A board, composed of seven members, that determines general monetary and credit policies and oversees the operations of the twelve district Federal Reserve banks and member banks throughout the country. Board members are appointed for fourteen-year terms by the President with the Senate's confirmation, with consideration given to geographical and major business interests in the selection process. *See* FEDERAL RESERVE SYSTEM, page 240.

Significance   The Board of Governors determines monetary policies through its control over the issuance of Federal Reserve notes by Federal Reserve banks, its fixing of the rediscount rate and, through its Open Market Committee, the purchase and sale of government and other securities. All of these activities have a profound effect on the amount of money in circulation and the credit available through Federal Reserve member banks, which in turn influences general economic conditions in the country. The Board also sets the margin requirements for purchases of securities, and conducts periodic examinations of Federal Reserve and member banks. Some students of government and finance would like to have its activities brought under the direct supervision of the President because of the close, important relationship of its activities to fiscal policies and the stability of the economy. Others consider it essential that the Board retain its independence from presidential control in order that its decisions be free from politics.

Bureau of the Budget   An agency in the Executive Office of the President, headed by a director who has primary responsibility under the President's direction for budget preparation and administration. The Bureau is divided into five major offices: budget review, legislative reference, management and organization, statistical standards, and financial management. *See* BUDGET AND ACCOUNTING ACT, page 254.

Significance   The Director of the Bureau of the Budget is empowered, under the Budget and Accounting Act of 1921, to "assemble, correlate, revise, reduce, or increase" the estimates from executive agencies. Broad fiscal powers flow from this grant, both in the planning and estimate stage and, following congressional approval of the budget, in the budget execution stage, when agency heads must obtain Bureau approval in financing their programs. In addition to its budgeting function, the Bureau carries on duties directed toward improving organization and management within the executive branch and acts as a clearinghouse for legislative proposals originating in the executive agencies. Since 1939, when the Bureau of the Budget was transferred from the Department of the Treasury to the Executive Office, it has become the President's major staff agency in fiscal and related matters.

Department of the Treasury   A major department of the national government, responsible for fiscal management and headed by a Secretary with Cabinet status. The Department of the Treasury was one of the original departments established in 1789.

Significance   Major responsibilities of the Department are to: (1) collect internal revenue taxes and customs duties; (2) administer the public debt; (3) keep central accounts for the entire national government; (4) coin and print money and protect against counterfeiting; (5) register and license ships engaged in foreign and interstate commerce; and (6) administer the narcotic control laws. Important administrative units include the Internal Revenue Service, Bureau of Customs, Bureau of Accounts, Secret Service, Bureau of Public Debt, and Fiscal Service. The Secretary of the Treasury is usually regarded as second only to the Secretary of State as a Cabinet adviser to the President. The Department plays a broad and significant role in formulating both monetary and fiscal policies for the national administration.

General Accounting Office (GAO)   An independent agency that controls and audits national government expenditures as an agent of Congress. The GAO is headed by the Comptroller General who is appointed by the President with the Senate's approval for a fifteen-year term and can be removed only through impeachment or a joint resolution of Congress. *See* COMPTROLLER GENERAL, page 235.

Significance   The major functions carried on by the GAO include: (1) prescribing accounting systems for federal agencies; (2) authorizing federal agencies to make specific expenditures (preaudit); and (3) making extensive investigations to determine the validity of the receipt and disbursement of public funds (postaudit). In short, Congress by law determines in general how public money shall be spent, and the GAO acts as an agent of Congress, checking on specific expenditures to ensure that each falls within the intent of Congress. Students of finance object to the system whereby the GAO makes both the pre-audit authorization and the postaudit check, holding that the President cannot reasonably be held responsible for executive-spending activities if the GAO can determine the validity and reasonableness of expenditures before they are paid.

Internal Revenue Service   A unit in the Department of the Treasury that has major responsibility for the collection of all taxes except customs duties. The Internal Revenue Service is headed by a Commissioner and operates through district offices, each headed by a director.

Significance   The Internal Revenue Service collects over $100 billion each year, mostly in individual and corporation income taxes. Collection costs average less than $.50 for each $100 of tax collected. Because of its discretionary powers in making decisions in specific tax cases, it has become an important agency in the lives of millions of Americans.

Tax Court of the United States   A special agency that hears controversies between taxpayers and the Commissioner of Internal Revenue, and has jurisdiction over excess profits proceedings. It is, in fact, not a court but a quasi-judicial administrative agency. The Court consists of sixteen "judges" appointed by the President with the Senate's consent, for twelve-year terms. Each judge heads a division and court is held in various places throughout the country.

Significance   The Tax Court provides a relatively easy and inexpensive means for taxpayers to appeal decisions made by tax officials. It relieves the regular courts of the tremendous burden of suits resulting from the far-reaching effect of federal tax programs. All decisions of the Tax Court, except those involving excess profits, may be appealed to a court of appeals and, by writ of certiorari, to the Supreme Court.

IMPORTANT CASES

Legal Tender Cases (Knox v. Lee; Parker v. Davis), 12 Wallace 457 (1871): Recognized the power of Congress to make Treasury notes (paper money) legal tender in place of gold or silver in payment of debt.

Significance   The case grew out of a wartime debt but, a few years later, the Court also upheld the issuance of paper money as legal tender in time of peace in *Juilliard v. Greenman,* 110 U.S. 421 (1884). In the *Legal Tender Cases* the Court recognized a new category of "resulting powers"—those powers that are not expressly granted nor implied from a single enumerated power but that arise from the aggregate powers of government.

Pollock v. Farmers Loan and Trust Co., 158 U.S. 601 (1895): Held the federal income tax law of 1894 unconstitutional on the ground that it was a direct tax and, therefore, Congress should have apportioned it among the several states according to population as provided in Article I, section 9 of the Constitution.

Significance   The *Pollock* decision was a reversal of earlier decisions by the Court in which the validity of income taxes not apportioned according to the population had been upheld. The inequity of levying income taxes on a population basis restrained Congress from enacting a new income tax law until 1913, when the Sixteenth Amendment was adopted. The Amendment side-stepped the dispute of whether an income tax law is a direct or indirect tax by ruling out the necessity of apportionment.

South Carolina v. United States, 199 U.S. 437 (1905): Upheld a federal tax levied upon wholesale and retail liquor sales by the state of South Carolina on the ground that exemption of states from federal taxes applies only when a state carries on strictly governmental functions, not when it engages in business of a private nature. The state had argued that because all profits from liquor sales went into the state treasury, it was exercising the sovereign power of the state and should be immune from federal taxes. *See* INTERGOVERNMENTAL TAX IMMUNITY, page 34.

Significance   The *South Carolina* case laid down the fundamental rule that state immunity from federal taxation does not apply when a state enters a commercial or proprietary field. The case has served to modify substantially the intergovernmental tax immunity rule laid down in *McCulloch v. Maryland,* 4 Wheaton 316 (1819). Generally, the courts will not intervene when Congress decides to tax a state or local proprietary function.

Veazie Bank v. Fenno, 8 Wallace 533 (1869): Upheld the validity of a ten percent tax levied by Congress in 1866 upon notes issued by state banks for the purpose of driving them out of circulation.

Significance   The *Veazie Bank* decision gave judicial acceptance to the use of a federal tax primarily for a nonrevenue regulatory purpose and it sanctioned the action of Congress in providing a uniform currency for the United States. The objective of the tax sustained in this case has been realized, and state bank notes have been out of circulation for many years.

IMPORTANT STATUTES

Budget and Accounting Act of 1921   A law that established a national budget system and created the Bureau of the Budget and the General Accounting Office. It provides for the formulation of an annual executive budget by the Bureau under direction of the President, and for the auditing of all government expenditures by the General Accounting Office under the direction of the Comptroller General as an agent of Congress.

Significance   Prior to the enactment of the Budget and Accounting Act of 1921, the budget system was a loose and haphazard process in which various executive agencies submitted requests to as many as twenty-four different House and Senate committees. No attempt was made to look at the financial picture from an over-all viewpoint, and the President had little or no voice in the entire process. Under the Act, a budget is prepared by fiscal experts under the direction of the President and is submitted as a single-package budget to Congress, where it is assigned to revenue and appropriations committees for study. Congress can now consider the budget as a total picture for the fiscal period of proposed expenditures and anticipated income. Execution of the budget by the spending agencies is done under the watchful eyes of the General Accounting Office, which carries on both preaudit and postaudit functions. The Budget and Accounting Act of 1921 is probably the most significant piece of fiscal control legislation to come out of Congress, and has served to bring considerable order out of former budgetary chaos.

Twelve

Government and Business

Antitrust Laws   Laws intended to regulate or prohibit combinations in restraint of trade, including monopolies, cartels, trusts, and interlocking directorates. *See* MONOPOLY, page 263; TRUST, page 268; ANTITRUST DIVISION, page 269; SHERMAN ANTITRUST ACT, page 278.

Significance   The objective of antitrust action by the government is to maintain and strengthen the free enterprise system by ensuring competition in business. Responsibility for the enforcement of antitrust laws is vested in the Antitrust Division of the Department of Justice and in the Federal Trade Commission. Since the enactment of the Sherman Act in 1890, the national government's antitrust policy has been vigorously enforced at times, while at other times it has been sporadically enforced or ignored. Enforcement has been greatly influenced by Supreme Court decisions limiting or expanding the scope of enforcement authority, by the antitrust philosophy of particular presidents and the "trust busters" of the Antitrust Division, and by the views and pressures of public opinion calling for action or accepting inaction. Much also has depended upon the circumstances of the times, antitrust action having been reduced during periods of war, defense programs, or strenuous foreign competition.

Bankruptcy   A procedure for discharging unpaid obligations through a court action that frees the individual from further liability for his debts. Bankruptcy proceedings may be initiated either by the insolvent debtor (voluntary bankruptcy) or by a required number of his creditors (involuntary bankruptcy). Such cases are usually handled by federal district courts under equity jurisdiction. The court appoints an officer who sells the bankrupt's assets and pays his creditors on a prorated basis.

Significance   Bankruptcy proceedings enable persons, both human and corporate, to wipe clean a slate of hopeless debt and start anew. Some provisions of this kind are indispensable to protect the credit structure of modern business enterprise. Major federal bankruptcy acts have been passed by Congress in 1898 and 1933, and, although state legislation in this field is possible, the federal law is comprehensive and takes precedence over state enactments.

Some critics of bankruptcy proceedings charge that it encourages financial irresponsibility and recommend more restrictive measures concerning voluntary bankruptcy.

Blue Laws　　Laws on the books of many states that prohibit certain business operations on Sunday. They often make exceptions for amusements or essential activities and for persons who observe a sabbath day other than Sunday.

　　Significance　　Blue laws are religious in origin and have been challenged as violations of religious liberty. Today, they are supported largely as welfare measures to encourage rest and relaxation. In 1961, the Supreme Court upheld a number of such laws on these grounds. Blue laws have not been rigorously enforced and permit many exceptions that render them ineffective in practice.

Blue Sky Laws　　State laws to protect investors in securities from misrepresentation and outright fraud. Blue sky laws commonly require that companies selling securities be certified by a state agency and furnish detailed information concerning their financial position.

　　Significance　　The term "blue sky" refers to the gullible investor who discovers that the securities he has purchased represent nothing of value but the blue sky above. Blue sky laws have been enacted in almost all states since the early part of the twentieth century. Although most states continue to offer some protection to buyers of securities, most of their functions have been taken over by the Securities and Exchange Commission, created by Congress in 1934.

Bond　　A certificate of indebtedness issued by a borrower to a lender as a legal promise to repay the principal of the loan plus accrued interest. Bonds are issued by private corporations, by all levels of government, and by many governmental agencies and corporations. Most bonds have limited negotiability in the security markets. *See* BOND, page 234.

　　Significance　　In recent years, bonds have greatly exceeded new stock issues in their importance in financing business expansion in the United States. Like stocks, the issuance of private corporation bonds is regulated by the Federal Securities and Exchange Commission and by regulatory agencies in most of the states. Unlike stockholders, bondholders are not part owners of the corporation but have merely lent their money to it for investment purposes.

Business Affected with a Public Interest　　Any privately owned and operated selling or service activity that, as a matter of public policy, has been brought under the regulatory power of government. Businesses affected with a public interest, such as public utilities, are regulated by government boards and commissions in regard to their services and rates. *See* PUBLIC UTILITY, page 266; *Munn v. Illinois,* page 276.

　　Significance　　Many regulatory bodies have been created by national, state, and local governments when policy makers have determined that the free competition of the marketplace has become an insufficient means of protecting the right of the public to obtain satisfactory products or services at reasonable rates. Through such regulation, Americans have decided that such businesses as public carriers and gas and electric companies may operate under conditions of monopoly or near monopoly without danger to the public interest. The doctrine of "business affected with a public interest" was developed by the Supreme Court in *Munn v. Illinois,* 94 U.S. 113 (1876).

Business Cycles   The rhythmic fluctuation of a free economy as changes occur in business activity. Business cycles, typically, involve movements from prosperity to recession or depression, followed by economic recovery and the completion of the cycle by a return to the previous high point of economic activity. A new cycle then begins. *See* DEPRESSION, page 261; FISCAL POLICY, page 241; MONETARY POLICY, page 244.

Significance   Business cycles were considered to be natural economic phenomena by classical economists, and their recurrence was regarded as inevitable. Since the 1930s, however, it is no longer considered to be politically feasible to allow the cycles to run their course, because of the heavy costs in unemployment and economic stagnation at low points in the cycles, and the ever-present dangers of inflation at the high points. Today, the national government increasingly employs fiscal and monetary policies to control the extremes of business cycle activity and inactivity and to promote general and continuing stability for the economy.

Business and Professional Organizations   Groups organized to promote the interests of business and the professions. The leading nation-wide organizations of businessmen are the Chamber of Commerce of the United States and the National Association of Manufacturers (NAM). The Chamber is a federation of more than 3000 local chambers of commerce representing almost three million businessmen. The NAM represents about 20,000 large industrial firms. In addition, businessmen are organized according to their trade or industry interests in numerous national and local trade associations. Leading professional associations include the American Medical Association (AMA), the American Bar Association (ABA), and the National Education Association (NEA). *See* PRESSURE GROUP, page 114.

Significance   Most business and professional organizations reflect conservative attitudes toward taxes, government spending, and welfare programs. The Chamber of Commerce and the NAM spend much effort on public education programs in support of the free enterprise system. The AMA's long battle against Medicare is an outstanding example of pressure group involvement in a major political controversy. While businessmen have traditionally remained aloof from open political involvement, contemporary labor efforts and success on the political scene have encouraged business interests to become directly active in politics.

Caveat Venditor   A term meaning literally, "let the seller beware." *Caveat venditor* involves the acceptance by government of a responsibility to regulate business operations for the protection of consumers. *See* UNFAIR TRADE PRACTICE, page 269.

Significance   The freewheeling business practices of the nineteenth century period of laissez faire and *caveat emptor* ("let the buyer beware") have given way, in the twentieth century, to numerous national, state, and local laws and enforcement agencies that operate in the interest of consumer protection. Businesses that sell impure foods or drugs, engage in false advertising, give short measure to buyers, sell dangerous items, or misrepresent their products, may be subject to civil or criminal action. National agencies that are particularly concerned with safeguarding consumer interests include the Food and Drug Administration of the Department of Health, Education, and Welfare, and the Federal Trade Commission. Regulation is intended to force business to present certain facts about their products for the information of the public, but sound investments and purchases still require careful buying methods by individual consumers.

Certificate of Public Convenience, Interest, and Necessity   Permission granted by a regulatory agency to an individual or group to conduct a particular type of business. The standard of "public convenience, interest, and necessity" has been established by Congress and state legislatures to guide regulatory agencies in issuing licenses and permits to public utilities and communication media. *See* FRANCHISE, page 261.

Significance   The public interest is rarely served by the presence of several telephone companies in one community, or by competing railroads or buses. Limited channels for television and radio make regulation essential lest the airways be jammed. Thus, the determination of which company will be given the right to a television channel or to engage in a public utility enterprise is a major problem facing regulatory agencies. A company granted such a privilege generally receives an asset of considerable financial value and influence, and is subject to continuing regulation of the quality of its service and the rates it may charge. Many agencies, state and national, have been charged with favoritism in the granting of certificates, necessitating constant oversight by the legislature and the public.

Commerce   The buying and selling of commodities, transportation and commercial intercourse, and the transmission of radio, television, and telephonic and telegraphic messages. The Constitution grants Congress the power to regulate interstate and foreign commerce, and commerce with the Indian tribes. The states retain the power to regulate intrastate commerce. *See* COMMERCE POWER, page 29; *Cooley v. Board of Wardens,* page 276; *Gibbons v. Ogden,* page 276.

Significance   The power of Congress to regulate interstate and foreign commerce has, throughout American history, proved to be one of the most significant powers of the national government. Through successively broader interpretations by Congress and the Supreme Court, the term "commerce" has come to include almost all forms of business activity, including manufacturing since 1937. Although many legal battles have been fought concerning the extent of the commerce power, the issue since 1937 has become largely a political question rather than a legal one, to be settled by Congress and the people and not, ordinarily, by the Supreme Court. Commerce that is intrastate may come under the regulatory power of Congress if it directly or indirectly affects interstate commerce. States may also regulate interstate commerce if such regulation does not impede the free flow of that commerce and has a reasonable relation to the protection of the public safety, health, morals, or welfare, and if the activity regulated does not require uniform national treatment.

Common Carrier   Any company that offers its services to the public for the transportation of goods or persons. Common carriers include airlines, railroads, bus companies, taxicabs, ships, pipe lines, and trucking lines.

Significance   Common carriers have been legally recognized throughout American history as "business affected with a public interest" because of the public's dependence upon their services. They may, therefore, be regulated for the public safety and convenience by the national, state, and local governments, each acting within its sphere of authority. National agencies involved in regulating interstate common carriers include the Civil Aeronautics Board, the Interstate Commerce Commission, the Federal Maritime Commission, and the Federal Power Commission. Regulation of common carriers by governments includes various aspects of their services and the rates they may charge.

Copyright   The exclusive right granted by the Copyright Office in the Library of Congress to the creative products of authors, composers, dramatists, photographers, and others. A copyright grant is made to anyone who wants one, following publication of his material and its submission to the Copyright Office. A copyright confers an exclusive privilege for a period of twenty-eight years, with the option of renewal for another twenty-eight-year period. Typical copyrighted items include books, newspapers, magazines, musical compositions, translations, cartoons, sermons, motion pictures, photographs, paintings, maps, and charts. The copyright power is based on the constitutional grant to Congress to promote science and the arts by granting authors "the exclusive right to their respective writings. . . ." See PATENT, page 265; TRADEMARK, page 268.

Significance   Copyrights are intended to foster creative efforts and to reward talent, and, like patents, they constitute an exception to the laws against monopolies. The Copyright Office makes no effort to enforce the exclusive grant, however, and the individual grantee must take civil suit or injunctive action through the federal courts when he believes his copyright has been infringed. The United States has entered into copyright agreements with most foreign states, but a few have refused to ratify reciprocal protection agreements.

Corporation   A business unit, chartered under state or federal law, owned by stockholders and legally regarded as an artificial person. Private corporations are owned by individual investors and public corporations are partially or wholly owned by government—national, state, or local. Corporations may enter into contracts and sue and be sued. See GOVERNMENT CORPORATION, page 186; BOND, page 257.

Significance   The corporation has become the major form of business enterprise in the United States. Individually owned and partnership businesses, although more numerous than corporations, are dwarfed by the corporations in terms of volume of business, numbers of employees, assets, and in the wielding of economic and political power. The corporate form has tended to promote urbanization, industrialization, and increasing impersonality in business life. National defense requirements, corporation mergers, and a high mortality rate for small, noncorporative business have all tended to accelerate the growth of huge corporations in recent years. National and state legislation extensively regulate the chartering of corporations, their financial and general business operations, and their impact upon competition in the market place.

Depression A business cycle period characterized by a serious economic slump, inadequate purchasing power, deflation, and high unemployment. Typically, major depressions have followed peak periods of prosperity when production facilities and credit have been overextended. *See* BUSINESS CYCLES, page 258.

Significance The American economy has experienced numerous depressions of serious proportions, but all previous ones were dwarfed by the great depression of the 1930s. Classical economic theory held that depressions are inevitable in a free enterprise economy and that self-correcting economic forces set in motion by the depression would in time provide adjustments without governmental interference. Today, economic theory and analysis are aimed at preventing a depression, and most economists believe that governmental monetary and fiscal policies can prevent or quickly remedy a serious depression if they are wisely used and properly timed. Four post-World War II economic recessions have been attacked with monetary and fiscal measures, and the serious downturns in the economy have been arrested and reversed before they could assume depression proportions.

Economic Planning The establishment by government of economic goals and the means for reaching them. Economic planning may be concerned with providing some protection against violent swings of the business cycle in a capitalistic economy. At the other extreme, it may involve total governmental control and direction of investment, production, consumption, and other economic forces. *See* COUNCIL OF ECONOMIC ADVISERS, page 270.

Significance The national government, since the depression of the 1930s, has increasingly used economic planning, primarily through the national budget, to fight recessions and to promote full employment. Long-range resources planning was first begun by the National Resources Planning Board, established in 1934, which was charged with studying economic trends and recommending national policies to avoid runaway booms or major slumps in the economy. In the Employment Act of 1946, Congress created a new planning group, the Council of Economic Advisers. The Council is charged with responsibility for short-term planning to recommend governmental policies that will give stability to the nation's economy, promote full employment, and avoid major booms and busts. In Communist and Socialist countries, economic planning is based on setting up national goals for a specific period, such as in a five-year plan, and the marshalling of the nation's work force and resources, often through authoritarian control, to achieve these goals.

Franchise A privilege conferred by government upon a private company to operate a public utility and to use public property for the welfare or convenience of the public. Franchises are granted by the national, state, and local governments to bus companies, railroads, telephone and electric power companies, pipe lines, and other private companies performing public services. *See* PUBLIC UTILITY, page 266.

Significance   A government grants a franchise when a condition of limited competition or natural monopoly exists and unrestricted competition is not practicable. In restricting competition, the government accepts a responsibility to regulate the service and rates of the franchised company to ensure that it operates in the public interest. Most franchises are granted by city governments, and franchise fees constitute a sizable source of municipal funds.

Holding Company   A corporation whose assets consist of stocks in operating companies, usually a controlling share in each of several allegedly competing companies (subsidiaries). Holding companies, although illegal under the common law, have been legalized by statute in many states. The policies and pricing of subsidiary companies are controlled through stock ownership and the membership of holding company officers on the boards of directors of subsidiaries.

Significance   In the late nineteenth and early twentieth centuries, holding companies were used to establish monopoly or near-monopoly pricing conditions in certain industries, especially in electric and gas utilities. By the 1930s, holding companies were recognized as a threat to free enterprise competition and to the welfare of consumers in the gas and electric industries. Congress enacted the Holding Company Act of 1935 to control the operations of such companies engaged in interstate and foreign commerce. One section of this law, the so-called death sentence provision, halted the pyramiding of holding companies by limiting them to the second degree, that is, only two holding companies are permitted beyond the operating level. The effect of the law in dissolving many of the complicated holding company structures that had been built up over the years has generally been salutary in revitalizing competition and keeping consumer prices at reasonable levels.

Interlocking Directorates   A means by which competing companies reduce or eliminate competition among themselves by having the same individuals as members of the boards of directors of their companies. *See* CLAYTON ACT, page 277.

Significance   Through interlocking directorates, companies supposedly in competition with each other could establish uniform pricing policies and take other actions of a monopolistic nature. The device came into use in the world of big business as a means of evading the provisions of the Sherman Antitrust Act prohibiting combinations in restraint of trade. This loophole was largely closed by the Clayton Act of 1914, which prohibits interlocking directorates in companies if any of them has a capitalization of $1 million and if they are engaged in interstate or foreign commerce and are natural competitors.

License   A certificate granted under law by administrative officials, permitting private individuals to engage in certain business or professional activities. Licensing power is exercised primarily by the state and local governments, but the national government also uses it to regulate such fields as atomic materials, securities, market exchanges, and radio and television.

Significance   Persons seeking a license must meet the requirements established by law. Discretion is exercised by administrative officials in choosing from among many qualified applicants for a limited number of licenses. The power to grant licenses includes the power to suspend, revoke, or refuse to renew licenses for cause. Licensing by government is often demanded by professional or skilled groups, such as physicians and beauty operators, to ensure proper standards and, in some cases, to restrict competition in the field.

Merger   The pooling of assets of two companies to form a single company. Various kinds of mergers are possible, including those between competing companies (horizontal), those aimed at gaining control of raw material suppliers (vertical-backward), those involving retail outlets (vertical-forward), and those of unrelated businesses (conglomerate).

Significance   For many years, mergers were regarded as reasonable business combinations not in violation of the antitrust laws. As a result of a rapidly increasing number of business mergers and growing pressure for governmental action, Congress enacted the Celler Antimerger Act in 1950 as an amendment to the Clayton Act. Mergers that reduce competition or that foster the growth of monopoly conditions are prohibited by the law. Many controversies have arisen concerning the application of the Celler amendment because its vague and general language leaves considerable discretion in the hands of enforcement officials. Most such controversies involve the question of whether a specific merger will increase or decrease competition. Companies often seek approval from enforcement officials prior to undertaking a merger.

Monopoly   A market condition characterized by the absence of competition and the artificial fixing of prices for services or commodities. *See* OLIGOPOLY, page 264.

Significance   Monopolies result when business firms establish conditions in which prices are controlled through mergers, holding companies, interlocking directorates, conspiracies to restrain trade, and collusive bidding. Under the Sherman Act of 1890, the Clayton Act of 1914, and the Federal Trade Commission Act of 1914, the national government seeks to break up monopolies and restrain their price-fixing techniques so as to foster real competition in the free enterprise system. In some cases, however, the national government has permitted and even encouraged monopolies, as, for example, in granting exclusive franchises to public utilities, in conferring patent and copyright privileges, and in fostering the export trade (Webb-Pomerene Act).

Nationalization   The transference of the ownership and operation of private enterprises to a national government. Nationalization (also called expropriation) may result from purchase or confiscation with or without compensation, and may apply to properties owned by citizens or foreign nationals.

Significance   Although American nationalization has been limited to the seizure of enemy assets during time of war, other democratic nations, such as

Britain, have nationalized some of their basic industries and communications, transportation, banking, and health facilities. Nationalization of private business and industry is a goal of the Socialists and Communists, and in many countries private assets have been confiscated without compensation to the owners. Fear of expropriation has been a significant factor in limiting American private investments abroad, especially in the newly emerging nations of Asia and Africa. American constitutional guarantees limit the nationalization powers of the national government, although private property may be appropriated by law for a public purpose and with the payment of just compensation to the private owners.

Navigable Waters   All waters within the boundaries of the United States that are or may be used as highways for interstate or foreign commerce, such as rivers, streams, lakes, and inlets. *See* ADMIRALTY JURISDICTION, page 198.
    Significance   The Supreme Court in its decision in the *Daniel Ball* case (10 Wall. 557 [1871]), declared that the jurisdiction of Congress extends to all natural waterways that can be used for the transmission of commerce among the states and with foreign nations. Although the beds of such waterways are under state jurisdiction, no state may constitutionally impede or obstruct the flow of commerce on the waters. Approval for construction of bridges over navigable waters by state or local governments must be obtained from the national government through the United States Corps of Engineers.

Oligopoly   A market condition wherein the supply of a commodity is controlled by a few companies, consequently limiting competition. Oligopoly is sometimes referred to as a situation of partial monopoly, because the market price can be fixed through collusion or passive competition. *See* MONOPOLY, page 263.
    Significance   Oligopoly conditions have tended to increase in many areas of the nation's economy in recent years, especially as a result of business mergers. Oligopoly constitutes an especially difficult enforcement problem in the national government's efforts to maintain effective competition in business, because competition appears to exist when it may not exist in fact.

Original Cost Theory   An approach used by government, in fixing rates, to determine a fair return in profits for public utilities. The original cost theory is based on ascertaining the total investment made by the stockholders when the corporation was organized, plus subsequent capital expansions, less depreciation. *See* RATE-MAKING, page 267; *Smyth v. Ames,* page 276.
    Significance   The original cost theory is usually favored by utility companies if their major investments have been made during periods of high cost. If made during periods of deflation, "reproduction cost" would be regarded more favorably. Federal regulatory agencies generally follow the original cost less depreciation theory, modified by the "prudent investment theory." Supporters of the original cost thesis argue that it is the only way of accurately computing a company's actual investment and that all other theories are hypothetical and subjective. Those who oppose original cost regard it as in-

accurate and unfair because of its failure to take inflationary and deflationary factors into account.

Original Package Doctrine   A limitation on the state taxing powers that exempts commodities from state jurisdiction so long as they remain in their original shipping containers. The Supreme Court applied the original package doctrine to products imported from foreign countries (*Brown v. Maryland,* 12 Wheaton 419 [1827]) and to those commodities produced in the United States and shipped in interstate commerce (*Leisy v. Hardin,* 135 U.S. 100 [1890]). *See Brown v. Maryland,* page 275.

Significance   The Supreme Court's original package doctrine was intended to restrain the states from imposing a burden upon the flow of interstate and foreign commerce. Otherwise, commodities could be subjected to a series of crippling taxes levied by each state that the commodities passed through on their way to their final destination.

Patent   An exclusive grant to an inventor by which the national government extends to an individual or corporation "the right to exclude others from making, using, or selling the invention throughout the United States" for a period of seventeen years. Patent grants are made only for bona fide "discoveries," and not for improvements upon existing inventions. They apply to any new machine, design, process, composition, substance, or plant variety. The Constitution grants Congress exclusive power to grant patents. Patents are granted by the United States Patent Office in the Department of Commerce. *See* COPYRIGHT, page 260; TRADEMARK, page 268.

Significance   The United States Patent Office has issued over three and one-half million patents since it was established by Congress in 1836. In recent years, patent applications have been made at the rate of 1500 each week, and there is a backlog of over 200,000 applications in various stages of processing. As the Founding Fathers intended, the monopoly granted to inventors has served as a major incentive in developing the thousands of useful products that typify the American economy. The United States has entered into patent agreements with most foreign states, although a few have jeopardized inventors' international patent rights by refusing to conclude reciprocal protection agreements.

Proprietary Function   A governmental activity involving business-type operations ordinarily carried on by private companies. Proprietary functions include such activities as supplying electricity and gas, recreational facilities, garbage collection, transportation, and operating a liquor business. *See* INTERGOVERNMENTAL TAX IMMUNITY, page 34; *South Carolina v. United States,* page 254.

Significance   Governments engage in proprietary functions to secure revenue, to provide proper regulation of certain activities, or to offer services that private companies cannot or will not provide. Neither level of government can tax the other level's purely governmental functions, but the problem of distinguishing between proprietary and ordinary governmental activities has been a troublesome one for the courts. For example, the supplying of water to a city was held by the courts to be a regular function of government, whereas the bottling and selling of mineral waters by a state was held to be a proprietary function.

Prudent Investment Theory   An approach used by government, in fixing rates, to determine a fair return in profits for public utilities. The prudent investment theory is based on ascertaining the original cost of investments in the utility and subtracting from this figure those that have been imprudent or wasteful. *See* RATE-MAKING, page 267; *Smyth v. Ames,* page 276.

Significance   The prudent investment theory is based on the assumption that it would be unrealistic to include imprudent or dishonest investments in calculating the rate base of a utility for determining a fair return on investment. The Supreme Court in recent years has favored the use of the prudent investment theory by federal regulatory agencies, although it has not tried to establish a single formula (*FPC v. Hope Natural Gas Co.,* 320 U.S. 591 [1943]). The prudent investment theory has also been favored by many state courts for use by state regulatory agencies.

Public Service Commission   A regulatory agency, found in each of the states, that regulates the rates and services of public utilities operating within the state. Public service commissions vary in size from one to seven members, with most states fixing the number at three. Private utility companies regulated by the commissions include gas and electric suppliers, buses, interurban railway transit systems, taxicabs, oil and gas pipe lines, telephone and telegraph services, and in some states, municipal utilities. Some of the larger cities have also established public service commissions, and in many other cities the city council functions in this role. *See* PUBLIC UTILITY, page 266.

Significance   Public service commissions are expected to regulate utilities in the public interest to provide good service and fair rates for consumers. In most states, their efforts are hampered by complicated, court-imposed valuation formulas for determining rates, by inadequate operating funds, and by politically appointed staffs. In some states, the regulated companies are accused of having an inordinate influence over the commissions, which undermines the latter's regulatory role and results in higher rates. Organized consumer groups in some states have successfully exerted political pressure to strengthen the regulatory function of commissions.

Public Utility   A privately owned business that performs an essential service for the community and is extensively regulated by government. Congress and the state legislatures establish general criteria for regulation and create government commissions to perform the regulatory function subject to review by the courts. Typical examples of public utilities include transportation facilities, electric and gas suppliers, communication services, and water suppliers. *See* FRANCHISE, page 261.

Significance   A public utility is given a license or franchise by government when noncompetitive conditions are desirable. When government grants franchises to private businesses to carry on operations in the public interest free from competition, it has a resulting responsibility to regulate their services and rates. This involves decisions over the types of businesses that can be regulated as public utilities, the respective regulatory spheres of the nation and the states, and the methods of calculating a fair return for the company in fixing rates.

Public Works   Improvements in public facilities financed or built by government for the public welfare and convenience. Public works include such projects as parks, bridges, public buildings, roads, sewers, dams, harbors, housing, hospitals, canals, reclamation, irrigation, and navigation. *See* FISCAL POLICY, page 241.

Significance   Public works projects not only provide facilities for public benefit; they are also useful in carrying out countercyclical fiscal policies to combat economic recessions. Economists suggest that public improvements be carefully planned in advance and, during an economic downturn, be quickly put into effect. Governments on all three levels generally cooperate in carrying out public works programs, with major financing usually provided by the national government. In addition to stimulating the economy by increasing purchasing power and reducing unemployment, public works can greatly strengthen the nation by meeting present and future needs. Critics charge, however, that some public works programs are enacted for political reasons (pork barrel legislation) rather than out of need.

Rate-making   The determination by governmental regulatory agencies of the charges that public utilities will be permitted to levy for their services to the public. Rate-making agencies usually fix only maximum rates, although minimum rates may be set to avoid rate wars. *See* ORIGINAL COST THEORY, page 264; PRUDENT INVESTMENT THEORY, page 266; REPRODUCTION COST THEORY, page 267; *Smyth v. Ames,* page 276.

Significance   Rate-making involves the problem of protecting consumer interests while permitting rates high enough for the utility to earn a fair return. Rates are usually fixed to give a return of from five to eight percent, but the difficulty remains of determining the base on which this profit is to be calculated. Utilities often appeal to the courts when they regard their return as too small. Theories of valuation on which rate-making has been based include original cost, reproduction cost, market value, and prudent investment; regulatory agencies generally follow the original cost approach, modified by prudent investment.

Reproduction Cost Theory   An approach used by government, in fixing rates, to determine a fair return in profits for public utilities. The reproduction cost theory is based on ascertaining the cost of reproducing the assets of a utility at current prices less depreciation over the period of their use. *See* RATE-MAKING, page 267; *Smyth v. Ames,* page 276.

Significance   The reproduction cost theory is favored by utilities during periods of inflation because higher prices tend to increase the size of the rate base on which rates and a fair return are computed. The case for the reproduction cost theory is based on its acceptance of current market conditions as the basis for rate-making, whereas the case against it is based on the view that a fair return can be accurately determined only if based on an actual investment figure (original cost theory) and not one established by government rate makers.

Restraint of Trade   The use in the business world of trusts, monopolies, price fixing, collusion, conspiracy, or other practices that hamper or eliminate a market economy based on free competition. The phrase is used in the Sherman Act of 1890 wherein it forbids any "conspiracy in the restraint of trade. . . ." *See* SHERMAN ANTITRUST ACT, page 278.

Significance   Although the laissez-faire theory of free enterprise calls for economic freedom from governmental controls, some measure of regulation of business and commerce has proved necessary to maintain free competition. Major federal statutes that have sought to prevent private actions in restraint of trade and free competition include the Sherman Act of 1890, the Clayton Act of 1914, and the Federal Trade Commission Act of 1914.

Subsidy   Financial aid bestowed by government upon private individuals to improve their economic position. Subsidies may be direct, as in the payment of sums of money to shipbuilders and farmers, or indirect, as in the tariff that protects American business, labor, and agriculture from foreign competition.

Significance   Although subsidies are granted to private individuals by all three levels of American government, the national government has been the most active. Since Alexander Hamilton first proposed subsidies in his Financial Program, they have been a continuing and significant function of the national government, amounting to billions of dollars annually in recent years. Major beneficiaries of governmental subsidies are or have been railroads, airlines, farmers, businessmen, home builders, defense contractors, the unemployed, and veterans. In some cases, subsidies to one group may imperil the economic position of another group, as, for example, the effect on railroads of extensive subsidies to airlines.

Trademark   A name, mark, or symbol used by a manufacturer or dealer to identify his product or service to the consuming public. Trademarks are granted by the Patent Office through a procedure similar to that for obtaining patents. Registered trademarks are valid for twenty years, provided registrants file affidavits with the Patent Office every five years attesting to their use, and are renewable for subsequent twenty-year periods. Trademark protection is left up to registrants who can take civil suit action in the courts when infringements occur. *See* COPYRIGHT, page 260; PATENT, page 265.

Significance   Like patents and copyrights, a trademark bestows a monopoly right upon an individual or company. Trademarks are significant not only to registrants, whose sales of products may be increased through such identification, but also to consumers, who are protected from a welter of confusion of similar marks and symbols when making purchases. In 1946, Congress enacted the Lanham Trademark Act, which revised and codified numerous federal statutes relating to trademarks.

Trust   Two or more corporations linked together by assigning the voting rights of a majority of stockholders in each corporation to a single group of trustees. The term is also commonly used to describe any huge corporation or group of corporations that pursues monopolistic policies in the production or supplying of goods or services. *See* SHERMAN ANTITRUST ACT, page 278.

Significance   The trust as a business combination was used extensively to reduce or eliminate competition among previously competing companies, until it was outlawed by the Sherman Act of 1890. The Supreme Court, however, subsequently modified the antitrust provisions with its "rule of reason," which applied the Sherman Act only to those combinations that are unreasonably restrictive of competition and in which a clear intention of monopoly can be shown. Many trusts continued to flourish until the late 1930s when the Department of Justice engaged in a vigorous trust-busting campaign. In recent years, the Department has turned its attention to preventing mergers and collusive practices that, like the trusts of an earlier period, tend to reduce competition.

Unfair Trade Practice   Any business activity that deceives or misleads the consumer and results in his being sold shoddy, dangerous, or overpriced goods or services. Examples of unfair trade practices include false and misleading advertising, misbranding, improper labeling, conspiracies to fix prices, collusive bidding, discrimination against buyers, price cutting to eliminate competition, and other practices in restraint of trade. *See* FEDERAL TRADE COMMISSION, page 273; CLAYTON ACT, page 277.

Significance   Unfair trade practices were outlawed by the Congress in two laws enacted in 1914, the Clayton Act and the Federal Trade Commission Act. The former forbids price discrimination, price cutting to restrain trade, and purchases of stock among competitors. The latter seeks to promote fair competition and, through the Wheeler-Lea Act amendments of 1938, outlaws unfair and deceptive practices and false advertising of foods, drugs, cosmetics, and other commodities. Both acts are administered by the Federal Trade Commission. Consumer interests are also protected by the Food and Drug Administration of the Health, Education, and Welfare Department, which safeguards against misbranding, adulteration, and false labeling.

Usury   The charging of interest in excess of the maximum rate permitted by law. State usury laws provide for civil and criminal actions against persons or lending institutions charging illegal interest rates.

Significance   All states have enacted usury laws, although the legal maximum rates permissible vary considerably. Provisions of usury laws are particularly effective in holding down interest rates charged by small loan companies and pawnbrokers. Usury laws have gained in importance as the American economy has become increasingly dependent upon consumer credit.

IMPORTANT AGENCIES

Antitrust Division   One of the major divisions of the Department of Justice, which has responsibility for enforcement of the antitrust laws.

Significance   The forcefulness with which the national government has carried on its antimonopoly programs has depended often on the person chosen by the President and the Attorney General to be placed in charge of the Antitrust Division. For example, when Thurman W. Arnold, a law professor dedicated to breaking up trusts, headed the Antitrust Division, almost as many legal proceedings were initiated in the five years of his tenure, from 1938 to 1943, as had been started in the preceding half century since the enactment of the Sherman Act. The Antitrust Division carries on its enforcement duties through both civil and criminal actions.

Civil Aeronautics Board (CAB)   A five-member independent regulatory agency that controls the business aspects of private airlines engaged in domestic and foreign transportation. Board members are appointed by the President with the Senate's approval for six year terms. The CAB was established under the Civil Aeronautics Act of 1938, which gave it responsibility for the "encouragement and development" of civil aviation. Its functions include the regulation of the economic aspects of domestic airlines and the operations of both domestic and foreign airlines in the United States. It grants permission to companies to fly specific routes, exercises jurisdiction over rates and fares, and regulates mergers and other business relations in the interest of maintaining competition.

Significance   The Civil Aeronautics Board's functions have increased with the growth of the airline industry. CAB decisions are vital to the economic interests of the airlines and to the convenience of the traveling public. Presidential approval is required for CAB decisions affecting foreign air transportation.

Council of Economic Advisers (CEA)   A staff agency in the Executive Office of the President. It consists of three leading economists who advise the President on measures to maintain stability in the nation's economy. The Council was established by Congress in the Employment Act of 1946 and was given responsibility by that Act to formulate proposals "to maintain employment, production, and purchasing power." The Council's recommendations are included in the President's annual economic report to Congress, in which he sets forth the economic problems facing the nation and recommends legislative solutions. *See* EMPLOYMENT ACT, page 277.

Significance   The Council of Economic Advisers' role as a leading staff agency reflects the increasing responsibility of the President to provide leadership in keeping the nation's economy healthy. The Council has played a significant role in recommending fiscal policies to help overcome several post-World War II recessions. Its influence depends upon its acceptance as a professionally competent body of advisers, but it must avoid detachment from political realities.

Department of Commerce   One of the twelve major departments of the national administration headed by a Secretary with Cabinet rank. The Department of Commerce and Labor, founded in 1903, was split in 1913 by Congress into the two separate departments of Commerce and Labor. Major units found in the Department of Commerce, and the main responsibility of each, include: (1) the Bureau of the Census, which conducts the decennial census;

(2) the Coast and Geodetic Survey, which maps coastlines and waterways; (3) the International Commerce Bureau, which promotes US business interests abroad; (4) the Maritime Administration, which administers grants to shipbuilders and operators; (5) the National Bureau of Standards, which maintains basic units for testing and measuring in business and industry; (6) the Community Relations Service which conciliates racial disputes; (7) the Patent Office, which examines and grants patents and trademarks; (8) the Weather Bureau, which provides meteorological data; and (9) the Area Redevelopment Administration, which provides aid to areas with substantial and persistent unemployment.

Significance   The Department of Commerce has major responsibility for providing services for the business community. It promotes and protects the interests of businessmen at home and abroad. It is primarily a service, rather than a regulatory agency. The Secretary of Commerce is, typically, a businessman or a person who has been identified as friendly to the business community.

Department of Transportation   One of the major departments of the national administration, headed by a Secretary with Cabinet rank. The Department, established in 1966, brought together more than thirty separate agencies and bureaus dealing with transportation, including the Federal Aviation Agency, which makes and enforces traffic and safety regulations for civil aviation, the Bureau of Public Roads which administers the federal aid highway program, and the Coast Guard.

Significance   The Department of Transportation has responsibility for developing a national transportation policy. Although several important agencies concerned with transportation, such as the ICC and Maritime Administration, were not included in the Department, the Secretary of Transportation will suggest policy guidelines to independent agencies. Safety in all forms of transportation is a major concern of the Department.

Export-Import Bank of Washington   A government corporation that guarantees private credit and makes direct loans to foreign and domestic businessmen to promote the flow of trade. The Export-Import Bank, originally chartered in 1934, is governed by a five-member bipartisan board appointed by the President with Senate consent.

Significance   The Export-Import Bank was originally created to foster trade between the United States and the Soviet Union and with Latin America, but its operations have become almost world-wide in scope. Its loans must be repaid in American dollars, and capital equipment needed by the party receiving the loan must be purchased in the United States. The Bank is an important contributor to aid programs for underdeveloped countries, financing the building of steel mills, roads, dams, manufacturing plants, and other projects.

Federal Communications Commission (FCC)   A seven-member independent regulatory commission that controls interstate and foreign communication via radio, television, telephone, telegraph, and cable. The FCC was created by and administers the Federal Communications Act of 1934. Under the Act, the FCC grants licenses to broadcasters, enforces regulations prohibiting indecent language and lotteries, and requires equal time for political candidates. The FCC has no power to regulate rates charged sponsors of radio and television programs, but Congress has designated telephone, telegraph, and cable services as "common carriers" and, therefore, subject to extensive regulation of rates and services. The FCC also implements provisions of the Communications Satellite Act of 1962.

Significance   The major responsibility of the FCC in recent years has been that of granting licenses to broadcasters. A limited number of radio frequencies and television channels are available. A television license, for example, is granted free by the FCC but may be worth millions of dollars to the licensee. As a result, the FCC has often had to select from a number of applicants who may bring various kinds of political pressure to bear on the commissioners. Although its regulation of broadcasting is exercised exclusively, it shares regulation of telephone services with state utility commissions. The latter control rates and services of independent telephone companies and local calls, whereas the FCC controls interstate long-distance calls and all telegraph and cable services.

Federal Deposit Insurance Corporation (FDIC)   A government corporation established in 1933 to insure depositors' accounts in participating banks up to $15,000 for each account. The FDIC insurance system is financed through annual assessments levied on the privately owned banks. Member banks of the Federal Reserve System must participate, and nonmember banks may request to join the program. The FDIC is directed by the Comptroller of the Currency and by two directors appointed by the President with Senate consent.

Significance   The FDIC program promotes stability in the banking system by maintaining the confidence of depositors that their money is safe. Prior to the establishment of the government's guarantee, "runs" on individual banks and general bank "panics" were quite common. They were difficult to control because banks do not normally keep enough cash on hand to meet widespread demands from depositors for their money. Because such fear is restrained by absolute guarantees of the national government offered through the FDIC, the banking system and, as a consequence, the entire American economy have achieved greater stability. All but a small fraction of the commercial bank and trust companies in the United States are insured by the FDIC. The Federal Savings and Loan Insurance Corporation (FSLIC) similarly insures each depositor's account for up to $15,000 in all federally chartered and in most state-chartered savings and loan associations.

Federal Maritime Commission (FMC)   A five-member independent regulatory agency that controls rates and services of water carriers engaged in foreign and domestic off-shore commerce. Members are appointed by the President with the Senate's approval, for four-year terms. The FMC's authority includes the approval of routes, the settling of disputes, and the prescribing of working conditions for seamen.

Significance   The Federal Maritime Commission was established in 1961 as an independent agency to make and enforce regulations relating to the merchant marine. Foreign shippers are freer from governmental controls than are coastal and inland waterway shippers under Interstate Commerce Commission jurisdiction. The Maritime Administration in the Department of Commerce aids shipbuilders and operators through the payment of "construction differentials" and "operating differentials" as subsidies to enable American shippers to compete with foreign companies. The FMC works with the Department of State to eliminate foreign discrimination against American shipping.

Federal Power Commission (FPC)   A five-member independent regulatory commission that controls the production and the interstate transmission and sale of electrical energy and the interstate transportation and sale of natural gas. Commissioners are appointed by the President with the Senate's approval for five-year terms. The FPC was created as a Cabinet committee in 1920, and given its independent status by the Federal Power Act of 1930. Its functions include granting licenses to private companies to build hydroelectric plants on navigable waters, determining wholesale rates for electric power transmitted across state lines, regulating security issues of private power companies, planning for multipurpose river basin development, developing power resources at government-built dams, and controlling pipeline transmissions and sales of natural gas.

Significance   National regulation through the FPC of electrical power and natural gas operations of private utility companies stemmed largely from the inability of state utility commissions to protect the public interest in these areas. The FPC undertakes extensive studies and detailed investigations to determine fair prices and reasonable services, rather than relying on information supplied by utility companies at formal hearings—a practice that characterizes much state regulation. The major issues in this area in recent years have been whether the national government or private utility companies should develop some of the few remaining sites for major dams, and the scope of natural gas regulation.

Federal Trade Commission (FTC)   A five-member independent regulatory commission established by Congress in 1914 to promote fair competition in business and to restrict unfair business practices in interstate and foreign commerce. Commissioners are appointed by the President, with the Senate's approval, for seven-year terms. The FTC enforces the Clayton and the Federal Trade Commission Acts of 1914. It seeks to prevent illegal combinations in restraint of trade, deception, price discriminations, price fixing, interlocking directorates, fraudulent advertising of foods, drugs, and cosmetics, and other business activities that reduce competition or endanger or defraud the consumer. The operations of the FTC include making rules and regulations to establish a code of fair competition, holding hearings concerning alleged violations, and enforcing decisions through cease and desist orders and injunctions granted by federal courts.

Significance   Most of the work of the FTC is carried on by persuading businessmen to cease some activity of doubtful legality. The Commission plays a relatively minor role in enforcing antimonopoly legislation and directs most of its efforts to protecting consumer interests by preventing deceptive advertising, fraud, and the sale of dangerous products. Although the duties of the FTC are varied, its underlying purpose is to maintain the free enterprise system by preventing corrupt practices.

Interstate Commerce Commission (ICC)   An eleven-member independent regulatory commission, established in 1887, that regulates the business operations, services, and rates of interstate carriers. Commissioners are appointed by the President and confirmed by the Senate for seven-year terms. The jurisdiction of the ICC extends to railroads, express companies, bus and truck companies, oil pipe lines, intercoastal and inland waterway carriers, and terminal facilities used in transporting goods or persons. The ICC enforces the Interstate Commerce Act of 1887 and six other supplementary statutes, plus numerous amendments. It employs a staff of over 2300 attorneys, investigators, economists, examiners, and technicians. Its responsibilities include fixing rates, both maximum and minimum, controlling poolings and consolidations of operating companies, regulating their sales of stocks and bonds, prescribing accounting systems, granting permits and licenses, and providing traffic management.

Significance   The ICC was the first of the independent regulatory commissions, all of which have come to play a major role in the national government's regulation of substantial sectors of the nation's economy. The ICC, like the others, performs a threefold function of making rules and regulations (quasi-legislative), administering them, and holding hearings concerning violations and disputes (quasi-judicial). Commissioners work in three-member panels to carry out most of the routine work of the ICC, with appeal to the full Commission possible. The role of the ICC has become increasingly difficult as competition among the various carriers has intensified in recent years. Decisions of the ICC can be appealed to the federal courts for review to ensure protection of property rights from arbitrary actions.

Post Office Department   One of the twelve major departments in the national administration. The Postmaster General who heads the Department is appointed by the President with the Senate's approval and is a Cabinet officer. The national chairman of the party that wins the presidency has often received the appointment in a new administration. The Post Office Department operates 34,000 post offices around the country. In addition to carrying the mail, the Department operates a parcel-post service, a system of registering, certifying, and insuring mail, money orders, C.O.D. and special delivery services, and sells government bonds.

Significance   The Post Office is one of the biggest business operations in the world. Each year the Department incurs a substantial deficit in its operations, resulting mainly from subsidies to many politically powerful groups. These subsidies include below-cost rates for certain types of mail, such as business advertising, books, newspapers, and magazines. Free postage privileges are granted to various groups, and rail, air, and other carriers are paid high prices to carry the mails. Although Congress has from time to time raised rates, they have not been raised high enough to overcome deficits. The postal service, however, provides a nation-wide network for the dissemination of information and for the distribution of articles of commerce and industry.

Securities and Exchange Commission (SEC)   A five-member independent regulatory commission established by the Securities Exchange Act of 1934 to regulate the buying and selling of securities (stocks, bonds, and so forth). Commissioners are appointed by the President, with the Senate's approval, for five-year terms. In addition to the Act of 1934, the SEC enforces the Securities Act of 1933, which compels full disclosure of information concerning new security issues, and the Public Utility Holding Company Act of 1935 under which the SEC tries to limit mergers and combinations of utility companies.

Significance   The establishment of the SEC and adoption by Congress of the Acts of 1933 and 1934 grew out of the shocking disclosures of deception, manipulation, fraud, and dishonesty revealed by a Senate investigation of causes of the stock market crash of 1929. The SEC does not guarantee the financial soundness or money-making possibilities of any security; it merely requires disclosure of all pertinent information to prospective buyers and forbids any attempts to manipulate prices.

Small Business Administration (SBA)   An independent agency, headed by an Administrator, established to make loans to small businesses and to assist them in obtaining government contracts. The SBA was given temporary status by Congress in 1953, and was expanded and made a permanent agency in 1958. Some of its operations since 1961 have been carried on through small-business investment companies around the nation. Principal functions of SBA include financing plant expansion and modernization, aiding disaster victims, helping businessmen to cut through red tape to secure government procurement contracts, and giving managerial advice to small firms. Applicants for loans must show they have been turned down by private banks.

Significance   The SBA was the first agency established for the specific purpose of aiding small business. There are approximately four million small businesses in the United States today with an annual turnover rate of about ten percent. The SBA utilizes a revolving fund that gives it a measure of freedom from dependence upon annual budget grants from Congress. Although the agency was criticized in its early operations for granting, mainly, large loans to sizable businesses, it has increased the number of its loans and reduced the average amount of each loan to about $40,000 in recent years.

IMPORTANT CASES

Brown v. Maryland, 12 Wheaton 419 (1827): Established the "original package" doctrine, which holds that the authority of Congress over foreign commerce does not end until the merchandise arrives at its ultimate destination, the contents of the package are sold or removed for the purpose of selling, and they become commingled with the general property of a state. The case invalidated a law of Maryland that had required importers of foreign goods to obtain a license before being permitted to sell them.

Significance   The original package doctrine established in the Brown case remains a significant factor in restricting state interference with foreign commerce. In *Leisy v. Hardin,* 135 U.S. 100 (1890), the Court expanded the original package doctrine to include products shipped in interstate as well as foreign commerce. The regulatory power of Congress continues, however, to be more extensive over foreign than over interstate commerce because of the vast powers exercised by the national government in foreign affairs.

Cooley v. Board of Wardens, 12 Howard 299 (1851): Upheld the right of the states to regulate interstate commerce if Congress has not covered the field with its regulations and if the subject regulated by the states is not of a nature to require uniform national regulation. The case involved local regulations for port pilots, which were upheld as a reasonable regulation of interstate commerce by a state since such regulation does not need a uniform national policy.

Significance   The *Cooley* case established the precedent on which a vast amount of state regulation of interstate commerce is based today. By permitting states to enter the field, the Court recognized that the national government would be unable to provide all of the regulations needed to control the flow of commerce. Under the *Cooley* rule, the permissible extent of state regulation of interstate commerce in the absence of federal regulation is left to the courts to decide.

Gibbons v. Ogden, 9 Wheaton 1 (1824): Nullified a state grant giving an exclusive right to use navigable waters within the state. The Court held that congressional control over interstate commerce includes navigation. It was the first case involving the commerce clause and the powers of Congress to regulate interstate commerce were broadly interpreted by Chief Justice Marshall and the Court. They defined interstate commerce to include not only traffic but all commercial intercourse.

Significance   The *Gibbons* case opened the door to a vast expansion of national control over commerce through liberal interpretations of the commerce power. Today, the powers of Congress to regulate interstate commerce include the regulation of transportation, communications, buying and selling, and manufacturing. Few areas of economic activity remain outside the regulatory power of Congress.

Munn v. Illinois, 94 U.S. 113 (1876): Held that a state can validly fix maximum rates for a "business affected with a public interest." Regulation of a privately owned grain warehouse by the state of Illinois was upheld on the ground that when a proprietor devotes his property to a public use, he "must submit to be controlled by the public for the common good. . . ."

Significance   The *Munn* case was a landmark in establishing the power of government to regulate businesses other than public utilities. Congress and state legislatures have continued to use the flexible criterion of "business affected with a public interest" to regulate many business activities.

Smyth v. Ames, 169 U.S. 466 (1898): Declared, in an historic rate-making case, that government regulatory agencies must consider a number of factors in fixing rates, rather than a single one. The facts in the case involved a dispute over rate-setting for Nebraska railroads, in which the governmental agency based its formula chiefly on "reproduction cost," and the railroads demanded that the rate base be "original cost." The Court held that many factors should be considered in determining fair value, including original cost, cost of improvements, value of securities, reproduction cost, earning capacity, and operating expenses.

Significance   Because due process requires that rates fixed by government for private businesses be fair and reasonable, the problem of determining the base upon which the fair return will be calculated is a basic one. In recent years, the Court has modified the *Smyth* decision, adopting the "prudent investment" theory as a guide and using a pragmatic approach to determine whether the rates permit companies to operate successfully (*FPC v. Hope Natural Gas Co.,* 320 U.S. 591 [1943]).

IMPORTANT STATUTES

Atomic Energy Acts of 1946, 1954   The Act of 1946 created the Atomic Energy Commission (AEC) to control and develop the uses of atomic energy. Private mining of fissionable materials was permitted, but all other aspects of atomic energy were kept under strict governmental control. The Act of 1954 modified the public monopoly by permitting private development and operation of atomic power plants and the use of nuclear fuels and the sale of by-products by private firms under government licensing. *See* ATOMIC ENERGY COMMISSION, page 352.

Significance   The first Atomic Energy Act placed atomic energy, which had been developed by the military, under civilian control. Growing foreign achievements in the atomic field awakened Congress to the need to stimulate more rapid development of atomic energy for industrial purposes. As a result, the second Act, which sought to unleash private energies within limits of governmental control, was passed. Because of the extremely high cost of producing electricity in atomic power plants, the government contributes a major portion of the cost in building private facilities. Considerable governmental effort is also going into research to try to develop cheaper power.

Clayton Act of 1914   A major antitrust act, aimed at increasing competition in business. Provisions of the Clayton Act forbid price cutting and other abuses that tend to weaken competition, restrict corporations from acquiring stock in competing firms or building interlocking directorates, make corporation officers individually liable for violations, and facilitate civil suit procedures by injured parties. Labor unions and agricultural organizations not carrying on business for profit are exempted from the provisions of the Act.

Significance   The Clayton Act was intended to supplement and reinforce the Sherman Act of 1890, which had been weakened by the Supreme Court's interpretation limiting its application to "unreasonable" combinations in restraint of trade. The Act was aimed at reducing the confusion surrounding the Sherman Act by more clearly defining unfair business practices. Enforcement of the Clayton Act, however, has been weakened through administrative unconcern and judicial tolerance, except for a few periods of vigorous enforcement by the Antitrust Division and the Federal Trade Commission.

Employment Act of 1946   An act that establishes responsibility for the national government to maintain stability in the nation's economy. A Council of Economic Advisers (CEA) was created by the Act and placed in the Executive Office to advise the President on economic matters. The Act requires the President to make an annual economic report to Congress setting forth the major economic problems confronting the nation and recommending appropriate legislation.

Significance   The Employment Act of 1946 was the first legislation to recognize a continuing responsibility of government to use its fiscal powers to promote the nation's economic well-being. Specific goals of the Act include the maintenance of high levels of production, employment, and purchasing power. Since 1946, many demands have been made to include price stability as an additional responsibility of government. Congress has created a Joint Committee on the Economic Report, with seven members from each chamber, to study the President's recommendations and to recommend legislative consideration of specific programs. Although some recommendations and decisions undertaken under the Act have been controversial, the acceptance by government of a responsibility to combat economic downturns has been generally accepted by the American public.

Sherman Antitrust Act of 1890

The basic federal antimonopoly law that forbids "every contract, combination . . . or conspiracy in the restraint of trade or commerce." Enforcement of the Act is provided through criminal penalties, civil suit action with triple damages to injured parties, injunction, and seizure of property. Responsibility for enforcement is vested in the Antitrust Division of the Department of Justice.

Significance   The Sherman Act was a recognition by Congress that, paradoxical as it might appear to be, governmental intervention in the free economy was essential to preserve competition and free enterprise. Soon after its enactment, the Act was seriously crippled in two major Supreme Court tests. In the first, the Court held that manufacturing trusts were not engaged in commerce and, therefore, could be regulated only by the states (*United States v. E. C. Knight Co.,* 156 U.S. 1 [1895]). In the second, the Court laid down the "rule of reason" by which not *every* combination in restraint of trade (as Congress had explicitly stated in the Act) was illegal, but only those *unreasonably* so (*Standard Oil Co. v. United States,* 221 U.S. 1 [1910]). To supplement and reinforce the Sherman Act, Congress has since adopted the Clayton Act of 1914 and the Federal Trade Commission Act of 1914. The history of the Sherman Act demonstrates the influence of the Supreme Court, the President, the Attorney General, and other high officials in interpreting the language of the Act narrowly or broadly and in vigorously or reluctantly enforcing it.

Webb-Pomerene Act of 1918

An act that exempts business associations engaged in export trade to foreign lands from the provisions of the antitrust laws. Such organizations must register with the Federal Trade Commission.

Significance   The Webb-Pomerene Act was enacted to promote American foreign trade and to put American exporters on a competitive basis with countries that have little or no effective antitrust or anticartel legislation.

Thirteen

Government and Labor

Arbitration   The submission of a labor-management dispute to an impartial board or individual whose decision is binding upon the parties to the dispute. A few states have passed statutes requiring compulsory arbitration of disputes in public utility enterprises, such as electric, gas, and water. *See* MEDIATION AND CONCILIATION, page 284.

   Significance   A large number of labor disputes are submitted to private, professional arbitrators. Many strikes are thereby avoided. Compulsory arbitration has been used in wartime, but both management and labor fear compulsory arbitration, since both prefer to keep the government out of labor disputes and to pursue their ends through collective bargaining. Compulsory arbitration procedures are provided under the Railway Labor Act to supplement, rather than substitute for, collective bargaining. These procedures have not, however, proved successful, and they have often been bypassed during a railroad labor dispute.

Boycott   An economic weapon used by labor to curtail the purchase of products from an employer. Two types of boycotts, primary and secondary, may be distinguished. A primary boycott involves withdrawal of patronage, and the urging of others to withdraw their patronage, from an employer with whom a union is having a labor dispute. A secondary boycott involves a refusal to deal with or patronize anyone who deals with the employer with whom there is a dispute. Secondary boycotts are outlawed by the Taft-Hartley Act of 1947 and, with certain exceptions, by the Landrum-Griffin Act of 1959. Most states also outlaw secondary boycotts.

   Significance   The primary boycott is lawful but often ineffective for a union. People may continue to cross a picket line to patronize a strikebound store and, in the case of large industrial plants, suppliers may continue to sell to the plant and dealers continue to sell its products. Labor prefers the secondary boycott, which enables it to bring pressure to bear upon others whose continued dealing with the strikebound plant hinders the successful conclusion of the strike. Secondary boycotts are, however, illegal since they interfere with the rights of persons not involved in the dispute, and public policy seeks to confine the dispute to the particular parties involved.

Child Labor   The employment of children below the legal age limit. The national government and most states prohibit the employment of children below the age of sixteen and, in certain hazardous occupations, below the age of eighteen. Children are permitted to work outside of school in nonhazardous jobs.

Significance   Until about 1910, large numbers of children ten to fifteen years of age were regularly employed. State governments then began to impose restrictions, but states that did not do so were at an advantage over those that did. Agitation for national regulation led to the passage of legislation. The Supreme Court, however, struck down a law aimed at banning products of child labor from interstate commerce (*Hammer v. Dagenhart*, 247 U.S. 251 [1918]), and another law which taxed such products (*Bailey v. Drexel Furniture Co.*, 259 U.S. 20 [1922]). In 1924, Congress submitted to the states a constitutional amendment that would authorize federal regulation of child labor. Strong opposition prevented its ratification, though, by 1937, twenty-eight states, eight short of the required three-fourths, had ratified it. A more liberal view of national power, however, resulted in the passage and Supreme Court approval of the Fair Labor Standards Act of 1938 (*United States v. Darby*, 312 U.S. 100 [1941]), which, among other things, prohibits child labor. Today, child labor poses no major problem, particularly in view of compulsory education laws.

Closed Shop   An industrial plant that agrees to hire only those persons who are members of a labor union. The closed shop is outlawed by the Taft-Hartley Act of 1947, although later legislation has modified this restriction with regard to the building trades. *See* UNION SHOP, page 285; RIGHT TO WORK LAW, page 284.

Significance   The closed shop is opposed by management because it allegedly places the hiring power in the union rather than in the hands of management. Approximately thirty percent of organized labor, largely in craft industries, were under closed shop agreements prior to 1947. Though forbidden by the Taft-Hartley Act, many establishments continue to operate as closed shops through the mutual agreement of the union and management who are reluctant to upset customary patterns.

Collective Bargaining   Negotiation between an employer and a union representing the employees. It is to be distinguished from negotiation between an employer and an individual employee. The right of workers to organize and to bargain collectively through their representatives has been the official policy of the United States since 1935. Collective bargaining imposes upon the employer and labor union an obligation to confer in good faith with respect to working conditions and to execute a written contract embodying the agreements reached. Refusal to bargain, on the part of an employer or a duly recognized union, may be adjudged an unfair labor practice. *See* WAGNER ACT, page 291; *NLRB v. Jones and Laughlin Steel Corp.*, page 288.

Significance   Official recognition of the principle of collective bargaining was the culmination of years of industrial strife in which unions sought recognition from employers as legitimate bargaining agents for employees. Both national and state labor-management relations laws were enacted to guarantee the right of collective bargaining in the interest of avoiding continued industrial unrest. The principle of collective bargaining is recognition of the inequality of bargaining power between an employer and an individual employee. National and state laws now extensively regulate the procedures by which agreements are to be reached, the administration of agreements, and the problems attending the breakdown of collective bargaining procedures.

Committee on Political Education (COPE)   The political action organization of the AFL-CIO. COPE combines the political tactics developed over the years by the CIO Political Action Committee (PAC) and the AFL League for Political Education. These were the political action organizations of the two labor federations prior to their merger into the new AFL-CIO in 1955. Funds for COPE's activities are raised through voluntary contributions of trade union members.

Significance   The Taft-Hartley Act of 1947 forbids the use of union dues for partisan political activity. This resulted in the establishment of political "education" committees financed through voluntary contributions. COPE has been active in state and national campaigns since 1956. It educates workers and the general public on candidates and on issues of interest to labor. Its activities have had a considerable effect on elections, especially in the industrial states. Opponents have criticized COPE on the grounds that, allegedly, members are pressured into making contributions and that its education consists, in reality, of partisan political propaganda.

Cooling-off Period   A period of time, stipulated by the Taft-Hartley Act of 1947, during which parties to a labor-management controversy may not engage in a strike or lockout. Under the Act, an existing collective bargaining contract can be terminated or changed only after sixty days' notice to the other party. If no agreement is reached within thirty days, the Federal Mediation and Conciliation Service must be notified. During the sixty-day period no strike or lockout is permitted. In the case of disputes threatening the national welfare, the Taft-Hartley Act authorizes the President to seek an injunction from the courts which maintains the status quo for eighty days. During this time, fact-finding and conciliation efforts are to be made and the workers given a chance to vote on the employer's last offer. If, at the end of the eighty-day period, no solution is reached, a strike or lockout may take place. Similar procedures are provided for the rail and air transport industries in the Railway Labor Act.

Significance   The sixty-day and eighty-day cooling-off periods are designed to give the parties to the dispute a chance to reach an amicable settlement without resort to disruptive practices. Ofttimes, in practice, the parties "warm up" rather than "cool off" during this period. Both labor and management tend to judge any governmental intrusion into collective bargaining arrangements according to its effect on their respective positions.

Featherbedding   A labor practice requiring an employer to pay for services that are not performed. Featherbedding is considered to be an unfair labor practice and is outlawed by the Taft-Hartley Act. An example of feather-bedding is a requirement that a radio station pay musicians who do not play, since phonograph records, rather than "live" musicians, are used. Feather-bedding may also take the form of deliberate slowdowns in production or insistence that a job be performed by a particular individual though others can do it as well.

Significance   The increasing automation of industry has caused concern in labor circles. Featherbedding practices are designed to maintain the employment of persons whose jobs are rendered useless by new techniques. Labor leaders defend the practice by comparing it to the businessman who restricts output to keep prices high, to professions that restrict the licensing of persons seeking to join the profession, and to farmers who are paid not to grow crops. Featherbedding practices are likely to be part of the labor scene except in times of full employment.

General Counsel   An official charged with the responsibility for the investigation and prosecution of unfair labor-management practices under the Taft-Hartley Act. His functions include supervision of all regional offices of the National Labor Relations Board and final authority to issue complaints in unfair labor practice cases. These functions were formerly vested in the National Labor Relations Board. The General Counsel is appointed by the President, with the Senate's approval, for a four-year term. *See* NATIONAL LABOR RELATIONS BOARD, page 287.

Significance   The office of General Counsel was created by the Taft-Hartley Act to meet the criticism that the National Labor Relations Board was both prosecutor and judge in unfair labor practice cases. The net effect of this move was to make the Board primarily a quasi-judicial agency to hear appeals from decisions rendered by trial examiners in cases brought by the General Counsel. In the early stages of this new development, some friction arose between the Board and the General Counsel, but basic policy matters remain in the hands of the Board.

Injunction   A court order to compel or restrain the performance of an act. In the field of labor, the injunction became a weapon in the hands of management to restrain the activities of labor unions during their formative period. For many years, the injunction was used to enforce the Sherman Antitrust Act against unions. The Norris-LaGuardia Act of 1932 outlawed the use of the labor injunction when labor pursues lawful ends by legitimate means. The Taft-Hartley Act of 1947, however, empowers the President to seek an injunction when a labor dispute threatens the national welfare. *See* INJUNCTION, page 212.

Significance   The labor injunction used prior to 1932 was based on the theory that organized labor was a conspiracy in restraint of trade and that, when a union conducted a strike, it threatened the property rights of the employer. The injunctive power exercised by an unfriendly judiciary made it virtually impossible for labor to pursue its goals. From 1890 to 1932, the major political aim of labor was to eliminate the injunction from labor-management disputes, and success was achieved in the Norris-LaGuardia Act. The return to the injunctive device in the Taft-Hartley Act caused resentment among labor leaders, and presidents have been reluctant to use this power. However, under the Taft-Hartley Act, the injunction can last only eighty days, after which labor is free to strike.

Jurisdictional Strike   A strike involving a dispute between unions rather than between a union and an employer. Jurisdictional strikes may occur over the question of which union has the right to represent the workers or over the question of which workers are to do a specific job. For example, both carpenters and metalworkers may claim the right to install metal framed windows, or one union may try to "raid" another union's territory. The Taft-Hartley Act and many state laws make the jurisdictional strike unlawful. *See* STRIKE, page 285.

Significance   Jurisdictional strikes generally are viewed with little sympathy by the public. The consumer and the employer suffer the consequences of a fight in which they are innocent bystanders. Unions, too, recognize that such strikes harm them in the public eye and have tried to reach voluntary agreements on problems likely to lead to jurisdictional disputes. Nevertheless, workers may be vitally affected by problems arising over which group is to do a specific job. Jurisdictional strikes still erupt from time to time but the number has diminished.

Labor Unions   Organizations of workers that seek to improve the economic status and working conditions of labor through collective bargaining and political action. The largest and most influential labor organization is the American Federation of Labor-Congress of Industrial Organizations (AFL-CIO), a federation of over 130 unions. The AFL-CIO has almost fifteen million members comprising about eighty percent of organized labor. The remainder of organized labor is in independent unions, such as the Teamsters, Mine Workers, Longshoremen, Railroad Brotherhoods and a number of smaller unions. *See* PRESSURE GROUP, page 114.

Significance   Labor unions and the AFL-CIO in particular are major forces on the American scene. The merger of the AFL and CIO strengthened the labor movement and increased its political power. Rivalry among unions and union leaders both within and without the AFL-CIO has, however, reduced its full potential as an economic and political force. Moreover, less than thirty percent of the working force is organized into unions and the percentage is decreasing as a result of an affluent society and a decrease in factory type employment. Organized labor's major objectives are improved working conditions, improved wages and hours, and extensive social welfare legislation. For the most part, labor unions have been identified with the Democratic party.

Lockout   Action taken by an employer to close down his plant to keep workers from their jobs in order to force them to accept his position in a labor controversy. Lockouts are lawful unless they violate a collective bargaining agreement or seek a goal that the law declares to be an unfair practice.

Significance   The lockout is to the employer what the strike is to the union—a major weapon to force agreement. Lockouts are not commonly used, but some labor authorities point out that what the public usually considers to be a strike may also be a lockout since the employer closes his plant by refusing to meet union demands.

Mediation and Conciliation   Terms used interchangeably to refer to the attempt of a third party to settle a labor dispute by bringing the parties together and persuading them to reach a compromise. Unlike arbitration, the mediator or conciliator has no power to make his suggested solutions binding upon the parties. *See* FEDERAL MEDIATION AND CONCILIATION SERVICE, page 287; NATIONAL MEDIATION BOARD, page 287.

Significance   Elaborate mediation and conciliation machinery has been established by the national government and most state governments. The Federal Mediation and Conciliation Service, an agency established in 1913 in the Department of Labor but given independent status by the Taft-Hartley Act, may be called into a dispute by either party, or it may offer its services. State mediation services operate only on a part-time basis in most states, but the larger industrial states have established full-time agencies. In the railway and air transport industries a federal agency, the National Mediation Board, has been established to mediate disputes in those critical areas of industrial relations.

Picketing   Patrolling the site of a business establishment by workers who are on strike. Peaceful picketing is a form of free speech protected by the First Amendment (*Thornhill v. Alabama,* 310 U.S. 88 [1940]). Under national and state laws, however, picketing may not be used to promote any purpose which is contrary to law or public policy. The Taft-Hartley Act and the Landrum-Griffin Act forbid picketing for such purposes as encouraging secondary boycotts or trying to force employers to recognize a union other than one already lawfully recognized.

Significance   Picketing by a labor group serves both the purposes of informing the public of the controversy and persuading customers and other workers to refrain from dealing with a business establishment. It is a potent labor weapon since many people will not cross a picket line, out of either sympathy for the strike or fear of retaliation. Labor leaders hailed the 1940 Supreme Court decision that made picketing a free speech right, but subsequent legislation and court decisions have placed numerous restrictions upon the practice.

Right to Work Law   A law that prohibits making union membership a qualification for employment. Nineteen states have constitutional or statutory provisions that a person may not be compelled to join a union or to remain a member of a union to hold his job. Right to work laws establish the principle of the "open shop." *See* CLOSED SHOP, page 280; UNION SHOP, page 285.

Significance   Right to work laws are designed to curtail the closed shop and union shop. Though a union shop is permitted by section 14 (b) of the Taft-Hartley Act, that Act also permits states to pass right to work legislation. These laws are prompted in part by exposures of union corruption and by concern for workers who are penalized by not holding union membership. Some states seek to attract industry by enacting right to work laws that greatly weaken labor unions. Labor leaders strongly oppose right to work laws. They argue that nonunion members benefit from the union's efforts and that the laws will destroy unions and the principle of collective bargaining. With the exception of the state of Indiana, no major industrial state has enacted a right to work law. An effort to have Congress nullify state right to work laws by repealing section 14 (b) was defeated by a filibuster in the Senate in 1965.

Strike   A stoppage of work by employees for the purpose of winning concessions from their employer on matters of wages, hours, or working conditions. The right to strike, except for purposes prohibited by law, is considered to be a fundamental right of free workingmen. Government employees, however, are not permitted to strike. National and state laws contain a variety of limitations on the right to strike. For example, strikes may not be used to promote a secondary boycott or other unfair labor practice. Procedures are also provided by law for cooling-off periods, injunctions, fact-finding boards, and mediation services in order to avoid strikes. *See* COOLING-OFF PERIOD, page 281; JURISDICTIONAL STRIKE, page 283; LOCKOUT, page 283.

Significance   The strike is labor's most effective weapon but is often damaging to both sides and to the public. A strike in one industry has an effect on other industries dependent upon the struck plants for supplies. The Taft-Hartley Act of 1947 permits the President to obtain an eighty-day injunction if a strike might cause a national emergency. Workers on strike are not considered to have given up their jobs and a lawful dispute may not be interfered with by "strikebreakers" or "scabs" who replace the striking workers. Many unions provide strikers with subsistence allowances during a strike.

Unfair Labor Practice   Activity by a labor union or an employer that is defined by law as constituting a threat to industrial peace. Unfair labor practices are defined in the Taft-Hartley Act of 1947. Employers are forbidden to interfere with the rights of unions to organize, to discriminate against union members, or to refuse to bargain collectively. Unions may not discriminate against or coerce employees who are not union members, or engage in such practices as secondary boycotts, featherbedding, jurisdictional strikes, charging excessive dues or fees, or refusing to bargain collectively. *See* BOYCOTT, page 279; FEATHERBEDDING, page 282; JURISDICTIONAL STRIKE, page 283; TAFT-HARTLEY ACT, page 290.

Significance   By listing unfair labor practices, Congress sought to cope with the more common causes of labor-management unrest. The Taft-Hartley Act represented a departure from previous legislation by listing unfair union tactics as well as unfair employer behavior. The National Labor Relations Board (NLRB) and its General Counsel are charged with the duty of policing unfair activities. Exactly what constitutes an unfair practice is often open to dispute since the law cannot cover every eventuality. Many NLRB decisions on unfair practices are appealed to the federal courts.

Union Shop   An establishment in which all newly hired workers must join the union after a specified period of time, usually thirty days. Unlike the closed shop, now outlawed, the employee need not be a member of the union in order to be hired. *See* CLOSED SHOP, page 280; RIGHT TO WORK LAW, page 284.

Significance   The union shop is the major form of union security permitted by law. About seventy-five percent of organized labor works in union shops. The union shop eliminates "free riders" who would benefit from collective bargaining agreements without supporting the union. Many employees object to being forced to join a union, but they must remain members in order to hold their jobs. The Taft-Hartley Act authorizes union shop agreements, but permits states to eliminate them through right to work laws.

Workmen's Compensation   An insurance program, in effect in all states, that provides compensation for workers injured on their jobs and for dependents of workers who are killed in the course of employment. In most states, the program is financed entirely by the employer, who must take out private or public insurance for this purpose. Occupational diseases are also covered in many states. An administrative agency is generally established to settle claims arising under the law with appeal to the courts possible. State laws vary with regard to types of employers and occupations covered.

Significance   Workmen's compensation has replaced the system that required an injured worker to bring a lawsuit against his employer to recover damages. In such lawsuits, the employer could be freed from liability if he could show that the injury was the fault of the worker or of another employee. Workmen's compensation is based on the theory that whatever the cause, workers cannot bear the financial burden of a lawsuit and that insurance is to be carried as a regular cost of production. Workmen's compensation laws have reduced hardship and have sustained families who might otherwise have to seek welfare aid.

IMPORTANT AGENCIES

Department of Labor   A major Department of Cabinet status that administers laws designed to promote the welfare of wage earners through improved working conditions and employment opportunities. The Department, established in 1913, is headed by the Secretary of Labor and is divided into four major operational units: (1) Manpower Administration, which appraises national manpower requirements to deal with unemployment, underemployment, the impact of automation, apprenticeship training, and aspects of the war on poverty, and administers the unemployment compensation program and the United States Employment Service; (2) Labor-Management Relations, which administers laws relating to welfare and pension plans, enforces the Labor-Management Reporting and Disclosure Act relative to internal affairs of labor unions, provides a wide variety of industrial relations services, and administers wage and hour laws; (3) International Affairs, which considers the effect of American labor problems on foreign policy and is responsible for American participation in the International Labor Organization; and (5) Labor Standards, which seeks to improve working conditions with special attention to industrial safety and health and the needs of women and children.

Significance   The Department of Labor was established to give labor a direct voice at the highest level of government to accord it equal political status with agriculture and business. Increased federal labor legislation and growing American international economic involvement have strengthened the influence and stature of the Department in meeting national and international problems related to labor and the economy in general.

Federal Mediation and Conciliation Service   An agency formerly within the Department of Labor but given independent status under the Taft-Hartley Act of 1947. The Service is headed by a director appointed by the President with the Senate's consent. The Service has no law-enforcement authority but relies upon persuasion to prevent strikes that will impede the free flow of interstate commerce. Professional mediators employed by the Service assist in the settlement of labor-management disputes and try to promote good relations between labor and management. The Taft-Hartley Act requires that employers and unions must file notice of any dispute not settled thirty days after either side has expressed an intention to terminate an existing contract. The Mediation and Conciliation Service then tries to conciliate the dispute, but neither side is compelled to accept the solution suggested by the Service. The Service may also offer to enter a dispute on its own motion or at the request of parties. The Service often helps in the selection of arbitrators when both sides accept arbitration.
     Significance   The Federal Mediation and Conciliation Service reflects government policy to prevent the disruptive influence of strikes whenever possible. The Service has been highly successful in carrying on its functions because of the high prestige of its employees and its independent status in the government organization.

National Labor Relations Board (NLRB)   An independent regulatory commission, established in 1935, which administers the Wagner Act and the Taft-Hartley Act relative to unfair labor practices and the designation of appropriate bargaining units. The NLRB consists of five members appointed by the President, with the Senate's consent, for five-year terms, and a General Counsel similarly appointed for a four-year term. The Board is authorized to issue cease and desist orders, to hold bargaining representative elections, and to seek court injunctions and other enforcement orders. The General Counsel conducts investigations, issues complaints, and conducts prosecutions before the Board. Actual hearings are held by trial examiners with final orders issuing from the Board. *See NLRB v. Jones and Laughlin Steel Corp.,* page 288.
     Significance   The NLRB, like other independent regulatory commissions, reflects the policy of utilizing an independent agency to perform quasi-legislative and quasi-judicial functions in important sectors of the economy. The NLRB has played a crucial role in the development of broad policies as well as specific rules to meet the complicated problems posed by the growth of labor unions and the increasing problems of labor-management relations in an industrial society.

National Mediation Board   An independent agency established in 1934, under an amendment to the Railway Labor Act of 1926, to mediate differences between management and labor in the railroad and airline fields and to determine bargaining representatives. The Board consists of three members appointed by the President with the Senate's consent. For the settlement of disputes growing out of the application of collective bargaining contracts, the National Railroad Adjustment Board, consisting of representatives of the unions and the carriers, is called into action. In the event of deadlocks in the Adjustment Board, the National Mediation Board appoints a referee. Parties may appeal to the courts for enforcement of any settlements reached through this procedure. If the dispute does not involve a collective bargaining agreement, and the National Mediation Board cannot effect a solution, the law authorizes the President to appoint a special fact-finding board and, if this fails, the President may place the carrier under government operation.

Significance   The National Mediation Board and the related procedures are designed to prevent strikes and lockouts in the crucial areas of rail and air transport. With occasional lapses, these procedures have proved effective and work stoppages in these fields are relatively rare. Every effort is made to avoid government-imposed solutions and to help the parties reach agreement.

IMPORTANT CASES

NLRB v. Jones and Laughlin Steel Corp., 301 U.S. 1 (1937): Upheld the National Labor Relations Act of 1935, which guarantees labor the right to organize and bargain collectively and establishes the National Labor Relations Board to regulate labor-management relations. The Act was upheld as a valid exercise of Congress' power to regulate interstate commerce.

Significance   The *NLRB* case reflected a major shift in attitude by the Supreme Court toward New Deal regulatory legislation. The Court asserted the right of Congress to regulate activities having "a close and substantial relation to interstate commerce" and to prevent strikes and other industrial disputes that might burden or obstruct the free flow of commerce. In its decision, the Court took a broad view of the power of Congress to meet the challenges of an industrial society. The case was a turning point for the American labor movement, and has been followed by extensive involvement by the national government in labor-management relations.

United States v. Darby Lumber Co., 312 U.S. 100 (1941): Upheld the Fair Labor Standards Act of 1938, which imposes wage-and-hour regulations upon businesses engaged in or producing goods for interstate commerce and places restrictions upon the use of child labor.

Significance   The *Darby* decision climaxed many years of national efforts to regulate wages, hours, and other conditions of employment in the face of hostile judicial decisions. The *Darby* case specifically overruled *Hammer v. Dagenhart,* 247 U.S. 251 (1918), in which the Supreme Court held unconstitutional a statute which barred goods made by child labor from interstate commerce. In the *Darby* case the Court repudiated long-held notions that Congress could not regulate production or control wages and hours. The decision virtually put an end to legal challenges to the power of Congress to regulate aspects of business which directly or indirectly affect interstate commerce. The decision also made it unnecessary to secure ratification of the proposed child labor amendment to the Constitution.

West Coast Hotel Co. v. Parrish, 300 U.S. 379 (1937): Supported a minimum wage law of the state of Washington. The Court held that a minimum wage law did not violate freedom of contract under the due process clause of the Fourteenth Amendment.

Significance   The *Parrish* case put an end to the use by the Court of the due process clause of the Fourteenth Amendment to restrict state regulation of working conditions. It specifically overruled *Adkins v. Children's Hospital,* 261 U.S. 525 (1923), in which the Court had struck down a federal law establishing minimum wages for women in the District of Columbia. In the *Parrish* case, the Court rejected the notion that wages were beyond legislative control. It also rejected the concept of freedom of contract, which the Court had in earlier decisions injected into the due process clause. Such regulation was upheld as a valid exercise of the police power in the interest of protecting the health, safety, morals, and welfare of the people.

IMPORTANT STATUTES

Fair Labor Standards Act of 1938   An act establishing minimum wages and maximum hours for employees engaged in interstate commerce and outlawing the use of child labor. An eight-hour day at $1.60 per hour is established as the basic requirement, with time and a half for work exceeding forty hours a week. Persons not engaged in interstate commerce are not covered unless state laws make similar provisions. Certain types of work are exempted from coverage, but Congress has progressively increased coverage over the years. *See United States v. Darby Lumber Co.,* page 288.

Significance   The Fair Labor Standards Act was designed to eliminate substandard working conditions and to minimize competition among the states which might be inclined to have lower standards in order to attract industry. The Act has also been successful in eradicating the worst aspects of child labor. Responsibility for enforcement of the Act is lodged in the Wage-and-Hour and Public Contracts Division of the Department of Labor. Earlier, in 1936, Congress passed the Walsh-Healey Act, which establishes minimum wages, maximum hours, and outlaws child labor for persons working on federal contracts. The Fair Labor Standards Act was patterned on the Walsh-Healey Act, but has broader coverage. The Equal Pay Act of 1963, an amendment to the Fair Labor Standards Act, requires employers to pay equal wages to men and women doing equal work.

Landrum-Griffin Act (Labor-Management Reporting and Disclosure Act of 1959)   Informally known as the Labor Reform Act of 1959, this law strengthens the Taft-Hartley Act's restrictions upon internal procedures of labor unions and provides a "bill of rights" for members of labor unions. The Act requires detailed reports to the Secretary of Labor on union finances and the operations of union constitutions and by-laws, and it makes misuse of union funds a federal crime. Ex-convicts, Communists, and labor officials with conflicting business interests are barred from holding union office. The "bill of rights" provisions secure the secret ballot in union elections, freedom of speech in union meetings, hearings in disciplinary cases, the right of members to sue the union for unfair practices, and authorize member access to union records.

Significance   The Landrum-Griffin Act was a direct result of investigations by the Senate Rackets Committee that revealed a variety of corrupt practices by some labor leaders. The Act is designed to protect the integrity of law-abiding labor unions as well as the rights of individual members. The provision barring Communists from union offices was declared unconstitutional as a bill of attainder (*United States v. Brown* 381 U.S. 437 [1965]). Both the Taft-Hartley Act and the Landrum-Griffin Act reflect a change in governmental policy since the Wagner Act of 1935, from promotion of labor interests to regulation of unions.

Norris-LaGuardia Act of 1932   An act that outlawed "yellow-dog" contracts by which workers agreed not to join unions, and limited the use of the injunction in labor disputes.

Significance   The Norris-LaGuardia Act was one of the first pieces of pro-labor legislation. Its main purpose was to free labor from two major weapons used against it and to enable labor unions to pursue lawful goals. The Act was instrumental in providing the climate in which labor could develop as an economic power. It led to the passage of the Wagner Act in 1935, which guaranteed the right of labor to organize and bargain collectively.

Taft-Hartley Act (Labor-Management Relations Act of 1947)   A major revision of the Wagner Act of 1935 that seeks to equalize the power of employers and labor unions. The Act places limitations upon labor union practices, regulates certain internal arrangements of unions, and strengthens the position of the individual worker. Provisions of the Wagner Act relative to unfair practices by employers against unions are retained. Among the major limitations placed upon unions by the Taft-Hartley Act are those outlawing the closed shop (but permitting the union shop), jurisdictional strikes, secondary boycotts, political expenditures, and excessive dues. The Act also permits unions and employers to sue each other for contract violations and provides for the use of the injunction and other "cooling-off" procedures in strikes that threaten the national welfare. Internal affairs of unions are regulated by requiring them to file reports on the use of union funds and organizational procedures. The National Labor Relations Board (NLRB) was increased from three to five members and the office of General Counsel was established to investigate and prosecute unfair labor charges.

Significance   The Taft-Hartley Act was a reaction to growing union strength, to allegations that the Wagner Act and the NLRB favored unions over employers, and to revelations of communism and corruption in some unions. The Act was passed over the veto of President Harry Truman and has been a major political issue since its enactment. Many observers are fearful of the extent to which the Act involves the government in labor-management relations and restricts the range of free collective bargaining for both labor and management. Many states have passed "little Taft-Hartley" acts. Nineteen states, under section 14 (b) of the Act, have passed "right to work" laws which have further limited the power of unions by curtailing the union shop. Both the national and state laws gave great impetus to the merger of the AFL-CIO in 1955, and have intensified the political activity of organized labor.

Wagner Act (National Labor Relations Act of 1935)   A major enactment of the New Deal period that guarantees the right of labor to organize and bargain collectively through representatives of its own choosing. The Act established the National Labor Relations Board (NLRB) to administer the Act. The Board is authorized to issue cease and desist orders to employers who commit unfair labor practices as defined by the law and to certify bargaining representatives for unions. *See NLRB v. Jones and Laughlin Steel Corp.,* page 288.

Significance   The Wagner Act was a boon to the American labor movement. Until the year 1947, when it was amended by the Taft-Hartley Act, union membership grew from four to fifteen million and the overwhelming majority of manufacturing plants were covered by union contracts. This growth was accompanied by increased economic and political power for unions. Criticism of the Act as being too one-sided in favor of organized labor, and discriminatory against employers and individual workers, led to the passage of the Taft-Hartley Act in 1947. Nevertheless, the Wagner Act has significantly altered labor-management relations in the United States. "Little Wagner" acts were also passed in many states to cover workers not engaged in interstate commerce. The underlying purposes of the law—to foster and protect the right of collective bargaining—remains basic to public policy in the labor field.

Fourteen

Agriculture and Natural Resources

Colorado River Compact   An interstate agreement concluded among seven states concerning their respective rights to the waters of the Colorado River and its tributaries. The Colorado River Compact was concluded in 1922 after years of negotiation and was approved by Congress in 1927. Parties to the compact are Arizona, California, Colorado, Nevada, New Mexico, Utah, and Wyoming. *See* WATER CONSERVATION, page 297.

Significance   The Colorado River Compact sought to alleviate a long-standing disagreement over the use of the Colorado River waters, permitted Los Angeles to draw an essential water supply from 300 miles to the east, and laid the groundwork for the building of the first huge reclamation dam, the Hoover Dam, by the national government. Droughts and rapidly expanding populations, especially in Arizona and California, have led to greatly increased demands for water, involving compact states in continuing legal disputes over the use of the Colorado River.

Columbia River Compact   An interstate agreement concluded in 1925 among four states—Idaho, Montana, Oregon, and Washington—concerning their respective rights to the waters of the Columbia River and its tributaries. *See* WATER CONSERVATION, page 297.

Significance   The Columbia River Compact helped lead to the construction of the huge, multipurpose Grand Coulee and Bonneville Dams by the national government. Programs of great benefit to the four compact states have been cooperatively developed, including flood control, reclamation, power production, improved navigation, and the conservation of the famed Columbia River salmon.

Conservation   The careful management and wise use of natural resources to prevent depletion and to maximize the production of wealth from their use. Conservation involves the protection, preservation, and replenishment as well as the planned use of land, forests, wildlife, minerals, and water by private individuals and national, state, and local governments. *See* SOIL CONSERVATION, page 296; WATER CONSERVATION, page 297; DEPARTMENT OF THE INTERIOR, page 298.

Significance   Conservation was recognized as a new problem area around the turn of the century. Apprehension over the squandering of the nation's natural wealth plus the crusading zeal of President Theodore Roosevelt led to the first conservation programs by the national government in the vast areas of the public domain. These were followed by state efforts, cooperative nation-state programs, and educational and publicly financed efforts in privately owned areas. The major impetus behind the conservation program remains with the national government, although some states have developed extensive programs covering water resources, mineral production, reclamation and irrigation, forest protection and reforestation, and protection of wildlife. Conservation has increasingly come to mean not only the preservation of existing natural wealth, but the planned use of resources to increase wealth and to turn unproductive areas into productive natural assets. Major conservation programs of the national government are carried on by the Departments of Agriculture and the Interior, and conservation and agricultural departments in state governments have primary responsibility for implementing state programs.

County Agent   The local official charged with promoting agriculture under the federal, state, and county cooperative extension program. The Smith-Lever Act of 1914 created the modern extension service under which the county agent program was developed.

Significance   County agents seek to improve agriculture by encouraging farmers to adopt new methods developed in laboratories and in agricultural research centers. They try to reach the ordinary farmer through advice, demonstrations, and exhibits, and the great increase in farm productivity testifies to their success over the years. The county agent has also been an important factor in many states in the development of the American Farm Bureau Federation, a leading farmers' organization. Although the early integration of the county agent system with the Farm Bureau has been ended, the county agent continues to work closely with the organization in some states.

Ever-normal Granary   The concept behind the national government's farm programs since 1938 that aims at securing a stable supply of, and stable prices for farm products through governmental action. The ever-normal granary system provides for accumulation of reserves of basic farm products by the government during periods of oversupply as a means of maintaining price levels. During droughts or other times of short supply, when prices rise above support levels, the government reverses the process by selling from its granaries to meet market demand and to stabilize price levels. *See* PRICE SUPPORT, page 294.

Significance   The ever-normal granary system seeks to maintain some semblance of equilibrium between supply and demand for basic farm products, while maintaining most of the traditional freedom of the farm economy. In the years since 1938, however, generally good weather, parity price support incentives and, especially, the scientific revolution in farm technology, all contributed to surplus production and resulted in huge accumulations of government owned farm products. Over the years, the government has been able to dispose of much of its granary holdings through domestic relief programs, the foreign aid Food For Peace (Public Law 480) program, and increasing demand in the domestic and foreign markets. Acreage controls with direct subsidies to individual farmers have also helped by reducing annual surpluses.

Farm Organizations   Groups organized to promote the interests of the farmer. The oldest and most conservative farmers' organization is the National Grange, which was most effective after the Civil War and now has most of its membership in the New England and Middle Atlantic States. The most powerful and energetic spokesman for the farmers' interest is the American Farm Bureau Federation, which represents all types of farmers throughout the country. The Farm Bureau, now a private organization, grew out of the promotional activities of county agents sponsored by the Department of Agriculture through the agricultural extension services. A third major group is the National Farmer's Union, representing the less prosperous farmers. The newest group is the National Farmer's Organization, which seeks to emulate the strike techniques of labor unions by having farmers withhold products from the marketplace to drive prices up rather than depend upon governmental subsidies. *See* PRESSURE GROUP, page 114.

Significance   Farm organizations have long been a political force, strengthened by rural overrepresentation in legislative bodies. The Farm Bureau and the National Farmer's Union represent the major differences among farmers today. While both support governmental research, extension services, and credit facilities for farmers, the Farm Bureau emphasizes free enterprise while the Farmer's Union supports production controls and subsidies. The declining number of farms and farmers in the United States and the trend toward urban dominance of legislatures pose threats to the continued success of farmers' organizations.

Parity   A governmental price policy designed to maintain a level of purchasing power for farmers equal to that of a previous base period that was favorable to agriculture. This means, for example, that if in 1910 a farmer was able to sell ten bushels of wheat and buy a bicycle with the receipts, at full parity today he should be able to work out the same exchange. Parity-support price levels are determined by Congress, and actual parity prices for specific crops are determined each year by the Department of Agriculture. *See* PRICE SUPPORT, page 294.

Significance   The concept of parity has become a significant part of the national government's farm program. It recognizes that the agricultural sector of the economy is basic to the well-being of the rest of the nation's economy, and any serious imbalance might result in a serious slump for the entire economy. Parity does not provide a maximum price, only a minimum, which has often been exceeded on the free market in recent years. Governmental price support programs have generally ranged from sixty to ninety percent of parity, depending upon the supply of each basic crop.

Price Support   A program of the national government to help stabilize agricultural prices near parity by buying up market surpluses. Price supports, which have been used since 1933, are accompanied by production controls. The Commodity Credit Corporation (CCC) and the Agricultural Stabilization and Conservation Service (ASCS) administer the price support program through outright purchases and, more commonly, by granting loans to farmers, their stored crops being the collateral. The individual farmer can, in effect, turn the loan into a government purchase of his crop by simply not paying it off. If, however, the market price of the commodity goes above support level, he may pay off his loan, redeem his stored crop, and sell it on the free market. *See* EVER-NORMAL GRANARY, page 293; PARITY, page 294; AGRICULTURAL ADJUSTMENT ACTS, page 300; *Mulford v. Smith,* page 299.

Significance   Important commodities that have come under the price support program include corn, cotton, rice, tobacco, wheat, wool, and milk. The price support program recognizes the significance of agriculture and demonstrates the extent of agriculture's power in national politics and the farm bloc in Congress. The basic problem of agriculture is to bring the supply of farm products into line with the demand for them. As a result of a technological revolution in farming methods in the 1950s and 1960s, productivity has increased to the point where the national government has a huge amount of farm surpluses valued at billions of dollars, with annual storage costs running into hundreds of millions of dollars. Various domestic and foreign disposal programs have helped diminish the size of the government's surpluses in the 1960s. In addition, price supports have been sharply cut and replaced by cash subsidies to farmers so as to keep American crops competitive.

Public Domain   Public lands owned by the United States government. The public domain consists of national parks and forests, grazing districts, Indian reservations, and miscellaneous holdings. The Bureau of Land Management in the Department of the Interior has custody over a large portion of the public domain. *See* HOMESTEAD ACT, page 301.

Significance   Most of the land area of the United States today, with the exception of the thirteen original states and Texas, was once under the proprietorship of the national government. Through many programs, including homesteads, state grants, sales, grants to railroads, aids to education, and grants to soldiers and sailors, the national government has divested itself of most of its public lands. The public domain now comprises approximately 412 million acres, about twenty percent of the nation's total land area. Most of these public lands are found in eleven Western states, in six of which more than half of the state's lands are held by the national government. In the state of Alaska, ninety-nine percent of the land remains part of the public domain. Considerable political controversy in recent years has concerned the leasing of vast areas of the public domain for exploitation by private parties.

Public Power   The production of electrical energy by government-built and operated dams and power plants. Millions of kilowatts are produced and sold by the national government, especially from generating plants on the Colorado, Columbia, and Tennessee rivers. Public power production has become one of the major functions of the huge governmental dams, along with reclamation, irrigation, navigation, and flood control. Many cities and towns also produce and sell public power. *See* TENNESSEE VALLEY AUTHORITY, page 298; *Ashwander v. TVA*, page 299.

Significance   Public power development by the national and local governments was negligible until the depression years of the 1930s. The case for public power is based on the multipurpose nature of governmental dams, and on the claims that water power is a public resource and should not be used for private gain, and that public power is necessary to build up underdeveloped regions. The case against public power holds that it is dangerous to free enterprise, that government facilities do not pay taxes or dividends, that the taxpayers of the entire nation subsidize the people of the regions with public power, and that where multipurpose governmental dams are necessary, a partnership should be worked out with private business for buying wholesale power and selling it to the consumers. Over four-fifths of the electricity used in the United States is produced by private companies.

Rural Electrification   The governmental program to bring electric service and telephone lines to rural people not serviced by private enterprise. The Roosevelt Administration initiated the electrification program in 1935 with the establishment of the Rural Electrification Administration (REA) by executive order. The telephone program was added by Congress in 1949.

Significance   The REA has encouraged rural electrification by making low-interest loans to farmer cooperatives and local governments to build transmission lines, and to private electrical companies engaged in wiring individual farms. When the program started, only ten percent of the nation's farms were electrified, whereas, today, almost all farms have light and power, and most have telephone service. Critics of the REA charge that the rural electrification and telephone program involves a considerable subsidy by the nation's taxpayers because of the low-interest loans, the high administrative costs, and tax exemptions to cooperatives. Supporters of the REA program defend it on the ground that private enterprise has refused to bring electrical services to the farmers because of the lack of profit possibilities, and they note that the improvement of farm conditions benefits the entire nation.

Soil Conservation   A cooperative program of the national government, states, local units, and individual farmers to preserve valuable top soil from being washed or blown away through erosion and dust storms. Primary responsibility for carrying out soil conservation programs is vested in the Soil Conservation Service of the Department of Agriculture.

Significance   Although government can spark soil conservation programs and provide some financing, their effectiveness depends almost wholly upon the efforts of individual farmers. Soil-conserving methods include proper drainage, crop rotation, terracing, contour plowing, and strip cropping. The national government has provided an incentive for individual farmers to cooperate by requiring all farmers participating in price support subsidy programs to use soil conservation methods. Current national programs seek to improve soil conservation and reduce agricultural surpluses by paying farmers to retire overworked cropland by planting soil-conserving grasses and trees.

Water Conservation   The planned use and protection of water resources. Water conservation programs include promoting the navigability of streams, flood control, irrigation, river basin development, pollution control, recreation, reclamation, hydroelectric power, and the use of water for home and industrial consumption. *See* COLORADO RIVER COMPACT, page 292; COLUMBIA RIVER COMPACT, page 292; CORPS OF ENGINEERS, page 297.

Significance   The Bureau of Reclamation of the Department of the Interior, the Soil Conservation Service of the Department of Agriculture, and the United States Army Corps of Engineers play significant and sometimes competing roles in developing the nation's water resources. Pollution control is carried on through federal and state programs, and through interstate agreements on waterways that flow through several states. The most pressing problem for the future is that of providing adequate supplies of fresh water for human consumption and industrial use. President John F. Kennedy initiated a program to develop practical means for converting salt water from the oceans into fresh water, a program since expanded and accelerated by the Johnson Administration.

IMPORTANT AGENCIES

Corps of Engineers   A branch of the United States Army charged with planning and constructing public works on navigable waterways. The Engineers construct dams and power-generating facilities on many major rivers and develop extensive flood-control projects.

Significance   The construction of governmental dams and other public projects involving multipurpose river development have often produced jurisdictional battles among the Corps of Engineers, the Department of Agriculture, the Department of the Interior, and advocates of valley authorities like the TVA. The Corps of Engineers with strong congressional support has been able to maintain its position as a major agency in the development of river programs.

Department of Agriculture   A major department of the national government that provides numerous services for farmers and regulates various aspects of agriculture and related fields in the interest of farmers and the general public. The Secretary who heads the Department is appointed by the President with the Senate's approval and serves as a member of the Cabinet. A variety of activities are carried on by the Department's major operational units: (1) The Agricultural Research Service conducts research in crop and livestock production and marketing. (2) The Federal Extension Service works cooperatively with land-grant colleges and county agents to provide research information to farmers. (3) The Forest Service protects the national forests from fire and disease. (4) The Soil Conservation Service conserves soil resources through programs of research, erosion control, reforestation, and flood control. (5) The Commodity Exchange Authority supervises trading on commodity exchanges where agricultural products are bought and sold. (6) The Commodity Credit Corporation and the Agricultural Stabilization and Conservation Service are responsible for the stabilization of agricultural prices. (7) The Federal Crop

Insurance Corporation insures farmers against loss or damage to their crops. (8) The Farmers Home Administration makes low-interest loans to low-income farmers to improve their crops or facilities. (9) The Rural Electrification Administration makes loans to finance the extension of electric power and telephone service to rural areas.

Significance   The farm economy is undergoing a scientific revolution in production resulting in huge surpluses, low prices for farm products, and an increasing need for governmental assistance. The Department of Agriculture is primarily concerned with maintaining stability in the farm economy, expanding agricultural markets, and controlling agricultural surpluses. Some critics point out that the Department is largely responsible for the great increases in productivity through its laboratory, experimental farm, and county-agent programs. Others have noted that with the population explosion in the United States and in the entire world, new agricultural technologies are essential.

Department of the Interior   A major department of the national government that has responsibility over a variety of affairs concerning the territories and properties of the United States. The Secretary who heads the Department is appointed by the President with the Senate's approval and serves as a member of the Cabinet. Some of the major operating units found in the Interior Department are the: (1) Fish and Wildlife Service, which improves commercial fishing, and hunting and fishing for sport through research and conservation programs; (2) Bureau of Mines, which promotes health and safety in privately owned mines and compiles statistics on mine operations; (3) Geological Survey, which surveys and classifies public lands and conducts geologic research; (4) Bureau of Indian Affairs which promotes health, welfare, and educational facilities for Indians; (5) Bureau of Land Management, which supervises the exploitation of natural resources of the public domain by private companies; (6) National Park Service, which develops and administers natural beauty spots and historic sites for the enjoyment of the American people; (7) Bureau of Outdoor Recreation, which maintains a continuing inventory and evaluation of recreational needs and resources; (8) Office of Territories, which promotes the economic, social, and political development of the peoples of overseas territories; (9) Bureau of Reclamation, which constructs and operates public facilities to generate electric power, promote flood control, and provide irrigation; and (10) Bonneville, Southeastern, and Southwestern Power Administrations, which market electric power generated by national dams and power stations in different sections of the country.

Significance   Most of the agencies in the Department of the Interior are concerned with conservation. Conservation as practiced by the Department means not only the preservation of land, water, forests, natural resources, and wildlife, but their wise and systematic use as well. Not only is the Department the custodian of the nation's natural resources, but its jurisdiction extends to islands in the Caribbean and South Pacific and to lands within the Arctic Circle.

Tennessee Valley Authority (TVA)   A major corporation of the national government established by Congress in 1933 to provide for the development of the Tennessee River and its tributaries. The TVA has responsibility for the generation, transmission, and sale of electric power, flood control, improvement of navigation, production of fertilizers, reforestation, reclamation, and soil conservation. The TVA operates under a board of three directors appointed by the President with the Senate's approval. Its operations cover an area of over 40,000 square miles in the states of Alabama, Georgia, Kentucky, Mississippi, North Carolina, Tennessee, and Virginia. Development projects are financed through the issuance of bonds by the Authority and through the sale of electric power to private companies. *See Ashwander v. TVA*, page 299.

Significance   The TVA is an outstanding example of regional development fostered by a single, independent government corporation. Almost thirty major dams have been constructed and others are planned. The flood-prone Tennessee River has been tamed. Navigation and farming have been improved and the cheap power supplied by the TVA has encouraged the industrial development of the entire region. The TVA is also a principal source of electric power for the national atomic energy and space programs. All essential features of the program have been sustained by the Supreme Court. Yet, in spite of its success, opposition remains. Many businessmen oppose the TVA as unfair, subsidized governmental competition with private power companies. It is often charged with being another step toward national planning and socialism. Some critics in other parts of the country oppose the use of government tax money to subsidize the people of a single region with cheap power. Much opposition has resulted from the attraction of industry away from other sections of the country to the Tennessee Valley. Private power companies operating in the area oppose the use of TVA rates as a "yardstick" to measure the fairness of the rates which they charge consumers. Despite the political controversy over TVA, several additional valley authorities have been proposed, including a Missouri Valley and a Columbia Valley authority, but none has received congressional approval.

IMPORTANT CASES

Ashwander v. TVA, 297 U.S. 288 (1936): Upheld the construction of major dams by an agency of the national government under the war and commerce powers, and upheld the authority of such an agency to build transmission lines and to sell electrical energy generated at the dams. The Court held that Congress could properly build huge dams if needed for national defense and to improve navigation, and that it could, under the Constitution, dispose of property belonging to the United States.

Significance   The *Ashwander* decision sustained the legal basis for the vast complex of the TVA and its multipurpose program. The case emphasizes the broad application of the commerce clause and the domestic implications resulting from a liberal interpretation of the war power.

Mulford v. Smith, 307 U.S. 38 (1939): Sustained the constitutionality of the Agriculture Act of 1938, holding that Congress may limit the amount of a crop sold in interstate commerce, and that the delegation of powers to the Secretary of Agriculture by Congress was proper since definite standards were laid down in the Act. It also held that Congress may validly exercise its power to regulate interstate commerce through a regulatory tax.

Significance   The *Mulford* case sanctioned the attempts by Congress and the Department of Agriculture to provide a more orderly marketing system for the basic crops of cotton, wheat, corn, tobacco, and rice. National government procedures involved under the Act include loans, marketing quotas, storage of crop reserves, and the parity concept aimed at securing fair prices for farmers. This case had the effect of overruling the Supreme Court's earlier decision in *United States v. Butler,* 297 U.S. 1 (1936), in which it held that national regulation of farm prices invaded the reserved powers of the states. Since the *Mulford* decision, the national government's handling of the farm problem has involved primarily political and economic rather than legal problems.

IMPORTANT STATUTES

Agricultural Act of 1965   An approach to the farm problem that combines low support prices with income supplements for farmers. The objective of the program is to achieve lower market prices so that output will be controlled and exports increased. A long-term land retirement program to reduce surpluses is included.

Significance   The Agricultural Act of 1965 seeks to reduce governmental subsidies progressively and to build better market demand on the lower prices that result. The Food for Peace (Public Law 480) program of selling American surpluses for foreign currencies is supplemented under the Act, with provisions for building the dollar-trade in agricultural sales abroad. Although the number of farmers in the United States in the decade 1955–1965 decreased from 3.7 million to 2.2 million, the amount of subsidies granted increased from less than $1 billion to more than $3 billion during the same period.

Agricultural Adjustment Acts of 1933, 1938   Broad agricultural programs sponsored by the Roosevelt Administration and enacted by Congress to maintain farm income through parity price supports and production controls for basic crops. After the first Agricultural Adjustment Act (AAA) had been declared unconstitutional by the Supreme Court in *United States v. Butler,* 297 U.S. 1 (1936), a second AAA, containing much of the first program but eliminating or modifying those sections that had failed the constitutionality test, was adopted in 1938. The 1933 Act was held to be an invalid use of the taxing power, whereas the 1938 Act was upheld as a valid exercise of the commerce power (*Mulford v. Smith,* 307 U.S. 38 [1939]). *See Mulford v. Smith,* page 299.

Significance   Most of the procedures for aiding agriculture that were initiated in these two AAA programs remain the basic approach used by the national government today. Features continued today include direct governmental payments to individual farmers for reducing acreage for soil conservation purposes, governmental loans on surplus crops when overproduction drives prices down, support of farm crop prices at a parity level, and establishment of acreage allotments and marketing quotas on basic crops when farmers choose them through a two-thirds majority vote in a national referendum.

Homestead Act of 1862   An historic act in which Congress offered 160 acres of the public domain to any person who would pay a $10 registration fee and live on the land for five years.

Significance   The Homestead Act opened up the vast areas of the public domain in the Midwest and West to farming. Millions of acres were parceled out to pioneering "homesteaders," and by 1910 restrictions had to be imposed to keep some governmental lands under public ownership. The Homestead Act contributed greatly to the growing strength of the nation by opening the West and encouraging land and home ownership.

Fifteen

Health, Education, and Welfare

Aid to Dependent Children   Financial aid provided under the categorical assistance program of the Social Security Act of 1935 for children who lack adequate support but are living with one parent or relative. Some provision also has been made for support of children in foster homes. The program is administered by the states with the assistance of federal funds and under regulations established by the national government. The program is supervised by the Bureau of Family Services of the Department of Health, Education, and Welfare.

Significance   The aid to dependent children program is designed to preserve a private home environment for children who otherwise would have to be put into orphanages, institutions, or foster homes. The program makes it possible for children to remain with a parent, grandparent, or other close relative and to receive the love and attention unavailable in even the best institutions.

Aid to the Blind   Financial aid given to the needy blind under the categorical assistance program of the Social Security Act. Payments are made by the states with funds provided by the states and the national government to persons whose eyesight deficiencies make it impossible for them to engage in normal work. The program is supervised by the Bureau of Family Services.

Significance   About one-third of the blind people in the United States are aided through this categorical aid program. Though the payments are not high, the blind are able to live outside of public institutions. The specific degree of eyesight deficiency which makes a person eligible for aid is determined by each state.

Aid to the Totally and Permanently Disabled   A program inaugurated in 1950 as part of the categorical aid program of the Social Security Act, which provides for financial aid to persons over eighteen whose physical condition makes it impossible to engage in gainful employment. The program is administered by the states with the assistance of federal funds under the supervision of the Bureau of Family Services.

Significance   As is true of the categorical aid programs which preceded it, the eligibility requirements for aid to the disabled are determined by each state. Most states have established broad categories of disability ranging from shut-ins to those with various disabilities who are unable to hold employment.

Categorical Assistance   Welfare programs provided under the Social Security Act. These programs include: (1) old age assistance, (2) aid to the blind, (3) aid to dependent children, and (4) aid to the totally and permanently disabled. Persons who fall within these categories and are in need of financial assistance may receive aid from their state from funds supplemented by federal grants. The programs also extend to the District of Columbia, Puerto Rico, Guam, and the Virgin Islands. *See* SOCIAL SECURITY ACT, page 313.

Significance   Categorical assistance establishes a continuing program of aid for major categories of destitute people. The states may establish their own requirements that individuals must meet to receive assistance, such as residence, conduct, and need. Categorical assistance has made it possible for many helpless people to continue living outside of public institutions. In former years, it was common for local governments to provide poorhouses or almshouses for the care of the needy. Congress requires that any state participating in the program must establish a state agency, staffed by the merit system, to conduct the program or to supervise local units which conduct the program. Persons denied aid must be given opportunity to appeal to the state supervisory agency.

Community Action Program   A "war on poverty" program created by the Economic Opportunity Act of 1964 to stimulate communities to mobilize their resources against poverty. Federal aid is given to local public and private agencies to undertake antipoverty programs that involve the poor themselves in operating the programs. Possible projects include literacy instruction, job training, vocational rehabilitation, homemaker services, job development and health services. *See* ECONOMIC OPPORTUNITY ACT, page 311.

Significance   The Community Action Program encourages public and private nonprofit agencies to engage in positive and varied programs to meet and, if possible, conquer the causes of poverty in the community. Many Community Action Programs have stimulated fresh approaches to the poverty problem other than direct handouts to the poor. Where, however, public agencies control the program, the danger exists that they may use it for political patronage, and concern has been voiced about the lack of sufficient involvement of poor people in the administration of community projects.

Federal Aid to Education   Various programs of federal grants-in-aid to the states for educational purposes. Such aid has taken the form of land grants for schools and colleges, grants for vocational education and vocational rehabilitation, school lunch programs, scholarship funds for science, mathematics and other programs in the interest of national defense, grants to veterans to attend school, and grants to areas with a heavy influx of students because of the establishment of a military base or other national facility. In recent years, numerous aids to higher education have been enacted by Congress, and, in 1965, the first general aid-to-education bill, providing substantial aid to elementary and secondary schools, was passed. *See* ELEMENTARY AND SECONDARY EDUCATION ACT, page 311; HIGHER EDUCATION ACT, page 312; NATIONAL DEFENSE EDUCATION ACT, page 313.

Significance   Much controversy has been engendered by general federal aid to education. Opponents point out that education has traditionally been a state and local concern, and that federal aid means federal supervision and control of the school system and curriculum. Supporters point to the wide variety of federal aids to education carried on over a long period of American history without undue federal interference. They claim that the states are in no position to finance the increasing need for better educational facilities. Deeply involved in the controversy is the issue relating to aid for parochial schools. Many persons oppose aid to religious institutions as a violation of the principle of separation of church and state. Others argue that all children should benefit from such aid, and, hence, no restriction should be placed on the type of school affected.

Indoor Relief   Care of the needy in public institutions. Indoor relief is usually provided for the aged, the chronically ill, and the mentally incompetent. Prior to 1935 and the passage of the Social Security Act, many poor but healthy persons were cared for in public almshouses, poorhouses, poor farms, asylums, county homes, or institutions of like names. Indoor relief has largely been replaced by "outdoor relief," which provides money, food, and medical care to persons who continue to live in their own homes. *See* OUTDOOR RELIEF, page 307.

Significance   Indoor relief is largely the responsibility of local governments. At one time, it was common practice to put all kinds of helpless people —dependent children, the blind, the aged, the sick—in the same institution. National and state programs now make separate provisions for many of these people under the categorical assistance program. Numerous public institutions are maintained, however, largely for the aged who are unable to care for themselves, and for other persons who cannot be provided for in private homes. Modern institutions now take the form of nursing homes, many of which are supported by local and state governments.

Job Corps   A program, authorized by the Economic Opportunity Act of 1964, that enables jobless youths from sixteen to twenty-one to work and study at training centers or in conservation camps. Emphasis is placed upon education, vocational training, and work experiences. The Job Corps is managed by the Office of Economic Opportunity, which contracts with local public and private agencies to establish training centers. *See* ECONOMIC OPPORTUNITY ACT, page 311.

Significance   The Job Corps is part of the Johnson Administration's "war on poverty." Its aim is to attack the causes rather than the effects of unemployment. Through the Job Corps program, it is hoped that school dropouts and underprivileged youth will become useful and productive citizens. While learning, Corpsmen receive living and travel allowances.

Land-grant College   An agricultural and mechanical college, or the agricultural and mechanical school of a state university, established under the provisions of the Morrill Act of 1862. The Morrill Act provided for the granting of land (amounting to nearly eleven million acres) by the national government to the states for the support of colleges to teach agriculture, engineering, and home economics. Since that time, Congress has continued to make money grants to these institutions, supplementing funds given by state and private agencies. Experimental stations for agriculture, and an extension service that carries education directly to the farmer in the rural areas, have also been established at land-grant colleges.

Significance   Most of the great state universities and agricultural colleges in the United States are a direct result of the land-grant policy. Congress did not exclude the teaching of other subjects from these schools and all of them provide education in the humanities and scientific fields. The agricultural and mechanical divisions, however, continue to receive special attention from Congress. The farmer has benefited most from the facilities made available through the land-grant college.

Maternal and Child Welfare Program   A feature of the Social Security Act of 1935 that provides for grants to the states for maternal and child health services, crippled children services, and general child welfare programs. Grants are made to the states not for payments to particular persons, as is true under the categorical aid programs, but for support of state welfare programs. Maternal and child health services include care of mothers before and after childbirth, and immunization of children against communicable diseases. Another program seeks to provide therapy and rehabilitation for crippled children whose parents lack independent means to care for them. Child welfare activities include counseling and care of neglected, mentally retarded, and emotionally disturbed youngsters, and care of delinquent children.

Significance   The maternal and child welfare program has had remarkable success in reducing infant and maternal mortality and has benefited thousands of crippled, neglected, and emotionally disturbed children. All states have established agencies to carry out these functions. Over-all administration is in the hands of the Children's Bureau of the Department of Health, Education, and Welfare.

Medicare   A health insurance program enacted in 1965 as an amendment to the Social Security Act to provide medical care for the elderly. Two health care programs are involved. One, which is compulsory and is financed by increases in the social security payroll tax, covers most hospital and nursing home costs, home health service visits, and diagnostic services for persons aged sixty-five or older. The second is a voluntary supplementary health program for persons over sixty-five, which covers a variety of health services both in and out of medical institutions and pays a substantial part of physician costs. The supplementary plan is financed by a small charge to the person enrolled and by an equal amount paid by the national government out of general revenue.

Significance   The passage of medicare in 1965 climaxed a twenty-year fight over what the American Medical Association and other opposition groups called "socialized medicine." The program recognizes that illness can quickly exhaust the resources of most families and that elderly persons, who suffer most health problems, cannot afford private health insurance. The medicare program represents a major step in social-welfare legislation, with social-insurance programs now covering most major hazards. In adopting the medicare program, the United States has followed the lead of most democratic states, some of which instituted public medical care programs in the nineteenth century.

Old-Age, Survivors, and Disability Insurance (OASDI)   An insurance program, commonly called "social security," administered by the national government under the provisions of the Social Security Act of 1935. Its major purposes are to provide a retirement income for elderly persons, income for workers who are totally disabled, and income for the widows and minor children of deceased wage earners. Specifically exempted from coverage are federal employees under the civil service retirement system, ministers (optional), state and local employees not authorized coverage by state law, and some persons whose incomes are not sufficient to qualify. All other persons are required to contribute a certain percent of their income that is matched by their employer. Self-employed persons also contribute. These contributions are credited to each worker's account and, upon death, retirement, or disablement, funds are provided in accordance with the formulas provided by law for each eventuality. Retirement usually takes place at the age of sixty-five, but one may retire at sixty-two with reduced benefits. Retired persons may continue to work but may have their benefits reduced if they earn more than $1500 a year. After the age of seventy-two, no limitations are placed on earnings. The program is administered directly by the Social Security Administration in the Department of Health, Education, and Welfare. *See* SOCIAL SECURITY CASES, page 311.

Significance   OASDI is a compulsory savings plan designed to meet the problems of an increasingly aging population. Modern health programs have contributed to a rapid increase in the number of persons over sixty-five. In addition, OASDI provides for the disabled and the families of deceased workers who would otherwise become public charges. Insurance has taken the place of public and private charity, and maintains the dignity of those who receive funds from the program. The program is a direct result of the depression of the 1930s, during which many people became destitute. Some persons object to the compulsory nature of the program and to the amounts spent on its administration. The program has, however, received the endorsement of both major parties and benefits and coverage have been regularly increased.

Old-age Assistance   Financial aid provided under the categorical assistance program of the Social Security Act for the needy aged who are not covered by the Old-Age, Survivors and Disability Insurance program. Old-age assistance is furnished through the states under grants-in-aid from the national government under supervision of the Bureau of Family Services. The program is in effect in all states, the amount granted to an individual varying with his need, the responsibility of relatives, and other requirements established under state laws.

Significance   Old-age assistance is designed to provide aid to those needy people who retired prior to the enactment of the Old-Age, Survivors and Disability Insurance program or whose occupations are not covered by the insurance program. Congress has extended the coverage of social security insurance to many more occupations in recent years. In future years, the need for the old-age assistance program should diminish considerably.

Outdoor Relief   Financial aid or food and medical care provided needy persons outside of public institutions. Outdoor relief programs are administered by state and local governments under a general relief program or with the aid of the national government under the categorical assistance program. *See* IN-DOOR RELIEF, page 304.

Significance   Outdoor relief is generally preferred to indoor relief unless the health or mental incompetence of an individual compels that he be placed under constant institutional care. Outdoor relief permits greater flexibility in administration and preserves the dignity of those in need of aid. One drawback of outdoor relief is that it may encourage persons to seek aid who, under the threat of having to go to a poorhouse, would make greater efforts to rehabilitate themselves. Yet, careful administration of the program can assure that only those in need are provided with aid. In this way, the needy can continue to maintain their homes and play a useful part in society.

Public Housing   Government construction and maintenance of dwellings for low-income families. Since 1937, and with increasing emphasis after 1949, the national government has given assistance to local governments to clear slum areas and to construct housing. Local governments need state authorization to participate in the program and the local community can reject public housing by referendum. A local housing authority must be established. It administers the funds provided by the federal government and floats bonds. Rentals are used to repay the federal loan and private bondholders. Rentals are kept very low and the federal government subsidizes the difference between costs and rental receipts. Only persons with limited incomes are eligible to occupy the housing. Some cities and states have undertaken their own public housing programs without federal aid. *See* HOUSING ACT, page 312.

Significance   The depression and World War II contributed to a housing shortage and continuing deterioration of slum areas. Rising costs have made it impossible for many low-income families to secure decent housing. Poor housing and slums increase delinquency, impair family ties, and are costly to the community in such things as welfare services and police and fire protection. Opponents of public housing object to the government competing with private industry. It is argued, too, that the availability of public housing discourages tenants to earn higher incomes since they may be forced to move if their income rises.

Unemployment Insurance   A program of insurance under the Social Security Act of 1935 that provides for payment of funds for a limited period of time to workers who are laid off or discharged for reasons beyond their control. The program is administered by the states under national supervision. Under the plan, Congress imposes a tax on the payroll of employers of four or more workers. Ninety percent of the revenue from this tax is credited to each state that comes under the act (all do), with the remainder used for administrative purposes. All proceeds of the tax are held by the national Department of the Treasury in separate state accounts to be paid out as needed by each state. Each state determines the amount to be paid to each unemployed person, for how long, and under what conditions. Generally, benefits amount to about $36 per week for twenty weeks and are provided to unemployed persons who register with the proper state agency and are willing to accept suitable employment. Most states penalize employers with poor employment records by raising their payroll tax. Over-all supervision of state plans is in the hands of the Bureau of Employment Security in the Department of Labor. *See Social Security Cases,* page 311.

Significance   Unemployment insurance, Medicare, and Old-Age, Survivors and Disability Insurance, comprise the major programs of social insurance in effect today. Unemployment insurance makes public relief unnecessary and preserves some purchasing power in the hands of the unemployed. Critics of the plan charge that it encourages laziness, and many oppose the compulsory nature of the plan. Supporters point out that unemployment tends to have a chain effect and that the loss of purchasing power endangers other jobs.

Urban Renewal   Programs conducted by cities to prevent the spread of urban blight, to rehabilitate areas that can be restored, and to clear and re- develop slum areas that are beyond repair. The Housing Act of 1949 and subsequent legislation provide for procedures by which cities can submit pro- grams to obtain federal aid. Aid is provided for planning and clearance pro- grams and for public housing. Federal mortgage insurance is made available to private investors in reconstruction and rehabilitation projects. *See* HOUSING ACT, page 312.

Significance   Urban renewal is designed to restore rapidly deteriorating cities and to make the city an attractive place in which to live and work. The growth of suburbia has cost cities a good deal in tax resources. Slum areas are a blight on a community and a drain on its financial resources. Suitable hous- ing is needed in most large cities to attract residents and to rehabilitate slum dwellers. Downtown areas need restoring to attract business concerns and customers. Industrial areas need to be developed to provide jobs. All of these problems, and the need to prevent future blight, are the underlying concerns of the urban-renewal program. It represents a major attempt on the part of the national government to gain the cooperation of both local governments and private capital to save the cities. Critics of the urban-renewal program charge that it uproots entire neighborhoods and deprives poor people of property in favor of investment capital, and that waste and politics mark the program.

Veterans Organizations   Groups organized to promote the interests of former members of the armed forces and their families. The largest and most influential group is the American Legion, with more than two million members, followed by the Veterans of Foreign Wars, with over a million members. Both organizations take firm stands on political issues and are basically conservative in outlook. The American Veterans Committee, with less than 30,000 mem- bers, supports liberal programs and generally opposes special benefits for veterans. Numerous other veterans organizations are based on religious, ethnic, specific war experiences, or military unit considerations. *See* PRESSURE GROUP, page 114.

Significance Veterans organizations have been successful at all levels of government in furthering the economic interests of veterans. Public benefits for veterans include bonuses and pensions, educational aids, civil service preference, loans and insurance, even burial allowances. With the heavy military involvement of the United States in the twentieth century, almost every American family has a veteran. Legislative bodies find it difficult to resist pressure from organized veteran groups. Veterans groups have been particularly active in promoting patriotism and military preparedness.

Vocational Rehabilitation The training of the physically and mentally handicapped for useful work. The national government provides grants-in-aid to the states for such programs under supervision of the Vocational Rehabilitation Administration in the Department of Health, Education, and Welfare. Another major program is in the hands of the Veterans Administration which cooperates with various state educational agencies for the training of handicapped veterans.

Significance Vocational rehabilitation is made available to any handicapped person who can become self-sufficient. If the person can pay for the service, he is required to do so, but those unable to pay are provided free training. The program has been expanded in recent years on the theory that it is better for the individual and for society to rehabilitate the handicapped than to provide a dole. The restored worker is not only able to sustain himself, but contributes taxes to the community as well.

Volunteers in Service to America (VISTA) A "domestic peace corps" established by the Economic Opportunity Act of 1964 to combat poverty in American communities. VISTA volunteers, paid only a subsistence allowance, work in community action programs, Job Corps and migrant-worker camps, Indian reservations, hospitals, and schools. *See* ECONOMIC OPPORTUNITY ACT, page 311.

Significance VISTA, patterned after the Peace Corps, offers opportunities for Americans to join the "war on poverty." Training programs for volunteers stress field experiences that contribute to program goals. The basic objective of VISTA is to raise the health and educational levels of poor people to eradicate the causes of poverty.

IMPORTANT AGENCIES

Department of Health, Education, and Welfare (HEW) A major department of the national government established in 1953 to unify administration of federal activities in the fields of health, education, and social security. The Department is headed by a Secretary who is a member of the Cabinet. Its major operating units include: (1) the Social Security Administration, which administers the Old-Age, Survivors and Disability Insurance, and the federal credit union programs; (2) the Welfare Administration, which includes the Children's Bureau and the Bureau of Family Services, which administers the categorical aid programs; (3) the Office of Education, which administers grants-in-aid for educational purposes; (4) the Public Health Service, which carries on far-flung programs in health and hospital care; (5) the Food and Drug Administration, which prevents misbranding and adulteration of food and drugs; and (6) the Vocational Rehabilitation Administration, which works with states to aid the physically and mentally handicapped.

Significance   The Department reflects the commitment of the national government to protect the public health and welfare through vast programs of social security, education, and disease prevention. Most of these programs, once highly controversial, are now accepted by both major political parties and by the American people.

Department of Housing and Urban Development (HUD)   A major department of Cabinet status, established in 1965, with responsibility for the housing, home finance, and community-development functions of the national government. The Department, headed by a Secretary, is organized into four major units: (1) Mortgage Credit and Federal Housing Commissioner, established by law as a separate unit within the department to administer programs related to the private mortgage market; (2) Renewal and Housing Assistance, responsible for urban renewal projects, rehabilitation loans, public housing, college housing, and programs for the elderly and handicapped; (3) Metropolitan Development, charged with metropolitan area planning for urban renewal, mass transport, water, sewer, schools and other urban problems; (4) Demonstrations and Intergovernmental Relations, established to plan demonstration low income housing and urban renewal projects and to serve as a clearinghouse for research and technical services for state and local problems.

Significance   Cabinet status for HUD climaxed years of effort to have the problems of metropolitan areas considered at the highest levels of government. It represents a national commitment to meet the growing crises in the highly urbanized areas of housing, urban renewal, and metropolitan planning. With more than seventy percent of the American people living in urban areas, HUD is likely to become an increasingly important center for governmental action programs.

Veterans Administration (VA)   An independent agency established in 1930 to coordinate the administration of various laws providing benefits for veterans and their dependents. Included are such programs as compensation for service or nonservice connected disabilities or death, vocational rehabilitation, education, home insurance, life insurance, hospitalization, care of disabled veterans, and burial of veterans. The agency is headed by an administrator appointed by the President with the Senate's consent.

Significance   The Veterans Administration's programs represent the aftercost of war. More than twenty million Americans are veterans and, if one includes their families, who are actual or potential beneficiaries, nearly one-half of the American people are concerned with the operations of this agency. Various suggestions to make the VA a part of a major department, such as Health, Education, and Welfare, have met resistance from veterans organizations which prefer the independent status of the VA.

IMPORTANT CASES

Social Security Cases: Two cases in which the Supreme Court upheld the Social Security Act of 1935. In *Steward Machine Co. v. Davis,* 301 U.S. 548 (1937), the Court upheld the unemployment insurance feature of the Act. The Court reasoned that the tax for relief of the unemployed was within the power of Congress to provide for the national welfare and that the states were not coerced to join the plan. In *Helvering v. Davis,* 301 U.S. 619 (1937), decided the same day, the Court upheld the Old-Age, Survivors and Disability Insurance provisions. The Court recognized the broad power of Congress to promote the general welfare and maintained that the scope of the general welfare was for Congress to determine. The Court denied that the tax on payrolls for Old-Age, Survivors and Disability Insurance benefited only a particular class of persons or invaded the powers of the states. *See* SOCIAL SECURITY ACT, page 313.

Significance   The Social Security Cases involved major interpretations of the general welfare clause of the Constitution. The decisions gave Congress an almost unlimited power to tax and spend for whatever purposes it deems necessary to promote the general welfare. These cases established the legal framework for the extensive system of social welfare measures carried on by the national government with the cooperation of state and local governments.

IMPORTANT STATUTES

Economic Opportunity Act of 1964   An act to help the poor become productive citizens through a "war on poverty." The Act places stress on education and training through such programs as the Job Corps, Neighborhood Youth Corps and work study programs. Community-action programs are encouraged under the Act to stimulate local action to meet the needs of low-income people. Loan programs are made available to farmers and small businessmen. VISTA (Volunteers in Service to America) has been established by the Act to aid in community welfare projects. Programs are administered by the Office of Economic Opportunity in the Executive Office of the President, the Department of Labor, and the Department of Health, Education and Welfare. *See* COMMUNITY ACTION PROGRAM, page 303; JOB CORPS, page 304; VISTA, page 309.

Significance   The Economic Opportunity Act is aimed at overcoming the causes of poverty by encouraging both community and individual programs of education and training for employment. While the Act provides for aid to older persons, stress is placed on programs for the young, including preschool children and college youth. Opponents of the "war on poverty" have criticized it for not involving sufficient numbers of low-income people and for its potential control by political machines. More basic criticism is aimed at the underlying purposes of the program and the enlarged role of the national government in meeting social and economic problems.

Elementary and Secondary Education Act of 1965   The first general federal aid-to-education law enacted by Congress. It provides federal aid to most of the nation's school districts. The Act authorizes aid on the basis of the number of children from low-income families in each district. It applies to both public and nonpublic schools. Other major provisions authorize grants for textbooks and library materials for all schools, educational centers to provide programs that individual schools cannot afford, and grants for improvement of educational research and administration.

Significance   The Elementary and Secondary Education Act of 1965 is a landmark in relations between the nation and the states, representing a commitment on the part of both to nation-wide equality of educational opportunity. Numerous, past efforts to enact such legislation failed because of fear of federal control of education, racial segregation in schools, and controversy over aid to nonpublic, church-related schools. Many opponents of federal aid were defeated in the Democratic landslide of 1964, the school segregation issue was no longer legally relevant, and the church-state issue was overcome by basing the school aid formula on benefiting low-income children rather than the parochial schools. Legal questions on federal aid to nonpublic schools, however, remain to be tested.

Higher Education Act of 1965   An act to broaden higher educational opportunities through federal aid. Major programs include scholarships, work-study programs, guaranteed low-interest loans, aid to developing colleges, aid to college and university community-service programs with emphasis on urban problems, aid for library resources, a National Teachers Corps to work in slum areas, and aid for fellowships for present and future teachers. In addition, the Act increases aid under the Higher Education Facilities Act of 1963, which authorized grants and loans for construction of public and private academic facilities.

Significance   The Higher Education Act of 1965 is a major extension of existing federal aids to higher education. A notable innovation provides scholarships for general undergraduate education. The Act's major purpose is to overcome rising costs of higher education for low- and middle-income families. Soaring enrollments in colleges and universities have strained the resources of most institutions of higher learning while the desire to secure a college education has become common in all classes of the population. The Higher Education Act, together with the Elementary and Secondary Education Act of 1965, commits the national government to extensive involvement in education from the preschool level through graduate education.

Housing Act of 1949   An act providing for federal assistance to local governments for low-rent public housing, slum clearance, and urban renewal. The Housing Act of 1949 continued a program, begun under the Housing Act of 1937, that had been interrupted by World War II. The 1949 Act called for the construction of 810,000 housing units over a period of six years but Congress reduced this figure in subsequent legislation. In amendments to the Act since 1949, the urban renewal aspects have been expanded and various specialized housing programs have been instituted, such as those for college dormitories, housing for the aged, and rent subsidies for the poor. Funds have also been made available for municipal public works, such as sewers and transportation. The Department of Housing and Urban Development supervises administration of the Act.

Significance   In the Housing Act of 1949, Congress declared its goal to be "a decent home and a suitable living environment for every American family." The national government is now committed to a "total" housing program that takes account of all aspects of community development. These programs result from an acute housing shortage for low-income families, slums and blight, and increasing urbanization which multiplies the service needs of millions of city dwellers and suburbanites. Many persons object to the intrusion of the national government into these areas, but Congress has continued to expand existing programs, encouraging the use of private capital when possible.

National Defense Education Act of 1958   An act to encourage education in science, mathematics, engineering, languages, humanities, social sciences, and teacher education. The Act provides for loans to needy college students, with preference given to those pursuing these courses of study; one-half the loan is forgiven if the student teaches for five years after graduation. In addition, the Act provides funds for graduate fellowships, and for public schools to purchase educational equipment and to improve guidance and testing services.

Significance   Congress enacted the National Defense Education Act in response to Soviet achievements in the field of science. This started a trend of greater national involvement in education. The Act is designed to serve national security needs by equalizing educational opportunities throughout the nation in critical subject matter fields. In order to meet the major objections to federal aid to education, the Act specifically provides that no national official may exercise any control over curriculum or personnel in any school system.

National Mental Health Act of 1946   A nation-wide program for the care and treatment of the mentally ill. The Act provides for grants-in-aid to the states for psychiatric personnel, community psychiatric services, and research into prevention and care of mental illness. The Act is administered by the Public Health Service in the Department of Health, Education, and Welfare.

Significance   Mental health is one of the most pressing health problems in the United States. Though more than half the hospital beds are occupied by the mentally ill, an acute shortage of trained personnel and facilities exists. Much progress has been made since the passage of the National Mental Health Act. The national government has also taken action to provide grants for hospital construction and for the control and treatment of other serious diseases such as tuberculosis, cancer, and heart diseases.

Social Security Act of 1935   The basic social-welfare legislation embodying social insurance, public assistance, and child-health and welfare services. Social-insurance programs include Old-Age, Survivors and Disability Insurance, Medicare, and unemployment insurance. Public assistance is provided under the categorical assistance program to the needy aged, blind, permanently and totally disabled, and to dependent children. Child-health and welfare services are provided under the Act for maternal care, crippled children, and general child-welfare services. With the exception of the Old-Age, Survivors and Disability Insurance and Medicare programs, which are financed and administered exclusively by the national government, all others are administered by the states under grants-in-aid from the national government. Responsibility for over-all supervision rests with the Department of Health, Education, and Welfare. In addition, the Social Security Act provides for widespread public health services through grants to the states under supervision of the Public Health Service in the Department of Health, Education, and Welfare. *See* SOCIAL SECURITY CASES, page 311.

Significance   The Social Security Act is the most comprehensive social welfare legislation passed in the United States. The program grew out of the experience of the great depression and reflected a basic change in public attitudes toward the needy and the role of the government. The Act, at first highly controversial, is now generally accepted by the American people; both major political parties have expanded the scope of benefits available under the law. The partnership of the national and state governments in the administration of the Act provides a leading example of cooperative federalism in action to meet common national problems.

Sixteen

Foreign Policy and
International Affairs

Aggression   An unwarranted attack by one state against another. Much of the literature of international law is concerned with the problem of identifying aggression and differentiating it from self-defense. The cold war has been characterized by nations arming and concluding alliances to protect themselves from aggression. The United Nations collective-security system exists to protect states from aggression. *See* COLLECTIVE SECURITY, page 319; SANCTIONS, page 335.

   Significance   The community of nations has seldom been able to agree on a definition of what constitutes aggression. On occasion, however, international bodies have identified and fixed responsibility for aggression. For example, individuals were punished for the crime of aggressive war in the post-World War II Nuremberg and Tokyo trials of Nazi and Japanese war leaders. The United Nations Charter does not define aggression; aggression has occurred when an authorized organ of the world organization makes such a determination through its voting procedure. Such was the case in 1950, when the Security Council branded North Korea an aggressor. The International Law Commission of the United Nations has tried for several years to establish objective criteria to be used in deciding whether acts of aggression have been committed. Extensive studies have been carried on but little agreement has been reached.

Alliance   A multilateral agreement by states to improve their power position by joining together in defense of their common interest. Most alliances are now characterized by an agreement to regard "an attack upon any member of the alliance as an attack upon all." Hence, an alliance is a way of informing friend and foe that an attack against any individual nation will precipitate a general war. Balance of power systems tend to create the need for alliances. *See* BALANCE OF POWER, page 318.

   Significance   Throughout most of American history, President George Washington's advice to "steer clear of permanent alliances" was carefully observed. Since the advent of the cold war, the United States has been catapulted into a position of leadership of the free world, unable to continue its time-honored policy of isolation. The United States has become the world's leading advocate of security through defensive alliances. Alliances have been concluded with over forty nations to forestall a Communist attack, or to meet it if it should occur. Mutual security alliances include the Rio Treaty, the North Atlantic Treaty (NATO), the South-East Asia Treaty (SEATO), a trilateral treaty with Australia and New Zealand (ANZUS), and bilateral pacts with Japan, the Philippines, Nationalist China, and South Korea.

Alliance for Progress   A program of foreign aid for Latin America developed by the Kennedy Administration. Congress authorized $500 million in 1961 to initiate the program. Nineteen Latin American countries—all except Cuba —are participating. Continued aid to these nations will be offered if internal economic reforms are instituted and if social progress moves forward with economic development. The Inter-American Development Bank was created in 1961 to play a major role in implementing the program through development loans. Its efforts are supplemented by the Development Loan Fund, the Export-Import Bank, and the Agency for International Development. *See* ORGANIZATION OF AMERICAN STATES, page 332.

Significance   The emphasis in the Alliance for Progress program is on securing progress in Latin America through close hemispheric cooperation. American help is intended to aid these countries in getting started on the road to self-sustaining growth. Closer economic ties leading to some measure of economic integration are encouraged by the program. Additional objectives include the strengthening of political relations through the Organization of American States (OAS) and the collective security system under the Rio Treaty.

Ambassador   The top-ranking diplomat sent by the government of a sovereign state as its official representative to another state. An ambassador is the head of an embassy in the capital city of the foreign state. Official relations between governments are carried on mainly through an exchange of ambassadors. *See* DIPLOMATIC IMMUNITY, page 321; PERSONA NON GRATA, page 333.

Significance   In the United States, ambassadors are appointed by the President and confirmed by the Senate. Personal and political considerations, such as campaign contributions and party service, may be important in making such appointments. The trend, however, is in the direction of appointing foreign service career diplomats. An ambassador is the personal representative of the President, and, as such, is charged with implementing the foreign policy of the administration in power in the United States. In addition to his official duties, much of an ambassador's time is spent in promoting better relations between the peoples of the two countries.

ANZUS Pact   A tripartite security treaty concluded in 1951 among Australia, New Zealand, and the United States. The treaty, which has no terminal date, declares that an attack upon any of the members would constitute a common danger and each would act to meet it according to its constitutional processes. *See* ALLIANCE, page 315.

Significance   ANZUS is an attempt to provide security against Communist encroachment in a large area of the Pacific. The Pact reflects a growing dependence upon the United States for leadership in providing security in the Pacific. In 1954, the security system of the ANZUS Pact was expanded into the South-East Asia Treaty Organization (SEATO) defense arrangement, but the ANZUS Pact remains in force.

Appeasement   A term used to describe concessions made to a warlike, potential enemy in the hope that these will satiate his appetite for expansion, and that peace will be secure. Prime Minister Neville Chamberlain's agreement at Munich to accept Adolf Hitler's demand for the partition of Czechoslovakia is regarded as a classic example of appeasement.

Significance   The fear of appeasement makes diplomatic negotiations extremely difficult. Successful diplomacy requires concessions from both sides. Frequently, the cry of "appeasement" can sabotage a diplomat's position. Concessions are played up while counterconcessions are overlooked. The problem of appeasement is particularly acute when diplomats are engaged in "open" or "public" negotiations.

Arbitration   A method of settling a dispute between states by judges selected by the parties to the dispute. The judges, who have standing as international jurists, must render a decision or award based on international law, and the parties agree in advance to accept the decision as binding. Arbitration dates back many centuries, but its modern use began with the famous *Alabama Claims* settlement between the United States and Great Britain growing out of Civil War controversies. *See* PACIFIC SETTLEMENT OF DISPUTES, page 333.

Significance   Many conflicts between states involving their secondary interests have been solved through arbitration. Generally, states are reluctant to submit disputes involving their *primary* national interests to an arbitration tribunal. Contrary to popular myth, states that have accepted arbitration have almost always abided by the decision of the tribunal. The main weakness of arbitration is the difficulty of getting states to accept it as a means of settling their dispute.

Attaché   A military, commercial, agricultural, or other official with diplomatic rank who is attached to an embassy or foreign mission.

Significance   Attachés seek to establish good relations with similar officials in the country to which they are accredited. They also comprise the eyes and ears of the United States in gaining specialized information concerning the conditions that exist in that country.

Balance of Payments   The net balance between total income and expenditures of a nation in its business and trade relations with the rest of the world. Included are all monetary transactions, such as imports and exports of goods, tourist expenditures, investments, and income from investments. *See* ECONOMIC NATIONALISM, page 322.

Significance   Nations usually seek to maintain a "favorable" balance of payments. This means that they strive to increase income over expenditure to the extent that balances of foreign currencies and gold can be built up. Nations with "unfavorable" or deficit balances are like individuals who spend beyond their income. In the short run, this situation may not be serious. If it persists, corrective action must be taken. This may take the form of higher tariffs, exchange controls, export subsidies, austerity programs, currency depreciation, or other kinds of state action. The United States has suffered from a deficit balance of payments for many years, resulting in an outflow of gold and sizable dollar balances into foreign hands.

Balance of Power   A system of power alignments in which peace and security may be maintained through an equilibrium of power between the rival blocs. Participating states enter into alliances with friendly states in attempts to protect and enhance their power positions. *See* ALLIANCE, page 315.

Significance   If the balance works well, peace will be maintained for a period of years. So long as a near equilibrium is thought to exist, neither side will dare to launch an attack upon the other. However, with the military build-up characteristic of a balance of power system, there is always the danger that war will result from border incidents, miscalculations, or causes other than planned attack. Historically, balance of power systems have kept the peace for short and long periods, but have often deteriorated into war. Today, a world-wide balance of power system exists between the Communist and the free-world camps. This system is accompanied by the greatest armaments race in the history of the world.

Bipartisanship   Close cooperation between the two major American political parties in dealing with foreign problems. Bipartisanship usually takes the form of frequent consultations between the leaders of both parties in Congress, and between these leaders and the President. During time of war or threat of war, when bipartisanship typically comes into vogue, the President may appoint members of the opposition party to key Cabinet posts.

Significance   Bipartisanship is a means by which a democracy can overcome its divisions and present a solid front to the world. "Partisanship ends at the water's edge" is a frequently repeated description of bipartisanship. Disadvantages resulting from such cooperation include the loss of the function of the "loyal opposition" within the government, and the lack of discussion of vital issues.

Central Treaty Organization (CENTO)   A Middle East alliance adhered to by Britain, Iran, Pakistan, and Turkey. Originally known as the Baghdad Pact, the name was changed and headquarters moved from Baghdad to Ankara when a neutralist government seized power in Iraq in 1958 and withdrew from the alliance. *See* ALLIANCE, page 315.

Significance   CENTO was established on American initiative to provide a mutual-security shield against Communist expansion in the Middle East. The United States participates in CENTO planning, is a member of CENTO committees, and provides military support to CENTO members, but has never joined the alliance. American guarantees of assistance to CENTO members in case of attack, however, are covered by NATO, SEATO, and, in the case of

Iran, by a bilateral pact. Growing polycentrism and neutralism among pact members threatens to reduce the CENTO arrangement to a mere formality.

Chargé d'Affaires The Foreign Service official temporarily placed in charge of an embassy or legation in the absence of the ambassador or minister.

Significance When the United States seeks to indicate displeasure with the actions of a foreign government, but does not wish to take the serious step of severing diplomatic relations, it usually withdraws its ambassador. Under such conditions, the chargé d'affaires assumes a position of grave importance. In this way, a "listening post" to the foreign country is kept open, as are the diplomatic channels.

Charter of the United Nations A multilateral treaty that serves as the constitution for the United Nations Organization. The Charter was drawn up and signed at San Francisco on June 26, 1945; it was ratified by fifty-one nations and put into effect on October 24, 1945, since designated United Nations Day. The document consists of a preamble and 111 articles that provide for the creation of six major organs and set out the powers to be exercised by each. (*See* Index: United Nations.)

Significance The Charter represents an effort by the community of nations to establish norms of international conduct by outlawing war, providing for the peaceful settlement of international disputes, and encouraging cooperation among nations in dealing with economic and social problems. Like the United States Constitution, the Charter has proved to be a flexible document, subject to broad interpretations. Without this feature of adaptability, the United Nations would probably have collapsed under the impact of the cold war.

Collective Security A world-wide security system by which all or most nations agree in advance to take collective action against any state or states that may break the peace by committing aggression. Collective security is based on the assumption that, normally, no nation or group of nations would dare to challenge the power of the world community, but, if an attack should occur, all nations would honor their commitments to take police action. The United Nations embodies the concept of collective security. Under Chapter VII of its Charter, the organization can take such action, including military, as may be necessary to preserve world peace. Primary responsibility is vested in the five great powers (U.S., USSR, Britain, France, China), each having the veto power in the Security Council. Since 1950, the General Assembly also has been empowered under the Uniting for Peace Resolution to authorize collective security action if the Security Council is stymied with a veto. Sometimes, collective security is also used to describe alliances established under a balance of power system. See SANCTIONS, page 335; SECURITY COUNCIL, page 337.

Significance The first universal collective security arrangement, the League of Nations, broke down in the 1930s under the impact of aggressions by the Axis powers, Germany, Italy, and Japan. Collective-security military sanctions were invoked by the U.N. in 1950 against North Korea for its attack upon South Korea. Although this police action left much to be resolved, the U.N. was successful in halting the aggression. In 1956, the world organization was faced simultaneously with an attack by the Soviet Union upon Hungary and an attack by Britain, France, and Israel against Egypt. Although the U.N. was able to cope with the latter successfully, in the Hungarian case only moral sanctions were employed because of a fear of general war.

Comity   Courtesies extended between nations in their formal relations with each other. Examples include extradition of fugitives in absence of a treaty, and immunity of diplomats.

Significance   Most acts of comity between nations are based on customary international practice. It is important that nations abide by certain principles of conduct so that their relations can be harmonious and fruitful. Comity is not regarded as binding in character or enforceable in court.

Consul   An official appointed by a government to reside in a foreign country in order to assist citizens of the appointing state and to advance their commercial interests. American consuls are members of the Foreign Service.

Significance   The United States maintains consulates in most of the important commercial cities of the world. Responsibilities of an American consul include jurisdiction over American vessels (the settling of shipboard disputes, sanitary inspections, sending mutinous and shipwrecked sailors home, and so on), granting visas to foreigners seeking entry into the United States, and opening up new business and trade opportunities.

Containment   A general policy adopted in 1947 by the Truman Administration to build "situations of strength" around the globe in order to contain Communist power within its existing boundaries. Underlying the policy was a belief that, if Soviet expansion could be stopped, communism would collapse of its own internal weaknesses. The policy was first applied in the Truman Doctrine of 1947 in a program of military aid to Greece and Turkey. *See* TRUMAN DOCTRINE, page 339.

Significance   Under general guidelines of containment policy, the Truman Administration embarked on vast new programs that included: (1) rearmament; (2) establishment of military bases around the world; (3) mutual security alliances with friendly powers; (4) an economic aid program to rebuild war-shattered economies in western Europe (Marshall Plan); and (5) a program of technical and economic aid to underdeveloped countries. Through these and other programs, Communist expansion was slowed down but not completely halted. American actions in South Vietnam in the 1960s are based on this policy of containing Communist power.

De Facto Recognition   The preliminary recognition of a new state or government by another state. It is usually followed by *de jure* or full, legal recognition with exchange of ambassadors. The term also refers to a theory advanced by some international jurists that new states and governments should be recognized if, in fact, they do exist. *See* RECOGNITION, page 000.

Significance   Premature granting of recognition to a revolutionary regime, or continued withholding of it from a government on ideological grounds, has produced much turmoil in the world. Today, Communist China and East

Germany are subjects of recognition controversies. Great Britain has maintained a *de facto* recognition of Communist China for more than fifteen years without an exchange of ambassadors. The United States has withheld recognition from Communist China but has in fact communicated with it through other nations and in conversations between the ambassadors of the two countries in Warsaw.

De Jure Recognition   Full, legal recognition of a new state or government by another state, usually accompanied by an exchange of ambassadors or ministers. Also, a theory that only those states and governments that have come into existence through peaceful, constitutional means are deserving of recognition. *See* RECOGNITION, page 334.

Significance   The *de jure* theory is used mainly by those nations which seek to preserve the status quo in the world. In an ideological struggle such as the present day cold war, rigid theories frequently give way to mere expediency as each side uses its power to recognize or to withhold recognition as a diplomatic weapon. Many nations in the world, including the United States, have refused to extend *de jure* recognition to Communist China.

Diplomacy   The total process by means of which states carry on political relations with each other. The machinery of diplomacy includes a policy-making foreign office (Department of State in the United States) and diplomatic missions abroad (Foreign Service). Diplomacy may be carried on through open or conference negotiations or in secret. Increasingly, diplomacy is undertaken by heads of state, a process commonly called "summit" diplomacy. *See* APPEASEMENT, page 317; DOLLAR DIPLOMACY, page 321; *Quid Pro Quo,* page 333; PACIFIC SETTLEMENT OF DISPUTES, page 333.

Significance   Diplomacy is an art that can be mastered only by skilled negotiators. A good diplomat knows how, when, and what to compromise and how to achieve maximum benefit from compromise. War may result if diplomacy fails.

Diplomatic Immunity   Under international law, ambassadors and other diplomatic officials are immune from the jurisdiction of the state to which they are accredited. The embassy grounds may not be trespassed upon by local officials unless permission is granted by the diplomat. He, his family, and his official staff are immune from arrest and from civil jurisdiction unless his own government waives this immunity.

Significance   The purpose of diplomatic immunity is to ensure that the diplomat will have the freedom to carry on effectively the relations between the two states. Though not subject to the laws of the state to which he is accredited, he nevertheless is expected to abide by them under normal conditions. A diplomat who misuses his immunity may be reported to his superiors for discipline or, in severe cases, his recall may be demanded by the government of the state to which he is accredited.

Dollar Diplomacy   A term used by Latin Americans to show their disapproval of the role the American government has played in using diplomatic and military power to open up foreign markets and to safeguard the financial interests of American businessmen. Under the Roosevelt Corollary of the Monroe Doctrine, American Marines were frequently sent into countries of Central America. Protectorates were established over Cuba, Haiti, Nicaragua, and Santo Domingo in the early part of the twentieth century. The term might also be used to describe any use of a state's political or military power to further the economic interests of its citizens abroad. *See* GOOD NEIGHBOR POLICY, page 325.

Significance   American relations with Latin America have considerably improved since the inauguration of the "Good Neighbor Policy" in the 1930s and the "Alliance for Progress" aid program of 1961. Treatment as equals and mutual solving of problems through the Organization of American States has greatly improved the position of the United States with the Latin American republics. Yet reservoirs of ill-feeling remain and are occasionally exploited by political leaders unfriendly to the United States.

Economic and Social Council (ECOSOC)   A major organ of the United Nations concerned with promoting higher standards of living and social justice throughout the world. The Council includes twenty-seven members elected by the General Assembly, nine chosen each year for three-year terms. Responsibilities include: (1) coordinating the activities of the Specialized Agencies, such as the World Health Organization (WHO) and the Food and Agriculture Organization (FAO); (2) administering United Nations functions in economic, social, educational, cultural, and related areas; (3) promoting world-wide observance of human rights and fundamental freedoms.

Significance   The Economic and Social Council has successfully coordinated the operations of diverse agencies in seeking to meet pressing social and economic problems. It has established regional Economic Commissions for Asia and the Far East, for Europe, for Africa, and for Latin America to make comprehensive studies and recommendations on how economic conditions can be improved. It has established various commissions to study international problems, including: Fiscal, Human Rights, Narcotic Drugs, Population, Social, Statistical, Status of Women, and Transport and Communications.

Economic Nationalism   An economic policy by which a nation seeks to attain economic prosperity or to correct a disequilibrium in its balance of payments by protecting the home market and/or opening up foreign markets through unilateral or bilateral governmental action. It is the opposite of a multilateral trading system with free flow of trade and free convertibility of currencies. It is characterized by extensive governmental control of trade and the subjection of economic matters to overriding considerations of political or military policy. Techniques employed by states pursuing policies of economic nationalism include: (1) austerity programs; (2) barter arrangements; (3) currency depreciation; (4) exchange controls; (5) export subsidies; (6) licensing; (7) quota restrictions; and (8) tariffs. *See* TARIFF, page 338.

Significance   A state cannot normally pursue a policy of economic nationalism without inciting retaliatory action from other states that have suffered harm from such policies. The great danger is that, once started, the process becomes cumulative, with action and counteraction building up to the point of stifling most trade. This is what happened in the 1930s, when the Smoot-Hawley

Tariff Act raised tariff rates to the highest point in American history in an effort to protect the home market from foreign competition. The action touched off extensive retaliation which precipitated a world trade crisis. Today, bloc trading systems, such as the European Economic Community (Common Market) and the Soviet bloc, tend to reduce restrictive trade practices among member nations but to encourage increasing economic warfare between blocs.

Executive Agreement   An international agreement between the President and foreign heads of state that, unlike a treaty, does not require Senate consent. Most notably, trade agreements are concluded under powers granted to the President by Congress. Others are concluded by the President acting under his constitutional powers over foreign relations. The Constitution makes no explicit provision for executive agreements. *See* EXECUTIVE AGREEMENT, page 167; TREATY, page 338.

Significance   Legally, an executive agreement is the same as a treaty. In recent years, the trend has been toward more agreements, fewer treaties. For example, in 1930, 11 agreements and 25 treaties were concluded; in 1958, there were 182 agreements and 3 treaties. Advantages of the executive agreement include avoidance of the power of the Senate to cripple or kill a treaty, and the maintenance of secrecy when desirable, as in a wartime agreement. Disadvantages include the frequent need for further implementation of the agreement by *both* houses of Congress through statutes and appropriations. When secrecy is involved, congressional and public suspicions may be aroused. When substantial public support is needed, presidents usually fall back on the treaty procedure.

Extradition   Return by one nation to another of a person accused of a crime. The process resembles that of interstate rendition, which occurs within the United States. In the international field, extradition usually depends upon treaty arrangements between the two nations concerned. Some international jurists regard it as a matter of reciprocal interest covered by customary international law in the absence of any treaty. *See* INTERSTATE RENDITION, page 36.

Significance   Because there is no international criminal law, without extradition a criminal could escape punishment by simply crossing a border. The whole process of law enforcement would become infinitely more difficult under such circumstances. States usually extradite persons sought by other states; however, political offenses are not generally recognized as ground for extradition. In the United States, the President is not legally empowered to extradite in the absence of treaty provisions.

Foreign Aid   The granting of economic or military assistance to foreign countries. American economic aid includes disposal of food surpluses, technical assistance, development loans, capital grants, and investment guarantees. The aid has been offered to over ninety countries bilaterally and to additional nations through United Nations and regional programs. Major programs in which the United States participates include the Alliance for Progress, the Peace Corps, the Colombo Plan, the Organization for Economic Cooperation and Development, the Asian, African, and Inter-American Development Banks, the World Bank Group (IBRD, IDA, and IFC), and the United Nations Development Program. Military aid, taking the form of weapons, training, and defense support (highways, airports, and so forth), is given on a selective basis to strengthen resistance to external or internal Communist aggression. Foreign economic aid programs are administered by the Agency for International Development (AID), and military aid by the Defense Department.

Significance   The United States has provided more than $120 billion in aid to foreign countries in the period 1941-1966. Aid programs started with Lend-Lease assistance to the Allies in World War II and in postwar years included the Marshall Plan to aid European recovery, the Truman Doctrine of military and economic assistance to Greece and Turkey to "contain" communism, and the Mutual Security Program of military aid to bolster NATO defenses in Western Europe. In the late 1950s and 1960s, most American aid has gone to developing countries to encourage their "self-help" efforts. New approaches include the encouragement of internal reforms by the Alliance for Progress, the offering of human resources through the Peace Corps, and the disposing of surplus food to needy peoples through the Food for Peace (Public Law 480) program. In recent years foreign aid has averaged $4 billion annually.

Free Trade   The elimination of all governmental regulations and controls so as to allow the free flow of commodities among countries. The theory is associated with Adam Smith, who believed that a free trade system would foster an international specialization that would result in higher productivity and standards of living for all nations.

Significance   Desirable as free trade appears in theory, all nations practice varying degrees of protectionism. Many economists still support the idea of free trade, but political considerations have tended to override economic theories. Many nations seek to obtain a measure of self-sufficiency, particularly in critical sectors of their economy, rather than becoming overly specialized. World peace and security are indispensable conditions to a system of free trade.

General Assembly   The major organ of the United Nations in which all members (121, in 1966) are equally represented. The Assembly has evolved into the focus for the multifold activities of the U.N. In one sense, it is a continuing international conference; in another, it is an international forum in which each member nation can discuss its international problems with all others. It is a "Town Meeting of the World," through which world public opinion can be aroused and brought to bear on a problem. Its functions directly or indirectly relate to almost all of the activities carried on by the world organization. Specific responsibilities include: (1) election of some or all members of the other five major organs; (2) an annual review of the activities of all segments of the organization; (3) control over the budget; and (4) decision-making and recommendations to members on all subjects within U.N. jurisdiction. Measures are adopted ordinarily by a simple majority vote, but "important questions," as defined by the Charter or as determined by a majority of the Assembly, require a two-thirds vote of members present and voting. The most important power of the Assembly—to deal with acts of aggression and breaches of the peace when the Security Council is stalemated by a veto —was not vested in the Assembly by the Charter, but was assumed by it in 1950.

Significance   Through an evolutionary process, the Assembly has become the sun of the U.N. solar system. Until, and unless, the great powers begin to cooperate more fully, the Assembly seems destined to overshadow the Security Council. With the admittance of many new members, mostly African states, the prestige and responsibilities of the Assembly have grown accordingly.

Good Neighbor Policy   American policy toward Latin America initiated in the early 1930s. President Franklin Roosevelt described the change in policy in his inaugural address in March 1933 as follows: "In the field of world policy, I would dedicate this nation to the policy of the good neighbor—the neighbor who resolutely respects himself and, because he does so, respects the rights of others. . . ." Although the policy was directed toward the world at large, it soon came into general usage as descriptive of the American policy of treating Latin-American nations as friends and equals. *See* ORGANIZATION OF AMERICAN STATES, page 332.

Significance   From the turn of the century until the adoption of the Good Neighbor policy, the United States played the role of "Big Brother" to Latin America. Unilateral actions, dollar diplomacy, and frequent military intervention characterized that policy. Terms such as "Yankee imperialists" and "Colossus of the North" came into common usage in Latin America to indicate displeasure with American policies. The Good Neighbor policy was an about-face, a repudiation of earlier actions. Since its inception, the policy has resulted in two military pacts of mutual assistance (the Act of Chapultepec of 1945 and the Rio Treaty of 1947), the creation of the Organization of American States (OAS), and a general improvement in relations between the United States and the Latin-American countries. The policy occasionally has been strained over United States relations with dictatorial regimes and over unilateral actions by the United States, such as the military intervention in the Dominican Republic in 1965.

Good Offices   A method of peaceful settlement by which a third nation seeks to bring two disputing nations into agreement. The state offering its good offices merely seeks to create favorable conditions under which the states in conflict can talk over their differences. Good offices does not include participation in the negotiations nor the offering of a suggested solution, although the disputing states may request them. When they do, good offices is converted into mediation. *See* PACIFIC SETTLEMENT OF DISPUTES, page 333.

Significance   Good offices can be a useful device in "breaking the ice" between disputing states by getting them to talk things over. Neither disputant may be willing to initiate proposals for such talks for fear of demonstrating weakness in its position. The third state that offers its good offices is playing the role of peacemaker on behalf of the world community. In recent years, the United Nations has generally taken over the role of offering good offices to disputing states, usually through the Security Council, the General Assembly, or the Secretary-General.

Ideological Warfare   One of the tactics used by the Communist and free-world blocs in the cold war. Each side seeks to achieve ideological conformity among its own people while trying to convert the large masses of mankind outside its borders to its "way of life." Ideology comprises the ideas and ideals of a political and economic system. The struggle involves competition between Soviet-style communism and dictatorship, and western-style capitalism and democracy. *See* IDEOLOGY, page 9.

Significance   The ideological war has developed an inclination toward "black and white" classification as each side tries to convince millions of peoples of the soundness and rightness of its position and the imperialistic, war-like, aggressive nature of the other side. Various psychological techniques are used in disseminating propaganda.

Inherent Powers   Powers exercised by the national government in foreign affairs that are neither expressed nor implied in the Constitution. They are derived from the concept that the United States exists in a world of many nations and, therefore, must possess powers to meet its international responsibilities. *See* INHERENT POWERS, page 34; *United States v. Curtiss-Wright Export Corp.*, page 342.

Significance   The inherent powers doctrine enables the national government to act in foreign affairs to protect the security and well-being of the American people. The extent to which such action would be permissible has not been specified, although the Supreme Court has stated (*United States v. Curtiss-Wright Export Corp.*, 299 U.S. 304 [1936]): "As a member of the family of nations, the right and power of the United States in that field are equal to the right and power of the other nations of the international family."

International Bank for Reconstruction and Development   A Specialized Agency of the United Nations, known informally as the World Bank, that makes loans to member nations for economic rehabilitation or developmental purposes. The Bank was created by the Bretton Woods Agreement of 1944 to promote the growth of world trade and higher standards of living by making loans when private capital is not available. The Bank's chief sources of funds are capital subscriptions from member nations and sales of its own bonds to private investors. By 1967, the subscribed capital of the Bank was more than $21 billion of which almost one-third was supplied by the United States. The Bank operates by insuring private loans or, if necessary, by providing the funds itself. As of 1967, over 100 countries were members.

Significance   The Bank has made several hundred loans to over seventy countries and territories, mostly in the underdeveloped category. Loans are made only after careful and detailed studies convince the directors of the soundness and usefulness of the ventures. To meet criticism of the Bank's conservative lending policies, the International Finance Corporation (IFC) was created in 1956 to invest in private enterprises and, in 1960, the International Development Association (IDA) was created to offer long-term, low-interest loans.

International Court of Justice (ICJ)   An international tribunal, known as the World Court, established as one of the six major organs of the United Nations to adjudicate justiciable disputes among nations and to render advisory opinions to organs of the United Nations. The World Court was established in 1945 under an agreement that was annexed to the United Nations Charter, and to which all U.N. member states are parties. Nonmembers of the U.N. may adhere to the agreement under conditions set by the General Assembly and the Security Council. Other states may use the Court if they accept its jurisdiction. The Court, with its headquarters at the Hague, has fifteen judges elected by the General Assembly and the Security Council, no two of whom may be nationals of the same state. Decisions rendered by the Court are final and, if any party to a case refuses to heed the judgment of the Court, the other party has recourse to the Security Council, which may decide on a course of action. *See* INTERNATIONAL LAW, page 327.

Significance   The usefulness of the Court has been impaired because its jurisdiction extends only to cases in which the states concerned have accepted such jurisdiction. No national court system could function under such limitations, and the International Court of Justice has suffered a lack of effectiveness as a result. Attempts to correct this weakness through compulsory jurisdiction under the "optional clause" (Article 36 of the Court's Statute) have largely been unsuccessful because of the reservation attached to the acceptance of compulsory jurisdiction by many nations, including the United States (Connally Amendment). Only about twenty cases have been decided by the Court. Unless leading members of the United Nations resolve their political differences, the Court will continue to play a limited role, having little impact on world affairs. Many people believe that world peace and security cannot be achieved without world law and an effective court system.

International Labor Organization (ILO)   A Specialized Agency of the United Nations that seeks through research and recommendation to improve working conditions throughout the world. Established in 1919, the ILO was the only major agency associated with the League of Nations in which the United States participated. The ILO is concerned with problems of full employment, labor standards, migration of workers, collective bargaining, social security, and workers' health. Its headquarters are in Geneva, and it functions through a General Conference comprised of delegates representing labor, employers, and government. Between annual conferences, an executive Governing Body supervises the operations of ILO committees and commissions and prepares the agenda for future conferences.

Significance   Although the ILO cannot make binding decisions, its recommendations have been adopted by many member countries, resulting in improved working and living conditions for millions of workers. Improvements in labor standards can best be accomplished when they are instituted simultaneously by many nations; otherwise those nations acting alone would place themselves at a competitive disadvantage costwise. In recent years, much of the ILO's activity has been directed toward the underdeveloped areas of the world. Hundreds of ILO experts have provided technical assistance to countries in Asia, Africa, Latin America, and the Middle East.

International Law   A body of rules and principles that guides the relations among nations and between governments and foreign nationals. Sources of international law include treaties, authority (for example, decisions of international courts), reason, and custom. Treaties are the most important source today, as custom was earlier in the development of international law. The law has been classified into three categories: peace, war, and neutrality, based on the nature of the law, and into public, private, and administrative, based on the different sources of the law. *See* INTERNATIONAL COURT OF JUSTICE, page 326.

Significance   Although international law evolved out of the European nation-state system, it has gained nearly universal acceptance by the world community of states. Some theorists reject the entire concept of international law, holding that law must be handed down by a sovereign authority, enforcement agencies must exist, and courts must provide sanctions against violators. Because none of these conditions exist in the state system, the existence of *law* is denied. Others refute this position by noting the universal acceptance of some elements of international law by the world community (such as diplomacy and commerce), and the general obedience of states to its rules. Today, with the world caught up in revolutionary ferment, international law has depreciated in importance, despite efforts of the United Nations to foster its growth and adherence to its principles.

Isolationism   The theory and practice of noninvolvement in the affairs of other nations. Isolationism as a political ideology is nurtured by geographical, ideological, and cultural separateness.

Significance   The United States pursued a policy of isolation during the nineteenth and part of the twentieth century. It was particularly operative in American intentions to remain aloof from the power struggles of Europe by remaining independent of Europe's system of entangling alliances. The doctrine was instrumental in conditioning the American public's belief that the United States should maintain neutrality during the early stages of World War I and World War II and not join the League of Nations. Since World War II, American isolationism has given way to a deep commitment to internationalism.

League of Nations   The first general international organization established to preserve peace and security and to promote cooperation among nations in economic and social fields. The League was created by the victorious powers of World War I in 1919 under the leadership of President Woodrow Wilson, but the United States did not join. The organization operated under a constitutional system established through its Covenant, a section of the Versailles peace treaty. A Council and Assembly were the major organs (similar to the Security Council and General Assembly of the United Nations) and subsidiary committees and commissions were established to deal with special problems in areas such as mandates, military affairs, and disarmament. A Secretariat, headed by a Secretary-General and staffed with international civil servants, provided continuity and expertness in record keeping and research. A World Court (the Permanent Court of International Justice, forerunner of the present International Court of Justice) and the International Labor Organization were independent of the League but worked closely with it. Sixty-one nations joined the League and its headquarters were at Geneva, Switzerland.

Significance   In its first decade, the League resolved many postwar problems and settled numerous disputes that threatened the peace. The great depression that swept across the world in 1929-1930 rekindled aggressive nationalism and reduced the League's effectiveness. Failure of the League to deal resolutely with the Japanese conquest of Manchuria in 1931, the Italian conquest of Ethiopia in 1935, and the Nazi aggressions in the late 1930s brought about its collapse. Most observers believe that the League's breakdown resulted not from internal constitutional weaknesses, but from the failure of key member states to support its principles and from the refusal of the United States to join. Despite its failure to maintain peace, the League did succeed in promoting extensive international cooperation in economic and social affairs and in developing new ideas and procedures for international organizations which have proved useful to its successor, the United Nations. The League voted itself out of existence in 1946.

Marshall Plan   A proposal made by Secretary of State George C. Marshall in 1947 for a vast program of American economic aid to reconstruct the war-devastated economies of western Europe. The United States Congress accepted the Plan and, in 1948, established the European Recovery Program under which sixteen nations of western Europe (later joined by West Germany) received $15 billion in grants and loans from 1948 to 1952. Under the Marshall program, the participating European nations on American request joined together in the Organization for European Economic Cooperation (OEEC) for the purpose of drawing up a collective inventory of resources and requirements. The USSR and other Communist countries were invited to participate, but rejected the offer. *See* FOREIGN AID, page 323.

   Significance   The Marshall Plan was successful in thwarting Communist aims of exploiting the economic collapse and political turmoil of the post-World War II era in western Europe. By 1951, all participating members had raised their production capacities beyond prewar levels. American attempts to promote the integration of European economies through the program were partially successful, especially on the Continent. The Marshall Plan was the first of a series of economic and military programs through which the United States has provided over $120 billion in grants and loans to over 100 countries.

Monroe Doctrine   A unilateral declaration of American foreign policy made by President Monroe in his annual message to Congress in December 1823, opposing any European intervention in the affairs of the American continents. He also reaffirmed the American intention to refrain from interfering in European affairs. The Doctrine was intended to stop the Holy Alliance from aiding Spain in a reconquest of the newly independent Latin-American republics. *See* RIO TREATY, page 335; ORGANIZATION OF AMERICAN STATES, page 332.

   Significance   The Monroe Doctrine at the time of its enunciation was largely meaningless because only the British fleet stood between the Holy Alliance and the reconquest of Latin America. Over the years, however, it developed into one of the basic tenets of American policy through restatements, corollaries, and the growing ability of a powerful United States to intervene actively whenever the Doctrine was challenged. Since the Declaration of Lima in 1942, and particularly in the Rio Treaty of 1947, the Doctrine has become a common principle by which the American republics have declared their determination to defend themselves against foreign intervention. In recent years, the Doctrine has been challenged by the existence of a Communist government in Cuba and its efforts to promote revolution throughout Latin America because of a conflict between those portions of the Doctrine ruling out foreign intervention and those guaranteeing that each Latin-American state may choose its own economic and political system.

National Interest   The concept of the security and well-being of the state, used in making foreign policy. National interest demands a "realistic" approach to international problems, based on the use of power divorced from moral principles and values. Conflicts of national interest in the state system are resolved through diplomacy, international law, international institutions, or, ultimately, through war.

Significance   The concept of national interest is hazy and subjective in its application. Exponents of a realistic approach argue that it reduces utopian expectations, recognizes the existence of power politics, produces a steady and sober involvement in world affairs, and limits a state to attainable objectives. Opponents argue that the strongest foreign policy is one built on a firm moral base, and that reliance on unilateral policies of national interest fails to provide for reconciliation of international interests.

Nationalism   Social and psychological forces that spring from unique cultural and historical factors to provide unity and inspiration to a given people through a sense of belonging together and of shared values. Nationalism binds together people who possess common cultural, linguistic, racial, historical, or geographical characteristics or experiences and who give their loyalty to the same political group. *See* NATION, page 11.

Significance   The spirit of nationalism subjects people to the intangible forces of group psychology and collective behavior, expecially when a crisis confronts them with a real or imaginary enemy. Nationalism tends to emphasize the separateness of and differences between groups, as for example, Germans versus French or Arabs versus Jews. Most modern wars have been products of extreme nationalism in which mass emotional enthusiasm has been marshaled for one nation against another. It has played a significant role in the march to independence of numerous peoples. Nationalism is waning in Europe, its seedbed, and waxing strong in the new states of Asia and Africa. Nationalism is also a powerful internal force that helps produce unity, loyalty, and durable political, economic, and social institutions.

Neutralism   A "third force" in the cold war power struggle, comprised of states that pursue policies of nonalignment with the free world and the Communist bloc. Most of the nations of Asia, Africa, and the Middle East and a few states in Europe have refused to join military alliance systems propagated by either the United States or Soviet Russia. Although some of these states profess ideological sympathy toward one side or the other, none has committed itself to any kind of military involvement.

Significance   Neutralist leaders have consistently emphasized that neutralism is a positive force that endeavors to prevent another catastrophic global war by encouraging a rapprochement between the East and West. Both rival power blocs have been seeking to win the favor of the neutralists. Some of these neutralist states, such as Sweden and Ireland, are ideologically identified with the West, whereas others, such as Yugoslavia and Ghana, are more sympathetic with the goals of the Communist bloc. Others, such as India and Burma, have tried to steer a middle course.

Neutrality   The legal status of a nation that does not participate in a war between other states. Under international law, such a state is free to defend its territory or neutral waters against attack by belligerents. Although public opinion and even the government of a neutral state may sympathize with one side or the other, to retain its neutral position a state may not engage in action that might favor one side in the war. Some states, such as Switzerland, Sweden, and Ireland, have espoused a doctrine of perpetual neutrality.
    Significance   The concept of neutrality has lost some of its meaning in modern times because of the increasingly ruthless nature of war, its expansion into global struggles, and the tendency of neutrals to show some favoritism based on ideological sympathies. In a future global war, neutrals may be placed in as great a position of danger as belligerents because of the possibilities of radioactive fall-out, the spread of poisonous gases, and the employment of biological warfare by belligerents.

North Atlantic Treaty Organization (NATO)   An organization established under the North Atlantic Treaty of 1949 to create a single unified defense force to safeguard the security of the North Atlantic area. Members agree under Article V of the Treaty to regard an attack upon any of them as an attack upon all, and, if an armed attack occurs, each will render such assistance as it deems necessary. NATO now includes fifteen members, the original twelve (Belgium, Britain, Canada, Denmark, France, Iceland, Italy, Luxembourg, Netherlands, Norway, Portugal, and the United States) and three states that joined NATO in the 1950s (Greece, Turkey, and West Germany). NATO's members seek, in addition to attainment of mutual security, "the further development of peaceful and friendly international relations . . . and to eliminate conflict in their international economic policies." *See* ALLIANCE, page 315.
    Significance   NATO provides the basic framework of the political-military structure of the west. Important questions, such as the rearmament of West Germany, the establishment of missile bases in western Europe, the employment of nuclear weapons, and over-all strategic and tactical strategy have been worked out through the political and military channels of cooperation established within the NATO framework. NATO's solidarity has tended to wax and wane over the years as the cold war grew more intense or cooled off through Soviet peace offensives. In recent years, France, under de Gaulle, has strained the alliance through independent actions aimed at wresting leadership from the United States. Other NATO members seek to implement more fully the treaty provisions calling for expanded political and economic cooperation. The future importance of NATO as a military "sword and shield" will be tested in 1969 when the pact comes up for renewal.

Organization for Economic Cooperation and Development (OECD)   An international organization created in 1961 to achieve expanded cooperation and joint action between the United States and western Europe and Canada. The OECD is an outgrowth of the Organization for European Economic Cooperation (OEEC), established in 1948 to decide how American aid granted under the Marshall Plan would be distributed. When the OEEC went out of existence in 1960, its membership included eighteen European nations which, with the addition of the United States and Canada, comprise the present membership of OECD. Fifteen of the twenty members of OECD are NATO allies—the United States, Canada, Belgium, Britain, Denmark, France, Greece, Iceland, Italy, Luxembourg, Netherlands, Norway, Portugal, Turkey, and West Germany. The other five are Austria, Ireland, Spain, Sweden, and Switzerland.

Significance   The objectives of the OECD are: (1) to encourage economic growth and financial stability for member nations; (2) to expand and improve Western aid to underdeveloped countries; (3) to expand trade among members and with the world through more liberal policies; and (4) to provide a forum in which members can consult on mutual economic problems. The United States was the main force behind the creation of the OECD. American policy makers are particularly concerned with overcoming the balance of payments deficit, with penetrating the Common Market and Free Trade Association trading blocs in Europe, and with ensuring that all Western nations carry their fair share of the program for aiding the underdeveloped countries.

Organization of American States (OAS)   A regional political organization, comprised of the United States and twenty Latin-American republics, that was created at the Bogotá Conference in 1948. The OAS consists of: (1) the Inter-American Conference, which meets every five years to decide general policies; (2) the Council, with each member state represented by an ambassador, which oversees the implementation of general policies of OAS; (3) the Consultative Meetings of Ministers of Foreign Affairs, which occur whenever urgent problems confront the OAS; (4) the Pan-American Union, which operates through its headquarters, in Washington, D.C., as a general secretariat of the OAS; (5) the Specialized Conferences, which are called periodically to enable the members to cooperate in dealing with technical problems; and (6) the Specialized Agencies, which are responsible for eliciting cooperation in economic, social, education, technical, and humanitarian problem areas. The OAS is a regional organization of the type encouraged by the United Nations Charter. Important provisions of the OAS Charter are concerned with the peaceful settlement of disputes among members, and with procedures for mediation, arbitration, and adjudication. The OAS also implements the Rio Treaty's provision to safeguard the hemisphere from attack. See ALLIANCE FOR PROGRESS, page 316; GOOD NEIGHBOR POLICY, page 325; MONROE DOCTRINE, page 329; RIO TREATY, page 335.

Significance   The OAS regional system has institutionalized the principles embodied in the Monroe Doctrine. All major hemisphere problems have been taken up since 1948 through the machinery of the OAS. Communist infiltration into Latin America has been a major problem for OAS organs. In 1962, the Castro regime of Cuba was expelled for promoting Communist subversion and revolution in Latin America. American unilateral military intervention in the Dominican Republic in 1965 created new strains in the OAS even though the United States' role was avowedly to prevent a Communist take-over and an OAS peace force soon assumed control. The major challenge facing OAS in the future will be that of meeting increasing Sino-Soviet-Cuban efforts to promote communism in Latin America.

Pacific Settlement of Disputes   The peaceful adjustment of international disputes by one or more of the following techniques: negotiation, inquiry, good offices, mediation, conciliation, arbitration, or adjudication. Pacific settlement may be employed through the traditional diplomatic channels, regional organizations or arrangements, or the organs or agencies of the United Nations. Chapter VI of the United Nations Charter sets out in detail the political procedures available to the Security Council and the General Assembly; Chapter XV delegates peaceful settlement responsibilities to the Secretary-General; and Chapter XIV prescribes the legal processes by which the International Court of Justice may attempt to settle justiciable disputes. *See* ARBITRATION, page 317; DIPLOMACY, page 321; GOOD OFFICES, page 325; INTERNATIONAL COURT OF JUSTICE, page 326.

Significance   War occurs not only as a result of planned aggression but also from failure to keep international disputes within peaceful bounds. The United Nations system has bolstered traditional and regional settlement channels by establishing the principle of member responsibility to settle all disputes peacefully and by providing permanent machinery readily available to take up disputes. The U.N. has a good record of settling or limiting the effects of many disputes, including those between India and Pakistan and between the Arab states and Israel, internal conflicts in Cyprus and the Congo, and various cold-war controversies.

Persona non Grata   An unacceptable person. *Persona non grata* relates particularly to the situation in which a nation declares that an ambassador or minister is no longer acceptable and requests his recall by his government.

Significance   Each nation is free to accept or reject any person accredited to it as a diplomatic agent. When a diplomat is declared *persona non grata,* his government may consider it an affront, but the procedure is generally recognized and accepted. Numerous incidents in recent years involving the declaring of diplomatic agents *persona non grata* have resulted from the cold war. In most such cases, retaliation has followed, with a diplomat of equal status declared *persona non grata* following the first dismissal.

Quid pro Quo   A diplomatic bargaining concept meaning, literally, something for something. Negotiations conducted on a basis of *quid pro quo* depend on mutual compromises for success. *See* DIPLOMACY, page 321.

Significance   Any nation unable to demand a *quid pro quo* in exchange for its own concessions is in an inferior bargaining (and power) position. Reciprocal concessions are particularly useful in reducing tariffs and other trade barriers through *quid pro quo* bargaining.

Ratification   The formal action of the President in giving effect to a treaty that has been approved by the Senate. The President or his representative meets with representatives of the other signatory parties and exchanges ratifications with them. The treaty then is officially proclaimed and becomes legally enforceable. *See* RATIFICATION, page 171; TREATY, page 338.

Significance   Contrary to popular belief, the Senate does not officially ratify a treaty when it gives its advice and consent. In giving its consent, the Senate may attach amendments or reservations that may influence the decision of the President on ratification. The Senate's amendments or reservations, under which portions of a treaty will not be considered binding on the United States, leave the President with three choices: (1) renegotiation of the treaty; (2) ratification with reservations, if acceptable to other signatories; or (3) refusal to ratify. In American history, over 900 treaties have been approved by the Senate and ratified by the President. In approximately 100 other cases, the Senate has either failed to act or has approved the treaties with reservations or amendments of such a nature that either the President or one of the signatories refused to ratify them. In addition, over 60 treaties have been rejected outright by the Senate, thus eliminating the question of ratification.

Recognition   The discretionary function exercised by the President of deciding whether or not the United States shall officially carry on relations with a new state or a new political regime in an existing state. *See* RECOGNITION, page 172; *De Facto* Recognition, page 320; *De Jure* Recognition, page 321.

Significance   Each state in the world must determine for itself if and when new states and governments are to be recognized. Premature recognition of a revolutionary regime may lead to a threat of war by the government fighting the insurgent group. Conversely, continued refusal to recognize an existing state or an established government may engender hostility toward the state that withholds it. American recognition policy has varied with different presidents but, since World War I, it has generally been one of withholding recognition from regimes distasteful to American citizens and of granting it to friendly governments. The world-wide ideological struggle has influenced presidential recognition policies in recent years. A major recognition controversy, linked also with the question of representation in the United Nations, has involved the refusal of the United States to accept Communist China into the family of nations. The United States also refuses to recognize Cuba, East Germany, North Korea, and North Vietnam.

Regionalism   Limited systems of international organization that enable groupings of states to deal cooperatively with political, economic, social, and military problems. Geographical proximity of states typifies most regional organizations, although a community of common interests alone, such as that found in the Commonwealth of Nations, can be the integrating force behind such movements. Regional organizations include the military-alliance systems of both the western and Soviet blocs, political systems such as the Organization of American States and the Council of Europe, and economic groupings such as the Common Market and the Free Trade Association.

Significance   Although the United Nations Charter encourages regionalism (Article 52), the prolific growth of regional organizations has had a limiting effect on the fostering of world-wide cooperation through the world organization. Supporters of regionalism point out that it represents a gradual approach toward world unity and is more realistic than either unilateralism or universalism because of the disharmony and conflict which exists in the world. Opponents argue that international problems are world-wide in scope and that increasing economic and security interdependence can best be met by a universal system.

Rio Treaty   The Inter-American Treaty of Reciprocal Assistance of 1947 by which twenty-one American republics agreed "that an armed attack by any State against an American State shall be considered as an attack against all the American States. . . ." The Rio Treaty was the first mutual security pact entered into by the United States and it became a model for all subsequent ones. The treaty establishes a hemispheric security zone stretching from the North Pole to the South Pole. If an attack occurs within the zone, members agree to consult upon collective measures to be undertaken while retaining freedom to act individually "in accordance with the principle of continental solidarity." The treaty also includes principles and means by which conflicts between American states can be settled peacefully. Decisions concerning implementation of the treaty are reached through the Organization of American States. *See* ALLIANCE, page 315; ORGANIZATION OF AMERICAN STATES, page 332.

Significance   The Rio Treaty has gained new importance as a result of increasing economic and political penetration into Latin America by the Soviet Union and Communist China. The major difficulty has been that posed by the establishment of a Communist regime in Cuba without a direct military attack by a nonhemispheric power. The Organization of American States, under the leadership of the United States, seeks to forestall further Communist take-overs in the hemisphere by including internal threats of subversion and revolution within the collective-security guarantees provided by the treaty.

Sanctions   A collective, punitive action involving diplomatic, economic, or military measures against a state. Under the United Nations Charter (Chapter VII), when the Security Council determines that a threat to the peace, breach of the peace, or act of aggression exists, members may be called upon to invoke military or nonmilitary sanctions against the lawbreaking state. Since the adoption of the Uniting for Peace Resolution in 1950, the General Assembly is also empowered to levy sanctions against an aggressor by a two-thirds vote. Sanctions may include such actions as breaking diplomatic relations, embargo or blockade, and the use of force. *See* COLLECTIVE SECURITY, page 319.

Significance   An international law-enforcement system, like a nation's, must provide enforcement action to be effective. The *threat* of collective sanctions may be more effective in preventing aggression than the enforcement system in dealing with actual aggressions. The League of Nations attempted only once to employ sanctions (an economic boycott was levied against Italy after its attack upon Ethiopia in 1935) but failed to deter the aggressor. The United Nations levied military and economic sanctions against North Korea in 1950 and applied economic measures against Communist China. Regional organizations may also employ sanctions, such as those undertaken by the Organization of American States against the Castro regime in Cuba.

Secretariat   An organized body of officials and civil servants who have the responsibility of fulfilling administrative, secretarial, and housekeeping functions for an international organization. The United Nations Secretariat is one of the six major organs of the world organization. Its formal structure includes a Secretary-General and eight Assistant Secretaries-General, each of the latter heading a major Department (Security, Economic, Social, Trusteeship, Legal, Information, General Services, and Administrative and Financial). *See* SECRE-TARY-GENERAL, page 336.

Significance   The success or failure of an international organization often depends on the efficiency of its secretariat and the capabilities and dedication of its staff. The United Nations has fostered the concept of an international civil service whose members serve the United Nations without regard for the views of their own countries.

Secretary-General   The chief administrative officer of the United Nations who heads the Secretariat. The Secretary-General is chosen by the General Assembly, upon recommendation by the Security Council, for five-year terms. The U.N. Charter, in an attempt to strengthen the office of Secretary-General over its League of Nations predecessor, gave him authority to place security questions before the Security Council. *See* SECRETARIAT, page 336.

Significance   The role of the Secretary-General has greatly expanded with the assignment of various political responsibilities in addition to his administrative duties. In theory, the position of Secretary-General is somewhat analogous to that of a city manager; in practice, however, it has evolved into a position of real leadership. Although he must operate within the framework of Assembly or Security Council resolutions, he has considerable decision-making power in implementing these resolutions. Trygve Lie of Norway, the first Secretary-General of the United Nations, provided effective leadership until a Western-Soviet split over the Korean War reduced his ability to function in that role. Dag Hammarskjöld of Sweden, who replaced Lie in 1953, further expanded the executive role of the office and maintained the support of all U.N. members until the Congo crisis of 1960. At that time, the Soviet Union charged Hammarskjöld with partisanship in his handling of the Congo situation. Following the death of Hammarskjöld in 1961, U Thant of Burma was appointed Secretary-General. Thant continued to develop the office as an agency of U.N. leadership and world influence.

Secretary of State   The leading Cabinet officer, who heads the Department of State and is charged with responsibility for formulating policies and conducting relations with foreign states. The Secretary of State has been recognized by statute as first of the Cabinet officials in the line of succession to the presidency following the Vice President, Speaker, and President pro tempore. His responsibilities include the direction and supervision of policy-making and administrative functions vested in the State Department in Washington, D.C., the diplomatic and consular services, and special missions and agencies abroad. *See* DEPARTMENT OF STATE, page 340.

Significance   The role of the Secretary of State as a decision-maker may be great or insignificant as the President may decide. Some presidents, like Woodrow Wilson and Franklin Roosevelt, largely ignored their secretaries of state and handled foreign policy matters directly and personally. Other presidents have delegated much responsibility to their secretaries of state in foreign affairs. Often in American history, the Secretary of State has become a political target of the opposition party.

Security Council   One of the six major organs of the United Nations, which was given primary responsibility for maintaining peace and security in the world. There are five permanent members—Britain, China, France, Soviet Union, and the United States—and ten nonpermanent members elected by the General Assembly for two-year periods, five chosen each year. Procedural and substantive decisions are made by an affirmative vote of nine members but, in the latter case, a negative vote cast by any permanent member constitutes a veto and stops all action. When considering peaceful settlement measures, a Council member that is a party to the dispute must abstain from voting. Nations that are not members of the Council may be invited to participate without a vote in Council deliberations if they are involved in a dispute being considered. Chapter VII of the Charter gives the Security Council the responsibility to "determine the existence of any threat to the peace, breach of the peace, or act of aggression. . . ." The Council can make recommendations or take enforcement action to restore peace and security.

Significance   The Security Council was given the most important responsibilities by the Charter on the assumption that the great powers would continue to cooperate in the postwar period to maintain peace and security. Instead, the major threats to world peace have involved great power rivalry, and over 100 vetoes have reduced the effectiveness of the Council. Some disputes and problems have been dealt with successfully by the Council, but few involving cold war questions have been resolved. As the Council's ability to act during crises faded, a new role was thrust upon the General Assembly, which has replaced the Council as the central organ of the United Nations. The importance of the Council today lies mainly in its role of providing the machinery for a continuous forum for great-power negotiation.

South-East Asia Treaty Organization (SEATO)   A military-economic arrangement based on the South-East Asia Collective Defense Treaty of 1954. Members who agree to take collective action whenever any of their number is threatened by external aggression or internal subversion in southeast Asia are Australia, Britain, France, New Zealand, Pakistan, the Philippines, Thailand, and the United States. SEATO headquarters are in Bangkok and include a council and a secretariat. *See* ALLIANCE, page 315.

Significance   SEATO was created through the efforts of Secretary of State John Foster Dulles to safeguard vital interests against Communist penetration in the southeast Asia area. The economic-cooperation sections of the agreement have been overshadowed by the military and anti-Communist provisions. Internal Communist threats, supported with military equipment provided by Sino-Soviet forces, have challenged the effectiveness of SEATO to maintain the security of the southeast Asia area. Although South Vietnam is not a member of SEATO, its territory is included in the area protected by the treaty.

Sovereignty   A legal concept that, in international affairs, means statehood, political independence, and freedom from external control. *See* SOVEREIGNTY, page 15.

Significance   The importance of sovereignty in the modern state system has come largely from the psychological effect it has had on the decision-making processes of states. It has been a difficult force to overcome in creating political, military, and economic international organizations with decision-making powers. Moreover, sovereignty remains one of the major legal and psychological obstacles to the effective operation of the United Nations system.

Status Quo   A descriptive term used by international political analysts to describe the foreign policy of a state that aims at preserving the existing distribution of power in the world. The concept is derived from the diplomatic term, *status quo ante bellum,* which is a clause typically inserted into peace treaties providing for the restoration of prewar conditions.

Significance   The term "status quo" is used as an analytical tool in seeking to understand and describe the motivations and actions of states in the struggle for power that characterizes the state system. States pursuing policies of revision provide the challenge that forces the status quo grouping to develop defensive policies and alliances. Since World War II, the United States has pursued a policy of the status quo, vis-à-vis the expansionist policies of the Soviet bloc.

Tariff   A tax levied on imports to help protect a nation's industry, business, labor, and agriculture from foreign competition, or to raise revenue. Tariffs are discriminatory if they apply unequally on similar products from different countries, and are retaliatory if motivated by the creation of trade barriers by other countries. *See* UNITED STATES TARIFF COMMISSION, page 341; RECIPROCAL TRADE AGREEMENTS ACT, page 343; TRADE EXPANSION ACT, page 344.

Significance   Tariffs have been used by the United States since 1789 as the principal means of protecting domestic producers from foreign competition. For many years prior to the adoption of an income tax, the tariff was also a primary source of revenue for the federal government. The United States has sought to encourage mutual reductions in tariffs through the Reciprocal Trade Agreement Act of 1934, the General Agreement on Tariffs and Trade of 1947, and the Trade Expansion Act of 1962.

Treaty   A formal agreement entered into between two or more sovereign states for the purpose of creating or restricting mutual rights and mutual responsibilities. The treaty process includes negotiation, signing, ratification, exchange of ratifications, publishing and proclamation, and treaty execution. Treaties having only two signatory states are called bilateral, whereas those with more than two parties are multilateral. Treaties may expire at the end of a specified time limit, when certain conditions have been met, or by mutual agreement. Renunciation of a treaty by one of its parties may occur when a state of war exists or when conditions have been substantially altered (*rebus sic stantibus*). In the United States, all treaties are negotiated under the direction of the President, with some members of the Senate occasionally participating under the constitutional provision that treaties be made "by and with the advice and consent of the Senate. . . ." Treaties must be approved by a two-thirds vote in the Senate, followed by presidential ratification if the Senate's version is acceptable. *See* EXECUTIVE AGREEMENT, page 323; RATIFICATION, page 334; *Missouri v. Holland,* page 342.

Significance   Multilateral treaties have become the major source of international law today. In the United States, treaties are part of the supreme law of the land and take precedence over state constitutions and laws. The courts have never declared a treaty to be unconstitutional. The Supreme Court has held that a treaty may increase the powers of Congress beyond the powers prescribed in the Constitution (*Missouri v. Holland,* 252 U.S. 416 [1920]). Increasingly, American presidents have come to depend on executive agreements rather than treaties; the latter are generally used only when strong congressional and public opinion support are essential to the success of the arrangements.

Truman Doctrine   The policy, adopted by President Harry Truman in 1947, that called for American support for all free peoples resisting armed subjugation by internal or outside forces. The policy was aimed expressly at halting Communist expansion in southeastern Europe and was expounded in a speech to Congress in which President Truman asked for an appropriation of $400 million for military and economic aid to Greece and Turkey. *See* CONTAINMENT, page 320.

Significance   The Truman Doctrine marked the first official acceptance of the "containment" philosophy of building up free-world strength to halt Communist expansionism. The Truman Administration followed it up with the development of the Marshall Plan (1947), a technical assistance program (1949), the North Atlantic Treaty (1949), and a mutual security program (1951). The Truman Doctrine, as applied to Greece and Turkey, was successful in helping the Greek loyalists to win the civil war and in building up Turkey as a bastion of free world strength with a modern army. The policy of containment of communism embodied in the Truman Doctrine has been continued by all succeeding presidents.

Trusteeship Council   One of the six major organs of the United Nations, which helps the General Assembly to supervise the administration of the international trusteeship system. Members of the Council include those nations that administer trust territories, permanent members of the Security Council, and elected members equal in number to the total of trust-administering states on the Council. Trust territories include the: (1) former mandates of the League of Nations; (2) Axis colonies; and (3) colonies voluntarily placed under trusteeship. No colonial power has yet volunteered to place a colony under the system. Council powers include considering reports, accepting petitions, and making periodic visits to trust territories. Administration of "strategic" trust territories is supervised by the Security Council, rather than by the Trusteeship Council, because of their military importance.

Significance   Through its supervisory role, the Trusteeship Council has helped most trust territories achieve self-government. Libya, Italian Somaliland, and Tanganyika, for example, have become independent states. South Africa, however, has refused to place its League of Nations mandate, Southwest Africa, under the trusteeship system, and little progress has been made toward the self-government of the three island groups under American strategic trust— the Marshalls, the Carolines, and the Marianas.

IMPORTANT AGENCIES

Agency for International Development (AID)   A semi-independent agency within the Department of State that directs economic and technical assistance aid programs to foreign nations. AID was created by Congress in the Act for International Development of 1961, replacing the International Cooperation Administration (ICA). AID administers the foreign aid program through developmental loans and grants, investment surveys and guarantees, and developmental research. AID is headed by an administrator who has a dual role as chief of the operating agency and political adviser to the Secretary of State and the President.

Significance   AID has become an increasingly important agency as the United States has stepped up its world-wide economic offensive to prevent the spread of communism to the undeveloped nations. Although military aid outweighed economic aid during the 1950s, the Kennedy and Johnson Administrations have stressed the expansion of economic programs. AID was created particularly to implement President Kennedy's Alliance for Progress program, but its operations are world-wide.

Department of State   The agency primarily responsible for making and executing American foreign policy. The Secretary of State, who heads the Department, is the President's official adviser on foreign-policy matters. The first responsibility of the Department is to formulate programs and policies for the United States in its relations with other nations. Next in importance are its duties of administering laws relating to foreign affairs and conducting the day-to-day relations with foreign countries. The latter responsibility is carried out primarily by the Foreign Service, which is administratively tied to the Department of State and has been undergoing a gradual process of integrating its personnel with that of the Department. Specific duties of the Department include: (1) negotiating treaties and agreements with foreign states; (2) carrying on extensive communications with foreign governments and American units abroad; (3) issuing passports and, through consular officials abroad, granting visas; (4) promoting cultural relations between foreign peoples and the American people; (5) carrying on propaganda and information programs overseas; (6) planning and administering economic aid programs. The Department and its Secretary are responsible to the President in carrying out these duties. Important policy-making and primary contact with field operations and foreign missions are carried on through six regional bureaus. These include the African, Inter-American, European, Far Eastern, and Near Eastern and South Asian Affairs Bureaus, and a Bureau of International Organization Affairs, each headed by an Assistant Secretary. The Agency for International Development and the Peace Corps are two important semiautonomous agencies within the State Department.

Significance   The Department is the major agency for foreign policy decision-making. The importance of its role may depend on the individuals who are President and Secretary of State. For example, President Woodrow Wilson chose to depend largely on his own abilities and those of close friends in making foreign-policy decisions. The main conflict over the role of the Department has involved the question of whether it should confine itself to policy making or be charged additionally with administering foreign programs. This problem has never been fully resolved, although today its primary responsibility is that of developing policy.

Peace Corps   An agency within the State Department that administers the foreign-aid program, adopted in 1961, under which American volunteers are sent to developing countries to teach and help improve living standards. By 1966, 12,000 Peace Corps volunteers were in training or in service in forty-six countries of Asia, Africa, and Latin America.

Significance   The Peace Corps employs a new approach to foreign aid in using human resources to help developing societies help themselves through person-to-person contacts. Despite some setbacks, most foreign governments have praised the Peace Corps and have requested additional volunteers. Twelve advanced countries have followed the American example by establishing similar volunteer programs.

United States Information Agency (USIA)   An independent agency, established in 1953, that has responsibility for administration of foreign information programs of the United States. The USIA operates a global network of communications media which beam propaganda programs all over the world. The agency works closely with the State Department and related agencies to harmonize its information programs with American foreign policy.

Significance   The USIA directs American governmental efforts in the psychological phase of the cold war. Activities include round-the-clock radio broadcasts in about forty languages, television programs, distribution and showings of documentary, feature, and newsreel films, and distribution of millions of leaflets, pamphlets, news bulletins, and related propaganda materials. The USIA has operated on the proposition that "truth is our weapon." Its information centers and libraries have often been damaged or destroyed in anti-American demonstrations abroad.

United States Tariff Commission   An independent agency that gives information to Congress and the President on American and foreign tariff and trade matters. The six members of the Tariff Commission, three from each of the major parties, are appointed by the President, with the Senate's approval, for six-year terms.

Significance   Congress has used the Tariff Commission as a means of keeping the President's tariff reductions, under the Reciprocal Trade Agreements Act of 1934 and the Trade Expansion Act of 1962, within some degree of congressional supervision and control. In the "peril point" provisions, the Tariff Commission indicates a rate for each imported product at which it might enter the American market in a quantity sufficient to threaten or injure domestic producers. Under "escape-clause" provisions, the Commission can recommend to the President that a trade agreement be adjusted when its investigations disclose that low tariff rates are threatening to injure or are injuring American producers. If the President rejects the advice of the Tariff Commission, Congress can override him and restore the higher tariff rate by a two-thirds vote in both houses. The escape clause has been invoked by the President to modify agreements with foreign nations on only a few occasions.

IMPORTANT CASES

Missouri v. Holland, 252 U.S. 416 (1920): Upheld the validity of a federal statute based on a treaty with Great Britain for the protection of birds and waterfowl migrating between Canada and the United States. The question was whether the national government could acquire, through a treaty, power to legislate on domestic matters otherwise reserved to the states. A similar federal law, antedating the treaty and the law in question in this case, had earlier been declared unconstitutional by the lower federal courts.

Significance   The decision in *Missouri v. Holland* means that the national government can actually add to its powers by concluding treaties with foreign states. Opponents of increasing federal responsibility have argued since 1920 that the case should be overturned because it almost obliterates the distinction between the national government's delegated and the state's reserved powers. This viewpoint crystallized in the 1950s in the Bricker Amendment proposal, which, if adopted, would have allowed treaties to become effective within the United States only through legislation valid in the absence of a treaty. Supporters of the decision point out that the alleged danger has not materialized and that to limit the treaty-making powers would constitute a greater danger to the country.

United States v. Curtiss-Wright Export Corp., 299 U.S. 304 (1936): Upheld the validity of a statute of Congress that delegated broad powers to the President to prohibit arms shipments to foreign belligerents. In question was a presidential proclamation levying an embargo on shipment of war matériel to either side in the Gran Chaco war between Bolivia and Paraguay. In the *Curtiss-Wright* case, the Court distinguished between permissible delegations of congressional lawmaking power in domestic areas and those in foreign affairs. The Court noted: "As a member of the family of nations, the right and power of the United States . . . are equal to the right and power of the other nations of the international family. Otherwise the United States is not completely sovereign."

Significance   The Court recognized in this case the full responsibility of the national government in foreign affairs and the importance of the President's role in this field. By authorizing congressional and presidential actions in foreign affairs that might not be valid in domestic matters, the Court recognized that, in addition to the enumerated and implied powers, a third category of powers, inherent in nature, may be exercised by the President in foreign affairs. The Court reaffirmed the primacy of the national government in foreign affairs in *United States v. Pink*, 315 U.S. 203 (1942), asserting that power over foreign relations "is not shared by the states; it is vested in the national government exclusively." Federalism, the Court noted, stops at the water's edge.

IMPORTANT STATUTES

Battle Act (Mutual Defense Assistance Control Act of 1951)   An act to prohibit trade with Communist countries in strategic goods and to deny American foreign aid to any nation that carried on such trade. The President is empowered to make exceptions if cutting off foreign aid would be contrary to American interests.

Significance   The Battle Act has resulted in a major reduction of American trade with the Soviet Union and other Communist countries. Much effort has been expended by American negotiators since 1951 to persuade allies and neutralist countries to cut off their strategic trade with the Communists. The policy was moderately successful for a few years, but most of the non-Communist nations of the world have progressively increased their trade with the Soviet bloc. The United States, itself, has expanded its trade with some Communist countries, such as Yugoslavia and Poland.

Reciprocal Trade Agreements Act of 1934   A broad tariff program under which the President negotiates trade agreements with foreign countries that provide for mutual reductions in tariff rates. It incorporates the "most-favored nation" principle, under which concessions contained in agreements apply to all other nations with which we have most favored nation arrangements. The original enactment in 1934 provided that tariff rates of the United States could be lowered or raised up to fifty percent of the existing rates, but renewals have given the President authority to seek additional cuts. Amendments to the Act include "peril-point" and "escape-clause" provisions. The peril-point amendment provides that the Tariff Commission inform the President and Congress at what level a tariff rate might allow imports to threaten or injure a domestic producer. Escape-clause procedures require that tariff rates be raised if they injure domestic producers. The Trade Expansion Act of 1962 expands the President's tariff-cutting powers, thereby strengthening the American bargaining position, especially with the European Common Market countries.

Significance   The Reciprocal Trade Agreements Act sought to increase the two-way flow of trade by transferring rate-setting powers from Congress, in which political considerations and logrolling tactics flourished, to the President, who was empowered to lower rates only on a *quid pro quo* basis. Agreements with forty-three countries are currently in force. Reciprocal bargaining has been facilitated through multilateral negotiations carried on through the General Agreement on Tariffs and Trade (GATT) system with a membership of sixty-six nations. Protectionist sentiment, however, has increased in the Congress in recent years as a result of growing competition from imports.

Rogers (Foreign Service) Act of 1924   The basic law that established the organization and functions of the Foreign Service as it exists today. The Rogers Act unified the diplomatic and consular services into an integrated Foreign Service, created a career service based on merit, and established the Foreign Service Institute. Subsequent amendments added in the Foreign Service Acts of 1946 and 1949 have sought to professionalize the Service. Additional changes based on the report of the Wriston Committee in 1954 have sought to "democratize" the Service and integrate its personnel with that of the State Department.

Significance   The Rogers Act initiated a series of reforms which have reshaped the Foreign Service over the years and developed it into a first-rate organization. Appointment to the Foreign Service today is open to most Americans, yet involves the most careful selection process developed by any government agency. The Foreign Service organization and the quality of its personnel have a direct bearing on making foreign policy and conducting foreign affairs.

Trade Expansion Act of 1962   A major revision of the Trade Agreements Act of 1934 to facilitate the reciprocal reduction of tariffs. The Act gives American negotiators unprecedented tariff-cutting powers. The major provisions of the Trade Expansion Act give the President power: (1) to reduce most tariffs by fifty percent and to eliminate some completely; (2) to reduce tariffs in general categories on an across-the-board basis rather than individually on an item-by-item approach; (3) to reduce tariffs and quotas on tropical products imported from developing countries; and (4) to establish domestic "trade adjustment" programs to moderate the impact of tariff cuts upon business and labor. The Act continues the "peril-point" and "escape-clause" provisions, which identify the levels of imports that constitute a danger to American industry and permit the President to invalidate a trade agreement that threatens substantial injury to American producers.

Significance   Congress enacted the Trade Expansion Act to provide tariff bargaining power to penetrate the tariff wall of the European Common Market. These negotiations, called the "Kennedy round," have continued since 1963 in the General Agreement on Tariffs and Trade (GATT) organization, but have met with only moderate success.

Seventeen

National Defense

Civil Defense   The protection of civilian populations from enemy attack. Civil defense operations are centered in the Office of Civil Defense (OCD) in the Department of the Army. The Director of Civil Defense, who heads the OCD, has been assigned responsibility for developing a shelter program, a defense against chemical, biological, and radiological weapons, a warning system, and measures to be undertaken following an attack. OCD has designated numerous structures as fallout shelters for protection against radioactivity following a nuclear attack and has stocked many of them with supplies; but the adoption of a major shelter program in the United States remains a controversial issue.

Significance   The advent of nuclear and other weapons of mass destruction raises the question of whether civil defense is practicable. Officials have estimated that a nuclear attack could result in 150 million American civilian casualties within a matter of hours. Those who favor a major shelter program believe that it would help to deter an attack because it would save millions of civilian lives and permit a subsequent mobilization of civilians as a second line of defense. Opponents claim that the cost of a national shelter program is prohibitive, that it would be ineffective against a massive attack, and that it might accelerate the arms race or encourage an American or Soviet strike.

Civilian Control   The American constitutional principle of civilian supremacy over the military to safeguard republican institutions. Civilian control is maintained through constitutional provisions that make the President commander in chief of the armed forces and grant Congress power to raise and support armies, make military law, declare war, and appropriate money for military expenditures for only two-year periods. The Second and Third Amendments buttress the principle by forbidding the quartering of troops without consent and by granting the people the right to keep and bear arms. Statutory enactments, such as the legal requirement that the Secretary of Defense and the Secretaries of the Army, Navy, and Air Force Departments must all be civilians, also encourage civilian control.

Significance   Civilian control is especially significant in a democratic nation that is beset by potential enemies and has built up a great military power. Several countries of the world today appear to be democratic but are controlled by military cliques. Some people in the United States have become fearful of the rising power and influence of the military during the period of the cold war, yet national defense considerations have increased the nation's dependence upon them.

Commander in Chief   The role of the President, as provided in Article II, section 2 of the Constitution, as supreme commander of the military forces of the United States and of the state national guard units when they are called into federal service. As commander in chief, the President exercises a vast array of "war powers." During periods of war or threat of war, he exercises both military and civilian powers related to defense. *See* PRESIDENT, page 169; WAR POWERS, page 352.

Significance   Under his war powers, the President can deploy American forces anywhere in the world and, as has happened many times in American history, order them into action against a foreign foe without a declaration of war by Congress. American military interventions—in Korea in 1950, in Vietnam since 1956, and in the Dominican Republic in 1965—without congressional declarations of war illustrate the extent to which a President can commit the nation to a course of military action under his powers as commander in chief.

Counterinsurgency   Military force employed against a revolutionary group trying to overthrow an established regime. Counterinsurgency operations describe the efforts of American and indigenous military forces to prevent a Communist take-over through revolution, guerrilla warfare, subversion, and related techniques.

Significance   Counterinsurgency operations have developed as a response to the Communist doctrine of promoting "wars of national liberation" enunciated in the late 1950s. In Vietnam, counterinsurgency operations are carried on by American, South Korean, Australian, New Zealand, and South Vietnamese units against Viet Cong guerrillas and North Vietnamese forces.

Court-martial   A military tribunal that conducts trials of military personnel accused of violating military law. A *summary* court-martial consists of a single officer who tries enlisted men for minor offenses. A *special* court-martial, which can only be convened by a commanding general, consists of three officers who may impose moderately severe penalties, such as six months at hard labor, bad conduct discharges, and reductions in rank. A *general* court-martial may be convened by the President or Secretary of Defense. It consists of five or more members, one-third of whom must be enlisted men if they are requested by the accused. Severe penalties, such as the death penalty, life imprisonment, or dishonorable discharge, may be imposed. *See* COURT OF MILITARY APPEALS, page 207; MILITARY LAW, page 349.

Significance   The court-martial has become an important part of the American system of justice because of the large numbers of Americans in the armed forces. During World War II, almost one-third of the nation's criminal cases were decided by courts-martial. Charges of unfair procedures and a lack of justice led Congress to establish a new Uniform Code of Military Justice in 1950, to provide for enlisted men to serve on *general* courts-martial, and to create a three-man civilian Court of Military Appeals to which convicted military personnel can appeal.

Declaration of War   A formal announcement by a nation that a state of hostilities exists with another nation. Constitutionally, only Congress can declare war. Under the usual procedure, the President requests a declaration of war, the Congress adopts it by joint resolution, and the President signs it.

Significance   In the conditions of modern war, Congress has lost most of its discretionary power to determine when and if war should be declared. Congress may merely recognize that a state of hostilities already exists, as in its declaration of war against the Axis powers following the attack upon Pearl Harbor in 1941. Moreover, the President, as commander in chief, may commit American forces to action without a congressional declaration of war, as when President Franklin Roosevelt ordered a naval convoy for merchant ships prior to America's actual entry into World War II. In the Korean War, American troops, ordered into action by President Harry Truman, fought from 1950 to 1953 under the United Nations banner without a formal declaration of war by Congress. In South Vietnam, Presidents Dwight Eisenhower, John Kennedy, and Lyndon Johnson committed increasingly large numbers of American troops to action and in 1965, President Johnson ordered bombing of North Vietnam, all without a congressional declaration of war. Today, with missiles and hydrogen bombs poised for attack, the decision to launch or repel an attack may be made by the President or, conceivably, by a military commander in the field, with Congress having little to do with the decision.

Deterrence   Retaliatory capability of a nation's military forces to discourage a potential enemy from launching an attack. The concept implies that a nation's military defenses are so large, so diversified, and so well protected that a first-strike by an enemy would not cripple its ability to retaliate decisively.

Significance   Nuclear weapons have made deterrence an effective and credible strategy. Even if most of a nuclear power's retaliatory capability were destroyed in an initial strike, the potential for mass destruction of enemy cities would remain. Deterrence implies that the people and industry of rival nuclear powers remain perpetual hostages to deter a planned attack by either. The United States' deterrent power includes intercontinental missiles protected by underground silos, polaris submarines with nuclear-tipped missiles, and the strategic bomber fleet, some of which is constantly airborne.

Intelligence   Gathering information about the capabilities and intentions of foreign governments. Most intelligence is secured by analyzing data found in governmental and private publications, but some requires the use of clandestine cloak-and-dagger methods. American agencies actively engaged in the gathering and/or analysis of intelligence include: (1) the Central Intelligence Agency (CIA), which carries on undercover activities around the globe and serves as a central focus for the receipt and evaluation of intelligence; (2) the National Security Agency (NSA), which engages in coding and decoding operations and electronic surveillance; (3) Army Intelligence (G2), which secures data on ground forces and new weapons; (4) Air Force Intelligence (A2), which covers air and space affairs; (5) the Office of Naval Intelligence (ONI), which ferrets out information on foreign navies and fleet movements; (6) the Bureau of Intelligence and Research (I & R) in the State Department, which obtains economic and political data and forecasts trends; (7) the Defense Intelligence Agency (DIA) of the Department of Defense, which evaluates the capabilities of allies and potential enemies; (8) the Atomic Energy Commission (AEC), which seeks data on nuclear weapons and detects nuclear test explosions; and (9) the Federal Bureau of Investigation (FBI), which obtains information on internal threats to security. The United States Intelligence Board, headed by the Director of the CIA, meets regularly to sift information gathered by intelligence agencies and to give a "national intelligence estimate" to the President. *See* CENTRAL INTELLIGENCE AGENCY, page 352.

Significance   Technological advancements in warfare have increased the need for governments to obtain vital information related to the security of the state. Intelligence objectives relate mainly to the military field, but states also gather data on political, economic, and social factors. Not only potential enemies but friendly and allied nations constitute the subjects of intelligence operations. Some critics charge that the multiplicity of American intelligence agencies leads to confusion and duplication. When intelligence failures permit a surprise attack—as at Pearl Harbor in 1941—or provide an erroneous assessment of a foreign situation—as in the abortive Bay of Pigs invasion of Cuba in 1961—the results may endanger a nation's vital security interests.

Limited War   Any war that is fought without the employment of all major weapons and for objectives other than the complete defeat of the enemy. Limited war involves the use of conventional military forces rather than of atomic superweapons.

Significance   In the Korean conflict of the early 1950s and the Vietnam war of the 1960s, the United States and other nations fought limited wars with conventional military forces. Efforts to contain limited wars from spreading into general world-wide conflagrations make decisive victories impossible to achieve. Many critics opposed American defense policies in the 1950s on the ground that too much emphasis was placed upon weapons of massive destruction at the expense of mobile tactical forces of the type needed to fight limited wars. This opposition was based on the belief that since neither the Soviet Union nor the United States would employ atomic weapons, the United States found itself in an inferior position to combat localized aggressions because of its overemphasis on atomic forces. The Kennedy and Johnson Administrations have sought to achieve a "balanced force" of conventional and nuclear weapons.

Martial Law   Military government established over a civilian population during an emergency in which military decrees supersede civilian laws and military tribunals replace civil courts. Martial law may be accompanied by the suspension of the writ of habeas corpus. Although the Constitution does not delegate specific power to declare martial law, it is implied from military and defense powers and can be invoked by the President when necessary for the security of the nation. In the states, the governor as commander in chief of the state militia may declare martial law during an emergency occasioned by internal disorders or a natural disaster. Vast discretion is vested in military officers in enforcing martial law. *See Ex parte Milligan*, page 354.

Significance   Martial law is sometimes erroneously used to describe the use of troops to aid civil authorities and civil courts in maintaining order, which is far more common than the suspension of civil authority. Rare occasions on which federal martial law has been invoked by the President include Abraham Lincoln's placing the southern and border states under martial law, and Franklin Roosevelt's placing Hawaii under it following the attack upon Pearl Harbor. Racial violence in recent years has often led governors to invoke martial law to restore order in local communities.

Military Government   Temporary government established by conquering military forces over occupied enemy territory. Areas occupied by American forces are governed under statutes enacted by Congress, supplemented by orders issued by the President as commander in chief. The military governor of a territory under military government exercises supreme legislative, executive, and judicial authority. Civil government operates to the extent permitted by the military governor.

Significance   Military government was used extensively by the United States and its allies during and following World War II in the occupation of enemy territory. Special army military government units were trained to perform occupation duties. Efforts were made to teach the enemy populace the principles and practices of democracy, in most cases successfully. Today, sovereignty has been restored and military government units have been withdrawn from most of these formerly occupied territories.

Military Law   Law, enacted by Congress, that governs the conduct of enlisted men and officers of the armed forces of the United States. Military law also establishes the procedures for trial by courts-martial for alleged infractions. *See* COURT-MARTIAL, page 346.

Significance   Prior to 1950, separate Articles of War applied to the Army, Navy, and Coast Guard. To secure uniformity, and in response to criticism concerning the lack of military justice, Congress, in 1950, enacted a single uniform code for all of the armed forces. This Uniform Code of Military Justice seeks to resolve the problem of balancing the needs for discipline with justice. It also permits the trial of servicemen by civil courts for off-duty offenses committed in the United States. Military law, however, does not ordinarily apply to civilians who are abroad with the armed forces (*Reid v. Covert*, 354 U.S. 1 [1957]) or to discharged servicemen for offenses committed while in the armed forces (*Toth v. Quarles*, 350 U.S. 11 [1955]).

Mobilization   Preparing a nation to meet an attack or to fight a war. Mobilization involves placing the armed forces in readiness, calling up reserves to active duty, putting the nation's economy on a war footing, establishing governmental controls over manpower, production, resources, and prices. Mobilization for modern war involves readying the totality of a nation's manpower and physical resources for military action. The Office of Emergency Planning in the Executive Office of the President is responsible for planning the nation's nonmilitary defense effort.

Significance   Mobilization is directed by the President whose constitutional authority as commander in chief is buttressed by vast delegations of emergency powers by Congress for the duration of the war or crisis. Under the stress of war or threat of war, the courts have not generally interfered with the President's exercise of mobilization powers. Mobilization by a nation during peacetime may decrease the possibility of war by calling a potential aggressor's bluff; conversely, it may increase the likelihood of war if other nations consider it a threat to their security.

National Guard   The volunteer armed forces of the states formerly called the militia. The Constitution provides for a cooperative system under which each state is responsible for appointing officers and Congress provides for organizing, arming, and disciplining the Guard. Each governor is commander in chief of his state's national guard and may call it out for emergencies, such as floods, fires, civil disorders, and racial riots.

Significance   During much of American history, state militias constituted a relatively powerful and autonomous group of armed forces. Since 1916, the militias have been organized as the National Guard, an auxiliary of the regular army subject to substantial national control. Congress may call the Guard into federal service at any time, and has done so during World Wars I and II and in other emergencies, such as in the 1962 Cuban crisis. The President, as commander in chief, decides when units will be called, and all state jurisdiction ceases when the Guard becomes part of the regular army.

Reserves   The Army, Navy, Air Force, Coast Guard, and National Guard units not on active duty but available to supplement the regular military services during emergencies. Reservists are divided into "ready reserves," "standby reserves," and "retired reserves." The ready reserve may be called to active duty by the President or Congress. The standby reserve is a pool of trained military personnel who can be called up only in case of war or an emergency declared by Congress. A third category, the retired reserve, can be recalled to active duty by Congress during a major emergency.

Significance   The reserves consist largely of men who have completed their active military duty and take weekly training and attend summer training camps. The role of reserves in modern warfare depends on the nature of the military situation. In a major atomic war, for example, decisive blows might be struck before reserves could be mustered. In a limited war, conversely, a reservoir of trained manpower would probably be essential. During the Berlin crisis in 1961, President John F. Kennedy called up some units of the ready reserves for one year of active duty to bolster the American military posture.

Selective Service   The conscription system under which the national government drafts men for service in the armed forces. Selective service is based on the constitutional provisions which give Congress the powers necessary "to raise" armies and "to provide" a navy. *See Selective Draft Law Cases,* page 355.

   Significance   The national government has drafted manpower for military service during and since the Civil War for wartime or emergency service. During World Wars I and II, millions of Americans were conscripted for military service. Peacetime selective service systems were also instituted by Congress in 1940 and again in 1948; the latter is currently in effect. Selective service activity has increased in the 1960s with larger draft quotas for the Vietnam war, resulting in anti-selective service demonstrations. The Supreme Court established a basic precedent in 1918 when it rejected the assertion that selective service violates the constitutional provision against "involuntary servitude" by holding that compulsory military service is, rather, an "involuntary duty" (*Selective Draft Law Cases,* 245 U.S. 366 [1918]).

Stockpiling   The accumulation of strategic raw materials for use during a national crisis. The United States has amassed a stockpile of about eighty essential raw materials and metals that must be obtained abroad or that might be needed quickly during an emergency. Stockpiled materials range from steel and aluminum to natural rubber, industrial diamonds, and such rare items as selenium and tantalum. The vast storehouse of agricultural products acquired by the national government under its price-support program buttresses the strategic materials stockpile.

   Significance   Stockpiling offers a country rich enough to indulge in the practice not only a hedge against future military demands but a powerful weapon for economic warfare as well. A stockpile has domestic as well as international implications. The Johnson Administration, for example, released quantities of steel and aluminum for domestic consumption to ward off inflationary price increases in the mid-1960s. The American stockpiling program gave impetus to the export earnings of some of the developing countries while the materials were being acquired; but when the buying program ceased, inflated productive capacities in these countries led to oversupply and a depressing of prices. The United States strategic-materials stockpile is currently valued at over $8 billion.

Unification   The integration of the military services of the United States. Under the National Security Act of 1947, the Army, Navy, and Air Force were unified under a single Department of Defense. *See* DEFENSE REORGANIZATION ACT, page 355; NATIONAL SECURITY ACTS, page 355.

   Significance   Critics of separate military departments charged that the system promoted interservice rivalries, prevented integrated planning, increased military costs, encouraged recruiting competition, promoted budget battles, and resulted in duplication and inefficiency. Supporters of independent departments claimed that a single military chief would be too powerful, that it would encourage a Prussian-type general staff system, that it would lead to charges of favoritism against the single head, and that the separate service approach had proved itself in World Wars I and II. Unification has not, in fact, eliminated interservice rivalries, and serious cleavages among the three branches, concerning such questions as basic strategy, budget allocation, and missile development responsibility, have continued.

War Powers   The authority expressly granted by the Constitution, implied from it, or inherent in the duty of protecting the nation from its enemies. War powers include those granted to Congress to tax and spend for the common defense, to declare war and make rules concerning captures, to raise and support armies and provide a navy, to enact military law, and to oversee the state militias. Moreover, the elastic clause permits Congress to do whatever is necessary and proper in executing these powers. The President, as commander in chief, has the inherent power to do whatever is necessary to protect the nation, subject to judicial scrutiny. In times of crisis, Congress delegates legislative powers to the President as "emergency powers."

Significance   Although defense and war powers are subject to constitutional limitations in the same way as other powers, they have been stretched to their limits during serious crises. Presidents Abraham Lincoln, Franklin Roosevelt, and Harry Truman regarded the war powers as a special and undefined category of powers that can be exercised whenever the security of the nation is threatened. Congress, the public, and the courts have generally accepted the primacy of the President's role and his exercise of vast powers during time of war. Under conditions of modern warfare, the war powers include control over the domestic economy as well as the military phases of the conflict.

IMPORTANT AGENCIES

Atomic Energy Commission (AEC)   An independent agency of the United States government with responsibility to foster research and development of atomic energy and to regulate all private efforts in the field. The AEC consists of five commissioners appointed by the President with the Senate's approval for five-year terms. Responsibility for enforcement of the Atomic Energy Acts of 1946 and 1954 is vested in the Commission. *See* ATOMIC ENERGY ACTS, page 277.

Significance   The AEC has been primarily concerned with developing and stockpiling a vast array of nuclear weapons. Its major research activities are carried on at Argonne National Laboratory at Chicago and at Brookhaven National Laboratory at Upton, New York. Its major production facilities are at Oak Ridge, Tennessee, and Richland, Washington. The AEC has become one of the major spending agencies of the national government with an annual budget of about $3 billion. Its activities are supervised by Congress through a Joint Committee on Atomic Energy.

Central Intelligence Agency (CIA)   An agency, headed by a Director appointed by the President with Senate approval, that functions under the National Security Council to coordinate intelligence activities in the interest of national security. The CIA evaluates raw intelligence data supplied by the Army, Navy, Air Force, the State Department, and other intelligence-gathering, civilian and military agencies. This information is disseminated among various units of the national government to aid in decision-making.

Significance   The CIA operations are supersecret in nature, and even most congressmen cannot inquire into its activities. Experts estimate that the major portion of intelligence information is secured through foreign publications and other materials of an open nature, with only a small amount of information obtained through clandestine "cloak-and-dagger" methods.

Department of Defense   A major department of the national government with responsibility to formulate military policies and to maintain the armed forces of the United States. Since 1961, it has assumed responsibility for civil defense functions. The Secretary who heads the Department of Defense is a civilian appointed by the President with the Senate's approval. He serves as a member of the Cabinet. The three major military departments of the Army, Navy, and Air Force are each headed by a civilian secretary responsible to the Secretary of Defense. The Chiefs of Staff of the Army and the Air Force and the Chief of Naval Operations are the top military officers in each service who advise the civilian secretaries. These three military leaders join with the Chief of Staff to the Secretary of Defense to form the Joint Chiefs of Staff, the nation's highest military advisory body. Other advisers to the Secretary of Defense include the Armed Forces Policy Council, composed of the civilian secretaries, the Joint Chiefs of Staff, the Director of Defense Research and Engineering, and a host of civilian and military individuals, boards, and committees to offer advice on a variety of defense subjects. The Commandant of the Marine Corps also attends meetings of the Joint Chiefs and the Policy Council.

Significance   The Defense Department has become the most important department in the national government in numbers of employees and amounts of money spent. Defense has over one million civilian employees, almost one-half of all national civil servants. In recent years, its annual budget has averaged more than fifty percent of all expenditures of the government. The Secretary of Defense ranks after the Secretaries of State and Treasury as Cabinet adviser to the President and in the line of succession to that office. Major expenditures of the Department fall into four categories: procurement of military items, salaries and benefits to personnel, operations, and research and development. Military bases are maintained around the world, and coordinated programs are worked out with the over forty nations with which the United States is militarily allied. Increasing emphasis is being placed on research and development as the technological race with the Soviet Union accelerates. Unity of command has been achieved through the National Security Acts of 1947 and 1949 and the Defense Reorganization Act of 1958, but interservice rivalries have not completely given way to unity of purpose, especially during budget-making.

National Aeronautics and Space Council (NASC)   A staff agency in the Executive Office of the President that advises the President on policies, plans, and programs concerning the American space program. Members include the Vice President of the United States, who serves as chairman, the Secretaries of State and Defense, the Administrator of the National Aeronautics and Space Administration (NASA) which carries out space program decisions, and the

Chairman of the Atomic Energy Commission. The NASC was established under the National Aeronautics and Space Act of 1958.

Significance   The Council was created to meet the challenge posed when Soviet scientists placed the first "sputnik" in space in 1957. The American failure to secure a "first" was blamed on many factors, among them the lack of a unified program to eliminate duplication and to achieve a common effort. Rival military space teams were brought into an integrated program directed by the civilian NASC and NASA agencies.

National Security Council (NSC)   A staff agency in the Executive Office of the President, established by the National Security Act of 1947, that advises the President on domestic and foreign matters involving national security. The Council is composed of the President, the Vice President, the Secretaries of State and Defense, and the Director of the Office of Emergency Planning. The Central Intelligence Agency (CIA) functions under the direction of the Council. The Council's main role is to assess and appraise the objectives, commitments, and risks of the United States in the interests of national security and to make recommendations to the President on specific policies and decisions.

Significance   The National Security Council is the highest policy-recommending body in defense and related fields. Whenever a serious crisis erupts anywhere in the world, the President usually summons the Council into an immediate session. The President is free to reject the advice of the Council, but this is unlikely because it is composed of the highest leaders of his administration in the defense and foreign-policy fields.

United States Arms Control and Disarmament Agency (USACDA)   An independent agency established in 1961 to conduct research and to develop disarmament policies. USACDA is headed by a Director, appointed by the President with Senate consent, who also serves as principal adviser to the President and the Secretary of State on disarmament matters.

Significance   USACDA was established in response to American and foreign demands that greater efforts be expended to reach a disarmament agreement. USACDA has carried on extensive "peace research" and has participated in thermonuclear and conventional disarmament negotiations at Geneva and the United Nations. Many of its studies are carried on by private and public institutions on a contractual basis. Major areas of negotiation and research include a ban on all nuclear testing, an antiproliferation treaty to prevent the spread of nuclear weapons among additional states, technical and political problems concerned with the enforcement of a disarmament agreement, and the development of new approaches to disarmament and arms control.

IMPORTANT CASES

Ex parte Milligan, 4 Wallace 2 (1866): Held that the suspension of the right of writ of habeas corpus and the trial of a civilian by a military tribunal while the civilian courts are operating violate the Constitution. The Court held that neither the President nor Congress could legally deny the accused a civil trial by jury in an area outside an actual theater of war.

Significance   The *Milligan* case reaffirmed the principles of civilian control over the military and the maintenance of due process of law free from military interference. There have been no further attempts to suspend the writ of habeas corpus in the continental United States. In 1941, following the attack upon Pearl Harbor, President Franklin Roosevelt placed the Hawaiian Islands under martial law and all civil courts were replaced by military tribunals. In a case after the war (*Duncan v. Kahanamoku,* 327 U.S. 304 [1946]), the Court held this action invalid.

Selective Draft Law Cases, 245 U.S. 366 (1918): Upheld the constitutional authority of Congress to draft men into the military forces. The Supreme Court rejected the argument that conscription is "involuntary servitude" in violation of the Thirteenth Amendment, holding that such service by the citizen was "his supreme and noble duty." *See* CONSCIENTIOUS OBJECTOR, page 58.

Significance   Although the *Selective Draft Law Cases* dealt with a wartime conscription measure, the constitutionality of the peacetime draft is also based on this precedent. During war and in peacetime, the Army has depended heavily upon the draft to supply needed manpower, whereas the Navy and Air Force have mainly used volunteers.

IMPORTANT STATUTES

Defense Reorganization Act of 1958   An act that sought to overcome administrative weaknesses in the Defense Department created by the National Security Acts of 1947 and 1949. The Act of 1958 made it clear that the Secretaries of the Army, Navy, and Air Force were under the direct authority of the Secretary of Defense. A direct line of command from the Secretary to operational units in the field replaced the earlier system whereby the Secretary communicated decisions through the Army, Navy, and Air Force Secretaries.

Significance   In the wake of Soviet space and missile successes, President Dwight Eisenhower proposed a sweeping reorganization of the defense organization. Congress accepted part of the President's proposals in the Act of 1958, but retained a legislative veto over the Defense Secretary's organizational changes, permitted the civilian and military heads of the three services to communicate directly with Congress, and specifically exempted the National Guard and Marine Corps from alteration, except by Congress. Although the Act of 1958 was designed to eliminate interservice rivalries over budgets and weapon development programs, controversy among the services has continued. The Act of 1958 expressly denied any power to the President to merge any of the military services or to create a military chief of staff system.

National Security Acts of 1947 and 1949   The Act of 1947 provided the nation's most comprehensive reorganization of its defense structure. It established a new National Security Organization and placed the three major military forces—Army, Navy, and Air Force—in a National Military Establishment under a single civilian Secretary of Defense. The National Security Council was established as a top-level advisory body. In the National Security Act of 1949 the National Military Establishment was replaced with a single executive department—the Department of Defense—and the National Security Council was transferred to the Executive Office as a staff agency to the President.

Significance   The National Security Acts of 1947 and 1949 were aimed at unifying and coordinating the efforts of the nation's armed services. Although the Act stated that the services were not to be merged, it called for "their integration into an efficient team of land, naval, and air forces." The authority given to the Secretary of Defense in the Act of 1947 proved insufficient to unify in fact three separate military services, each largely autonomous in its operations and protective of its traditional role. The Act of 1949 sought to reduce these interservice rivalries further by strengthening the hand of the Secretary of Defense over the military departments.

Eighteen

State and Local Government

Alderman   A member of a city council. The term originated in England and was used in the American colonies to designate officials chosen by the common council of the city to exercise judicial power and to share in the governing of the city. In the nineteenth century, when bicameral legislatures were common in cities, one house was designated as the Board of Aldermen, the other, as the Common Council.

Significance   The commission and council-manager plans of city government have been accompanied by the use of the terms commissioner or councilman to designate members of the city legislative body. Where used, the term alderman is generally associated with cities in which ward systems of representation for the city council function under a mayor-council plan of government.

Annexation   The addition of territory to a unit of government. Annexation usually denotes the addition by a city of land adjacent to it, to meet the problems of metropolitan expansion. Procedures for annexation are established by state law and generally require an affirmative vote of both the central city and of the area concerned. In a few states, as in Virginia and Texas, areas may be annexed by action of the city alone or through judicial procedures. *See* METROPOLITAN AREA, page 370.

Significance   Annexation is viewed as one solution to the problems caused by the urbanization of fringe areas of a city. Through annexation, a community seeks to eliminate conflicts of authority and duplication of services, and to protect orderly city growth, which is hampered by the existence of numerous units of government. Fringe-area dwellers often fear high city taxes and prefer to retain their identity as a community. Cities that annex residential fringe areas not having the broad tax base provided by business and industry, and with soaring needs for costly services, find the annexed areas to be costly for city taxpayers. Also, many annexed areas lack proper planning and zoning, posing special problems for the city administration.

Attorney General   The chief legal officer of the state. The office of attorney general is elective in forty-two states. He serves as legal adviser to the governor

357

and to state agencies, represents the state in legal proceedings, and may have general supervisory powers over local prosecuting attorneys. *See* ATTORNEY GENERAL, page 200.

Significance   Opinions of the attorney general have the force of law unless they are overturned by a court. Many students of state government argue that the office should be appointive, since the governor should have full confidence in his chief legal adviser, similar to that placed by a client in his attorney. The state attorney general holds an office that frequently leads to the governorship or to a judicial appointment.

Board of Education   The state or local governing body for public education. State boards of education establish state-wide educational and teacher certification standards, determine curricula, and control state educational funds. Most state boards are appointed by the governor; others are elected by the people or appointed by the state legislature. Each state board of education works closely with a state superintendent of schools who is in most cases elected by the people, although the trend is toward appointment by the board. Local school boards are chosen by popular vote in school districts in most states, with a few appointed by the city council. The local school board determines policy but leaves much responsibility in the hands of a school superintendent whom they appoint. Local school boards determine teacher salaries, curricula, and building needs.

Significance   Boards of education administer the largest share of state and local expenditures. The independent status of most boards of education is in keeping with the tradition that schools be "kept out of politics." Schools, however, develop "politics" of their own and no public agency spending huge sums of money is "out of politics." Typically, school boards are controlled by the same political group that dominates other governmental functions of a community and are subjected to considerable community pressures to have the school reflect the views of the community.

Borough   A municipal corporation, generally smaller than a city. Boroughs are found mainly in Pennsylvania, Connecticut, and New Jersey, and resemble villages or towns of other states. Borough is also the named assigned to major local government divisions in Alaska, comparable to counties. The city of New York is divided into five boroughs: Manhattan, Brooklyn, Queens, Bronx, and Richmond.

Significance   The term borough is a holdover from England and colonial America. In New York City, the boroughs represent an attempt to decentralize the operations of that huge metropolis. The use of the term in the constitution of Alaska represents a noteworthy departure from tradition. In order to avoid some of the pitfalls of county government and to adapt local government to their peculiar needs, the people of Alaska provided for the creation of boroughs that would embrace an area and population with common interests and that would have a high degree of home rule.

Charter   The basic law of a local governmental unit that defines its powers, responsibilities, and organization. Charters are granted, under state constitutional or statutory provisions, to municipal corporations and, in some states, to counties or townships. Charters may be provided by: (1) special act of the legislature applicable to one city, (2) general laws applicable to all cities within a certain classification, (3) optional charter laws whereby a city may choose a charter from a group provided by law, or (4) home rule whereby the people of a city draw up their own charter. *See* SPECIAL ACT, page 374; GENERAL LAWS, page 367; OPTIONAL CHARTER, page 372; HOME RULE, page 368.

Significance   In one sense, every unit of local government has a "charter" composed of the local government provisions of state constitutions, statutes, and the common law. Many cities, or other municipal corporations such as villages, do not have *a* charter in the form of a *document,* particularly when they operate under special acts or general laws. A charter document is generally found in cities operating under home rule and, sometimes, under optional charters. All local governments are subject to the state constitution and laws, and all actions taken under a charter must conform to these higher laws and to the charter as well.

City   A municipal corporation, chartered by the state, that is usually larger than a village, town, borough, or other incorporated area. The term is a legal concept and exactly what constitutes a city is defined by state law. This is generally based on population but may be based on assessed valuation.

Significance   Cities are generally accorded more authority over fiscal matters and services than are other incorporated units. Cities, too, are organized differently, with the mayor-council plan, commission plan, and council-manager plan generally made available by state law. Most Americans live in cities and their suburbs, and city culture is replacing the traditions of a rural society. Cities have long fought for greater freedom from state control and the trend is toward giving cities home rule.

City Council   The policy-making and, in some instances, administrative board of a city. The structure and powers of city councils vary with the plan of city government. In the weak-mayor and commission plans, the council plays a large role in lawmaking and in the direction and control of administrative departments. In the strong-mayor and council-manager plans, the council's job is largely in the realm of lawmaking, with only general oversight of administration. In all cases, the most important jobs of the council are to pass ordinances that determine public policy, and to exercise control over the purse strings. Other functions, which vary from city to city, may include serving as a board of review for tax assessments, issuing licenses, and making appointments. Members of city councils are elected, on a partisan or nonpartisan basis, from wards or districts, at large, or by a combination of both. *See* COMMISSION PLAN, page 361; COUNCIL-MANAGER PLAN, page 364; MAYOR-COUNCIL PLAN, page 370.

Significance   City councils are, typically, unicameral bodies, most commonly of five or seven members, but they range up to fifty. The commission and council-manager forms of city government, which replaced the cumbersome and often corrupt bicameral city councils, have raised the prestige and quality of councilmen. Each state determines by law the structure and powers of city councils.

City-County Consolidation   The merger of county government with all other units within the county to form one unit of government. The plan is suggested as one solution to the problems of a metropolitan area, particularly when it coincides with the county boundary. *See* METROPOLITAN AREA, page 370.

Significance   City-county consolidation simplifies the government of a metropolitan county by eliminating duplication of services and allowing for area-wide planning and administration of services. In many areas, such as Philadelphia, Boston, and New Orleans, city and county boundaries are actually or substantially the same. Where several units are involved, residents of smaller municipalities and rural parts of the county tend to resist consolidation. They fear increased costs and want to maintain their individual identity. The consolidation of Baton Rouge, Louisiana, and Nashville, Tennessee, with their counties are examples of successful consolidations. As a solution to metropolitan problems, however, the city-county consolidation plan does not meet the problems of areas that overlap counties or extend through many counties or even states.

City-County Separation   Political separation of the city from the county. Cities are generally part of the county in which they lie and the city residents pay county taxes and receive certain county services. More than thirty cities in Virginia, and the cities of St. Louis, Denver, Baltimore, and San Francisco, are separated from their counties and provide their residents with county services. *See* METROPOLITAN AREA, page 370.

Significance   City-county separation is designed to increase the efficiency of the urban area and to eliminate overlapping government. The urban area, however, tends to continue to spread beyond the city limits. Moreover, the rural areas of the county and smaller municipalities are left without the financial help of the city, and the county must continue to provide services. These problems have been met in part in Virginia by permitting the judiciary to adjust boundary lines to meet urban growth. At one time, city-county separation was considered a solution to metropolitan problems, but, except for the state of Virginia, it is rarely used today.

Classification of Cities   The grouping of cities by a state legislature according to population for the purpose of enacting laws or city charters. The practice of classification results from the requirement found in most state constitutions that the legislature must deal with local governments by general law rather than by special act applicable to one unit. Since general laws may result in putting all cities, large and small, into a uniform mold, legislatures have classified cities and passed general laws applicable to each class. *See* GENERAL LAWS, page 367.

Significance   A classification must be reasonable, and attainable by others not yet within the group. For example, state legislatures have tried to evade the purposes of general-law requirements by creating classes based on location in such a way as to have the effect of a special act applicable only to one community. However, laws applicable to cities with populations exceeding one million, for example, may actually apply to one city, but, theoretically, other cities may reach that population figure. Classification schemes are used to determine forms of government as well as specific powers which a city may exercise. The courts determine whether a scheme of classification is reasonable.

Commission Plan   One of the forms of city government in the United States wherein both legislative and executive powers are exercised by a commission of three to nine members. Variations in structure are found around the country, but the essential ingredients of the commission plan include: (1) the concentration of legislative and executive powers in a small group elected at large on a nonpartisan ballot; (2) the collective responsibility of the commission to pass ordinances and control the purse strings; (3) the individual responsibility of each commissioner to head a city department, such as public works, finance, and public safety; and (4) the selection of the mayor from among the commissioners but reducing the office to that of ceremonial leadership. *See* CITY COUNCIL, page 359.

Significance   The commission plan enjoyed great popularity from its inception in Galveston, Texas, in 1901 until about 1920. Its simplicity and its resemblance to business corporation organization appealed to reformers who sought an end to the long ballot and the extremes of partisan politics in municipal government. As its defects became apparent, however, its popularity declined. A major defect is the failure to separate legislative and executive authority, with the result that there is little check on spending and administration is in the hands of amateurs. The lack of a chief executive makes it difficult for the voter to fix responsibility, and, in turn, the city suffers from the absence of political leadership. Furthermore, trying to fit the number of city agencies to the number of commissioners leads to rigidity in organization. To meet these defects, many cities followed the lead of Des Moines, Iowa, and added the initiative, referendum, and recall to the plan, as well as a merit system for selection of governmental employees.

Congressional Township   A six-mile-square area of land established under laws of Congress for the purpose of surveying the land. The system was started by the Confederation Congress in 1785, and was applied to the land in most states. Excluded are the original thirteen states and Maine, Kentucky, Tennessee, Vermont, West Virginia, and Texas. Under the law, land is divided into townships six miles square and each township is divided into thirty-six mile-square sections. Each section is further subdivided into quarter sections and less. By the assignment of numbered base lines, similar to the longitude and latitude patterns on maps, any parcel of land may be easily identified. *See* TOWNSHIP, page 377.

Significance   The congressional township system of land survey was instituted to replace the haphazard "metes and bounds" method of identifying tracts of land wherein landmarks were used rather than precise, numerical points of reference. Accurate records, particularly for real estate transfers, are made possible by the congressional township plan. A congressional township is not a unit of government and, frequently, the township will overlap county and state boundaries. Many township units of government, however, do follow the congressional township line, accounting for the six-mile-square civil township. Congress reserved one section of the township (section 16) for the support of public schools and many states provide that the proceeds from this section constitute a permanent fund for school purposes.

Consolidation   The union of two or more units of government to form a single unit. Consolidation is often recommended as a solution to metropolitan area problems, but it is also recommended in rural areas as a means of reducing the large number of local governments in existence. State constitutions or statutes designate consolidation procedures, generally requiring the separate consent of all units. *See* METROPOLITAN AREA, page 370.

Significance   In the metropolitan areas, consolidation has the same benefits and meets the same opposition as do annexation proposals. It eliminates conflicting authority and duplication of services but meets opposition from suburban communities desiring to retain their identity. In rural areas, consolidation is viewed as a means of strengthening counties and townships that were established many years ago and no longer contain sizable populations or the means to carry on governmental functions efficiently. By joining together, it is expected that services may be improved and much confusion eliminated. None the less, legal intricacies, tradition, and the opposition of vested interests militate against consolidation. Many school districts, however, established prior to modern means of transportation, have found it desirable to consolidate in order to realize the benefits of larger enrollments and school plants, although this, too, meets strong opposition.

Constitution, State   The organic law of a state that defines and limits governmental power and guarantees the rights of the people. Each state has a constitution and its provisions may not conflict with the United States Constitution. Since state governments have all powers not delegated to the national government, state constitutions, typically, are filled with restrictions on legislative and executive power rather than grants of authority. *See* MODEL STATE CONSTITUTION, page 371.

Significance   State constitutions tend to be unduly lengthy and filled with details better left to statutes. The authority of the legislature and executive is, typically, restricted in taxation, expenditures, and administration. Local governments and major state services, such as education and highways, tend to be frozen into a specific mold. These defects, among others, have led to considerable agitation for state constitutional reform, since the people's representatives often have their hands tied by the constitution in their attempts to meet day-to-day problems. This has resulted in the frequent amendment of many state constitutions and the thorough revision of others. Proponents of constitutional reform seek a document more like the national Constitution, with emphasis on fundamentals rather than details. Strong opposition to change, however, comes from those whose interests are protected by specific provisions as well as from many who tend to view a constitution as a sacred document.

Constitutional Amendments, State   Changes in or additions to a state constitution. Amendment procedures are detailed in each state's constitution. Generally, two proposal methods are available—legislative, by an extraordinary
majority, and initiative of the people. Ratification by the people is usually accomplished by simple majority vote, but a few states require an extraordinary
majority. Under the initiative method, permitted in thirteen states, the voters
draw up a petition with a specified number of signatures (eight or ten percent
of the voters) requesting the desired change. If the petition is in order, the
proposal goes on the ballot for ratification by the people.
     Significance   Most state constitutions have been amended numerous
times to meet changing conditions or the desires of strong interest groups. The
legislative proposal method has been used most often because it is simple and
inexpensive compared to a constitutional convention. The requirement of extraordinary majorities, however, often makes it difficult to propose controversial
measures. Unlike the national Constitution, however, state constitutions have
required frequent amendment because of their inflexibility. The initiative
method serves as an important weapon for the people when the legislature
fails to respond to their demands. It tends, however, to be abused by pressure
groups, and many such proposals are rejected. Many states with extremely
difficult amending procedures suffer from outmoded organization and procedures in the daily workings of government. Often, the average citizen fails
to realize that his state constitution is a stumbling block to effective government.

Constitutional Commission   A group of citizens selected by the legislature
and/or the governor of a state to study the state constitution and to make
recommendations for change.
     Significance   Constitutional commissions have been used in a number of
states when revision of the constitution has been under consideration. The most
notable instance took place in Georgia, in 1945, where a commission, established by the legislature, had its proposed revision of the entire constitution
ratified by the people as a single amendment to replace the old constitution.
In other cases, a commission has served as an educational medium, prior to the
calling of a constitutional convention. In still others, the legislature submitted
to the people specific proposals of a commission as amendments. Through the
commission device, a group of leading citizens, making use of expert advice,
can contribute to better understanding of constitutional problems.

Constitutional Convention   A body selected by the people to rewrite the
constitution. Most state constitutions make provisions for the calling of a
constitutional convention but, even if no provisions are made, the power to
call a convention is considered to be inherent in the people in their sovereign
capacity. Ten states provide for a mandatory, periodic submission to the people
of the question of whether they wish to call a convention. The procedures for a
constitutional convention generally involve: (1) the placing of the question on
the ballot by the legislature, usually by an extraordinary majority unless it be
mandatory for that year; (2) the election of delegates, should the people approve the call; (3) the meeting of the convention which has deliberations

similar in method and procedure to legislative bodies; and (4) the submission of the new constitution to the people for ratification.

Significance   A constitutional convention is an historic event; over 200 have been held in the United States. About sixteen states have held just one convention, but some states have held ten or more. The most recent conventions have been held in Missouri (1945), New Jersey (1947), Tennessee (1953), and Michigan (1961). The new states of Alaska and Hawaii framed their constitutions in conventions held in 1955 and 1950 respectively. Constitutional conventions are expensive and many people fear that vested interests or long-standing practices will be disturbed. Yet, conventions represent the highest voice of the people and have tended to attract able citizen talent. The voter is brought into the picture at several stages and the entire process has an excellent educational effect. The provision for the mandatory call of a convention is based on the assumption that each generation should have the opportunity to revise its basic law.

Constitutional Officer   A public official, usually in the executive branch, whose office is established and required by the constitution. State constitutions generally name numerous state and local officials and designate their terms of office and duties. For example, most state constitutions provide for the election of such state-wide officers as secretary of state, attorney general, state treasurer, and state auditor. On the local level, the constitution may require election of such officers as sheriff, county clerk, township supervisor, and highway commissioner.

Significance   Constitutional officers present one of the troublesome aspects of state government today because they enjoy much immunity from legislative power and may resist direction from the chief executive, particularly when they belong to different political parties. Reform of state and local government is difficult since these offices cannot be abolished without constitutional change. Supporters of provisions for constitutional officers maintain that they reduce concentration of power in the chief executive and retain greater control in the hands of voters.

Council-manager Plan   A form of city government in which the city council appoints a professional administrator, a manager, to act as the chief executive. With variations from city to city, the essentials of this plan are: (1) a small council or commission of five or seven members elected at large on a non-partisan ballot, with power to make policy and to hire and fire the manager; (2) a professionally trained manager, with authority to hire and fire his subordinates, who is responsible to the council for efficient administration of the city; and (3) a mayor chosen separately or from within the council, but with no executive functions. The council must refrain from bypassing the manager by interfering with his subordinates or in the details of administration, and the manager must follow the policies outlined by the council. A merit system for selection of employees is generally used under this plan. See CITY COUNCIL, page 359.

Significance   The council-manager plan is a product of the twentieth century and about 2000 cities use the manager system. A small percentage of cities have abandoned the plan after trying it, usually because of lack of citizen understanding of its operations. More than one-third of cities over 5000 population, and about one-half of those over 25,000, use the manager plan, but only four over 500,000 (Cincinnati, Dallas, San Antonio, San Diego) have adopted it. Advantages of the plan include its simplicity, clarification of responsibility for both policy and administration, and its use of experts to adopt and utilize modern techniques of budgeting, planning, and over-all administration. The profession of city manager has gained in status and many universities train managers. The manager may also be of invaluable aid to the council and the public in suggesting policy alternatives. Opponents of the plan criticize the lack of a strong political leader, particularly essential in large cities where strong mayors play this role, and charge that the manager plan is undemocratic since the executive is appointed. The council is responsible, however, to the people and has full control over the manager. The plan is now well established in the United States and is growing in popularity.

County   The major unit of local government in the United States, except in Connecticut, Rhode Island, and Alaska. Louisiana has county units but calls them parishes. Alaska has a new major division of local government called a borough. Connecticut abolished counties in 1959. In New England, counties are relatively unimportant for governmental purposes. Otherwise, county governments exist as principal agencies of the state for state-wide purposes, and as important units of local government. There are over 3000 counties in the United States ranging from three in Delaware to 254 in Texas. Their powers and functions vary from state to state and within states as well. Generally, counties perform such functions as law enforcement, maintenance of courts, highways, schools, and welfare agencies. In urban areas, counties may perform a variety of services usually handled by cities. Counties are governed by a board that differs in composition from state to state. Counties have a large number of elected officials, such as sheriff, clerk, coroner, attorney, auditor, register of deeds, surveyor, and treasurer.

   Significance   Counties were originally established as administrative subdivisions of the state and for local governmental purposes. The number of counties and their organizational patterns have undergone almost no change through the years and tradition militates against change. Many are densely populated and integral parts of metropolitan areas. Others have lost population and are thoroughly rural. The metropolitan counties are faced with the need to expand their services; the rural counties find it difficult to support their regular functions. Thus, in one case, the county has achieved new importance while, in the other, means are sought to relieve it of its burdens. Most counties suffer from outmoded administrative organization, the lack of a chief executive, the long ballot, and the spoils system.

County Board   The governing body of the county. The official title of this body varies from state to state with as many as twenty-seven different titles used. Most common are "board of commissioners," "board of supervisors," and "county court," but the term county board is the popular one. About two-thirds of the county boards are composed of three to five commissioners or supervisors who are elected by the voters of the county. In states with township government, the board is composed of township supervisors and representatives of cities within the county and usually numbers about twenty-five. In several states the board is composed of county judges. The board administers state law in the county, levies taxes, appoints numerous officials, and supervises the general affairs of the county.

Significance   County boards are important strongholds of political power. The growing importance of the county in urban areas has added to the powers and influence of these boards. In some areas, they have not been adequate to meet new responsibilities and many persons advocate the use of a county manager. Because many boards are composed of persons with other responsibilities, no individual has over-all responsibility for the county. Boards are also handicapped by the large number of elected county officials over whom they exercise little control.

County Clerk   A county official who is popularly elected in more than half the states. His principal duties include acting as secretary to the county board, supervision of elections, issuance of various business certificates and licenses, and handling of birth, marriage, and death records.

Significance   The county clerk's office tends to become a central clearing house for county affairs, and the clerk is often an important political figure. The nature of the office has led some observers to consider it the logical place to vest principal administrative supervisory duties in the absence of a regular county executive.

County-manager Plan   A plan patterned after the council-manager plan used in many cities. The county-manager plan envisages a small county board for policy determination and an appointed, professional manager to serve as the executive officer of the county. Fewer than thirty of the more than 3000 counties in the United States have adopted the manager plan.

Significance   The county-manager plan is designed to overcome the defects common to most counties—the long ballot, the lack of an integrating executive officer, and the spoils system. General public apathy and a tradition-bound attitude toward county government have made for slow adoption of the plan. Constitutional provisions also make it difficult for counties to reorganize. Such reforms as county home rule or optional charters will probably be necessary before the county-manager plan can spread. Supporters of the plan hold that, in both urban and rural counties, it can make the operations of county government more efficient and clearly fix responsibility. Critics argue that, since the county is principally an administrative arm of the state, the manager would obstruct state supervision of county activities.

Dillon's Rule   A rule enunciated by Judge John F. Dillon, an authority on municipal corporations, to the effect that a municipal corporation can exercise only those powers expressly granted to it by state law, those necessarily implied from the granted powers, and those essential for the purposes of the organization. If any doubt exists, it is to be resolved against the local unit, in favor of the state.

Significance   Dillon's Rule underscores the subordinate relationship of local government to the state. The rule applies to all local units. Local government is a creature of the state and has only those powers permitted by state constitutions and laws.

Functional Consolidation   The cooperation of two or more units of local government in providing services to their inhabitants. Several counties may join together for common administration of health services, or two cities may agree to have a common water supply or sewerage system. *See* METROPOLITAN AREA, page 370.

Significance   Functional consolidation can help metropolitan areas, with their complex of overlapping governments, as well as rural areas, which lack financial resources. It provides a satisfactory alternative to complete consolidation of units which often meets strong opposition. Another form of consolidation of functions takes place when a state takes over a service, such as highways or education, and relieves local units of these burdens. Functional consolidation has made headway in metropolitan areas, since it serves to solve technical problems while permitting units of government to retain their separate political identity.

General Laws   Laws applicable to all local government units of a similar type. Most state constitutions now provide that the legislature may pass only laws of general application rather than special acts applicable only to one unit. To allow for variations in the needs of small or large units of government, the legislatures often classify units according to population and then pass general laws applicable to that classification. *See* CHARTER, page 358.

Significance   General laws relieve the burden on the legislature by making it unnecessary to deal with each unit individually. More important, it restricts the favoritism and political in-fighting that characterized the special-act system and permitted the legislatures to make decisions for individual cities. Often, however, the legislature's classifications are so specific as to apply, in fact, to a single unit of government.

Governor   The chief executive officer of a state. In all states, the governor is elected by the people, serving for four years in most, and for two years in others. About one-half the states limit the governor to one or two terms in office. A governor's executive powers include the power of appointment and removal (although this is severely restricted in most states), preparation and execution of the budget, the power to issue executive orders, and general law enforcement. In the legislative field, governors enjoy considerable power through exercise of the veto power (in all states but North Carolina), and in all but nine states the governor may veto items in appropriation bills. A governor may call the legislature into special session and, in several states, he may limit the special session to consideration of specified subjects. Like the President, the governor may exercise influence over the legislature through his party leadership, messages, and direct appeals to the people. Most governors have the power to pardon and grant reprieves to convicted persons. They also serve as commanders in chief of the National Guard of the state except when it is called into national service. Governors may be removed from office by impeachment and, in a few states, by the recall.

Significance   The office of governor is one of considerable prestige and political power and has been steadily growing in influence. One of the major difficulties of the office is the requirement in many states that the governor share his executive authority with several other elected officials. In this respect, the governor is a weaker executive than the President since the governor may not have control over many high executive officials. Reorganization movements have sought to strengthen the appointive and removal powers of the governor by reducing the number of elected officers and eliminating the many boards and commissions that characterize state government. Recent trends also include increasing the governor's term of office, and expanding his budgetary, management, and personnel powers.

Home Rule   The power vested in a local unit of government, usually a city, to draft or change its own charter and to manage its affairs. Home rule limits legislative interference in local affairs. More than half the states permit some degree of freedom for cities, but only twelve have granted it to counties. Home rule may be required or permitted by the state constitution or be granted by the legislature without specific constitutional authorization. Under home rule, the voters choose a commission to draft a charter that may be approved or rejected by the voters. This is in contrast to the granting of charters by the legislature under special acts, general laws, or optional plans. The city under home rule has control over its local problems provided it does not violate the state constitution or general laws of the state. *See* CHARTER, page 358.

Significance   Home rule introduces a measure of federalism into state-local relations to modify the usual unitary relation. The legislature is relieved of the burden of handling a variety of local problems that are best handled by those most intimately affected by them. Moreover, it strengthens democracy and local self-government, and increases citizen interest. The major problem of home rule is the determination of what constitutes a *local* problem. The attitude of the legislature and of the courts determines the effectiveness of home-rule provisions.

Incorporated and Unincorporated Areas   The legal status of a local unit of government. Incorporated units include cities, villages, and, in some states, towns and boroughs. Unincorporated units include counties, townships, New England towns, and school districts. Incorporated areas are also called municipal corporations and unincorporated places are known as quasi-corporations.

Significance   Though variations are found in the laws of the states, incorporated units or municipal corporations have a distinct legal entity and are usually created at the request, and for the benefit, of the inhabitants of the area. Incorporated units have a charter granted under special, general, or optional laws, or under home rule. As municipal corporations they usually have a large measure of self-government and provide services needed by the residents. Unincorporated units or quasi-corporations are created by the state constitution or laws without regard to the wishes of the inhabitants of the area and are primarily designed to carry on state services. The distinction between incorporated and unincorporated areas is rapidly disappearing in many states, as unincorporated units are increasingly given powers formerly reserved for incorporated areas.

Lieutenant Governor   The elective official in thirty-nine American states who succeeds to the governorship when that office is declared vacant. Typically, the lieutenant governor presides over the state senate and casts the deciding vote in case of a tie. He is elected at the same time and for the same term as the governor. In some states he serves as an ex officio member of the governor's administrative council and several boards and commissions.
    Significance   The lieutenant governor, like his counterpart, the Vice President in the national government, performs his most important function by being available to take over as chief executive. When the governor is temporarily absent from the state, the lieutenant governor usually takes over until the governor's return. In states without a lieutenant governor, the president pro tempore of the senate or the secretary of state succeeds to the office of governor.

Local Option   Authority vested in local units to approve, reject, or select specific or alternative forms of action. Local option often refers to the power of local units to determine by popular vote whether or not liquor will be served in the community. It may also be used to describe the action taken by communities to select a charter from those made available by state law.
    Significance   Local option provides a means whereby state governments are prevented from imposing the same controls over all units of local government. This has proved to be popular in the case of liquor sales, since each community may decide for itself whether it will be "wet" or "dry." Local option is in accord with traditional American theories of local self-government.

Mayor   The chief executive and/or the ceremonial leader of a city. The role of the mayor varies with the form of city government. Under the strong-mayor–council plan, the mayor has extensive executive power including control over appointments and removals of city officials and the veto power. Under a weak-mayor–council plan, the mayor has limited executive powers. The mayor in the commission and manager plans is largely a ceremonial figure. *See* MAYOR-COUNCIL PLAN, page 370.
    Significance   The power and prestige of the mayor varies not only with the structure of city government but with the personal qualities and political influence of the individual. In most cities, the mayor is a part-time official, but in cities like New York and Chicago his responsibilities are greater than those of many governors. In all cities, people look to the mayor for leadership in municipal affairs.

Mayor-administrator Plan   A plan of city government in which an administrative officer is appointed to assist the mayor in managing the affairs of the city. The plan has been adopted in a number of large cities to free the mayor for broader policy-making duties while using expert aid to supervise the routine administration of city government. The administrator, called the chief administrative officer, is appointed by the mayor with or without council approval and may have extensive appointment and removal power over administrative officials. His duties include budget supervision, coordination of city agencies, personnel direction, and the giving of technical advice to the mayor.

Significance   The mayor-administrator plan is a recent development used in large cities under a strong-mayor plan of government. The plan makes use of some of the features of the city manager form while retaining the political leadership of a strong mayor. It differs from the council-manager plan in retaining the position of strong mayor and in making the administrator responsible to the mayor rather than to the council.

Mayor-council Plan   A plan of city government in which the mayor is elected to serve as the executive officer of the city and an elective council serves as the legislative body. Wide variations exist from city to city but the plan usually takes the form of a weak- or strong-mayor–council plan depending upon the position of the mayor in the system. *See* STRONG-MAYOR PLAN, page 375; WEAK-MAYOR PLAN, page 379.

Significance   The mayor-council plan reflects the traditional separation of powers between the legislative and executive branches. While the role of the mayor is the key to the nature of any specific application of the plan in a city, the council, in all cases, plays a major role as the legislative body. In recent years, the mayor-council plan has lost ground to the council-manager plan, particularly in small and middle-sized cities. In large cities, however, the plan continues to be in use with the strong-mayor plan favored over the weak-mayor plan. More than one-half of American cities still use some form of the mayor-council plan.

Metropolitan Area   A large city and its surrounding suburbs, which are socially and economically integrated although composed of separate units of government. The term metropolitan is derived from the Greek terms "mētēr" (mother) and "polis" (city). In 1960, the Bureau of the Census identified 212 metropolitan areas, and new areas have since been added. These include each city of 50,000 population or more and the county and other outlying areas which are socially and economically a part of it. The Census Bureau calls these "standard metropolitan statistical areas." New York and Chicago have been identified as "standard consolidated areas" because of the highly complex nature of these regions which combine several contiguous standard metropolitan statistical areas. *See* ANNEXATION, page 357; CITY-COUNTY CONSOLIDATION, page 360; CITY-COUNTY SEPARATION, page 360; CONSOLIDATION, page 362; FUNCTIONAL CONSOLIDATION, page 367; METROPOLITAN FEDERATION, page 371; URBAN COUNTY, page 378.

Significance   Approximately seventy percent of the American people live in metropolitan areas although these occupy only about ten percent of the land area of the United States. This phenomenon of the twentieth century has brought with it a host of political, social, and economic challenges. Metropolitan areas are characterized by numerous governmental units sharing such major problems as transportation, housing, sewage disposal, and water supply. In recent years, the central city has been losing population to the suburbs, creating severe governmental and fiscal problems for both areas. Proposed solutions to the metropolitan problem include annexation, consolidation, federation, and functional consolidation. None of these proposals has, as yet, proved satisfactory, due largely to the reluctance on the part of the people to change established patterns. On the national scene, the metropolitan areas have had a strong political impact resulting in the establishment of the Department of Housing and Urban Development. New representational patterns in state legislatures stemming from court decisions on reapportionment have altered the balance of political power in favor of metropolitan over rural areas. About eighty-five percent of the total population increase between 1950 and 1960 took place in the metropolitan areas, and nearly seventy percent of this growth was in suburban regions.

Metropolitan Federation   A proposed solution to the problems of metropolitan areas that would create a central metropolitan government to handle problems of the entire metropolitan region, reserving to the local units control over local matters. The plan is based on the principle of federalism which is in effect at the national-state level. The plan has been put into effect in Toronto, Canada, but no American area has adopted it, although the metropolitan government of Dade County (Miami), Florida, resembles a federation. Under a federated plan, the metropolitan or central unit might handle such common problems as highways, air terminals, water supply, sewerage, and air pollution. The local units could continue to act in the areas of police, schools, and other matters which the people desire to retain as strictly local functions. *See* METRO-POLITAN AREA, page 370.

Significance   Federation is viewed as one of the more practical means of solving metropolitan problems because it does not destroy the identity of local units. At the same time, area-wide services can be provided to units unable to finance them alone. The plan is flexible, since functions can be arranged as need demonstrates and new units can be added as they become part of the metropolitan area. It is difficult, however, to determine what constitutes an area-wide or local problem. Further, the plan simply adds another unit of government to an already large number. Disagreement is apt to arise over proper representation of local units in the metropolitan government.

Model State Constitution   A proposed state constitution prepared by the National Municipal League. Highlights of the Model include a unicameral legislature, a strong executive, and a unified court system with judges appointed by the governor. It also provides for modern techniques of budgeting, financing, auditing, and personnel management; for home rule for cities and counties, the initiative and referendum, simplified amendment and revision procedures, and a brief bill of rights. The Model is brief compared to most state constitutions and is restricted to fundamentals. *See* CONSTITUTION, STATE, page 362.

Significance   The Model State Constitution is now in its sixth revised edition (1963). Its periodic revision demonstrates the need for adapting state constitutions to meet changing conditions. The Model is not likely to be adopted by any one state and it contains numerous highly controversial items. Yet, it is designed to stimulate discussion by presenting some guidelines proposed by experts. The major aim of the Model, however, meets with general approval from students of government, namely, a state constitution limited to fundamentals and with clear assignment of responsibility coupled with flexibility of action.

Optional Charter   A plan in effect in about one-third of the states that permits a city to choose a charter from among several provided by state law. Typically, cities may choose various forms of the mayor-council plan, the commission plan, or the council-manager plan. *See* CHARTER, page 358.

Significance   The optional-charter plan represents a compromise between complete legislative domination of cities through special acts and home rule. It permits cities to choose their own forms of government by public referendum. The plan is, however, unlike home rule in that the legislature may change the content of the options at any time. Under home rule, the city itself frames and changes its charter.

Ordinance   A legislative enactment of a local governing body. Ordinances have the force of law, but the term is to be distinguished from the statute-making power of national and state legislatures. Ordinances are issued under authority granted by the sovereign power and, in the case of local governments, must comply with state constitutions, charters, and general laws.

Significance   The subordinate position of local government in its relations to the state is underscored by the fact that the former has only ordinance-making rather than statutory power as that term is generally understood. An interesting sidelight of the use of the term ordinance is that Congress under the Articles of Confederation had only ordinance-making power, demonstrating the sovereignty of the member states.

Planning   Preparation and execution of projects for the future economic, social, and physical development of a community. Planning may be nation-wide or state-wide in situations in which it encompasses all types of governmental problems, but it is more often associated with the physical development of municipal governments. This includes planning street layouts, parks, public utility routes, and the zoning of areas for residential and commercial purposes. In recent years, emphasis has turned from purely physical aspects of city planning and beautification to social and economic concerns such as urban redevelopment and housing. In metropolitan areas, stress is now being put on the need for county-wide or regional planning to provide orderly development. Sound planning must take into consideration population and economic trends as well as future fiscal needs. Many cities and states have official planning agencies. *See* ZONING, page 379.

Significance   The American people have been slow to accept the concept of planning, conceiving of it, perhaps, as similar to the planned economies associated with socialism. Lack of planning has, however, resulted in waste of natural resources and the need for expensive corrective action. The failure of most communities to provide for suitable streets and parking facilities to meet the demands of the automotive age is a major example. Today, planning is generally accepted as a necessary aspect of governmental operations although many communities still resist it. A large number of cities now have master plans for future growth and require that new developments fit into the master plan. Planning is now considered to be a professional specialty, with many colleges and universities offering courses of training.

Register of Deeds   A county officer, sometimes called recorder of deeds, who is elected in about half the states. His major duty is to record and preserve legal documents relating mainly to real estate ownership and transfers. This function is designed to protect landowners and prospective purchasers of land against flaws in titles to property.

Significance   Few students of government support the idea of electing a register or recorder of deeds. The position is an important one but is not of a policy-making nature. Some counties have adopted modern techniques of recording legal papers through microfilm or other technical processes, but most continue to keep records in longhand in bound volumes.

School District   A governmental unit for the maintenance of schools. In about half the states, school districts are administratively and financially independent and do not follow township, city, or county lines. The town or township plan is dominant in New England and the county plan in the South. In Delaware and Hawaii, the entire state comprises one school district. Typically, school districts are governed by elective boards, which choose a superintendent to administer the system. In some areas, the school is part of city government, and the board is selected by the mayor or council. Approximately one-third of all local units of government are school districts and they account for almost one-half of all local governmental expenditures.

Significance   In 1942, school districts comprised more than two-thirds of all local governments. There has since been a dramatic decrease in the number of districts (from 108,000 to 30,000), and this trend continues. All over the country, small school districts are being consolidated to make larger, more efficient schools. The strong tradition of independent school districts is based on the assumption that schools should not be part of the politics of regular governments nor tied financially to other units. Some authorities claim, however, that the independent school district develops a "politics" of its own and tends to detract from the financial needs of other units.

Secretary of State   A state official elected by popular vote in thirty-nine states and appointed by the governor or legislature in others. His major duties include the preservation of official documents, administration of elections, issuance of business licenses and certificates of incorporation, and registration and issuance of motor vehicle licenses. He is also keeper of the state seal.

Significance   The office of secretary of state is not considered by political scientists to be one that justifies popular election. The office has few, if any, policy-making responsibilities, but its elective position reduces the governor's control over state administration. Appointment by the governor is generally recommended. In most states, the secretary of state enjoys political prominence because his name is affixed to numerous documents, such as driving licenses; many secretaries go on to higher office.

Special Act   Legislation applicable to one unit of local government. The special act system prevailed from colonial times to the middle of the nineteenth century and is still in use in several states. Through special acts, state legislatures grant charters to municipalities, amend the charters, and pass legislation on a wide variety of purely local problems. *See* CHARTER, page 358; GENERAL LAWS, page 367.

Significance   Special acts have the virtue of flexibility but are often abused. The net effect of much special legislation is to vest complete authority over a local unit in the legislative representative from that area since other representatives rarely interfere with his desires. Often, "ripper" acts are passed in such states; these abolish particular local offices, such as that of city manager, although such action may be contrary to local wishes. Special acts put a great burden on the legislature and, in some states, more than half the legislation is special in nature. Most states now forbid special legislation by requiring general laws or by permitting home rule. In a few states, the people of an affected area may reject special acts by popular vote.

Special District   A unit of local government established to provide a single service. About one-half of the special districts in the United States are for fire protection, soil conservation, and drainage. Other common types of special districts provide cemetery, sewer, water, housing, and mosquito abatement services. A school district may be classified as a special district but the Census Bureau and political scientists classify it separately. Special districts are usually created to meet problems that transcend local government boundaries or to bypass taxation and debt restrictions imposed upon local units by state law. The number of special districts has more than doubled since 1942 (8,000 to 19,000), and they now comprise about twenty percent of all local units. The special district is created under state law, usually requiring the consent of the people in the district, and is governed by a small board which has taxing and bonding authority.

Significance   The dramatic increase in the use of the special district device illustrates the inability of existing units of government to meet modern needs. Tax and debt restrictions can be evaded and high costs shared by several units without upsetting traditional governmental boundary lines. Paradoxically, while attempts are underway to decrease the number of local units of government, the special district is adding to the complexity of local government. The device, however, has strong appeal to interest groups that want to keep a function separate, and to many people who believe that a special district keeps a function "out of politics."

State Aid   Funds provided to local governments by the state in the form of grants-in-aid or shared taxes. State grants go primarily to school districts for educational purposes and to counties for welfare and highway functions. Shared taxes are administered by the state, which gives a portion of sales or income taxes to local units, including cities. *See* TAX SHARING, page 250.

Significance   Local units must rely heavily upon the general property tax for income. Since this source has proved insufficient, state aid has increased substantially in recent years and accounts for about thirty percent of local revenues. Grants-in-aid are usually accompanied by state supervision of the expenditure and a requirement that the local unit put up a matching amount or some percentage of the grant. Such grants have improved local government standards while retaining some measure of local control. Shared taxes are usually free of state controls but, since tax collections vary from year to year, local units cannot depend upon specific amounts.

State Auditor   A state official elected in thirty-one states and appointed by the governor or legislature in others. In some states, the title "comptroller" is used. His major duty is to act as a watchdog over expenditures of state agencies by postauditing accounts. In some states, however, he has preauditing and accounting duties as well. *See* AUDITOR, page 233.

Significance   The position of auditor is essential for ensuring accountability of public expenditures. Political scientists, however, doubt the wisdom of electing this official or of having him appointed by the governor. Selection by and responsibility to the legislature is considered the most desirable situation, because the auditor's job is to ensure that expenditures have been made in accordance with the legislature's enactments.

State Treasurer   A state official popularly elected in forty-one states and chosen by the governor or legislature in others. His major duties are the safekeeping of state funds and the payment of bills on proper warrant. In some states, he has tax collection responsibilities as well.

Significance   The popular election of a treasurer is viewed as unnecessary by students of government. Financial matters, except for auditing, should be centralized in a finance office headed by an appointee of the governor. This would make the governor clearly responsible for the handling of state funds.

Strong-mayor Plan   A plan of city government in which the mayor is given complete executive authority. Its major features include: (1) election of a mayor as chief executive; (2) concentration of administrative power in the hands of the mayor, including powers of appointment and removal; (3) a veto power over the city council; and (4) strong budgetary controls in the hands of the mayor. *See* MAYOR-COUNCIL PLAN, page 370.

Significance   The strong-mayor plan is used in most large cities and is favored by political scientists over the weak-mayor plan. The main advantages of the plan are the centralization of authority and the clear fixing of executive responsibility. The plan permits the mayor to exercise strong political or policy-making leadership, a particularly desirable condition in large cities with their variety of competing interests. In contrast to the weak-mayor plan, the strong-mayor plan encourages the use of modern administrative techniques and the appointment of able subordinates. Few people, however, combine top administrative and political talent. In several large cities, the mayor-administrator plan is in use to free the mayor from attention to administrative detail.

Superintendent of Public Instruction   An official elected in more than half the states to supervise the public school system of the state. In some states, he is known as superintendent of schools or commissioner of education. In several states, he is chosen by the state board of education, and in a few, by the governor. In most cases, the superintendent serves on the state board of education and acts as its chief administrative officer. His duties generally include the establishment of standards for schools, curriculum development, setting up teacher qualifications, and control of state administered school funds. In some states, his authority extends to other educational institutions, such as state teachers colleges and community colleges.

Significance   The superintendent of public instruction holds a position of major responsibility because of the value placed upon education in the United States. Because of the high professional standards desirable for this office, many educators and political scientists favor the superintendent's appointment by an elected or appointed board of education, or by the governor.

Supervisor   The chief elective officer of the township (called trustee in some states) and a member of the county board of supervisors. The supervisor has over-all responsibility for township government and presides over the township board. He represents his township on the county board and may serve as tax assessor. *See* TOWNSHIP, page 377.

Significance   In states with township government, the supervisor is an important political figure, who exercises considerable influence at the county and state levels. The growing urbanization of many townships and counties has forced new challenges upon township supervisors whose functions were originally designed for a rural society.

Town   The major unit of local government in New England. The term is used in some states to designate a township or a small urban area but is generally used by political scientists to designate the New England town. With the exception of some incorporated cities, all six states of New England are divided into towns; this division includes both the rural and urban portions of each particular area. The town is responsible for most of those governmental services provided in other states by counties and cities. The town is governed by all the inhabitants through the town meeting and, between meetings, by a board of selectmen and other town officers. In many towns, however, representatives are chosen for town meetings, and some utilize a town manager.

Significance   The New England town developed in the colonial period and is deeply rooted in tradition. Growing populations and urbanization of many towns has put a strain upon governmental arrangements suitable for a frontier, rural society. Representative town meetings, special finance and budget committees, and town managers now characterize many towns.

Town Meeting   The governing authority of a town or township. All qualified voters may participate in the election of officers and in the passage of taxes or other legislation. Town meetings are used in New England towns and in many midwestern townships.

Significance   The town meeting represents direct democracy in action. It is a product of rural society, however, and has lost much of its vitality in recent years. Areas with large populations cannot hold meetings of all qualified voters; no building can accommodate them and the meetings are unwieldy.

Often, people are apathetic and power falls into the hands of the few who do attend or to those who "pack" the meeting. Many midwestern townships have abolished the town meeting. In New England, representative town meetings are held; as is customary for most legislative bodies, these town meetings are comprised of delegates elected by the voters.

Township   A unit of government, usually a subdivision of a county, found in sixteen states, principally in the midwest and in the northeast. The term "midwestern township" is often used to distinguish it from the New England town. Townships vary in shape and size but tend to cover an area of thirty-six square miles as a result of the congressional township system of identifying land. Some townships have an annual town meeting and all are governed by a township board, usually consisting of three members. Municipal areas are usually excluded from the township territory but in some states, villages or towns remain part of the township. Township functions tend to be rural in nature, such as maintaining roads, cemeteries, and drains, minor law enforcement, and assessment of property. In urban areas, however, townships have taken on numerous urban services, such as police and fire protection, and public works. In some states, the township is the unit for school administration. *See* CONGRESSIONAL TOWNSHIP, page 361.

Significance   With some exceptions, township government has declined in importance. A product of frontier society and the New England town, it is too small for efficient administration. Modern communication makes it unnecessary as a subdivision of easily accessible county offices. Duplication of services in small areas results. Some states, such as Oklahoma and Iowa, have tranferred most township functions to the county. Although there are 17,000 township governments, a general lack of interest in them seems to characterize many areas. In some states, the township has gained strength by taking on municipal functions. Most political scientists favor abolition of the township as a unit of government and transfer of its functions to the county or, in some cases, to nearby city governments.

Uniform State Laws   Laws proposed by the National Conference of Commissioners on Uniform State Laws, a few of which have been adopted by all or many states. Among those proposals that have had wide adoption are the Negotiable Instruments Act, the Warehouse Receipts Act, the Stock Transfer Act, others relating to sales, partnerships, bills of lading, and some traffic, criminal, and family matters. The National Conference has proposed over 100 uniform laws since its inception in 1892, but it has met with only minor success. The Conference consists of three Commissioners from each state, usually lawyers, appointed by the governor. The Council of State Governments acts as secretariat for the Conference. *See* HORIZONTAL FFDERALISM, page 33.

Significance   The wide diversity of state laws under the federal system has proved vexing to many people. Persons doing business in several states are often inconvenienced and confused. Confusion exists, too, in such matters as marriage and divorce and traffic laws. The increasing mobility of business and private persons has increased the need for more uniformity. The effort has been retarded by apathetic state legislatures and by the desires of many states to gain an advantage over others by having less stringent rules concerning business transactions or divorce, for example, in order to attract more business to the state.

Urban County   A proposed solution to metropolitan area problems that involves the transfer to county governments of functions exercised by several units of government within the county. Several counties in California have taken over the functions of law enforcement, health services, tax assessments and collections, and prisons. Dade County, Florida, has been established as a metropolitan or urban county. Municipalities within that county, including Miami, have transferred to the county power over traffic problems, planning, sewerage, water supply, and other county-wide problems. The urban county plan is to be distinguished from city-county consolidation, which contemplates the complete merger of county government with all other units within the county. See METROPOLITAN AREA, page 370.

Significance   Most metropolitan areas lie within a single county. This facilitates the transfer of functions, since the county is an established unit of government. No new government need be created nor need any unit be abolished. Metropolitan areas are, however, rapidly spreading beyond county lines. Most county governments are poorly organized and have made little progress in the use of modern administrative techniques or of the merit system of personnel management. Most are ill-equipped to handle urban services without considerable reform.

Village   A small urban area, called a town or borough in some states, that is a municipal corporation but one with less authority and simpler organization than a city. The term "village" is a legal concept, varying in meaning from state to state in which the designation is used. Village status may be based upon population but many villages are larger than regular cities. Villages usually are governed by a small council and a village president or mayor. Limitations are placed by the state upon the taxing and borrowing powers of villages as well as upon the types of functions which they may perform.

Significance   Village government developed to accommodate the needs of trading centers in rural areas. Since the county or township could not provide needed services, such areas were permitted to incorporate as villages for limited purposes, such as street maintenance or water supply. Villages may attain city status by a vote of the people or by special act, but many people prefer the lesser designation and the informality of village organization. Increased population may, however, compel change to city status in order to get greater taxing and service authority.

Ward   The division of a city for purposes of electing members to the city council. The ward system is favored in the larger cities, but most cities use an at-large system of electing councilmen, particularly those using the commission or council-manager forms of government. A number of cities now use a combination of both methods, selecting some councilmen from wards and others at large.

Significance   The ward system has declined in recent years but still has many adherents. It provides a more representative council, since the voter can know his representative more intimately and, in turn, the councilman will know more about his ward. This system is particularly favored by minority groups and labor interests who seldom gain representation under the at-large system. The main disadvantage of the ward system is the emphasis it tends to place on special interests of neighborhoods rather than on the interest of the community as a whole. Further, it makes it more difficult to get qualified candidates and leads inevitably to gerrymandering and logrolling tactics. These factors have led to the growth of the at-large system or a combination of both ward and at-large elections.

Weak-mayor Plan   A plan of city government in which the mayor must share his executive authority with other elected officials and with the city council. Most cities under the mayor-council plan use the weak-mayor form rather than the strong-mayor plan. The major features of the weak-mayor plan include: (1) a long ballot in which the people choose numerous department heads and boards and commissions for administrative purposes, as well as the mayor; (2) a limited power of appointment and removal in the hands of the mayor; (3) the appointment of numerous officials by the council alone; (4) a weak, or complete absence of a veto power for the mayor; and (5) direct participation by the council in administrative matters, including preparation of the budget. *See* MAYOR-COUNCIL PLAN, page 370.

Significance   In spite of its wide use, political scientists frown upon the weak-mayor plan. The long ballot, the difficulty of fixing responsibility because of the lack of a responsible executive, the lack of coordination, and the use of outmoded administrative and personnel techniques that characterize the plan, lead to a poor quality of municipal government. Yet, the plan, which is rooted in the traditions of Jacksonian democracy, prevents the concentration of power and establishes an elaborate system of checks and balances.

Zoning   The division of a city or other unit of government into districts and the regulation, by law, of the uses of the land. Zoning is concerned with the nature of buildings (residential, industrial, or commercial), their height and density, and the uses which can be made of particular tracts of land. Zoning laws are enacted under the police power of communities to protect the health, safety, and welfare of the people. A zoning board of appeals is usually created to grant exceptions and variances to persons who might suffer undue hardships under a zoning regulation. *See* PLANNING, page 372.

Significance   Comprehensive zoning has been in effect only since the 1920s and still meets resistance in many areas in which the people object to legislative and administrative control of their property. Zoning, however, protects property values in residential areas by forbidding industrial or commercial uses of property, and it contributes to the beauty of a community. Zoning makes possible better planning and administration of public services, such as fire protection and traffic supervision, and contributes to the health and well-being of a community by segregating industrial plants from residential areas. Zoning must be carried out with careful regard for constitutionally protected property rights.

IMPORTANT AGENCIES

Council of State Governments   An agency maintained by the state governments to serve as a secretariat, research agency, and clearing house for the improvement of state legislative, executive, and judicial administration. It has encouraged interstate cooperation and the general improvement of federal-state relations and state-local relations. The Council is composed of Commissions on Interstate Cooperation that are found in each of the states and that include legislative and executive officials. The Council serves as the secretariat for the American Legislators Association, the Governors' Conference, and similar organizations of chief justices, attorneys general, court, budget, purchasing, parole, and juvenile officials. It publishes a monthly magazine, *State Government,* and the biennial *Book of the States.* Its headquarters are in Chicago.

Significance   The Council of State Governments has sponsored conferences and research in problems of common state concern from crime control to fisheries. It has promoted better interstate relations and has influence in Washington and in the state capitals. Its journal, *State Government,* carries informative and up-to-date information on state government developments and problems and the *Book of the States* is a major reference work on state and local government.

Index

Index

Page references in **bold** type indicate main entry in dictionary.